U0495753

澳门基金会

※

北京外国语大学

中国海外汉学研究中心

※

大象出版社

合作项目

卫三畏文集
Selected Works of Samuel Wells Williams

卫三畏在东亚——美日所藏资料选编

Samuel W. Williams in East Asia: Selected Archives from the United States and Japan

（卷上）

陶德民　编

中原出版传媒集团
大地传媒

大象出版社
·郑州·

图书在版编目(CIP)数据

卫三畏在东亚：美日所藏资料选编 / 陶德民编.— 郑州：大象出版社，2016. 7
(卫三畏文集)
ISBN 978-7-5347-8923-6

Ⅰ. ①卫… Ⅱ. ①陶… Ⅲ. ①卫三畏 (Samuel Well Williams 1812-1884) —生平事迹 Ⅳ. ①B979. 971. 2

中国版本图书馆 CIP 数据核字(2016)第 188335 号

卫三畏文集
卫三畏在东亚——美日所藏资料选编
陶德民 编

出 版 人 王刘纯
责任编辑 李光洁
责任校对 钟 骄
封面设计 意拓设计
版式设计 凌 青

出版发行 大象出版社(郑州市开元路 16 号 邮政编码 450044)
发行科 0371-63863551 总编室 0371-65597936
网 址 www.daxiang.cn
印 刷 北京汇林印务有限公司
经 销 各地新华书店经销
开 本 787mm×1092mm 1/16
印 张 59
字 数 1180 千字
版 次 2016 年 12 月第 1 版 2016 年 12 月第 1 次印刷
定 价 228.00 元(上、下卷)
若发现印、装质量问题，影响阅读，请与承印厂联系调换。
印厂地址 北京市大兴区黄村镇南六环磁各庄立交桥南 200 米(中轴路东侧)
邮政编码 102600 电话 010-61264834

主编序言

陶德民　张西平　吴志良

2008年8月8日，在北京奥运会开幕的当天，新落成的美国驻华使馆举行了剪彩仪式。美国国务院历史文献办公室为此发行了纪念图册，题为《共同走过的日子——美中交往两百年》，其中把1833年抵达广州的卫三畏(Samuel Wells Williams, 1812—1884)称扬为美国“来华传教第一人”，虽然他并非是第一个来到中国的美国传教士。图册对卫三畏在促进美中两国人民的相互了解方面所作的贡献作了这样的概括和评价：“传教士成为介绍中国社会与文化的重要信息来源，因为他们与大部分来华经商的外国人不一样，这些传教士学习了中文。例如，美国传教士卫三畏就会说流利的广东话和日语。他曾参与编辑英文期刊《中国丛报》，供西方传教士及时了解中国的最新动态，方便在美国的读者了解中国人的生活。卫三畏还编辑出版了《汉英拼音字典》（即《汉英韵府》——序者）和分为上下两卷的历史巨著《中国总论》。时至今日，他依然被公认为对19世纪的中国生活认识得最为精透的观察家。”

图册中也提到“蒲安臣于1862年成为第一个常驻北京的美国代表，在促进中国的国际关系上扮演了更为积极的角色。蒲安臣迅速结识了一批清政府的主要改革派官员，其中就包括咸丰皇帝的弟弟，设立了中国第一个外务部（应为总理各国事务衙门—序者）的恭亲王奕訢，”以及他1867年辞去驻华公使后作为清朝使节率团访问欧美，与当时的美国国务卿签订《蒲安臣条约》一事。“该条约扩展了中美两国的往来领域。条约规定，两国人民享有在彼此国家游历、居住的互惠权，并可入对方官学；中国领事在美国口岸享有完全的外交权利；鼓励华工移民美国；美国政府支持中国的领土主权。”其实，蒲安臣的卓有成效的外交活动及其维护正义的外交主张，与当时担任使馆秘书兼翻译的卫三畏的鼎力相助是分不开的。卫三畏的儿子卫斐列后来倾注极大热忱为蒲安臣撰写传记，其重要原因之一也在于此。

今天，当我们出版这部文集以纪念卫三畏诞辰200周年，并重新探讨其经历和成就之际，有必要思考这样一个问题，即卫三畏一生所体现的诸多志趣和倾向之中，什么是值得我们加以特别关注的呢？虽然这是一个“仁者见仁，智者见智”的问题，多数人恐怕都不会对以下见解持有异议，即卫三畏在对华态度上所发生的“从教化到对话”的某种转变可以说是他留给后世的最重要的精神遗产之一。而这恰恰可以从耶鲁大学校园里留存至今的两件文物上得到印证。

第一件文物是该校公共大食堂(Commons Dining Hall)墙上的卫三畏肖像画，它其实是设在纽约的美国圣经协会所藏同一油画的一个复本。如所周知，卫三畏的在华生涯大抵分为两个阶段，作为传教士的前22年(1833—1855)和作为外交官的后20年(1856—1876)。在前22年的最后一段时间里，他还作为首席翻译官随同佩里将军的舰队两次远征日本，在改变日本锁国政策的外交谈判过程中发挥了重要作用。佩里将军对其语言天赋和交涉手腕的赏识，无疑是卫三畏转而步入为期20年的外交生涯的一个契机。1877年辞职回国后不久，他受聘为耶鲁大学的中国语言文学讲座教授。1881年春被遴选为美国圣经协会会长后，他便提出希望有才华的画家制作自己的肖像画，并将其献给圣经协会。结果，由耶鲁大学艺术学院的韦约翰教授制作的油画所呈现的是这样一个形象：等身大的卫三畏站立在放有纸、笔和一个中国式花瓶的桌子边上，目视前方，手持1858年《中美天津条约》的文本。

很显然，这样的构图反映了卫三畏本人的意思：他一直把基督教传教自由的条款得以列入1858年《中美天津条约》看作自己毕生的最大成就。这是因为当时负责谈判的美国公使列卫廉对是否要在条约中加入该条款并不经意，只是在卫三畏的坚持之下才获得了最后的成功。此一事实，不仅可见于耶鲁大学斯德龄纪念图书馆附属档案馆所藏卫三畏的亲笔日记，也可以由当时协助他进行谈判工作的丁韪良牧师后来所写的《花甲忆记》得到证实："那份现在成为条约荣耀之处的条款是卫三畏博士提出的。"在预定签约的6月18日即"决定命运的那天早上，卫三畏博士告诉我他一夜未眠，一直在考虑这份宽容条款。现在他想到了一种新的形式，可能会被对方接受。他写了下来，我建议我们应当马上坐轿子直接奔赴中方官邸解决这个问题。……中方代表接见了我们，他们当中的负责人稍作修改，就接受了卫三畏博士的措辞"(详见陶德民《从卫三畏档案看1858年中美之间的基督教弛禁交涉——写在〈基督教传教士传记丛书〉问世之际》)。1876年夏天，美国国务院接受卫三畏的辞呈，在正式解职通知中对他赞扬有加："您对中国人的性格与习惯的熟悉，对该民族及其政府愿望与需求的了解，对汉语的精通，以及您对基督教与文明进步事业的贡献，都使您有充分的理由自豪。您无与伦比的中文字典与有关中国的诸多著作已为您赢得科学与文学领域内相应的崇高地位。更为重要的是，宗教界不会忘记，尤其多亏了您，我们与中国订立的条约中才得以加入自由传教这一条。"而卫三畏则在复信中坦承，这一嘉许是"最最让他感动与满意的"(见卫斐列著，顾钧、江莉译《卫三畏生平及书信——一位美国来华传教士的心路历程》)。顺便提到，在1858年6月19日，亦即《中美天津条约》签订的第二天，美国驻日总领事哈里斯便与德川幕府的代表签订了《美日修好通商条约》。卫三畏闻讯后，又不失时机地向美国的新教诸团体提出派遣牧师赴日传教的建议，并得到了切实的响应。所以，对美国基督教会的东亚传教事业来说，卫三畏确实是一位有功之臣。

那么，卫三畏是基于一种什么样的信念而企图以基督教义来教化东亚的所谓异教徒的呢？试举一个例子。1853年7月16日，在佩里将军初访日本，成功向日方递交美国总统国书一周之后，卫三畏曾从停泊在江户湾的军舰上给他在土耳其传教的弟弟W. F. 威廉斯写了一封长信，其中指出："佩里告诉日本官员，他将在次年率领一支更大的舰队以求得到他们对所提要求的回答，即所有前来访问或遇难流落日本海岸的美国人应得到善待，美国汽船在一个日本港口得到煤炭以及有关物资的补给。这些是我们花费巨大开支和派出强大舰队到日本水域的表面上的理由，而真正的理由是为了提高我们民族的名誉和得到称扬我们自己的材料。在这些理由的背后并通过这些理由，存有上帝的目的，即将福音传达给所有国家，并将神旨和责任送达这个至今为止只是在拙劣地模仿耶稣之真的民族。我十分确信，东亚各民族的锁国政策决非根据上帝的善意安排，其政府必须在恐怖和强制之下将之改变，尔后其人民或可自由。朝鲜人、中国人、琉球人和日本人必须承认这唯一活着的和真实的上帝，他们的锁国之墙必将为我们所拆除，而我们西方的太平洋沿岸城市正开始派出船队前往大洋的彼岸。”从卫三畏对佩里访日使命的解读来看，他固然赞成打开东亚各国的大门，但更重视把上帝的福音传入各国人们的心扉，期盼由此引发一系列的变革。因为他认定上帝所代表的真善美的品格和力量是美国等基督教国家所拥有的绝对优势和无比强势的源泉（详见陶德民《十九世纪中叶美国对日人权外交的启示——写在日本开国150周年之际》）。

然而，卫三畏在以后长期驻节北京的岁月里，逐步加深了对中国的悠久历史和深厚文化传统的了解，使他在对华态度上开始发生“从教化到对话”的某种转变。而这一点可以耶鲁校园里的另一件艺术杰作来作为象征，那就是在卫三畏于1884年2月16日去世两周之后，在举行其丧礼的巴特尔教堂（Battell Chapel）东北角中心位置安装的一块非常别致的彩色纪念玻璃。玻璃的中央写有《论语》中的七个汉字：“敏则有功，公则说。”（意思大体为，勤勉能积成事功，公道则众人心悦诚服。）玻璃的下方用英文记载了卫三畏的名字、生卒年份以及他一生所扮演的角色与身份，即“传教士、学者、外交官、耶鲁学院中文教授”。这块玻璃由纽约的路易斯·第法尼公司（Louis C. Tiffany & Co.）负责制作，其别出心裁的设计显然是出于卫三畏生前的授意。

卫三畏选用孔子的话作为自己一生的概括，可谓恰如其分。勤勉能积成事功的道理，可以从他孜孜不倦编纂而成的《中国丛报》、《中国总论》以及《汉英韵府》等多种刊物和名著得到了解。公道则众人心悦诚服的道理，则充分体现在了他辞职回国之际所受到的各界朋友的赞扬。他在信中告诉他的妻子，“临行前威妥玛于周六、西华于周一为我举办了两次特别宴会，我见到了北京的所有名流，并受到了他们的盛赞。然后，似乎是为了区别于外交聚会，丁韪良、艾约瑟、怀定先后请我吃饭。我告诉过你，我在丁韪良家见到了所有的传教士，那真是一次令人难忘的聚会”。“接连不断的登门送别者中有三四位是总理衙门的官员，京城中最位高权重的大官也来为我送行。除了亲王之外，我都是在办公室里会见他们，彼此依依惜别。九位官员每人赠我一柄折扇作为纪念，这充分显示了中国人的友善”。不仅北京的新教传教士们发给他一封送别信以示友谊与敬意，上海的同仁也发给他一封相似的信，恰如其分地总结了他在中国的生活：“您长期担任美国使馆秘书、翻译，九次代理公使的职务，这些工作给了您许多重要的机遇，使您得以把知识、经验用于为中国人造福、为您自己的国家谋利，尤其是为基督教在中国的传播效力。对您工作中表现出的高度责任感，我们不胜钦佩。”对这些热情洋溢的赞美之辞，卫三畏则表示自己的所作所为只不过是在执行上帝的旨意，“我在传教过程中与同伴们相处融洽、身体健康、工作愉快，为此我要虔诚地赞美造物主”。

在某种意义上说，卫三畏选用孔子的话来概括自己的一生，也显示了他对中国文化传统的敬重之意。而这种敬重之意，可以由1879年他为反对加州的排华风潮而撰写的《中国移民》中的一节得到佐证：“当加州的法庭想用立法来反对中国人时，它将中国人等同于印第安人的简单态度是颇为古怪的。生理学家查尔斯·匹克林将中国人和印第安人归为蒙古的成员，但加州的最高法院却认为‘印第安族包括汉族和蒙古族’。这样在概念错误的同时，它还支持了一种错误的观点。它把现存最古老国度的臣民和一个从未超越部落关系的种族相提并论；把这样一个民族——它的文学早于《诗篇》和《出埃及记》，并且是用一种如果法官本人肯于学习就不会叫作印第安语的语言写就，而它的读者超过了其他任何民族的作品——与最高的写作成就仅是一些图画和牛皮上的符号的人群混为一谈；把勤奋、谨慎、技艺、学识、发明等所有品质和全部保障人类生命和财产安全的物品等同于猎人和游牧民族的本能和习惯。它诋毁了一个教会我们如何制作瓷器、丝绸、火药，给予我们指南针，展示给我们茶叶的用处，启迪我们采用考试选拔官员的制度的民族；把它和一个轻视劳动，没有艺术、学校、贸易的种族归为同类，后者的一部分现在还混迹于加州人中间，满足于以挖草根过活。”虽然卫三畏在赞扬中国人的同时，也表达了他对印第安人的歧视态度，他的观点还是得到当时耶鲁学院全体教授的同情，他们纷纷签名支持他起草的请愿书，呼吁海斯总统否决1879年的反移民法，其中包含这样的警告：如果我们的政府首先改变条约的规定，中国政府也可以根据国际法取消治外法权，致使美国在华公民失去领事的保护。此外，1878年中国北方发生大饥荒时，身处太平洋彼岸的卫三畏利用他对美国在华传教士和商社的影响，不遗余力地推动救灾。他还试图劝说国会归还1859年中方赔款余额的一部分来帮助缓解灾区的困境。而早在1860年，他就曾建议国务院用这笔赔款余额在中国建立一所美中学院，以培养中方的翻译、通商和外交人才。这个建议得到了新上任的总统林肯的同意，只因为当时的国会未予批准而搁浅。卫三畏这个未能实现的建议完全可以称之为后来退回庚款吸引中国学生留美的先驱性方案。

卫三畏还对亲眼目睹的中国同时代的缓慢而确凿的变化做了一定的正面评价。1883年7月，即辞世的半年多之前，卫三畏在儿子的帮助下终于完成了《中国总论》这一巨著的修订工作，在增补版的序言中他写下了如下字句：“我在1833年到达广州时，和另外两位美国人作为‘番鬼’向行商经官正式报告，在他的监护之下才得以生存。1874年，我作为美国驻北京公使馆秘书，跟随艾忭敏公使觐见同治皇帝，美国使节站在与‘天子’完全平等的地位呈上国书。由于一生之中的这两次遭遇，并念念不忘在思想和道德上的重大进步是使一个孤傲的政府从强加于人的姿态改而听从他人所必需的，毫不足怪的是，我确信汉人的子孙有着伟大的未来，不过，唯有纯正基督教的发展才是能使这一成长过程中的各个冲突因素免于互相摧残的充分条件。无论如何，这个国家已经度过被动时期，这是肯定无疑的。中国不可能再安于懒散隔绝—像过去那样，以过于自负的态度俯视其他国家，就像面对她所无需劳神的星星一样。”

如果说，17世纪的礼仪之争最后是以天主教士在康熙禁令之下被逐出中国告终的，那么，这场可谓19世纪的礼仪之争则是以“天朝上国”在第二次鸦片战争之后所做出的巨大让步来结局的，包括废除以夷相称、公使驻京、平身觐见皇帝而不必行三跪九叩之礼。卫三畏的字里行间所透露的，既有在礼仪上争得与最古老“中央王国”之“天子”平等地位的自豪，又有从其所信奉的上帝的立场针砭这个王国“懒散隔绝”和“过于自负”的高傲。联系到上述 1853 年他给在土耳其传教的弟弟 W. F. 威廉斯的长信，可见这时的卫三畏虽然在其对华态度上开始了“从教化到对话”的转变，但并未把“异教徒”放在完全对等的位置上，特别是在道德和精神的层面上。在这个意义上说，自以为占据着道德精神的制高点，只有基督教可以拯救中国的卫三畏也难免“过于自负”的诟病。这就是笔者在前文中提到其转变时，始终不忘加上“某种”一词来予以限定的缘故。

尽管如此，卫三畏在序言中宣称，修订版“坚持初版序言中所述的观点——为中国人民及其文明洗刷掉古怪的、模糊不清的可笑印象”。卫三畏相信，在传教“事业取得成功的基础上，中国作为一个民族，在道义和政治两方面，将会得到拯救。这一成功有可能和人民的需要同步前进。他们将会变得适应于自己着手处理问题，并且和外国文明以多种活动形式结合起来。不久，将会引进铁路、电报和制造业，随之而来的是中国人民中成百万地受到启发，无论在宗教、政治和家庭生活的每一方面”。这种力图呈现中国文明及民族的美好品质和衷心期待中国在对外交往中日益开放进步的善意态度，自然是应该予以充分肯定的。

从卫三畏的例子不难联想到，身处所谓“轴心文明”(主要以几大世界性宗教作为标识)的人们往往患有“老子天下第一”的自恋症，而以“居高临下”的态度傲视其他人，难以免俗和根治。反观我们自己，历代国人的“华夷之辨”又何尝不是如此?而时至今日，仍不乏“宅兹中国”的自尊和输出“天下体系”的自负。但也不必悲观，因为这个五彩缤纷的世界本来就是由形形色色、各有偏好的人们构成的。他们之间有相辅相成的关系，也有相反相成的因素。虽然各派宗教和文化的代表自以为有“替上帝传教”或“替天行道”的使命，谁都无法垄断真理和剥夺他人的信仰，也不能指望按照自己的面貌来彻底改造他人。其出于宗教或政治动机的种种努力的后果，客观上会推动各国和各民族之间的交往和融合，并推动人类文明的进步和升华，则是毫无疑义的。从这一点来看，卫三畏一生的变化过程所显示的方向对我们建构今日地球村的和平共处规则还是不乏启迪作用的，那就是要逐渐学会把“老子化胡”的心态改为“相敬如宾”的心理，对异民族、异文化和异文明采取更加宽容、尊重和善于调适的态度，以便用文明对话来取代文明对抗，从而把亨廷顿认为不可避免的“文明冲突”消弭于萌芽状态和无形之间。

机构名称及书名的缩略语（按汉语拼音顺序）

D.A.B.: *Dictionary of American Biogrophy.* American Council of Learned Societies Scribner / 1937

东大史料　东京大学史料编纂所

ILN: *The ILLUSTRATED LONDON NEWS.*

NARA　The National Archives and Records Administration 美国国家档案馆

日译版《远征记》　《ペリー艦隊日本遠征記》 FRANCIS L. HAWKS 著／オフィス宮崎译，栄光教育文化研究所／ 1997

外交史料　日本外务省外交史料馆

耶鲁档案　*Samuel Wells Williams Family Papers,* Manuscript and Archives, Sterling Memorial Library, Yale University

英文版《远征记》　*Narrative of the Expedition of an American Squadron to the China Seas and Japan: Performed in the Years1852, 1853, and 1854, under the Command of Commodore M.C.Perry, United States Navy, by Order of the Government of the United States.*

真田宝物馆　日本長野県松代市真田宝物馆

目 录

卷首

第 1 部分　会员证书与自传

第 2 部分　鸦片战争前后

图像部分

文献部分

第 3 部分　远征琉球与日本

（1）琉球

图像部分

文献部分

（2）横滨

图像部分

文献部分

第 5 部分　耶鲁执教及身后哀荣

附录一　裨治文相关资料

附录二　卫三畏家族文书目录 (Guide to the Samuel Wells Williams Family Papers)　耶鲁大学图书馆 …… 769

附录三　编者相关论文及《每日新闻》报道

5. “Negotiating Language in The Opening of Japan: Luo Sen's Journal of Perry’s 1854 Expedition.” *JAPAN REVIEW*，NICHIBUNKEN，2005 年 1 月 ………… 850
6. “Yoshida Shōin’s Encounter with Commodore Perry: A Review of Cultural Interaction in the Days of Japan’s Opening” 『東アジア文化交渉研究』別冊 1，関西大学文化交渉学教育研究拠点 ,2008 年 3 月 ………………………………………… 879
7.< 黒船のもたらした「広東人」旋風一羅森の虚像と実像 > in *Image and Identity: Rethinking Japanese Cultural History*，山地俊秀 Jeffrey Hanes 共編，神戸大学経済経営研究所「現代経済経営シリーズ 1」，2005 年 3 月 ……………………… 896
8.< ペリーの旗艦に登った松陰の「時間」に迫る——ポウハタン号の航海日誌に見た下田密航関連記事について > 『東アジア文化交渉研究』第 2 号，関西大学文化交渉学教育研究拠点，2009 年 3 月……………………………………… 907

后记 …………………………………………………………………………… 917

目录附记

卷首

图 4 转载自沖縄県史ビジュアル版 4 『ペリーがやってきた』，沖縄県文化振興会公文書館管理部史料編集室編，沖縄県教育委員会 / 1999

图 5 Telly H. Koo, *The Life of Anson Burlingame*, Ph.D. dissertation, Harvard University / 1922

第 1 部分

1.2.3 上海社会科学院历史研究所研究员

第 2 部分

图 8 山口栄鉄著『異国と琉球』本邦書籍 / 1981；山口栄鉄編著『琉球：異邦典籍と史料』榕樹書林 / 2000

2.1.1 张西平主编：《中国丛报》英文影印本，广西师范大学出版社 / 2008

2.6 相原良一著『天保八年米船モリソン号渡来の研究』野人社 / 1954；经向故相原良一教授原工作单位横滨市立大学联系查询，仍无法找到其遗属，谨此说明。

第 3 部分

（1）琉球

图 1 *The ILLUSTRATED LONDON NEWS*，MAY 7. 1853

图 12 山口栄鉄著『琉球異邦典籍と史料』月刊沖縄社 / 1977

3.1.17 转载自沖縄県史ビジュアル版 4 『ペリーがやってきた』，沖縄県文化振興会公文書館管理部史料編集室編，沖縄県教育委員会 / 1999

（2）**横滨**

图 13 樋畑雪湖　樋畑翁輔筆『米國使節彼理来朝圖繪』／吉田一郎／1931，经向原著者故乡的真田宝物馆联系查询，仍无法找到其遗属，谨此说明。

图 18 長谷川亮編『象山先生遺墨選集』（佐久間象山先生遺墨顕彰会昭和八年）／陶德民藏本

3.2.2.1 松浦章　内田慶市　沈国威『遐邇貫珍の研究』關西大學東西學術研究所研究叢刊 24，関西大学出版部／2004

3.2.2.2 『大日本古文書幕末外国関係文書附録之一』東京大学史料編纂所編／1913

3.2.2.3 王晓秋点／史鹏校《罗森等早期日本游记五种》湖南人民出版社／1983

3.2.4 国立国会図書館蔵 , 国立国会図書館ウェブサイトより

3.2.5 "國立"歷史博物館 "國立"中央圖書館 美國聖若望大學亞洲研究中心編印《包遵彭先生紀念論文集》

3.2.6 『大阪大学文学部紀要』第 22 巻 /1982

第 4 部分

4.5 日本英学史学会纪要『英学史研究』第 8 号 ／ 1976

4.7.2 Ph.D. in East Asian Religions, Princeton University

4.7.3 《西昌学院学报》第 19 卷／2004

4.7.4 *Americans in Eastern Asia*. New York：The Macmillan Company ／ 1922

图 1　卫三畏肖像

图 2　卫三畏墓碑　山口荣铁摄

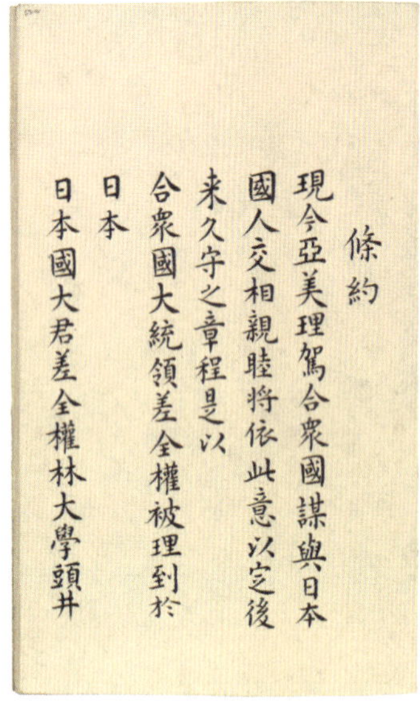

條約

現今亞美理駕合衆國與日本國人交相親睦將依此意以定後来久守之章程是以

合衆國大統領差全權被理到於

日本

日本國大君差全權林大學頭井

图 3　1854 年《美日和亲条约》汉文本首页　美国国家档案馆藏

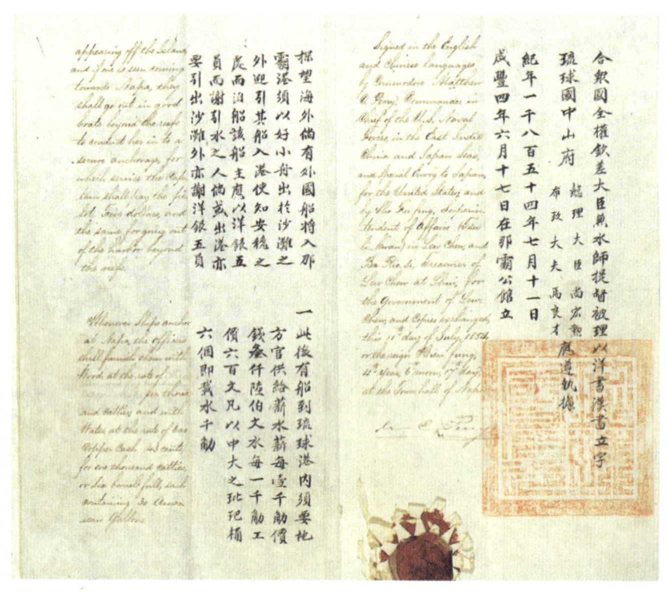

合衆國全權欽差大臣兼水師提督被理以洋書漢書立字

琉球國中山府　總理大臣尚宏勳　布政大夫馬良才

紀年一千八百五十四年七月十一日

咸豐四年六月十七日在那霸公館立

Signed in the English and Chinese languages by Commodore Matthew C. Perry, Commander in Chief of the U.S. Naval Forces in the East India, China and Japan Seas, and Special Envoy to Japan, for the United States; and by Sho Fu-fing, Superintendent of Affairs (Tsu-li-kwan) in Lew Chew, and Ba Rio-si, Treasurer of Lew Chew at Shui, for the Government of Lew Chew; and Copies exchanged, this 11th day of July, 1854, or the reign Hien-fung, 4th year, 6th moon, 17th day, at the Town hall of Napa.

M. C. Perry

探望海外倘有外國船將入那霸港須以好小舟出於沙灘之外迎引其船入港使知安穩之處而泊船該船主應以洋銀五員而謝引水之人倘或出港亦要引出沙灘外亦謝洋銀五員

一此後有船到琉球港內須要地方官供給薪水薪每壹千觔價錢叁仟陸伯文水每一千觔工價六百文凡以中大之秕杷桶六個即載水千觔

appearing off the Island, and if one is seen coming towards Napa, they shall go out in good boats beyond the reefs to conduct her in to a secure anchorage, for which service the captain shall pay the pilot Five dollars, and the same for going out of the harbor beyond the reefs.

Whenever Ships anchor at Napa, the officers shall furnish them with Wood at the rate of … for three … catties, and with Water at the rate of … Copper Cash … for one thousand catties, or Six barrels full, each containing 30 American Gallons.

图 4　1854 年《琉美条约》最后部分　日本外务省外交史料馆藏

图 5　蒲安臣使团合影（中间站立者为蒲氏）

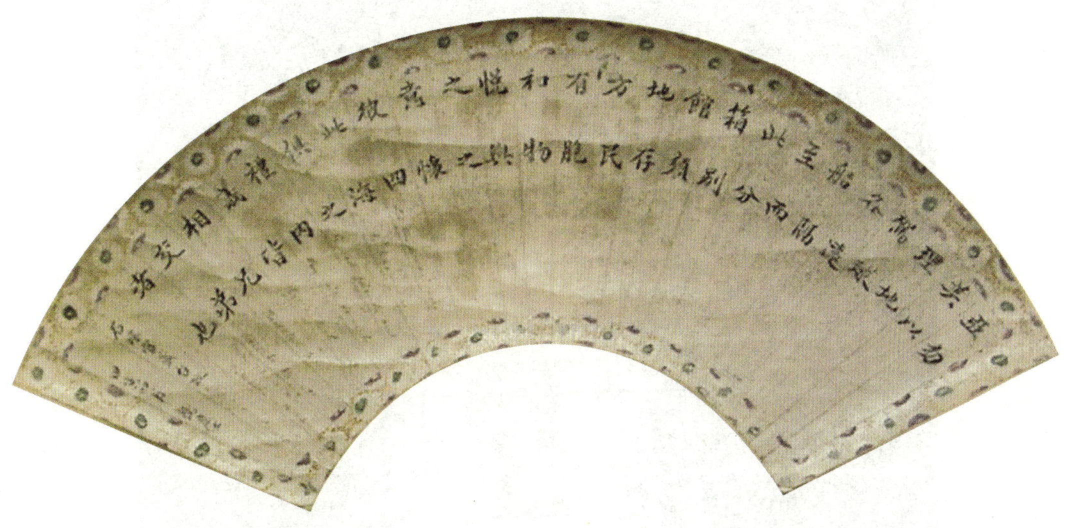

图 6-1　卫三畏赠北海道松前藩官员扇面陈述美国外交方针
罗森以儒学语言题写　市立函馆博物馆藏

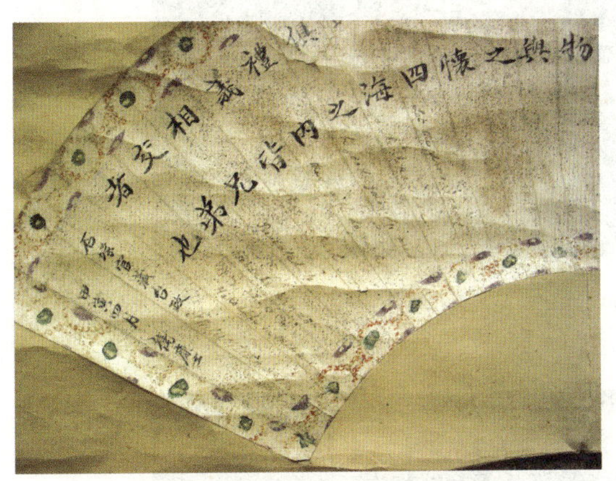

图 6-2　扇面左侧题辞　卫三畏手书英文与罗森手书落款

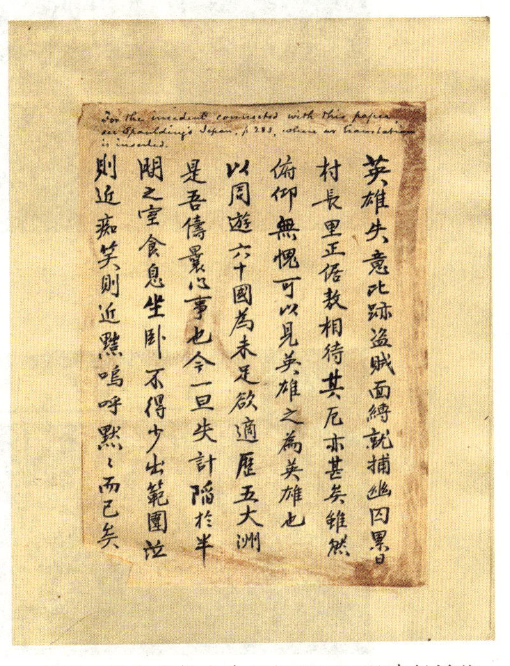

For the incident connected with this paper see Spalding's Japan, p. 283, where a translation is inserted.

英雄失意北跡盗賊面縛就捕幽囚累日村長里正倨傲相待其厄亦甚矣雖然俯仰無愧可以見英雄之為英雄也以周遊六十國為未足欲適歷五大洲是吾儕曩日之事也今一旦失計陷於半閒之室食息坐卧不得少出範圍泣則近痴笑則近黠嗚呼默默而已矣

图 7　罗森手抄本吉田松阴下田狱中投诉状
卫三畏贴在其日记封皮内侧并加注

图 8-1　巴特尔教堂（Battell Chapel）彩色纪念玻璃上的《论语》字句

图 8-2　彩色纪念玻璃下部写有传教士、学者、外交官、中文教授等文字

图 9　美国圣经协会会长纪念油画“卫三畏手持天津条约”之副本悬挂于耶鲁大学 Commons Dining Hall　陶德民摄

PORTRAIT OF DR. S. WELLS WILLIAMS.

The hall in which the Managers of the Bible Society hold their stated monthly meetings is rich in memories and suggestions of the past. The sides of the room are lined with cases full of volumes which illustrate the work which has been done in varied ways at home and abroad during the threescore and ten years which have passed since the Society began its organic life, and on the walls above are hung the portraits of those who from time to time have presided over the deliberations of the Board, or have been conspicuous in the conduct of its work. Boudinot, Jay, Varick, Smith, Frelinghuysen, and Bradish represent its Presidents; Mason and Milnor, its Secretaries; Pintard and Nitchie, its departments of finance and manufacture; while the portraits of Bexley, Teignmouth, and Shaftesbury are constant reminders of a close alliance with the kindred society beyond the sea.

Of its more recent Presidents, Mr. Lenox, Dr. Allen, and Mr. F. T. Frelinghuysen, the Society, unfortunately, has no portraits; but the late Dr. Williams, shortly after being elected to the presidency, announced his intention of having his portrait painted by some skilled hand and presented to the Society. That purpose has reached its consummation, and the painting, by Prof. John F. Weir, N. A., of the Yale College Art School, was formally received by the Board at the last meeting. It is of life-size, representing Dr. Williams as standing and holding in his hand a copy of the Chinese and American treaty of 1856, in the negotiation of which he had a part, while a table near by holds a Chinese vase, with writing implements and manuscripts. Certain characters faintly delineated in the background are a Chinese poem in praise of the vocation of a scholar.

It is interesting to note that up to the time of his death, Dr. Williams had been for half a century the living link between Dr. Robert Morrison and the generation of missionaries who followed him; and included in his gifts to the Society is a framed engraving, which bears the following inscription:

NEW HAVEN, Nov. 2, 1881.

This engraving of Robert Morrison engaged in his work of translating the Bible once belonged to him. After his death in 1834, his son, John Robert, gave it to the Mission of the American Board at Canton, then consisting of Messrs. Bridgman, Stevens, Williams, and Parker. Three of these having left or died, it fell to me as a cherished souvenir of the two Morrisons. The Chinese who stands in the picture, Mr. Chau, was also my assistant for a year or more; his likeness is very exact.

I give this picture to the American Bible Society as a memento of the two Morrisons and myself.

S. WELLS WILLIAMS.

At the instance of Mr. A. D. F. Randolph, the following Minute was adopted by the Board of Managers:

On occasion of receiving the beautiful portrait of the late S. Wells Williams, LL.D., a former President of the American Bible Society, which by his own direction and during his lifetime was painted expressly for the Society—the Board of Managers record anew their high appreciation of this eminent missionary and scholar, and their great satisfaction that they and their successors in office are to have constantly before them so fit a memorial of one whose missionary life in China began before that dark land was open to the entrance of the gospel, and whose last will and testament, made fifty years later, devised liberal things for the circulation of the Holy Scriptures throughout that empire.

It is directed that the painting referred to be hung on the walls of the Managers' Room, amidst other portraits of distinguished men who have taken part in the earlier and later management of the Society's affairs, and that a copy of this Minute be forwarded to the son of Dr. Williams, and published in the *Bible Society Record.*

In advocacy of the adoption of this Minute, Mr. Randolph spoke substantially as follows:

It is unusual for a public institution to receive a portrait of one of its benefactors under precisely these circumstances. The more common method is to request an officer or benefactor to sit for his portrait; and perhaps it might be said—for this is indeed a hard, materialistic age—by one destitute of that fine fibre essential to comprehend the high motives that impelled the act, that it was, after all, but the result of an ambitious purpose to perpetuate the name of the donor.

No one who knew Dr. Williams in his earlier or his later life, no one at all familiar with the great principles which controlled all his actions, would attribute to him any such unworthy motive.

There is indeed a touch of pathos in the thought that our venerated friend in the days of his enforced leisure planned and perfected this additional gift to our Society. He was long and intimately connected with various societies of learning; he was the friend and correspondent of many wise and distinguished men connected with these institutions, but not of these did he think in such a connection as this, when his eyes began to turn more frequently toward the border-land; for this Society ever lay nearer to his heart than the institutes of science and philosophy. He did not so plan that this product of the painter's art should adorn the galleries of one of those, but rather that it should be placed on these sequestered walls beyond "the madding crowd's ignoble strife." Himself a versatile scholar, a linguist, and a lexicographer, a statesman, philanthropist, and a man of affairs, he was in full sympathy with all the developments of human intelligence and human advancement, with a wise appreciation of each progressive movement of his time. Yet he ever set a priceless value on the one Book, the Book of God, in the clear light of which he had continually walked, out of which he had ever drawn the wisdom and strength that had enabled him in a long, eventful, and busy life, to rejoice with hope, and to "endure as seeing Him who is invisible."

An American writer has said that the best gift to one whom you love is something that is a part of yourself. So our departed friend, in this precious and fitting legacy, has given us another proof not only of his loyalty to the history and work of this Society, but of his undying love for it.

第1部分

会员证书与自传

[1864 Nov 10]

American Geographical and Statistical Society.

New York, 10 November 1864

At a Meeting of the Society, held this evening.

Archibald Russell Esq Vice President in the Chair.

It was

Resolved – That S. W. Williams Esq, Secretary of the Legation of the United States to Pekin, be and he is hereby Elected an Ex Officio – Member of the Society

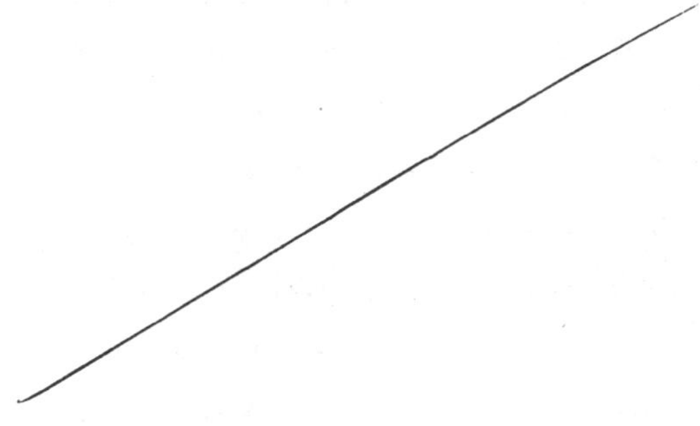

I Certify this to be a true extract from the records of the Society. **Witness** the Seal of the Society, this Tenth day of February 1865

Wm Coventry H Waddell

Recording Secretary.

(Sir) Harry Parkes [1865 Feb 10]

North-China Branch of the Royal Asiatic Society.

Shanghai, February 10th 1865

To

S. Wells Williams Esq. LL.D.

Peking

Sir,

I have the honor to inform you that at a public meeting of this Society, held on 13th December 1864 you were elected a Corresponding Member.

In communicating to you this Resolution the Council earnestly invite your able co-operation in the promotion of the objects of the Society. These consist in the collection and dissemination of information respecting China, Japan and the neighbouring countries, and the formation of a suitable Library and Museum. As it is desirable to give a practical character to the proceedings of the Society, its investigations will not be confined to literary and scientific subjects, but will be extended to all useful topics connected with industry and natural productions, commerce or useful arts, while the itineraries, charts or observations of travellers will be preserved for future explorers. The Society relies largely upon the support which it hopes to receive from its Corresponding Members, and will always welcome the advice or suggestions which their experience so well qualifies them to offer. Approved papers will be published with as little delay as possible, and copies of all printed transactions will be furnished gratuitously to Corresponding Members.

I forward herewith the Society's Journal for the past year, and have the honor to subscribe myself,

Sir,

Yours very faithfully,

Harry S. Parkes

President.

[NOTIFICATION OF ELECTION.]

The California Academy of Sciences

Has, at a Regular Meeting held at San Francisco, on the 17th day of November 1873 elected

S W Williams L L D

a Corresponding member of the Academy.

Geo. Davidson President.

Charles G. Yale Recording Secretary.

Connecticut Academy of Arts and Sciences,

New Haven, Conn., Nov 22d 1877

To

Prof. S. Wells Williams

Sir:

I have the honor to inform you that you were elected an active member of the

CONNECTICUT ACADEMY OF ARTS AND SCIENCES,

at a meeting held Nov. 21st 1877, and will be entitled to the privileges of membership on complying with the requirements of the Constitution, a copy of which I enclose.

The stated meetings of the Academy are held at Sheffield Hall on the third Wednesday of each month, at 7 1-2 o'clock P. M.

C. Hargers

Secretary.

(1881 Mo. 3)

Bible House, New York
March 5th, 1881

S. Wells Williams L.L.D.
New Haven

Dear Sir:

You have been elected President of the American Bible Society by the unanimous vote of its Board of Managers

We have the honor to be appointed a committee to notify you of the election and solicit your acceptance of the office.

It gives us pleasure to make this communication, and to express the earnest wish of the Board that you will take the place assigned to you, and thus aid in carrying on the great work of promoting the circulation of the Holy Scriptures through the world, by the united efforts of christians, of many denominations but partakers of like precious faith and all loyal to the same Holy Book.

Your early and favorable reply will greatly oblige the Society.

Respectfully and truly yours

Fred^k H. Wolcott,
Edward W. Gilman.
Charles Tracy } Committee.

Written for W. L. Kingsley
April 1878 - Too long

Samuel Wells Williams was born at Utica, N.Y. on the 22d of September 1812. His father, William Williams, was an eminent printer and publisher in Central New York, and during the fifteen years ending in 1832 carried on the largest bookselling business west of Albany. He was the eldest of sixteen children, and received the common school education ~~of~~ in the town Academy till he was 19, when he entered the Rensselaer School at Troy, then under the charge of Prof. Amos Eaton. This institution owed its foundation to the liberality of the Hon Stephen Van Rensselaer, but at this date he had almost reached the conclusion that it had no further mission, as the number of students had dwindled to one small class of six or seven. Mr Williams went through the regular course of studies in the natural sciences, and graduated in Sept. 1832.

While at the Rensselaer School, a proposal was made to him to take charge of the printing-office which was connected ~~in connection~~ with the ~~recently~~ Mission of the American Board at Canton recently established in that city. The Missionary ~~topic~~ cause was one which had long been familiar to him from the great interest taken, from the ~~foundation~~ formation of that Society, in its objects and operations by his parents. ~~from the establ~~ It is recorded that his mother, ~~had a~~ not long ~~short~~ time before her death in 1831, had attended a religious meeting where a collection was taken up for Foreign Missions, and she dropped a slip of paper into the plate on which she had written, "I give two of my sons." This early education in the details of the missionary enterprise made personal participation in the work seem more like a natural result, and Mr Williams readily agreed to the proposal to go to Canton.

More thorough acquaintance with the printer's trade having been obtained during the winter, in June 1833 he embarked from New York the ship "Morrison," in company with Rev Ira Tracy, and landed at Canton, Oct. 25th. The Mission then consisted only of Rev Mr Bridgman, while the total force of Protestant Missions in the Chinese Empire amounted to two missionaries, Dr. Morrison & Mr Bridgman, and two converts. All foreigners were obliged to live apart from the people in the western suburbs outside of the city walls, and among other means adopted by the authorities to keep them still more apart was to make it dangerous for educated natives to teach them to read & speak the Chinese language. The reality of this obstacle to free intercourse is indicated by the permission found in the 18th article of the American treaty of 1844 for American citizens to learn Chinese & buy books.

Mr Williams relates that the man whom

he employed as a sien-shang to acquire the language, used to bring a shoe every day to the house to exhibit in case a suspicious visitor should come into the room. The only work which was then done in the printing-office was to publish the Chinese Repository, a monthly periodical started by Mr Bridgman, aided by Dr Morrison & his son & others, intended to embody and diffuse accurate information respecting the Chinese people. As it was not safe to open an office at Canton to print Chinese books, the Mission decided in 1835 to send Mr Williams to Macao, where the Portuguese authority could protect such efforts, there to complete the printing of Medhurst's Chinese Dictionary of the Hokkeen Dialect, which had been left unfinished by the East India Company. This was completed in May 1837.

While carrying this book through the press, Mr Bridgman was preparing a work to aid students in the Canton Dialect, in which Mr Williams assisted. In July of that year, he went to Japan in the ship "Morrison", at the invitation of C. W. King, one of her owners, who wished to take advantage of the presence in Macao of seven castaway Japanese to return them to Yedo & see what openings could be found for trade or intercourse. This voyage was then really ~~considered~~ a very venturesome expedition for a merchant vessel in consequence of the entire want of charts for all the ports of Japan except Nagasaki. The ship stopped three days at Napa in Lewchew, and then proceeded to the Bay of Yedo. The officials having learned privately soon after she anchored that she was entirely defenceless, took no pains to find out what was her real object in thus suddenly intruding herself into waters where no foreign ship was known ever to have before ventured; and brought down four small cannon to the beach opposite. Even while she was coming up the Bay they intimated their designs by firing at her, and one of the shot fell so near as to make it necessary to anchor, and was thus the indirect means, probably, of preventing her from running on a reef of rocks. Early in the morning the four cannon opened upon the ship, Her ~~when~~ small crew ~~whose~~ had much ~~hard~~ labor to get in the anchor, but happily got out unharmed ~~and~~ before any serious damage was suffered; and Mr King tried to carry out his benevolent designs by making a second attempt to land the ~~seven men~~ at

Kagosima in the southwest part of Japan. Repulsed here in the same way, he returned to Macao, and the men were distributed here & there to earn their living. Mr Williams employed two ~~of them~~ in his printing-office, and was induced by the ability of one of these to read ~~his own language~~ Japanese to begin its study.

The way for direct mission work among the Chinese was still closed. ~~and~~ An attempt to get portions of the Scriptures printed at Canton had resulted in the imprisonment of two of the block-cutters, and there seemed no better way of ~~wor~~ ~~prosecuting his proper work than~~ ~~for~~ Mr Williams to print or prepare books designed to aid others in learning the language. ~~The work~~ labor of Mr Bridgman's work ~~was~~ ~~thus far on~~ prepared his Chinese Chrestomathy had now ~~gone~~ so far that the printing was commenced in October 1837, It was ~~and~~ completed in May 1841, a small folio volume of 736 pages, of which Mr Williams wrote ~~prepared~~ nearly one-half; the expenses of printing were partly defrayed by an English merchant. While this work was progressing the monthly issue of the Chinese Repository was kept up, and a translation ~~begun~~ of the Gospel of Matthew into Japanese begun by him in order to aid the returned sailors to understand its further instruction of his Japanese workmen was completed. There were only two or three copies of these translations made by them, and none have been preserved.

In Nov. 1844, Mr. Williams ~~returned~~ visited the United States, returning by way of Egypt and Palestine, which were then suffering from the ambitious wars of Mehemet Ali and his son Ibrahim, so that travelers in ~~them~~ were ~~was~~ not altogether safe when going through them. On reaching New York in Oct. 1845, he was successful in enlisting the effective aid of Hon Walter Lowrie, the Secretary of the Presbyterian Board of Missions, in obtaining a font of movable Chinese type cast from steel punches cut by Beyerhaus of Berlin. A careful examination ~~selection~~ of the ~~most~~ ~~common~~ characters in the Chinese language showed that by cutting punches for the few hundreds most commonly used, and for those which could not be divided perpendicularly, that ~~3000~~ the remainder could be formed by combining ~~combination~~ ~~of~~ the radical & primitive to make a new character, so that about 3000 ~~pieces~~ matrices would suffice to form over twenty thousand serviceable types.

In order to raise part of the funds for this enterprise, Mr Williams delivered many courses of lectures upon China, and the cutting of the punches was begun in 1847, though the type was not ready for use till 1857. The lectures thus delivered were rewritten and published in Nov. 1847, in two octavo vols, under the title of the "Middle Kingdom." Of this work, a resident in China, well competent to judge, has recently remarked, "Though printed nearly thirty years ago it has still a value in the full & accurate instruction it contains on all subjects relating to China that no book of later date has taken from it, & it is therefore still a standard book of reference for every student & Chinese scholar." The greater portion of it ~~was~~ has been translated into German & Spanish.

As a mark of ~~its~~ app[illegible] the faculty of Union College conferred ~~[illegible]~~ the honorary degree of LL.D. on the author.

Mr Williams was married Nov. 25. 1847 to Miss Sarah Walworth of Plattsburg, N. Y. and embarked for Canton with his wife in June 1848, reaching that city in September. His associate, Rev. Dr Bridgman, had removed to Shanghai to assist in the version of the New Testament jointly undertaken by a Delegation of the Protestant missionaries in China, and he accordingly took the editorial charge of the Chinese Repository. He also began the preparation of a Dictionary of the Canton dialect, ~~[illegible]~~ to the extent to which that ~~branch~~ patois of the Chinese language is spoken, and the increasing openings for missionary work among the Cantonese, ~~making~~ made it very desirable to ~~fix~~ furnish a convenient manual to help in learning it. The new openings for trade and intercourse at other ports had now so much diminished the position of Canton as their center, that it was deemed advisable to suspend the publication of the Chinese Repository in 1851, at the end of its 20th volume, in which full topical and subject indices render the contents of the whole series accessible. This work was carried on for twenty years under the joint charge of Dr Bridgman & Mr Williams; It was never any direct expense to the Mission, and ~~during~~ furnishes for that period, ~~furnishes~~ a reliable record of the foreign intercourse with China, as well as much accurate & valuable information upon the government, resources and languages of China & Japan.

In April 1853, the Expedition to Japan sent by the United States under Commodore Matthew C. Perry to bring about better relations with that secluded country, reached Hong-kong. Mr Williams was ~~invited~~ asked to accompany it as the Japanese & Chinese interpreter, as he was the only American who could read and speak both of those languages; and the Com- ~~Having~~

modore had determined to employ only such in the squadron. Having made arrangements for the conduct of the printing-office during his absence, he embarked in the U. S. sloop "Saratoga" in May, and reached Napa on the same day that the other three ships came in from Shanghai. The fears of the Lewchewan rulers as to the designs of such a formidable force were soon allayed, and they agreed to furnish such supplies as the islands afforded. The squadron, two steamers towing the two corvettes, soon left them for the Bay of Yedo; and anchored off Uraga. The Japanese authorities were perplexed by the demands of its commander, but after a short discussion agreed to receive the President's Letter, and consider its contents. The interview for this purpose was held on a beach half a mile or more north of the same spot where sixteen years before the Japanese had placed their guns to drive away the "Morrison"; and the contrast indicated very plainly that a new era was dawning in the land of the Rising Sun.

On the return of the squadron in February 1854, the negotiations were resumed. The Japanese were disinclined to admit more foreigners to their shores except under restrictions similar to those practiced at Nagasaki, but the negotiations were concluded on the 31st of March by signing the treaty of Kanagawa, which admitted the American flag & American consuls to the two ports of Simoda & Hakodadi. On his return to China from visiting them, to arrange the mode of trade, Com. Perry stayed at Napa long enough to negotiate & sign a Compact on the 12th of July with the Regent of Lewchew, stipulating for the kind treatment and relief of American ships in need of supplies. In all these conferences, Mr Williams bore a prominent part, and his ability to converse with the Japanese on shore and in their villages, answer their inquiries as to the real designs of the Expedition, and aid them in carrying on the little trade allowed at first, did much to allay their fears, and initiate the coming intercourse.

On returning to Canton, his principal work was carrying the Tonic Dictionary of the Canton Dialect through the press, printing each sheet as fast as the copy was ready. It was completed in July 1856, making an octavo volume of 900 pages, and proved to be a convenient manual for all students of the language. A fourth edition of the Commercial Guide was published the same year; it was entirely rewritten and much enlarged from the previous edition.

In July 1855, Mr Williams was appointed Secretary of Legation and Chinese Interpreter by President Pierce, in place of Peter Parker, who was made U. S. Minister to China. This appointment was made ~~at the suggestion of Com. Perry~~ without his knowledge, but as Dr Parker reached China soon after, time was ~~allowed~~ ~~obtained~~ available for Mr Williams to finish the two works then ~~on~~ in the press before entering upon all the duties of his new position. In October 1856, the troubles with the English authorities about the Lorcha "Arrow" began at Canton, and in the fire of December 15th the printing office belonging to the Mission and all its books and types were burned. This included about 6000 volumes of the various books already printed, a hundred sets of the Repository, and the font of Chinese type cut at an expense of more than $10.000 by the East India Company for Dr Morrison's Dictionary, among them. This office had been conducted by Mr Williams for 22 years. ~~and in such a manner that~~ During this time it had issued nineteen different publications aggregating about 30,000 volumes of all kinds, without any direct ~~ex~~ outlay by the parent Society in America; Nearly all of them were in English, and seven were to aid in learning the language.

The arrival of Hon. Wm B. Reed in 1857 ~~was~~ as U. S. Minister was in the midst of the excitement caused by the proceedings of the British authorities against Gov. Yeh at Canton. An embargo had been laid by the former on American & all foreign trade at that port without any declaration of war, and the irritation of all parties was ~~increasing~~ increased by the ~~menacing~~ difficulty of learning what were the complaints & wishes of the British. In ~~May~~ February 1858, the representatives of England & France having invited those of the United States and Russia to join them in a peaceful representation to the court of Peking, which failed of any direct effect, these four Powers appeared off the Pei-ho Forts. The first two ~~attacked those forts, and~~ soon forced their way up to Tientsin, and all ~~of them~~ four soon after opened negotiations with the Chinese high commissioners at Tientsin, which resulted in ~~a many~~ establishing ~~foreign ministers in Peking, and~~ better relations with the Imperial Court. In these negotiations, Mr Williams aided Mr Reed, and was ~~successful~~ instrumental in getting the article into the American Treaty which permitted the free exercise of the Christian religion among the Chinese people. He also had charge of all the details of ~~the~~ investigati~~ng~~ ~~into~~ the losses of American citizens at Canton and elsewhere; and after Mr Reed's departure ~~to~~ in December, the duty of arranging ~~for~~ the manner of paying the awards. On the arrival of Mr. Ward as U.S. Minister in 1859, it was agreed with the British & French plenipotentiaries that all should proceed to Peking in company there to exchange ratifications. But the Chinese general Săngkolinsin had determined to defend Tientsin from a second capture, and the Allies were repulsed at the Pei-ho Forts in their attempt to ascend the river. The American Mission proceeded to the Capital alone, by going north of Tientsin, & and ~~another way, and~~ were there ten days engaged most of the time in a ~~singular~~ discussion about the performing ~~manner~~ of performance ~~of~~ the ceremony of knocking head when appearing before the Emperor. Mr Ward refused to kneel, or make any approach to such a gesture, & left the city to exchange treaty ratifications at Peh-tang. An account of this visit was given by Mr. Williams in the Eclectic Magazine for April 1861.

~~Mr. Williams, has m~~ The Legation now returned to the south of China, where the atrocious coolie trade was assisted by ~~involving~~ American ships carrying away the kidnapped men. One ship was ~~complained~~ charged with having such on board, and Mr Williams superintended ~~attended at~~ the examination of over three hundred men, all of whom were released and sent home. In March 1860, having obtained leave of absence, he visited the United States. ~~going by way of San Francisco in a ship carrying the Chi nese coolies~~ going by way of San Francisco and carrying the ratified Treaty to Washington. This visit was made ~~during the excitement pre ceding the Southern rebellion~~ made while the British & French forces were advancing on Peking, ~~and~~ establishing their Legations in that capital, and placing the future relations of China with all foreign nations on a basis of equity and treaty rights.

In Sept. 1861, Mr Williams returned to ~~reached~~ China with his family, and Mr Burlingame arrived the next month ~~in October~~. It was too late in the season to go to the capital ~~Peking~~, and the Legation therefore ~~was~~ remained in the South till July 1862, when it was transferred to Peking. During this interval, Mr Williams rewrote the fourth and latest ~~prepared an entirely new~~ edition of the Commercial Guide, in an octavo volume of 670 pages, adapted to the ~~new~~ new political & commercial changes, and including those recently made with Japan, Siam & the Philippine Is. This made it an entirely new work, and it still remains a the most valuable aid to the foreign merchant ~~in carrying on his trade~~ in these details. A compilation of all the treaties between ~~those~~ these eastern ~~same~~ countries and the United States, with the decrees issued by the American Ministers in China was published by him for the reference ~~of~~

In June 1863, the American Legation was settled at Peking. The losses sustained by American citizens had been all paid ~~up~~ in full by the Chinese, ~~and they had~~ There was no desire ~~to excite~~ for another quarrel between ~~them~~ China and any foreign nation, but rather to help her to quell the Taiping rebellion which was rapidly depopulating the central provinces. From 1863 to ~~1872~~ 1871, Mr Williams remained at Peking, ~~and~~ During the intervals of official duty as Chinese Secretary, he ~~was~~ occupied himself in preparing a Syllabic Dictionary of the Chinese Language; in the Court Language, which was ready for the press in Dec. 1871. The Minister, Hon F F Low, took much interest in the completion of this work, and readily gave permission for him to repair to Shanghai to print it. The ~~whole~~ body of it was completed in June 1873, when ~~it~~ the author returned to Peking to prepare the necessary indexes, ~~and this was~~ The toil of examining the proofs had materially impaired his health, so that the change was very necessary. The Dictionary is in one quarto volume of 1336 pages, and has proved to be of great use to missionaries & other students of the Chinese language. The cost of printing and ~~stereotyping~~ publication was all defrayed by the author.

In November 1874, the American Minister B.P. Avery presented his letter of credence to the Emperor of China, and this ceremony was one of great interest to Mr Williams, to whom the long discussion held with Kwei-liang in 1859 ~~was~~ on the mode of audience on such occasion was still fresh. It also indicated ~~marked~~ the peaceful settlement of the last perplexing question with the Imperial Government, and a comparison of it with the questions which ~~were~~ demanded their settlement ~~on his landing~~ at Canton in Oct 1833, was both instructive & encouraging & showed how great had been the progress in establishing better relations during the interval.

In March 1875, Mr Williams ~~returned~~ left Peking for a visit to the United States ~~on a leave of absence~~ and this second travel through Europe after an interval of thirty years exhibited almost as great a change in political affairs there as had been seen in China. On ~~his~~ returning to his post in May of the next year, he decided to resign the situation he had held in the Legation for twenty-one years; ~~The chief the blue book~~ the official Register of the State Department for that year showed that no other officer ~~one~~ out of the country had been that length of time ~~as long~~ in its ~~service~~ diplomatic service. During this period he had acted as Chargé d'Affaires nine times, making nearly five years altogether. He had also built a house to accommodate the Legation on a manner more like those of other foreign nations, as there were ~~none~~ no dwellings suitable among the natives. The letter of resignation having been accepted, and the appointment of his successor Chester Holcombe ~~having~~ received SWWilliams left Peking Oct 25th just forty-three years from the day he landed at Canton. So far as he knew, ~~there was~~ not a foreigner remained ~~living~~ in China who was there when he arrived; & most of the missionaries in the country were younger than that date. The retrospect of the great progress made in promoting and enlarging the plans for the instruction & welfare of the people and government of the Empire was a source of deep gratitude. The Protestant missionaries in Peking & Shanghai united in farewell ~~in~~ letters, ~~to him~~ expressive of ~~these things~~ ~~and~~ their friendship for him and appreciation of the aids his books had given them in their work.

On reaching the United States in December, Mr. Williams took up his residence in New Haven. ~~There~~ A proposal had been made to him by his friends several years before to leave China, and take a professorship of Chinese in Yale College, but the Dictionary was not

and nothing was done about it.
then completed, The ~~appointment~~ matter was now reconsidered, and the appointment was made by the Faculty & Corporation of the University in June 1877 to the newly constituted chair of Chinese Language & Literature. It is the first one established in the country.

[*From "The Chinese Recorder," June,* 1889.]

S. Wells Williams, LL.D.

[THE following brief autobiographical sketch has a certain interest in being the only detailed account of his life which the late Dr. Williams is known to have written. It was prepared in 1878, and is noteworthy as furnishing his own mature opinions upon the principal events in his career.]

Samuel Wells Williams, the oldest of the sixteen children of William Williams, was born in Utica, New York, September 22, 1812. He received a common-school education in the Town Academy, and at the age of 19 entered the Rensselaer School at Troy, then under the charge of Prof. Amos Eaton. This institution owed its foundation to the liberality of the Hon. Stephen Van Rensselaer, but at this date he had almost reached the conclusion that it had no further mission, as the number of students had dwindled to one small class of six or seven. Mr. Williams went through the regular course of studies in the natural sciences, and graduated in September, 1832.

While at the Rensselaer School, a proposal was made to him to take charge of the printing-office which was connected with the Mission of the American Board, recently established in Canton. The missionary cause was one which had long been familiar to him from the great interest taken in that society by his parents. It is recorded that his mother, not long before her death in 1831, had attended a religious meeting, where a collection was taken up for foreign missions, and she dropped a slip of paper into the plate, on which was written, "I give two of my sons." This early education in the details of the missionary enterprise made personal participation in the work seem a natural sequence, and Mr. Williams readily agreed to the proposal to go to Canton.

2

More through acquaintance with the printer's trade having been obtained during the winter, in June, 1833, he embarked from New York in the ship *Morrison*, and landed at Canton, October 25. The mission then consisted only of Rev. E. C. Bridgman, while the total force in China amounted to but two missionaries—Bridgman and Morrison—and two converts. All foreigners were then obliged to live apart from the people, outside of the city walls, and among other means adopted by the authorities to isolate them was that of forbidding educated natives to teach them the language. The man employed by Mr. Williams as *sien-shăng*, to acquire the colloquial, used to bring a shoe every day to the house to exhibit in case a suspicious visitor should enquire his business with the "barbarian." The only work which could then be done in the printing-office was the publication of the *Chinese Repository*. It being unsafe to keep the office in Canton, the mission, in December, 1835, sent Mr. Williams and his press to Macao, there to complete the printing of Medhurst's Dictionary of Hokkiën Dialect, left unfinished by the East India Co. This was completed in May, 1837. While carrying this book through the press Mr. Williams also assisted in preparing Bridgman's Chinese Chrestomathy.

In July of that year he went to Japan in the ship *Morrison*, at the invitation of one of her owners, who wished to take advantage of the presence in Macao of seven castaway Japanese to return them to Yedo and see what opening could be found there for trade or intercourse. This voyage was then really a very venturesome expedition for a merchant vessel, in consequence of the entire want of charts for all the ports of Japan, except Nagasaki. Upon reaching the Bay of Yedo, the officials, having learned privately that the ship was wholly defenceless, took no pains to learn the real object of thus intruding herself into waters where no foreign ship had ever before ventured, but brought four small cannon to the beach. Even while she was progressing up the bay they intimated their hostility by firing at her, one shot falling so near as to make it necessary to anchor. Early in the morning the guns again opened upon the ship, and her small crew had much labor to get up the anchor before any serious damage was suffered. Mr. King tried to carry out his benevolent design by making a second attempt to land the Japanese at Kagosima, but being again repulsed the vessel returned with them to Macao, where they were distributed here and there amongst the foreigners to earn their living. Mr. Williams employed two in his printing-office, and was induced by the ability of one of these to read Japanese, to begin the study of that language.

3

In China no way for direct mission work was yet opened. Mr. Williams' best work seemed still to lie in the printing and preparing of aids towards learning the language, and with this in view he devoted what time he could to the exercises in the Chrestomathy, which was issued in May, 1841, and of which Mr. Williams compiled about one-half; the expenses of printing were partly defrayed by an English merchant. As soon as this was out, and in addition to the continued editorial work on the *Repository*, he began the writing and printing of the Easy Lessons in Chinese, completed 1842, a small manual after the method of Ollendorf. Following this he wrote his English and Chinese Vocabulary in the Court Dialect, published in January, 1844, and designed to facilitate the intercourse between foreigners and natives at the newly-opened ports. Another smaller publication, called the *Chinese Commerical Guide*, and intended to furnish foreign merchants with useful information respecting trade and navigation under the new treaties, was compiled by Mr. Williams; the same year he finished a translation of Genesis, designed for the further instruction of his Japanese workmen. Only two or three MS. copies of this and a previous translation of Matthew were made, and none have been preserved.

In November, 1844, he visited the United States, returning thither by way of Egypt and Palestine. On reaching New York in November, 1845, he was successful in enlisting the effective aid of Hon. Walter Lowrie, the Secretary of the Presbyterian Board of Missions, in obtaining a font of movable Chinese type from steel punches cut by Beyerhaus of Berlin. A careful examination of the characters in the Chinese language showed that by cutting punches for the few hundreds not commonly used, and for those which could not be divided perpendicularly, the remainder could be formed by combination in such a way that about 3,000 matrices would suffice to form over twenty thousand serviceable types. To raise a part of the funds for this enterprise, Mr. Williams delivered many courses of lectures upon China throughout the United States, and the cutting of the punches was begun in 1847, though the type was not ready for use until 1857. The lectures thus delivered were re-written and published in November, 1847, in two volumes, under the title of the *Middle Kingdom*. Of this work a resident in China, well competent to judge, remarked as long after its issue as 1877, "Though printed nearly thirty years ago it has still a value in the full and accurate instruction it contains on all subjects relating to China that no book of later date has taken from it, and it is therefore still a standard book of reference for every student and Chinese scholar." The greater portion of it was subsequently translated into German and Spanish. As a mark of approval the faculty of Union College conferred upon the author the honorary title of LL.D.

Mr. Williams was married November 25, 1847, to Miss Sarah Walworth, and embarked for Canton with his wife in June, 1848, reaching China in September. His associate, Dr. Bridgman, had removed to Shanghai, and he accordingly took upon his return to the printing-office the entire editorial charge of the *Chinese Repository*. He also began the preparation of a Dictionary of the Canton Dialect, for the extent to which that patois is spoken, and the increasing openings for missionary work among the Cantonese made it very desirable to furnish a convenient manual to help in learning it. The new openings for trade and intercourse at other ports had now so much diminished the position of Canton as their center that it was deemed advisable to suspend the publication of the *Repository* in 1851, at the conclusion of its 20th volume. During the twenty years in which this work was carried on under Messrs. Bridgman and Williams it was never any direct expense to the mission, while it furnished for that period a reliable record of the foreign intercourse with China, as well as much accurate and valuable information upon the governments, resources and languages of China and its neighboring lands.

In April, 1853, the Expedition to Japan sent by the United States under Commodore Perry, to bring about better relations with that secluded country, reached Hongkong. Mr. Williams was asked to accompany the squadron in the capacity of Japanese and Chinese interpreter, since he was the only American who could read and speak both of those languages, and the Commodore had determined to employ only his countrymen in the squadron. Upon their arrival at Napa they soon succeeded in allaying the fears of the Lewchewan rulers as to the designs of such a formidable force, and presently induced the natives to furnish such supplies as the islands afforded. The fleet then repaired to the Bay of Yedo, where the Japanese authorities were perplexed by the demands of its commander, but after a short discussion agreed to receive the President's letter and consider its contents. The interview for this purpose was held on a beach but half a mile from the spot where sixteen years before the Japanese had placed their guns to drive away the *Morrison*, and the contrast between that experience and this indicated very plainly that a new era was dawning for the land of the Rising Sun.

Upon the return of the ships by agreement, in February, 1854, the negotiations were resumed. The Japanese were disinclined to admit foreigners to their shores, except under restrictions similar to those practised at Nagasaki, but the negotiation was finally concluded on the 31st of March, by signing the treaty of Kanagawa, which admitted the American flag and American Consuls to the two ports of Simoda and Hakodadi. In all these conferences Mr. Williams was necessarily closely engaged, and his ability to converse with the Japanese on shore, in town and farm, answering their natural inquiries as to the real designs of the Expedition and aiding them to carry on the little trade allowed at first, did much to allay their fears and initiate the coming intercourse.

Once more in Canton his principal work was carrying through the press his Tonic Dictionary of the Canton Dialect already begun, printing each sheet as fast as the copy was ready. It was completed in July, 1856, an octavo of 900 pages, forming a convenient manual for all students of the language. A fourth edition of the *Commercial Guide* was published the same year, entirely re-written and much enlarged from the previous issue. In July, 1855, Mr. Williams had been appointed United States Secretary of Legation and Chinese Interpreter, in place of Peter Parker, who was made Minister to China. This appointment was made without his knowledge or consent, but, time being allowed him to finish the two works then in press before entering upon all the duties of his new position, he accepted the place provisionally upon obtaining the consent of his Mission Board. In December, 1856, upon the commencement of hostilities between the English and Chinese, the printing-office belonging to the mission, with all its stock of books and types, was burned, some 6,000 volumes in all of the various books printed there. During the twenty-two years while this office had been in charge of Mr. Williams it had issued nineteen different publications, many of them aids to learning the language, aggregating about 30,000 volumes, without any direct outlay by the parent Society in America.

The arrival of Hon. Wm. B. Reed as U. S. Plenipotentiary, in 1857, was in the midst of the excitement caused by the proceedings of the British authorities against Governor Yeh at Canton. Without any declaration of war an embargo had been laid by the former on American and all foreign trade at that port, and the irritation of all parties was increased by the difficulty of learning what were the complaints and wishes of the British. In February, 1858, upon invitation of England and France, the envoys of the United States and Russia joined them in a peaceful representation to the court of Peking, which failing of any direct effect, these four powers together repaired to the mouth of the Pei-ho. Soon after the destruction of the forts there the four ministers opened negotiations with the Chinese High Commissioners at Tientsin, which resulted in establishing better relations with the Imperial court. In these negotiations Mr. Williams, while aiding Mr. Reed, was personally instrumental in getting the article into the American treaty which permitted the free exercise of the Christian religion among the Chinese people. He also had charge afterwards of the details of investigating the losses of American citizens at Canton and elsewhere ; and upon Mr. Reed's departure, in December, the duty of arranging for the manner of paying the awards. On the arrival of Mr. J. E. Ward as U. S. Minister, in 1859, it was agreed with the British and French Plenipotentiaries that all should proceed to Peking in company, there to exchange the treaty ratifications. But the Chinese General San Ko Lin-sin had determined to defend Tientsin from a second capture, and the allies in their attempts this time to ascend the river were repulsed at the Pei-ho forts. The Americans, being non-belligerents, proceeded by land to the capital alone and remained there ten days, engaged most of the time in a discussion about performing the ceremony of the *kotow* when appearing before the Emperor. Mr. Ward refused to kneel or make any approach to such a gesture, and finally left the city without an audience to exchange ratifications at Peh-tang. An account of this visit was afterwards written by Mr. Williams for the Journal of the China Branch of the Asiatic Society.

In March, 1860, after superintending the examination and release of over 300 coolies kidnapped on board of an American vessel in Hongkong, he returned to the United States *viâ* San Francisco, carrying the ratified treaty to Washington. This visit was made while the British and French forces were advancing on Peking and establishing their legations there, placing the future relations of China with all foreign nations on a basis of equality and treaty right. The American legation was transferred to the capital in 1862, after the return of Mr. Williams and the arrival in China of Mr. A. Burlingame as minister. Before this move Mr. Williams had again re-written his *Commercial Guide*, adapting it to the recent political and commercial changes and issuing it in a fifth edition, which still remains as an aid to foreign merchants in these matters.

From 1862 to 1871 Mr. Williams remained at Peking, and during the intervals of official duty as Secretary and Interpreter occupied himself in preparing a Syllabic Dictionary of the Chinese Language in the court dialect. The work was put through the press at Shanghai, under the author's personal supervision during

7

the years 1872 and 1873; at the end of this toil he returned much prostrated in health to Peking. This Dictionary, a quarto volume of 1,336 pages, has proved to be of good service to missionaries and other students of the Chinese language. The cost of printing and publication was defrayed by the author. In November, 1874, the American Minister, B. P. Avery, presented his letter of credence in person to the Emperor of China. This ceremony was one of great interest to Mr. Williams, in whose mind the long discussions held with the Chinese Commissioners on this subject in 1859 were still fresh; it marked the peaceful settlement of the last perplexing question with the Imperial government, and a comparison of its gravity with that of the questions demanding settlement upon his first landing at Canton, in 1833, was both instructive and encouraging as indicating the progress in establishing better relations between China and the West during this interval.

After a furlough in 1875, when he made a second journey through Europe to America, Mr. Williams returned (1876) to Peking and resigned his post in the legation. He had held his situation for twenty-one years, a longer time than any other officer then in the diplomatic service of his country; during this period he had acted as Chargé d'Affaires nine times, a service altogether of nearly five years as head of the legation. He had also, out of his private funds, built houses to accommodate the legation in a manner suitable to its pretensions and more like the establishments of other foreign nations, there being no native dwellings in Peking that could well be used. Upon his final departure from the capital, October 25, 1876, just forty-three years from the day he reached Canton, there was not so far as he knew a single foreigner in China who was there when he arrived. The retrospect of the great progress made in promoting and enlarging the plans for the instruction and welfare of the people and government of the empire was a source of deep gratitude. The Protestant missionaries, both in Peking and Shanghai, united in farewell letters expressive of their friendship for him and appreciative of the aids his books had furnished them in their work.

Returning to the United States in December of this year Mr. Williams took up his residence in New Haven, Conn. A proposal had been made to him several years before to take a professorship of Chinese in Yale College, but his determination to remain in China and finish his Dictionary had prevented his accepting the offer; the appointment being now renewed he was installed in the newly constituted chair of Chinese Language and Literature by the faculty and corporation of the University in June, 1877, as the first professor of this sort in the country.

8

[Mr. Williams spent the remaining years of his life in New Haven. The chief occupation of this period was the entire revision of his *Middle Kingdom*, which was issued from Scribner's press, practically re-written and greatly enlarged, in October, 1883. A considerable number of essays, lectures and contributions to periodicals, mostly on topics relating to Eastern Asia, were the work of his busy pen before his health failed and he was obliged to stop writing in 1882. He died at his home, February 16th, 1884, and was buried at his birth-place, Utica, New York.]

卫三畏自传(1)

马军 译

1812年9月12日，卫三畏（萨谬尔·韦尔斯·威廉姆斯，Samuel Wells Williams）出生在纽约的尤蒂卡（Utica），是老威廉姆斯（ William Williams）的第16个孩子。他在城内的公立学校读完了小学。19岁那年，进入了特洛伊（Troy）的伦塞拉尔（Rensselaer）学校，该校由阿莫斯·伊顿教授（Prof. Amos Eaton）主管，创办人是慷慨的斯蒂芬·范·伦塞拉尔（Hon. Stephen Van Rensselaer）。当时，学校差点关闭，因为学生已降至6、7个人。卫三畏在那里接受了正规的自然科学教育，于1832年 9月毕业。

在伦塞拉尔学校时，有人曾建议卫三畏去负责美国公理会（Mission of the American Board）新近设在广州的印刷所。对这个差会，他的父母付诸了极大的热忱，卫三畏长期以来耳濡目染。据说他的母亲在 1831年去世前不久，曾参加过一个为海外教会募捐的宗教会议。她将一张长纸条放入盘中，上面写着“我捐献两个儿子”。由于从小深受宗教浸染，长大以后，卫三畏便很自然地投身于传教事业。于是，他决定接受建议前往广州。

卫三畏花了一个冬季熟悉印刷业务。1833年6月，他从纽约出发坐马礼逊号（Morrison）船去广州，同年10月25日到达。教会在广州只有裨治文牧师（E.C. Bridgeman）一人，即使在全中国，当时也不过还有马礼逊牧师（Robert Morrison）和另两个皈依者。(2)中国当局对外国人实施了隔离措施，全部外国人都住在城外，当局还禁止中国文人向他们教授汉语。卫三畏雇的教口语的“先生”，每天都要把鞋子带到房间里摊开，因为疑心重重的检察者总想查他和“蛮夷”有什么交易。当时印刷所能够做的唯一工作是出版《中国丛报》（Chinese Repository）。在广州办印刷所颇不安全。1835年12月，卫三畏和《丛报》迁往澳门。在那里，于1837年5月印刷完成了麦都思（W.H. Medhurst）的客家话词典，这是东印度公司遗留下的工作。(3)与此同时，卫三畏还协助裨治文准备出版他的中文选读。(4)

是年7月，卫三畏应马礼逊号船主之请前往日本，此行是为了送 7名落难的日本人返回江户。船主亦想借此机会寻找可以通商的口岸。对一条商船来说，这次航行风险很大。因为除了长崎，他们并没有其它日本港口的海图。抵达江户湾时，虽然明知该船毫无抵抗能力，船上的人还是很想探寻这个外国船只前所未到的水域。结果，岸边出现了日本人的四门小炮，并且开炮示警。一发炮弹落在船舷附近，船不得不抛锚停航。清晨，日本人再次开炮，为使船只免遭重创，船员尽力收起了铁锚。仁慈的金先生（Mr. King）决定改驶鹿儿岛，想在那里送7名日本人上陆，结果同样被挡了回来。日本人只得随船返回澳门，然后解散，依靠西方人维持生计。卫三畏的印刷所雇佣了其中2人，这给了他学习日语的机会。(5)

在中国依然无法直接传教，卫三畏所能做的是尽力抽出时间，继续印刷和编辑汉语读本。读本出版于1841年5月，约有一半出自卫三畏之手。一个英国商人支付了部分的印刷费用。紧接其后，他除了照旧承担《中国丛报》的编辑工作外，还在1842年编印完成了一份奥伦多尔夫（Ollendorf）式的《简易汉语教程》（Easy lessons in Chinese）。之后，他又用官话写了一本《英华韵府例举》（ An English and Chinese Vocabulary in the Court Dialect），出版于1844年。为了便于新开口岸中外人员的交往，卫三畏编辑了另一本名为《中国商务指南》（Chinese Commercial Guide）的书籍，旨在向外商提供新条约下贸易和航海的有用知识。同年，他又完成了《旧约·创世纪》的翻译，目的是进一步向他的日本雇员传教。此前只有二、三个手稿和《马太福音》的译本，但是都没有保存下来。

1844年11月，卫三畏经埃及、巴勒斯坦返回美国。次年11月，抵达纽约。他成功地获取了长老会（Presbyterian Board of Missions）干事娄理华（Hon. Walter Lowrie）的大力支持，得到了一副由柏林拜尔豪斯（Beyerhaus）厂钢压的中文活字。经仔细检查后发现，通过冲压有几百个汉字不能正常使用，有一些则不能作垂直分割。剩余的通过组合，大约3000个字模可作成2万多个可用的铅字。铅字的冲压1847年就已开始了，但直到1857年才投入使用。为了替业务筹集一部分资金，卫三畏还在美国各地作了许多有关中国的演讲。演讲稿经整理后于1847年11月出版，共2卷，书名是《中国总论》（The Middle Kingdom）。关于此书，一个在华居民在1877年（即此书出版后很久）极为正确地指出："虽然此书的出版已近30年了，但是仍有很大价值，它收录的信息全面、精确，涉及到中国问题的所有方面，其价值非其他书籍所能替代。所以对中外学者来说，这是一部标准的参考书"。该书的大部分被翻译成德文和西班牙文。联合学院（ Union College）为了表示对此书的赞赏，决定授予卫三畏名誉法学博士学位（LL.D）。

1847年11月25日，卫三畏和萨拉·沃尔沃思小姐（Miss Sarah Walworth）结婚。1848年6月他携妻坐船返回广州，同年9月到达。此时，他的同事裨治文博士已去了上海。所以，他承担起印刷所和《中国丛报》的编辑全责。他开始准备编写一本广东话词典。在这个方言区域，对广东人的传教工作刚刚开始，因此急需一本便利的手册。由于其他通商口岸的开辟，广州的中心地位已大大下降了。所以在1851年，《中国丛报》决定停刊。此时该刊已发行了20册。20年间，这本杂志在裨治文和卫三畏的主持下，从未接受过任何方面的直接津贴。该刊积累下那个时期中外关系的可靠纪录，还有关于中国政府、资源、语言和它邻近地区精确的、富有价值的信息。

1853年4月，由培理海军准将（Commodore Perry）指挥的派往日本的舰队到达了香港，它旨在与那个封闭的国家建立良好的关系。舰队要求卫三畏随行，担任日语和汉语翻译。因为他是唯一能够读、写这两种语言的美国人，所以准将决定雇佣他。到达那霸以后，他们成功地消除了琉球国王对这支强大舰队的恐惧。不久，又促使土人从岛上向他们提供给养。随后，舰队驶往江户湾。面对准将的要求，日本当局颇感窘迫。经简短的谈判后，日本人同意接受美国总统的信件，并答应对其内容给予考虑。为此在海岸边举行了一次面谈，地点就在 16年前日本人开炮驱逐马礼逊号船的半英里处。两次情形的对比鲜明地表明，这个"日出之国"的新时代来临了。

1854年2月，舰队按约定重新来到日本。谈判再度开始。日本人不愿让外国人进入他们的海岸，即使在长崎也必须置于严格的控制。 3月31日，谈判最后达成协议，签署了神奈川条约。允许星条旗和美国船只出现在下田和函馆。在所有这些谈判中，卫三畏紧密介入，他在海岸、城镇、农地和日本人交谈，回答他们提出的有关舰队真实意图的问题，帮助他们作一点获准的贸易，在消除恐惧和推动交往中作了许多工作。

一回到广州，卫三畏的主要工作是《英华分韵撮要》（Tonic Dictionary of the Chinese language in the Canton Dialect）的印刷，写好一页就印一页，到1856年全部完成，8开本， 900页。对学习语言的人来说，这是一本便利的手册。《中国商务指南》的第四版也在同年出版，与前一版相比，作了全面的修订和补充。 1855年7月，卫三畏接替伯驾（Peter Parker）出任美国公使馆头等参赞和翻译，伯驾被任命为驻华全权公使。这此任命预先并未征得卫三畏的同意，不过在就任前，他尚有充足的时间在印刷所里完成两部著作。在得到教会方面的首肯后，卫三畏暂时接受了任命。1856年12月爆发了英国和中国间的战争。属于教会的印刷所，连同成捆成捆的书籍和铅字都被焚毁了，那里有6000册各种印书。在卫三畏主持的22年里，这个印刷所已经出版了19种出版物，其中许多有助于汉语的学习，其总数有3万册，然而印刷所却没有用过美国母会的一分钱。

1857年，列卫廉（Hon. Wm. B. Reed）出任美国驻华全权公使。此时，人们正沉浸在兴奋之中，因为英国当局针对广州的叶总督采取了行动。未经任何宣战，前者即下达了美国和所有外国在广州的贸易禁令。由于不清楚英国的抱怨和意图，各方面颇感愤怒。1858年2月，应英、法两国的邀请，美国和俄国代表加入了他们的和平使团。直接的努力失败后，四强一起转向白河河口。攻破炮台后不久，四位使节在天津与中国高级官员开始谈判，结果取得了良好的成效。在这些谈判中，卫三畏帮助了列卫廉。为将"允许基督教在华自由传教"写入条约，他亲自发挥了作用。而后，他还负责详细调查美国公民在广州等地的损失。当12月列卫廉去职后，卫三畏负责安排赔偿事宜。1859年华若翰（Mr. J. E. Ward）就任美国驻华全权公使，他获准和英、法全权公使一起到北京换约。然而，中国僧格林沁将军决定保卫天津，以防止它第二次陷落。这一次联军想溯河而上，但是却被白河炮台挡住了。美国人没有参加战斗，经陆路到了北京，在那里呆了10天。许多时间用于讨论觐见皇帝时的礼仪。华若翰拒绝磕头，所以未见到皇帝就离开了北京，在北塘换了约。卫三畏写的有关这一事件的记载，后来刊发在《亚洲文会北中国支会报》上。

1860年3月，卫三畏经旧金山回美国华盛顿换约。此前，他曾在香港监督检查和释放被绑架在一条美国船上的300多名苦力。与此同时，英法联军正向北京挺进，在那里设立了公使馆。由此，未来的中外关系得以建立在一个平等、有条约保护的基础上。美国公使馆于1862年进驻北京，此时卫三畏已回到了中国，蒲安臣（A. Burlingame）也已出任驻华公使。在此之前，卫三畏对《中国商务指南》又作了修订，以适应政治、商业形势的变化。这已经是第五版了，在许多方面对外商依然有所帮助。

1862年至1871年，卫三畏住在北京，担任头等参赞和翻译。他利用空闲时间，编写了《汉英韵府》（A Syllabic Dictionary of the Chinese Language）。1872至1873年此书在上海付印，作者亲自监督。这是一件艰苦的工作，他搞得精疲力尽，最后回到北京。这本8开本词典，共1336页，实践证明，它对传教士和其他学习中国语言的人是极富帮助的。印刷和出版费用，由作者支付。1874年11月，美国驻华公使艾忭敏（B. P. Avery）亲自向中国皇帝递交国书，它标志着与清政府的最后一个"疙瘩"得到了圆满解决。这一仪式引起了卫三畏的极大关注。1857年曾就此问题与中国官员举行过漫长的谈判，卫三畏对此记忆犹新。此事的重要性与1833年他第一次到广州相比，同样富有益处和鼓舞人心。这标志着中西关系的进步。

1875年，卫三畏利用休假，从欧洲到美国又作了一次旅行。1876年回北京后，便辞去了在公使馆所任的职务。他在这个位置上干了21年，比美国任何一个外交官都要长。其间，他九次代理馆务（ Chargéd'Affaires），加在一起几乎有5年时间。由于北京的中国式房子都不尽人意，他便用公款为公使馆修建了与其他国家同样规模的房舍。1876年10月25日，卫三畏最后一次离开北京，而43年前的这一天，他正好到达广州。当时，他在中国仅认识一个外国人，今天则远非昔比。回顾中国政府和人民教育、福利发展中的巨大进步，换来的是深深的感激。北京和上海的新教教士们在告别信里，动情地表达了他们的友谊，同时也赞美卫三畏的著作，这些书对他们开展工作曾有过很大的帮助。

同年12月，卫三畏回到了美国，居住在康涅狄格州的纽黑文（ New Haven ）。由于在中国立下了完成词典的决心，因此当耶鲁大学请他就任中文教授时，他并未马上接受。几年以后，他终于应邀出任该校的中国语言文学讲座教授。讲座开设于1877年6月，在美国属于首创。

卫三畏的余生是在纽黑文度过的。其间，他主要对《中国总论》作了完整的修订。1883年10月，修订本由斯克里布纳（Scribner）出版社出版。卫三畏失去健康以前，在各种刊物上发表了许多散文、演讲稿和文章，内容大多数是关于东亚的。1882年他因病被迫搁笔。1884年2月16日，卫三畏在家中去世。就在他生日的那一天，被埋葬在纽约的尤蒂卡。

译者注：

(1) 此文实际上是卫三畏的自传，刊《教务杂志》（Chinese Recorder）第20期，1889年，第241-248页。文中最后一段是原编者在卫三畏去世后添加的。译文标题为译者所加。有关卫三畏的生平材料还可参见：一、卫福德 （Frederick Wells williams，卫三畏之子）：《卫三畏传》（The Life and Letters of Samuel Wells Williams, LL.D.Missionary, Diplomatist, Sinologue），1889年纽约、伦敦版。二、Muhlenberg Bailey：《已故本会通信会员卫三畏名誉法学博士》（Samuel Wells Williams,LL.D. Late Corresponding Member of the Society），载《美国地理协会杂志》（ Jour. Am.Geog.Soc.）第16册，1884年，第186-193页。三、《卫三畏博士》（Samuel Wells Williams,LL.D.），载《远东》（The Far East），I，No.6， 1876年，第140-142页。四、卫福德编：《卫三畏日记》（The Journal of S.Wells Williams, LL.D），载《亚洲文会北中国支会报》（1911年），第32-32页。
(2) 裨治文（1801-1861年），美国公理会教士。1830年来华，1832年创办《中国丛报》，1844年参与签订《中美望厦条约》， 1857-1859年任上海亚洲文会会长，一生写有许多关于中国的文章。马礼逊（1782-1834年），英国伦敦会教士，汉学家。1807年来华，在东印度公司广州办事处任职。1816年随阿美士德勋爵使团到北京，任翻译。
1833年任英国驻华商务基督署翻译。主要汉学著作有：《汉语语法》（A grammar of the Chinese language，1815年版）、《汉英字典》（Dictionary of the Chinese language，18131823年版）等。
(3) 麦都思（1796-1857年），英国伦敦会教士，汉学家。这里指的是他的《汉语客家话词典》（Dictionary of the Hokkeen dialect of the Chinese language,according to the reading and colloquial idioms）。
(4) 指的是裨治文的《粤语中文选读》（Chinese chrestomathy in the Canton dialect with English translation and notes,1841年澳门版）。
(5) 卫三畏关于此次航行的文章有：一、《莫礼逊号航行日本、琉球概述》（Narrative of a Voyage of the Ship Morrison, Captain D. Ingersoll, to Lewchew and Japan, in the months of July and August 1837），载《中国丛报》第6册，第209-229页、第353-380页。二、《从琉球到日本的航行中收集到的自然史标本》（ Specimens of Natural History, collected in a voyage to Lewchew and Japan），载《中国丛报》第6册，第406页。

WILLIAMS, SAMUEL WELLS (Sept. 22, 1812–Feb. 16, 1884), missionary, diplomat, and sinologue, was born in Utica, N. Y., the eldest of the fourteen children of William Williams, 1787–1850 [*q.v.*], a printer and bookseller, and Sophia (Wells) Williams. His parents were of old New England stock. Both were deeply religious and active in the work of the church. Because of his mother's ill health, he spent much of his childhood at his grandmother Wells's home at New Hartford, N. Y. As a boy he was studious and somewhat reserved; he early developed the interest in botany which he retained through life. He attended several schools, including one in Paris, Hill, N. Y., and the Utica High School. In 1831–32 he was a student at Rensselaer Polytechnic Institute in Troy. His father, asked to nominate a printer for the Canton press of the American Board of Commissioners for Foreign Missions, suggested him, and he accepted. He spent several months in 1832–33 studying the printing trade under his father's direction, and in June 1833 sailed for China.

Protestant missions among the Chinese were then twenty-six years old and were carried on by a small group who in China itself could maintain a precarious foothold only at Macao and Canton. Williams spent his first months in Canton, studying Chinese and Portuguese, managing the printing press, and contributing to the *Chinese Repository*, which had been recently initiated by Elijah Coleman Bridgman [*q.v.*]. In 1835 he and the press moved to Macao. Within the next decade, in addition to his direction of the press and his assistance with the *Chinese Repository*, he aided Bridgman in preparing *A Chinese Chrestomathy in the Canton Dialect* (1841) and compiled *Easy Lessons in Chinese* (1842), *An English and Chinese Vocabulary in the Court Dialect* (1844), and a *Chinese Topography* (1844), and edited *A Chinese Commercial Guide* (2nd ed., 1844). From 1845 to 1848 he was in the United States. There (Nov. 25, 1847) he married Sarah Walworth, by whom he had three sons and two daughters. Out of lectures which he gave during this sojourn in the United States grew the first edition of his *The Middle Kingdom* (2 vols., 1848), which for more than a generation was the standard book in English on China. In 1837 he had been a member of the *Morrison* party which attempted, unsuccessfully, to repatriate some shipwrecked Japanese. From one of these he learned enough Japanese to prepare in it a translation of the Gospel of Matthew. Because of this acquaintance with the language he was asked to accompany the Perry expedition as an interpreter, and in that capacity visited Japan in 1853 and in 1854. In 1856 he accepted an invitation to become secretary and interpreter of the American legation to China. At about the same time he completed his *A Tonic Dictionary of the Chinese Language in the Canton Dialect* (1856). His connection with the legation lasted until 1876. He helped negotiate the American treaty of Tientsin (1858), being responsible for the insertion in that document of the clause granting toleration to Christianity; he accompanied the party which went to Peking (1859) for the purpose of exchanging the ratifications of the treaty; he took up his residence in Peking (1863), being several times in charge of the legation in the intervals between ministers; he assisted Sweden (1870) in obtaining a treaty with China; and he compiled his much-used *A Syllabic Dictionary of the Chinese Language* (1874).

On his retirement to America he took up his residence in New Haven, Conn., becoming (1877) professor of the Chinese language and literature at Yale. The position was largely honorary, as the salary was small and he had no students. In spite of failing strength, however, he used the time to revise and enlarge his *Middle Kingdom* (2 vols., 1883), a task in which he was assisted by his son Frederick Wells [*q.v.*]. He actively opposed the restriction on Chinese immigration, and served as president of the American Bible Society and the American Oriental Society. Earnestly religious, he maintained his active interest in missions to the very last. Although he was a specialist on China and the outstanding American sinologist, his inquiring mind led him to range widely over the field of human knowledge, and he had a vast store of information on a great variety of subjects. Well-built, active, and wiry, but never especially robust, by temperate and regular habits and unremitting diligence he accomplished an enormous amount of work.

[G. H. Williams, "The Geneal. of Thomas Williams," in *New Eng. Hist. and Geneal. Reg.*, Jan. 1880; F. W. Williams, *The Life and Letters of Samuel Wells Williams* (1889); *Biog. Record . . . Rensselaer Polytechnic Inst.* (1887); ann. reports, Am. Board of Commissioners for Foreign Missions; H. Blodget, in *Chinese Recorder*, May–June 1884; Noah Porter, in *Missionary Herald*, Apr. 1884; obituary in *N. Y. Tribune*, Feb. 18, 1884.]

K. S. L.

WILLIAMS, FREDERICK WELLS (Oct. 31, 1857–Jan. 22, 1928), writer and teacher, was born in Macao, China, the son of Samuel Wells Williams [*q.v.*] and Sarah (Walworth) Williams and the descendant of Robert Williams who emigrated to Roxbury, Mass., from Norfolk County, England, in 1637. Most of his boyhood to the age of twelve was spent in China, chiefly in the American legation in Peking; and this fact, together with his father's long life and distinguished service in that country, determined his major interests. For a year he was in the public schools of Utica. Then for four years he prepared for college at the Hopkins Grammar School at New Haven, Conn. He graduated from Yale College in 1879 and spent the two and a half following years in study in Europe, in Göttingen, Berlin, and Paris. Returning to New Haven, he gave most of the succeeding two years to assisting his father in the revision and enlargement of the latter's *Middle Kingdom* (2 vols., 1883), for more than a generation the standard general work in English on China. In 1883–85 he was assistant in the library at Yale. On Nov. 19, 1885, he was married to Fanny Hapgood Wayland and with her he spent a year in Europe. From 1887 to 1893 he was the literary editor of the *National Baptist*, which was directed by his father-in-law, H. L. Wayland.

In 1893 he returned to Yale, this time to teach Oriental history, and he served on the Yale faculty until 1925. In his teaching he covered Central Asia, India, and the Far East and did much to stimulate interest in fields then generally neglected in the curriculums of American colleges and universities. It was to China, however, that he devoted the major part of his attention. Most of his books and numerous articles were on some phase of the history or problems of that country. Of these the chief were *The Life and Letters of Samuel Wells Williams* (1889) and *Anson Burlingame and the First Chinese Mission to Foreign Powers* (1912). From its inception in 1901 he was associated with Yale-in-China, the Yale foreign missionary society, which developed at Chang-sha a secondary school, a college, a hospital, a school of nursing, and a medical school. As chairman of its executive committee and its board of trustees he gave to it a large share of his time up to the very week of his death. To his wise counsel, his steadfast friendship for all those who served in Chang-sha, and his quiet courage in the recurrent crises that overtook the young enterprise, the undertaking owed much of its success. Aside from his connection with Yale-in-China, his life was that of a member of a university community. As secretary of his college class he devoted much attention to keeping in touch with its members and compiled *A History of the Class of Seventy-Nine, Yale College* (1906). Through his interest in literary matters he held membership in various clubs, which brought him in contact with those of like mind, and he was a member and vestryman of the St. John's Episcopal Church at New Haven. His home was much frequented by those concerned with the Orient and with literature. At the time of his death he had gathered what was one of the best private libraries on China in the United States. Calm and unhurried, he gave the impression on those who knew him of being not so much of a specialist as a cultivated gentleman, widely read and urbane. He died in New Haven.

[Autobiog. sketch in *A Hist. of . . . 1879, ante*; *Who's Who in America*, 1926–27; *Bulletin of Yale Univ. . . . Obituary Records . . . 1927–28* (1928); G. H. Williams, *The Williams Family* (1880), reprinted from *New England Hist. and Geneal. Register*, Jan. 1880; *N. Y. Times*, Jan. 23, 25, 28, 1928.] K. S. L.

第2部分

鸦片战争前后

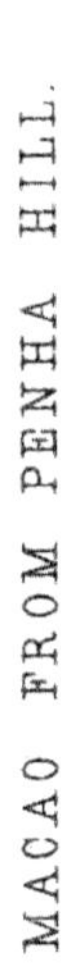

MACAO FROM PENHA HILL.

JESUIT CONVENT, MACAO.

CHINESE TEMPLE MACAO

マカオにあるプロテスタントの墓地

From nature by Heine Figures by Brown.

Lith. of SARONY & Co New York.

VIEW OF HONG-KONG FROM EAST POINT

FISH MARKET CANTON

American Consulate, and Port of Shanghai.

日本への門戸、キリスト教伝道の拠点

米船モリソン号で来琉した
ピーター・パーカー(左)と
カール・ギュツラフ(下)

両人は後のベッテルハイムの
先輩格で、特にベッテルハイ
ムがパーカー宛にしたためる
琉球宣教報告は貴重な記録。
ギュツラフはモリソン号以前、
アムハースト号でも来琉

澳门街景　陶德民摄

Templo de Kun Iam: a mesa onde foi assinado no século passado o tratado sino-americano. (GCS-23/7/1984

《望厦条约》签订处　澳门档案馆藏

List of Articles by S. Wells Williams in the Chinese Repository.

Alphabetical list of all the provinces, departments + districts in China.
Vol. XIII. pp. 320, 357, 418, 478, 513

Descriptive list of the largest towns + divisions in extra-provincial China.
Vol. XIII. 561.

Topography of the Province of Honan. Vol. XX. 546.

Topography of the Province of Yunnan. Vol. XVIII. 588.

Topography of the province of Kweichau. Vol. XVIII. 525.

Topography of the province of Húpeh. Vol. XIX. 97.

Topography of the province of Húnán. Vol. XIX. 156.

Topography of the province of Shánsí. Vol. XIX. 220.

Topography of the province of Sz'chuen. Vol. XIX. 317, 394.

Topography of the province of Kánsuh. Vol. XIX. 554.

Topography + divisions of extra-provincial China, ranges of the mountains, &c. Vol. XX. 57.

Course of the Yellow river, or Hwáng-ho. Vol. XIX. 499.

Notices of the Sagalier river + the island of Tarakai, opposite its mouth. Vol. XIX. 289.

Course + topography of the Chú Kiáng, or Pearl river, also called the Canton river. Vol. XX. 105, 113.

Visit of the U.S. brig Dolphin to the port of Kilung in Formosa for coal. Vol. XVIII. 392.

Journal of a trip overland from Háinán to Canton, in 1819 by J. R. supercargo of the Friendship. Vol. XVIII. 225.

Klaproth's account of the Chángpeh Shán, or Long White Mts. of Manchuria. Vol. XX. 296.
Death of Táukwáng, & papers connected with the accession of Hienfung to the throne. Vol. XIX. pp. 165, 231, 282.
Translation of the oath of the Triad Society, & account of its formation. Vol. XVIII. 281.
Account of the Miáutsz', & justice of the dealings of the Chinese with them. Vol. XIV. 106, 113.
Insurgents in Kwángsí. Vol. XX. pp. 53, 111, 224, 286, 492.
Illustrations of men & things in China. Vol. IX. 366, 506, 635; X. 104, 172, 472, 519, 613, 662; XI. 325, 434; XVII. 591.
Diet of the Chinese, & cost of living. Vol. III. 457.
Anecdotes from Chinese authors to illustrate human conduct, with a moral. Vol. XVII. 646. XVIII. 159.
Festivals given by the emperors Kánghí & Kienlung to old men in the empire. Vol. IX. 258.
Revenge of Miss Sháng Sánkwán. Vol. XVIII. 400.
Example of revenging a father's death. Vol. VIII. 345.
Examples of twenty-four filial children. Vol. VI. 130.
Three examples of female constancy. Vol. VI. 568.
Review of Lukcháu's Nü Hioh, or position & education of females in China. Vol. IX. 545.
Description & translation of a Shau Ping, or Longevity Screen. Vol. XIII. 535.
Explorers in the natural history of China, & sketch of the geology near Canton. Vol. III. 83.
Agriculture of the Chinese. Vol. III. 121.

Mode of raising rice. Vol. III. 231.
Description of the bamboo & palm. Vol. III. 261.
Description of the tea plant. Vol. VIII. 132
Review of Loureiro's Flora Cochinchinensis. Vol. V. 118.
Review of Gutzlaff's China Opened. Vol. VIII. 84.
Specimens of natural history collected in a voyage to Lewchew & Japan. Vol. VI. 406.
Chinese account of the lion, cat, &c., Vol. VII. 595.
Chinese account of the horse & ass. Vol. VII. 393.
Chinese account of the tapir & pangolin. Vol. VII. 44.
Description of the rhinoceros, elephant &c., Vol. VII. 136.
Dragon & other fabulous animals of the Chinese, & their ideas respecting them. Vol. VII. pp. 212, 250.
Account of the cormorant. Vol. VII. 541.
Chinese account of the bat & flying squirrel. Vol. VII. 90.
Chinese ~~account~~ notions of bees & wasps. Vol. VII. 485.
Proverbs & metaphors among the Chinese drawn from the habits of animals. Vol. VII. 231.
Notice of P. P. Thoms' work on ancient Chinese vases of the Sháng dynasty. Vol. XX. 489.
Chinese weights & measures. Vol. II. 444.
Popular ideas of the Chinese relating to the powers & operations of nature. Vol. X. 49; XI. 434.
Pagodas in & near Canton; their uses & the times of their erection. Vol. XIX. 535.
Notice of the Parisian font of Chinese types, & of an experiment of block stereotyping. Vol. III. 528.

Specimen of three-lined diamond Chinese type made
in Hongkong, & Chinese movable type. Vol. XX. 281.
Movable metallic types among the Chinese. Vol. XIX. 247.
Description of the Chinese bellows. Vol. IV. 37.
Description of the common agricultural implements used
by the Chinese. Vol. V. 485.
Memoir & account of the cultivation of hemp & the manufacture of grasscloth; by N. Rondot. Vol. XVIII. 216.
Erman's Travels in Siberia, & visit to Kiakhta. Vol. XX. 18.
Narrative of a mission of inquiry to the Jewish synagogue
in Kaifung fu in 1851. Vol. XX. 436.
List of foreign works ~~about~~ upon China, of a philological
nature, translations, travels &c., Vol. XVIII. 402, 657.
Table of sounds in three dialects of China. Vol. XI. 28.
Remarks on, & alterations proposed in the system of orthography for Chinese. Vol. VII. 490.
Thom's Esop's Fables rendered into the Chángchiū &
Tiéchiū colloquial, by Dyer & Stronach
Vol. XIII. 98.
Chhòng Sè Toan &c., with remarks on Romanizing the
Chinese language. Vol. XX. 472.
Biot's Essay on the history of public instruction in
China, & of the corporation of letters. Vol. XVIII. 57.
Vocabularies for Chinese to learn English. Vol. VI. 276.
Bazin's Théatre Chinois, ou choix de Pièces de Théatre
composées sur les empereurs Mongols.
Vol. XVIII. 113.

Ying Hwán Chi-lioh, or General survey of the Maritime Circuit, by Sü ~~Kiyii~~ Kiyii Vol. XX. 169.

Yung Yuen Tsiuen-tsih, or collection of Garden of Banians, & examination of an alleged forgery. Vol. XX. 340.

Translation of a ballad on picking tea. Vol. VIII. 195.

Macgowan's Philosophical almanac in Chinese & account of the electric telegraph. Vol. XX. 284.

T. T. Meadow's translations from the Manchú, & an essay on the language. Vol. XVIII. pp. 697, 617.

Description of the articles of export & import known in the trade of Canton. Vol. II. 447.

Paper money among the Chinese, & description of a bill from Fuhchau. Vol. XX. 289.

Extent of the fur trade, & an account of the fur-bearing animals. Vol. III. 548.

Execution of Kwoh Siping for dealing in opium. Vol. VI. 607.

Essay on the opium trade by N. Allen, M. D., Vol. XX. 479.

Combinations & preparations to prevent entrance of English into Canton in April, 1849. Vol. XVIII. 162.

Question of entry into the city of Canton considered & papers relating thereto. Vol. XVIII. ~~162~~ pp. 216, 335.

Jargon spoken in foreign intercourse ~~with~~ at Canton. Vol. IV. 428.

Review of Ides' ambassy to Peking. Vol. VIII. 520.

Assassination of H. E. Gov. Amaral of Macao, & papers connected therewith. Vol. XVIII. pp. 448, 532; XIX. 50.

Account of the Hiáng-fan, a Mohammedan mosque & burying-ground near Canton. Vol. XX. 47.

Emperor's rescript on peace, & a manifesto against the English at Canton. Vol. XI. 627.

Disturbances at Canton & death of Sü Aman caused by an American. Vol. XIII. 333.

Interview between Gov.-Gen. Sü & H. E. John W. Davis in 1848. Vol. XVII. 540.

Translation of a memoir on smelting copper. Vol. IX. 86.

Notices of the people of Japan, by Mrs. Busk; (notes by S. W. W.) Vol. IX. pp. 291, 369, 489, 620; Vol. X. 10, 72, 160, 205, 279, 309.

Voyage of the ship Morrison to Lewchew & Japan in 1837. Vol. VI. pp. 289, 353.

Visits of English ships to Japan. Vol. VII. 588.

Embassy to the Pope from Japan. Vol. VIII. 273.

Cruise of the U. S. sloop-of-war Preble, Commander J. Glynn to Napa, & Nagasaki. Vol. XVIII. 315.

Loss of the French whaler Narwal on Corea & efforts of M. Montigny to recover the crew. Vol. XX. 500.

Worship of ancesters among the Chinese, & account of funerals &c. Vol. XVIII. 363.

Mythological account of Hwuen-tien Shángti, with notices of his worship. Vol. XVIII. 102.

Testimony of the truth of Christianity given by Kiying ~~chau~~ & remarks by Bishop Boone. Vol. XX. 41.

Position & operations of the Protestant missions at the five ports & Hongkong in 1849. Vol. XVIII. 48

List of Protestant missionaries sent to the Chinese up to Jan. 1852, & present position of their missions. Vol. XX. 513.

Church at Amoy, & trip up the Min. Vol. XVIII. 444.

Report of Lockhart's hospital at Shánghái, & Macgowan's at Ningpo, 1848. Vol. XVIII. 505.

Proceedings of missionaries at the several ports, & of the delegates upon the version of the Testaments. Vol. ~~XIX~~ XIX. 544.

Proceedings relating to the Chinese version, report of a committee of the Am. Bible Society &c. Vol. XX. 216.

Staunton on rendering the word God, & Medhurst on the True Meaning of the word Shin. Vol. XVIII. 607.

Reply to letter from Rev. Messrs. Medhurst, Milne & Stronach, on the Chinese version of Bible Vol. XX. 485.

Illustrations of Scripture. Vol. VIII. 640; XVII. 537.

Index to the Chinese Repository 20 vols. vol XX

107

THE

CHINESE REPOSITORY.

VOL. XX.—APRIL, 1851.—NO. 4.

ART. I. *The Ying Hwán Chí-lioh* 瀛環志畧 *or General Survey of the Maritime Circuit, a Universal Geography by His Excellency Sü Ki-yü of Wútái in Shánsí, the present Lieutenant-governor of Fuhkien.* In 10 books. Fuhchau, 1848.

THIS work has justly been designated a "step taken in the right direction," and we hope it is the prelude to further publications of the like stamp by Chinese scholars, which shall make known to the magnates and literati of the Middle Kingdom the position, resources and designs of other nations of the earth. The distinguished author is a native of the district of Wútái 五臺 or Five Towers, in the northern part of Shánsí; but we have no means of learning anything of his early history. He temporarily held the office of judge of Kwángtung in March, 1843, as stated on page 328 of Vol. XII, but was shortly after transferred to the same post in Fuhkien, and sent to Amoy as commissioner to determine where the residences of foreigners should be. He arrived there in Jan. 1844, and through means of the admiral, sub-prefect, and other officers at that station, heard much of the foreigners settled there. He had probably already planned the present work, for Rev. Mr. Abeel says, referring to him (see p. 236, Vol. XIII), "that he is the most inquisitive Chinese of a high rank I have yet met;" he also mentions in the same journal that he supplied him with maps and geographical information. In May of the same year, he was again at Amoy, when Mr. Abeel gave him further instruction in geography and history, spending an afternoon tête-a-tête with him.

"He is as free and friendly," Mr. Abeel says in his journal, "as it is possible for him to be. That he has gained considerable knowledge is very evident; but he is far more anxious to learn the state of the kingdoms of this world, than the truths of the kingdom of heaven. The maps he has constructed are by no means accurate. He aims more at obtaining general ideas of countries—their size, political importance, and commercial relations, especially with China—than at tracing the lines of latitude and longitude, and thus fixing the exact position of places. England, America and France have been subjected to a more careful examination than the other countries of the world."

Though Mr. Abeel is the only foreigner's name acknowledged as having assisted the author, we know that others have aided him from time to time; and we think it just possible that he derived some of his information through a Chinese from Hiángshán, who had at that time recently returned from a four years' sojourn in the United States, where he had learned to read and write English tolerably well. This young man was engaged as interpreter by Capt. Smith of H. M. S. Druid, but his knowledge of his own language and the Amoy dialect was so imperfect that his interpretation was not very satisfactory in communication with either commoners or officials. We think it not unlikely that this young man may have been called on by Judge Sü to translate the compends of geography and history he had brought with him from New York, a service which he was quite able to perform *vivâ voce* in his own dialect. Sü's candid acknowledgment of the aid rendered him by Mr. Abeel stands in pleasant contrast to the meanness of the author who appropriated the entire tract of Sir George Staunton on the mode and benefits of Vaccination.

The Ying Hwán Chí Lioh is printed in large type, on a post folio page, and is usually bound up in six volumes, presenting a fair specimen of Chinese typography, in which the author's care to have his production make a good show is apparent, for it was printed at his own expense, and in the city of Fuhchau is only to be had at his own office or the shops of his agents. In giving a synopsis of the contents of this Geography, we will first let the author explain the manner in which he collected and digested his materials, and the care he took to verify his information; his diligence, care, and candor are, we think, well exhibited in the following unpretending preface; and though to write otherwise in such a connection would be considered in very ill taste among Chinese literati, we are willing to give him credit for a remarkably docile and inquiring cast of mind for a Chinese officer.

"A geography without maps can not be plain, and minute maps can not be drawn if persons do not go and examine the region. The world has a certain form, and its various indentations and projections can not be learned by merely thinking about them. The Occidentals are clever in traveling to remote parts, and as their ships wander over the four seas, on reaching a place, they take out a pencil and there draw a map of it, so that their maps alone are worthy of credit. In the year 1843, I was at Amoy on public duties, and there became acquainted with an American named Abeel, who was a scholar well acquainted with western knowledge, and able to converse in the dialect of Fuhkien. He had with him a book of maps beautifully drawn, but unhappily I did not know their characters; I had ten or more sheets of them copied, and then asked Abeel to translate them for me; I thus partially learned the names of each country, though I was so hurried I could not find time to learn them thoroughly.

"The next year I was again at Amoy, when I saw two maps on rollers which his honor the prefect Koh Yung-sang had purchased; one of them was about three feet, the other nearly two feet large, and both were more complete and fine than the book Abeel had, and were accompanied with several volumes in Chinese by foreigners. I also sought for all kinds of writings on this subject, and if their style was not clear and such as scholars would admire, I made extracts from all of them upon slips of paper of what was worthy of being retained; and whenever I saw men from the West, I improved the opportunity to ask them concerning the accuracy of my notes, and to learn respecting the shape of every country beyond our frontiers, and their present condition; in this way, I gradually ascertained an idea of their boundaries, which I attached to the maps, and with the verified selections I made from the various writings I had, I formed chapters, which gradually grew into the size of volumes. If I met with a book or a newspaper, I added, corrected, and altered my notes, sometimes revising them many ten times. In this way have I done from 1843 till now, for five years, winter and summer, in the intervals of official duties, making this pursuit my relaxation and amusement, and hardly omitting a day in which I did not do something at it.

"My friends Chin Sz'pú, the treasurer, and Luh Chun-jü the judge of Fuhkien, seeing the result of my labors, begged me to preserve the sheets carefully, and they afterwards corrected unclassial, expressions its and divided the whole into ten books. Other official friends also borrowed it to examine, and many begged me to get it printed, calling the performance *Ying Hwán Chi-lioh*, or General Survey of the Circuit of the Seas. This is a brief explanation of the manner in which this work was produced.

"Fuhchau, September, 1848. Sü Ki-yü of Wú-tái hien in Shansí."

The opinion formed of this performance by his friends and the fellow officers to whom he showed it, is not too high, but we only quote the shortest of the four prefaces prefixed to the work, that by the treasurer referred to above; one of the others was written by H. E. Liú Yunko, the then governor-general of Fuhkien and Chehkiang.

I.

To W.F. Williams

Canton, Feb. 19, 1835 ✓
— Nov 24 '35 ✓
— Dec 17, '35 ✓
Macao Jan 15, 36 ✓
Macao Apr 2, 36 ✓
— July 13 36 ✓
— Aug 31 '36 ✓
— Feb 22 '37 ✓
— May 15 '37 ✓
— May 12, '38 ✓
— Aug 31, '38 ✓
— May 17 '39 ✓
Canton June 21 '39 ✓
Macao Aug. 29 '39 ✓
— Nov 30 '39 ✓
— Apr 5, '40 ✓
— — 28 '40 ✓
— June 15 " ✓
— July 29 " ✓
— Nov 30 " ✓
— Jan 2 '41 ✓
— May 31 " ✓
— July 1 " ✓
— Sept 29 " ✓
— Apr. 5, '42 ✓
— " 18 " ✓
— Sept 2 " ✓
— Jan 20 '43 ✓
— Feb 28, " ✓
— Mch 20 " ✓

(✓ - S.W.W. to W.F.W.)
(* - Sarah W. Williams to W.F.W.)
(‡ - Sarah W. Williams to W.F.W. and Sarah (Pond) Williams)
(# - S.W.W. to Sarah (Pond) W.)
(□ - Sarah W. Williams to Sarah P. Williams)
(× - S.W.W. to W.F.W. and Sarah (Pond) Williams)
(◇ - S.W.W. to W.F.W. and H.B.W.)
(○ S.W.W. to W.F.W. and C.P.W.)

June 22, 1840 ✓
Oct. 26, 1840 ✓
March 29, 1841 ✓
May 15, 1841 ✓
June 15, 1841 ✓
July 28, 1841 ✓
Dec 10, 1841 ✓
May 25, 1842 ✓
June 25, 1842 ✓
Aug. 15, 1842 ✓
Feb. 12, 1843 ✓
May 29, 1843 ✓
June 15, 1843 ✓
Sept. 27, 1843 ✓

Macao, Nov. 20, '43 ✓
— Dec 18 " ✓
— Mch 31, '44 ✓
— May 1, '44 ✓
R. Nile Mch 10 '45 ✓
Canton Feb 24 '49 ✓
— Mch 26 '49 ✓
— Apr. 21 '49 #
— July 24 '49 ×
Macao Sept 12 '49 ×
Canton Oct 28 '49 ✓
— Mch. 29, '50 ×
— May 22 " ×
— July 20 " ×
— Nov 27 " ×
— Jan 28 '51 ×
— Feb 25, 51 ✓
— Apr 23 '51 ×
— Sept 21, " ×
— Dec 25 " ×
— Apr 22 '52 ×
— July 21 " ×
— Oct 28 " ×
— June 21 " ×
— Dec 20 " ×
— Jan 26, '53 ×
— Apr 16 " ×
Yedo Bay July 16 " ×
Canton Aug 20 " ×
— Sept 24 " ✓
— Dec 6 " ✓

Jan. 24, 1844 ✓
March 19, 1844 ✓
Dec. 22, 1845 ✓

1 undated ✓

March 24, 1852 □

II

衛廉士 to W. F. W.

Lewchew, Jan. 30, '54 × with Sarah W.W. VS
Yokohama Mch. 20 " × " March 25, '54 ✱
April 8, '54 ✱
Lewchew July 13, " ×
Canton Oct 9 " ×
— Mch 12 '55 (?) ✓
— Aug 8 " ✓
— Oct 12 " ✓
— Dec 13 " ✓
— Feb. 13, '56 ✓
— May 8 " ✓
~~— July 8 "~~
— July 22 " ✓
Shanghai Oct 7, '56 (×) ✓
Macao Jan 27 '57 ✓
— Mch 13 " ✓
— Apr. 25 " ✓
— June 22 " ✓
— July 23 " ✓
— Aug 20 " ✓
— Nov. 11 " ✓
— Jan 26, '58 ✓
— Mch 10 " o
Hongkong " 19 " ✓
G. of Pichili Apr. 30 " ✓
— May 25 " ✓
— July 9 " ✓
Nagasaki, Sept 22 " ✓

Shanghai, Oct. 22, '58 ✓
Hongkong Dec 7, '58 ✓
Macao, Jan 11, '59 ✓
Canton Mch 12 " ✓
Macao Apr 24 " ✓
Shanghai June 13 " ✓
Peiho July 5 " ✓
Peking July 29 " ✓
Shanghai Sept 2 " ✓
Kiahing Oct 11, " ✓
Kwanshan Nov 5 " ✓
Macao Dec 28 " ✓
Hongkong, Mch 6, '60 ✓
St. Albans, Sept 7 " ✓
Schenectady, Dec 22 " ✓
Macao, Nov 15 '61 ✓
— Jan 13 '62 ✓
— Mch. 13 " o
China Sea Apr 25 " ✓
Taku Nov. 16 " ✓
Macao Feb 12 '63 ✓
— — 27 " ✓
Peking Sept. 12 " ✓
— July 23 " o
— Nov 24 " ✓
— June 1 '64 ✓
— Aug 12, " ✓
— Dec 1 " ✓
— — 5 " ✓

August 29, 1865 ✓
Oct. 25, 1865 ✓
May 26, 1866 ✓
June 28, 1866 ✓
August 17, 1866 ✓
Jan. 12, 1867 ✓
Nov. 7, 1867 ✓

Miss. Herald on S.W.W.
1834 - p. 159 - arrival [wrong]
1835 - 412.
1836 - 203.
1837 - 212
1838 - 203. (Jap. trip)
1839 - 52. (Macao). 463
1840 - 81. 115.
1843 - 57. 256.
1844 - 217.
1845 - 9 - 155
1846 - 11
1848 - 67 (mid. K.) 248.
1849 - 9 - 33. 54 (Bible tr.)
1850 - 52. 393.
1851 - 138.
1852 - 86. 125.
1853 - 163. 243
1854 - 45. 178 (Lew chew)
1855 - 70. 86. 117. 250.
1856 - 308. 323.
1857 - 164. 403.
1858 - 60. 366.

At "The Club" in New Haven the following subjects were discussed by S.W.W.

Apr. 11, 1877. China
Feb. 6, 1878. China
Nov. 6, — Afghanistan
Mar. 12, 1879. The late Chinese Bill
Oct. 1, — The Southern Exodus
Nov. 26, — Sovereignty of Loo Choo Ids.
June 9, 1880. Extra Territorial Jurisdiction
Apr. 13, 1881. Nihilism.
Jan. 12, 1882. Mormonism

SWW Articles + Essays (B)

Treaties with China
~~Life (for Yale Book)~~
Perpetuity of Ch. Inst. (first sketch)
Tea Culture
Women in China
Chinese Language
Mission Work in China
Addr. to Linonian Soc on China (Feb 24 '79)
Confucianism + Xnty
On Learning Chinese
Perpetuity (another sketch)
On word God in Chinese (Bibl. Sacra)
~~Russia + China~~
Female Educ. in Ch. + Transl of Primer for girls

&c &c &c

Princeton Lectures

ASIATIC SOCIETY MEETING.

Dr. S. W. Williams on "Canton prior to 1840."

Having in last week's issue given the business part of the Annual Meeting of our local branch of this Society, we now proceed to give Dr. Williams's address.

Dr. Williams, who was received with great applause, said—Mr. President, and Ladies and Gentlemen:—The treatment of a subject like this is not very easy, considering that there will be many who would like to have particular information upon certain things, and others who would desire to be informed on other points; but I shall endeavour, in going over the details of those years, to give such an idea of the mode of living and the character of the foreign community, and its relations with the Chinese, as will in some measure supply a description of the way in which Foreigners lived and traded and went about in those early days. When I arrived, after a passage of 127 days, we brought three days latest news from America. It was the season when most of the tea ships arrived, and news was then thought to come in very rapidly, as it was seldom at that time of year that more than a week or two elapsed without some ship arriving. Within the next two years, however, there was one interval of nearly 80 days, during which we heard nothing from either England or America, and one ship brought, in that case, nearly three months' additional news from those countries. When our ship arrived, and had anchored in the the waters near Lintin Island, one of the first things that happened was the coming of a boatload of cassia from Canton, to be put on board at the outside anchorage, so that when the ship arrived, the dunnage for the tea she was to take in would be ready for her. This was brought down out by the Chinese. We had to send over to Macao, 20 miles, to get a pilot, and when we went up river we had the native pilots furnished by the Chinese Government from the Pilot Office at Macao. At Whampoa lay the large fleet of the East India Company. At that time the Company had received notice that it was in future to be a political, instead of a trading Company, and this being the last season, they had a large number of ships at Whampoa—the finest fleet, perhaps, to be seen anywhere in the world—some of which had from 70 to 90 men on board; the number of ships at Whampoa, stretching along three miles, was about 125 in all. None were allowed to go up to Canton; indeed, it was only some seven years after, that there was known to be a passage by which they could get up, so carefully had the Chinese kept Foreigners ignorant of the channels. When we went to Canton, it was always by ships' boats, manned by the crews, unless we got out a pass for a dollar-boat. These, which by the way always cost $4, were furnished by the compradore of the ship, and

deed, it was only some seven years after, that there was known to be a passage by which they could get up, so carefully had the Chinese kept Foreigners ignorant of the channels. When we went to Canton, it was always by ships' boats, manned by the crews, unless we got out a pass for a dollar-boat. These, which by the way always cost $4, were furnished by the compradore of the ship, and
you had to report at two or three "chop-houses," along the way up. But most of the ships had their own boats, and as there were so many sailors, lascars especially, I have often seen over 100 together, who frequently for want of accommodation turned the boats upside down, in warm weather particularly, and found a sleeping place underneath or prepared their meals by it. Opposite the Factories a small creek ran in shore, and boats came up to the tidewaiter's station at its head, to land their passengers. The word *Factories* was applied to the foreign dwellings at Canton, not because any work was carried on, but because *factors* lived in in them. This was an old name which had been known in India and the Archipelago. As soon as the ship I was in arrived, it was reported to the Hong Merchants, that such a ship had come to Olyphant & Co., as well as the names and number of the passengers who were to stay at Canton—and these Hong Merchants became security for our good conduct. We never saw these men, but they became official security to their Government for our good behaviour, and that we should not do anything against its interests. At that time there were only 5 or 6 Hong Merchants, who were really insolvent, for the system was a contrivance on the part of the Chinese Government to secure the collection of the duties, and they became responsible for so much duty as the Government was pleased to collect from the commerce. The trade that year was, as I have said, a very large one, and the East India Company had the largest portion of it.

At the time of my arrival at Canton, Mr. Plowden was what was called President of the supercargoes of the East India Company; Mr., afterwards Sir John, Davis being also one of them. There were 22 or 24 of these supercargoes in all, and of these, one-half or three-fifths were generally resident at Canton. Of the foreign firms that did business apart from the Company, there are five and, I believe, only five that still exist, viz.:—Messrs. Jardine, Matheson & Co., Dent & Co., and Turner & Co., British; and Messrs. Russell & Co. and Olyphant & Co., American. The residents of Canton numbered about 250 more or less, and, as a contrast to the state of things at present, I may state that there was but one German and two Frenchmen. There were a good number of Parsees, British subjects. Among the 250 residents there was not one lady; such foreign families as were in China stayed down at Macao, and it was not till 1843 or 1844 that any foreign families were allowed to reside at Canton. I learned that, before I arrived, a Mr. Bannerman attempted to take his family up to Canton with him, and so apprehensive was he of what the Chinese might do in consequence, that he had guns brought up from the ships and placed up and down among the Factories to defend himself and others.

The Factories were a series of 13 "Hongs," quite different from anything that can be seen in this part of China. They were placed close side by side each other, forming as it were a row or "terrace" fronting the river, but each Hong consisted of a series of buildings placed one behind the other from the river backwards for a depth of from 550 to 600 feet to the first street running parallel with the river. They were, in fact, modelled on the Chinese ground plan for the building of extensive houses, viz., court within court in as long a series as may be possible or desirable. The approach to those in the rear was through the basement of those in front. The interval between the houses was from 30 to 60 feet, or more. The upper storeys of these buildings were divided off by partitions. Some of them had only two stories, but that in which I lived had three. The old Factories had been entirely destroyed by fire in 1822, but they were rebuilt at the expense of the Hong-merchants who owned most of them.

Of these Hong-merchants the chief was Howqua, who was in many respects a very remarkable man. These merchants were the imtermediaries between the Chinese authorities and foreigners. When foreigners wished anything from the Chinese authorities, the plan was to draw up a petition and take it to a certain gate of the City known as the Oil Gate, where it was received by a policeman, or some low official who was generally on hand. But sometimes the Hong merchants refused to receive or transmit such petitions. On one occasion a Scotchman named Innes, a man of great energy, brought a petition to the Oil Gate, but the Hong merchants having got a hint of its purport refused to receive it. He waited at the Gate all day, but they persisted in their refusal. As night approached, he gave orders to his boy to go and fetch his bed, as an indication that he intended to stop there all night, and when the merchants came to know that, they received his petition. On another occasion before my arrival Mr. Jardine, the head of Jardine, Matheson & Co., having taken a petition to the gate in question got rather hard usage, some one having struck him a rap on the head. He, however, never stirred, or gave any indication that the blow had hurt him, from which circumstance he came to be known and spoken of by the Chinese, during all his subsequent stay in China, as (鐵頭老鼠) *teet tow lo shu*, "the iron headed old rat." This gate,—a very small one in the Southern Wall of Canton City—I have myself very frequently visited, but never with a petition.

As I have already said, there were no ladies at Canton till after the ratification of the Treaty at Nankin in 1843. Shortly after I arrived in Canton, Mr. Plowden left for England and Mr. Davis (afterward Sir John) took charge. He was the last of the East India Company's Presidents. I can not tell what number he held in the series, but as the E. I. Company was established about A.D. 1,600, he must have had a long line of predecessors during the interval of over 230 years. Of the merchants trading at Canton who were British subjects, most accepted a Consular commission from the Governments of other countries, as prior to 1834 the East India Co. had the exclusive privilege of trading, and all British subjects must be under them. There were 13 Factories for the 250 residents above mentioned, and the area covered by the Factories was exactly that of the base of the Great Pyramid—12 acres. Facing the river in front of the houses there was a small opening or square which had been gradually gained from the river, which became a favorite place of resort for hucksters and beggars, the latter being attracted to the spot by the Parsees frequently distributing alms in the neighbouring streets. From this open space a series of shops ran up through the Factories for a depth backward, as I have said, of about 500 or 600 feet. The Factories extended abreast of the river for over a 1,000 feet. They were known as the Creek, Dutch, English, Parsee, Old English, Swedish, Austrian, Paou-shun, American, French, Spanish, and Danish. That known as the "Creek" Factory was occupied by Jardine, Matheson & Co. In the Factory Block there also stood one native and indeed throughout his life he was chiefly engaged in the service of the British Government, though he also did a large amount of mission work. The font of Chinese type which had been cut at great expense for the printing of Morrison's Dictionary was just before this time brought up to Canton, but so great were the fears of the Cantonese printers that their officials would find out that they worked with foreign type, that the font had ere long to be taken back to Macao for safety, in case the authorities should on any pretext come to examine the factories.

That the fear of such a visit of inspection was not groundless, was proved by a circumstance that occurred about that time. The East India Company had so arranged the large factory occupied by them that they had managed at great expense to lay out a garden on its river front, extending to about half an acre, which was nicely kept and afforded a very pleasant promenade in summer time, as, being walled in, it was free from the intrusion of beggars and hucksters. This garden they had enlarged by extending their wall so as to include some land that had silted up from the river and was dry at low water. Soon after this acquisition had been made, the Fuyuen of Canton suddenly appeared one morning in front of the Factories, having with him a large band of attendants, several of whom were armed with shovels, with which they forthwith began to shovel this new piece of garden into the river, reducing the Company's pleasure ground to its original size. The mud thrown into the river was carried down a short distance and there collected, and being increased by subsequent siltings, formed the nucleus of a bank. The Governor having, as he flattered himself, effectually put an end to such foreign encroachments, returned into the City, but the Hong-merchants rather laughed at what he, no doubt, thought a very valorous exploit.

When I arrived in Canton, I found there some men who had lived many years in China. Among these was Mr. Thomas Beale, the father of Mr. Beale subsequently of Dent, Beale, & Co's. This gentleman told me that in 1799 he had gone up to Chusan to take delivery of something left there by H.M.S. *Lion*, which brought out Lord Macartney's Embassy. You thus see that the present times are connected with those of that Embassy by only two lives. Mr. Beale had at that time lived some 35 years in China without ever having left the country. He had collected at his residence in Macao a fine garden and splendid aviary, which was deservedly a great celebrity when I first saw it, there were 200 birds in it, about 20 of them being large and magnificent pheasants. But about 2 years afterwards the birds were attacked by a kind of murrain, brought on probably by a sudden change of the weather, and most of them died—a disaster greatly to be lamented. Mr. Beale was the first to send to England the "Reeves" Pheasant, which he had procured from the interior at great expense. He had also a number of "Modallion" Pheasants and several other rare kinds which he was the first to collect. From the interior of the aviary rose two large *longan* trees, among the branches of which the birds might disport themselves, while in the centre of it was a pond where the various kinds of ducks could indulge in their specific propensities. It was altogether a most interesting collection.

According to the usage then, the tea trade was over by the 1st of July, and then every one who possibly could, made for Macao, where the families of the leading employes of the East India Company resided, as well as 8 or 10 others. Thus during July, August and September most of the residents at Canton were to be found at Macao. Indeed, a gentleman who had been Consul at Canton told me that in one season, 1805, only two foreigners were left at Canton—that is excluding the Parsees who were not so migratory. This general resort of foreigners to Macao at the end of summer and the beginning of autumn made the arrival of the tea ships from home about the end of August a time of great interest, which was still further enhanced by the arrival at the same time of the cotton ships from India. Hongkong was then little known. In fact there were very few who had been there. At Macao there was at the time I am speaking of, a very interesting old gentleman, who remained there till he died. He was a Swede named Ljungstedt, who wrote a most laborious history of Macao, which is indeed the only thorough account of that Colony that we yet possess. He had been Agent for the Swedish East India Company. There was also resident there Chinnery, an English artist, who has left us many memorials of his life both in India and China. He also died in Macao.

As soon as the monopoly of the East India Company expired in 1833, there naturally came a great influx of foreigners, chiefly from England or India who established new firms, and from 1834 to 1842 and 1843, there were few places in the East that could compare with Canton for the high grade, intelligence and enterprise of its merchants. Among them were numbered such names as those of Mr. Jardine, Mr. Lancelot Dent, Mr., now Sir James Matheson, Mr. C. W. King of Olyphant & Co., Mr. J. C. Green and Mr. A. A. Low of Russell & Co.'s, and Mr. Robert Inglis. On the death of Dr. Morrison in 1834, many of these took the greatest interest in the formation of the Morrison Education Society as a memorial to that great and good man, and Mr. L. Dent, Mr. Jardine, Mr. Matheson and Mr. Olyphant especially, continued for many years to give it the benefit of their valuable counsel and support. Another valuable institution, started about this time, was the Medical Missionary Society of Canton. This was initiated by Dr. Parker, of Canton, in 1835; and the same gentlemen as those above named contributed greatly to its maintenance and success. Mr. Turner also, the founder of the house of Turner & Co., continued till his death in 1839 to take interest in both these Societies.

The Superintendent of British Trade in the person of Lord Napier having been so badly treated at Canton, the Office of the Superintendency was removed to Macao to await the advent of better days. It remained there for some years, a clerk only being kept at Canton to receive ships' papers and such other official business as might be necessary. During the years 1837 and 1838, commenced the remarkable proceedings of the Chinese Government with a view to putting down the opium trade. The movement appears to have originated with Hü-Nai-tsi. He was connected with the Board of Rites, but his reputation for character and talent is unknown. This man about 1836 or 1837 drew up a memorial to the Emperor in which he called attention to the rapid growth of the traffic in the prohibited article of opium, and proposed in order to put a stop to the wholesale smuggling of the article to legalise the trade. Considering the limited opportunities of the writer to acquaint himself with such a subject, his arguments were very creditable. The importance of the subject being recognised, the Emperor Taoukwang issued a circular to the chief dignitaries throughout the Empire enclosing a copy of Hü-Nai-tsi's memorial, and asking them to state their several opinions whether his proposal to legalise the trade should be accepted or rejected. It was two years before all the replies were received, and then it was found that the majority of voices were for rejecting the proposal. They declared that they had carefully examined into the effects of opium on the country and people, and found it to be so injurious in demoralising the people, and draining the country of its wealth that they held it best that decisive steps should be taken to put down the traffic. It was this response to his circular that determined the Emperor to appoint for the carrying out of the anti-opium policy the celebrated commissioner

Lin.

Lin, who was appointed anti-opium Imperial Commissioner, had previously been Fuyuen (Governor) of this (Kiangsu) province, and his memorials in the *Peking Gazette* had already drawn attention to him as a man of superior ability. Dr. Morrison told me that Lin's memorial on the effects of a severe inundation in this province of Kiangsu was one of the ablest state papers he had ever read. Lin had taken the trouble of travelling over the province and making personal investigation into the condition of the people, and his memorial was that of a man who had seen and heard for himself what he wrote. Lin, armed with full powers to deal with the opium question, came down to Canton. But before his arrival some steps had been taken towards suppressing the trade. The Governor of Canton some 2 or 3 years previously had obtained—no doubt through the Hong merchants, who made their selection of names, probably, to suit their own purposes—the names of 9 or 11 of the principal foreign dealers in opium, and in the list were the names of 3 who had never had transactions in the drug. It must certainly be admitted that throughout all these troubles, the Hong-merchants were placed in a very difficult situation; they had, in fact, to act as a sort of buffer between the Governor-General and Hoppo and the Foreigners; on the one hand, they wished to please the foreigners who gave them trade, and, on the other, they very naturally feared to offend the Viceroy who might take their lives. The part they had to play, therefore, was not an easy one. The foreigners, whose names were thus given to the Governor were subsequently ordered to leave the country. And when Lin came to Canton the Chinese did not fail to remark that not one of the 9 or 11 remained there,—they had all either returned home or had removed to Macao. Mr. Jardine was one of them, and Mr. Gordon who had then gone home, and some others; while another of them, Mr. Turner, had just died at Macao—a fact which the Chinese, as is their wont, did not fail to ascribe to the anger of Heaven against men who had engaged in such a trade.

When Lin arrived, he soon gave proofs that he was thoroughly in earnest in his resolution to faithfully discharge the trust committed to him, but how to set about it he was as ignorant of as one can well imagine. The trade in opium was very dull at the time; the fact being that people were afraid to deal in it, and so it happened that the stock on hand was very large. Lin adopted the plan of keeping himself incog. for a fortnight or so after his arrival, during which he used all diligence in endeavouring to collect information about the opium trade; but the information procured was as incorrect as might have been expected to be got from such a people by this method. He never communicated with Capt. Elliot, nor sought to learn from the foreigners, the information on the subject they were not unwilling and able to furnish. But, proceeding in the underhand manner just described, Lin suddenly came to a resolution as to the course of action he would pursue, and one day foreigners in Canton suddenly found themselves shut up as they had been immediately after Lord Napier left Canton. About 4 p.m. one day a man went up and down through the Factories, calling out in Chinese, and warning every Chinese servant to leave; and in two hours there was not a single native servant in all the 13 Factories. A line of boats was also placed in the river abreast of the Factories, so that escape from that side would be impossible. The residents by this time must have numbered about 300. I have several lists of them in my house in Peking, but not in Shanghai. All these 300 residents had, for the time, to depend on the assistance of the Parsees' servants, who, knowing a little of the Cantonese dialect, were able to go into the adjoining markets and purchase some things. But the supplies they bought were inadequate, and we had to make a careful inspection of our store-rooms and larders to see what resources were left us; and what between laying tables, washing dishes and trying to cook, we considered we had rather a hard time of it. It was no small privation to be forced to go down ourselves and carry unfiltered water from the river. By-and-by the Governor took pity on us and sent us some bullocks, pigs and poultry. These, however, the foreigners refused to touch, and, indeed, some of them were allowed to starve at our doors. I suppose the Hong merchants gave the Governor a hint that that was hardly the way to get on with us. At all events greater freedom was soon allowed, and facilities were afforded us to procure wood and water, which, especially the latter, had been almost unprocurable. We were, indeed, put to many a strange shift. This state of blockade lasted for a little less than 3 months.

Capt. Elliot was at Macao when these occurrences took place, and as soon as he heard of it he came up to Canton and took the management of affairs, and Lin was no doubt glad to have some responsible head of affairs to deal with. It is not necessary that I should follow in detail the history of the measures and negotiations which led Captain Elliot to surrender to Lin, under protest, 20,283 chests of opium, being all the drug at that time remaining in the hands of British merchants in Chinese waters. All this immense quantity was brought together at a place a little below the Bogue Forts, in the summer of 1839. While these negotiations were going on, the foreigners were kept within their own bounds very strictly; but within these limits there was no restraint on their personal liberty. Business was, of course, entirely suspended; but no one suffered any other loss or damage; no one fell sick; and the ships at Whampoa were kept supplied with food throughout the three months blockade. At length when Capt. Elliot had given up the opium, foreigners were permitted to leave, and some of them were told never to return, though who these were I am here unable to mention.

Few of the foreign officials who have come to China have been superior in talent, or better fitted than was Capt. Elliot to fulfill the important duties devolving upon him. Having lived in the country for five years (he came in 1834), he had obtained a very good idea of Chinese character, and how they could be suitably dealt with. He had also the advantage of having as his interpreter and advisor Mr. John R. Morrison, Dr. Morrison's son, a man whom it was impossible to know without loving, and who, born in the country and familiar with the Chinese from childhood, was in some respects better qualified than even his father to act in these capacities. Mr. Morrison was a man whom I remember with a respect and love that I feel it hard to describe. He received me when I came to China with that kindness which never failed to leave an impression. Captain Elliot and Mr. Morrison recognised clearly the ideas the Chinese have on the subject of their unchallengeable supremacy over all other nations—ideas that appear to have grown up in the earliest periods of their history and are to be found in all their writings. And, indeed, it was hardly to be wondered at, if they felt themselves vastly superior to the handful of foreigners who dwelt in the Canton Factories, intent only on trade, which, as you know, is the lowest of the four categories into which the Chinese divide human professions and pursuits. Indeed, the foreign residents themselves appeared to have to some extent imbibed the same ideas, partly in consequence of the way the Chinese officials treated them, and partly because of the position in which we allowed ourselves to be placed relatively to the Chinese. It was by no means pleasant to live among a people cherishing such self conceited and supercilious notions regarding us.

Before this time an incident occurred which I may relate, both as illustrating the power of officials over the Chinese people, and for other reasons which will appear. As a warning to all of the fate to which those who dealt in opium made themselves liable, a native who had sold opium near Macao was one day taken outside of the gates of that city, and there, in the presence of thousands, put to death by strangling. That, however, was not considered enough. Soon after, another poor wretch was condemned to a similar death, and he was brought for execution to the front of the Foreign Factories. A few of the foreigners interfered and would not allow the execution to take place there. The yamun runners, therefore, were forced to hurry the hapless man into one of the side streets close by, where they put him to death by strangling, and carrying the body back to the yamun, reported the matter. Attracted by the event, a great crowd, probably 2,000, appeared in front of the Factories in a state of great excitement because the foreigners had dared to interfere with the execution of their law, and soon began to show signs of anger. In front of the Old English Hong and Messrs. Russell & Co.'s there was a wooden balustrade, the pillars of which were speedily torn out to be used as bludgeons, and immediately thereafter they began to throw such bricks as they could get hold of. Soon there would have been a riot and the Factories would in that case have been almost certain to be plundered. But word had been sent to the Chifu, who, quickly getting into his chair, hastened to the spot, and arrived just in time to prevent the pillage from commencing. His only attendants were 6 or 7 runners similar to those we see around an ordinary mandarin's chair. With these he came into a small street known as Hog Lane, running between some of the Factories down to the river, got out of his chair and simply waved his hand towards the surging crowds. The effect was instantaneous. The immense mob dispersed before that mute gesture like a flock of sheep before a mastiff. The attendant lictors seized some half a dozen of the rioters, threw them on the ground and gave them a bambooing; and all things assumed their usual quiet appearance. This incident occurred in 1839, just before the arrival of Lin, and excited the native authorities a good deal, as it was the first hint they had of foreigners having the spirit to offer resistance and repel force by force.

After the short interval of private preliminary investigation referred to above, Lin issued some of his Edicts, in which he gave public announcement of the views entertained by the Emperor as to the opium traffic, and after issuing one or two of them, he shut us up as already described. Capt. Elliot felt that now at length the time had come to bring all previous disputes and misunderstandings to a clear issue, and his superior ability and the justness of his appreciation of the difficulty was shown by his clear recognition that nothing but access to the Central Government could put an end to the complications that had grown up; that by taking the responsibility of complying with Lin's demand and giving up all the opium he would as it were force the British Government to take the matter up and carry it through to a definite settlement; and that till this was done further progress was both impossible. It should be kept in view that all the foreign relations of China had been managed hitherto by the Hong-merchants working with the E. J. Co. a corporate body of merchants, both intent only on preserving and enlarging their trade; and for this state of things, the Hong merchant system proved sufficient. But as the trade was thrown open to general competition, a new state of things arose, and new arrangements became necessary, and Captain Elliot's move in the surrender of the opium was really the first beginning of that basis on which foreign relations in China are now conducted. And looking back over what has happened since then, I am disposed to think that what Captain Elliot did was the best thing that could have been done in the circumstances, having regard to the nature of the whole question at issue. Capt. Elliot, it should be mentioned, was personally much opposed to the opium traffic. He had carefully examined the whole subject in its various bearings, and had come to the conclusion that the trade was one that must exert a most hurtful influence on the Chinese, unless they could exercise a strong moral restraint on the use of the drug, which was not at all likely.

When Lin had got possession of the opium by the consent of Captain Elliot, he caused an immense tank, many acres in extent, to be made, at the place above indicated. It was made by simply enclosing a portion of the beach by embankments. This tank was filled with salt water, into which the whole number of chests were thrown, and were, of course, speedily destroyed. While Lin was superintending the destruction of the opium, he sent a messenger to Macao to request Dr. Bridgman to go up and see him. The Chinese portion of the Mission Press had already been taken to Macao, and the rest went there as soon as foreigners were allowed to leave Canton. British subjects were all ordered to leave Canton by Captain Elliot, and by the 1st of June all had left. Only a few American merchants and others remained, by means of whom trade continued to be carried on; vessels arriving to British merchants stopped at Macao and were reconsigned to some of those of other nationalities remaining at Canton. Dr. Bridgman was sent for by Lin at the suggestion of a former pupil of the Doctor's, who spoke English very well, and who was kept employed by Lin in translating into Chinese such portions of foreign newspapers as were of interest for him. And here I may observe that of all the Chinamen I have ever seen, Lin was decidedly the finest looking and the most intelligent. He was, indeed, a very superior man for a Chinese, and if he had only been better informed he might have brought the difficult business intrusted to him to a much more creditable issue than he did; but this his ignorance and the self-conceit that accompanies ignorance prevented. I saw him only once. He was naturally much elated at his rank, and the absolute power entrusted to him to do whatever he pleased in putting down the opium traffic, led him to commit acts of rashness which recoiled upon himself. At the point to which my remarks have now brought me, Lin began to be conscious of this, and to feel that the question with which he had to deal was a much bigger one than he had supposed; too big for him to handle without assistance, and so he sent for Dr. Bridgman.

Dr. Bridgman went up and remained at the Bogue for a day or two. Lin wanted him to carry a letter to Capt. Elliot. This Dr. Bridgman agreed to do provided Lin would make him aware of its contents; but Lin declined to do this, and was told by Dr. Bridgman that he would not carry letters like a common postman. Lin then agreed to write the letter, but when Dr. Bridgman called to take leave, it was not ready, and it was never sent. Lin, however, did write a letter to the Queen of England, the original of which was taken to England I think, by a ship named the *Royal Saxon*. A copy of it was afterwards procured and a singular document it was. It showed how fully he appreciated the perplexities of the situation he was in, and how helpless he felt to extricate himself from it. He implored the Queen to put a stop to the opium trade.

Between the expiry of the East India Company's monopoly in 1833 and the year 1839, the intercourse and trade of foreigners with China had largely increased and was greatly stimulated by the cruise of the *Lord Amherst* in 1834. The supercargo of that ship was Mr. Hugh H. Lindsay, who had been a servant of the E. I. Co. and who became the founder of Messrs. Lindsay & Co.; Dr. Gutzlaff accompanied him as interpreter. The *Lord Amherst* cruised along the coast, trading, surveying, and observing, and thus added greatly to the information previously possessed of the configuration and trading capacities of the coast. Indeed, it is curious in the light of what we now know, to look back and think how dense was the ignorance of the best informed before that cruise of places now so familiar as Amoy, Chinchew, Foochow, Ningpo, Chusan and Shanghai. They were till then almost literally unknown to us. From that time onwards the coast of China as far north, at east, at Shanghai, was traversed by an ever increasing fleet of small vessels almost wholly occupied in the contraband opium trade, which, however, were continually adding to our knowledge of the coast and of the requirements of the Chinese.

One remarkable feature of the time now under review was the small number of foreigners who were students of Chinese. I can, in fact, remember only five, during the time that Lin was Commissioner; leaving out of view the Portuguese of Macao, few of whom, however, knew anything of the character. One of the five referred to was Mr. Robert Thom, at that time an assistant in Messrs. Jardine, Matheson & Co.'s, but who afterwards became H. M. Consul at Ningpo and died there in 1846; another was Mr. John R. Morrison, already referred to; and a third was Dr. Gutzlaff. These three were the only men who were available to the British Government as interpreters. But they were all men well qualified for the duties of such a post. And when Captain Elliot and Admiral Elliot afterwards had a conference with Kishen and other high functionaries at Taku, it was found that Mr. Morrison had no difficulty either in understanding or in making himself understood. But it was a very distinct fact that the authorities at Canton during a long course of years, by their intimidation of natives who aided us to learn it, did much to prevent foreigners from acquiring a knowledge of the language. In order to procure and preserve accurate information, and help in this direction Dr. Bridgman commenced and with myself carried on the *Chinese Repository* for 20 years.

Between my arrival at Canton and 1840, there were two foreign newspapers published. The first of these was the Canton *Register*: the other was the Canton *Courier*. The latter, however, had rather a short life. It criticised somewhat severely certain measures of the East India Company, the Company stopped taking the 12 copies for which it had subscribed, and the *Courier* collapsed. For, in those days, there were few or no advertisements to supplement the income from subscriptions. In fact, there were only two places that could be called shops where foreign articles were to be bought; one kept by Markwick, the other by Edwards, and of these Markwick's was by far the better. There was a chaplain who officiated in winter at Canton and in summer at Macao. Dr. Bridgman had a service all the year round at Canton. Dr. Morrison used to conduct a Chinese service in summer at Macao and at Canton in winter, to which only his servants and a few others came, as it were by stealth.

Besides the *Register* and *Courier* already referred to, there was started at Canton in 1836 the *Canton Press*, between which and the *Register*, a good deal of healthy controversy was kept up and much information was diffused about the Chinese, obtained chiefly through the Morrisons, a considerable portion being translations from the *Pekin Gazette*. From these newspapers, as well as from one published at Malacca Mr. Robert Inglis, a partner of Messrs. Dent & Co., spent much of his time in making extracts, which he reproduced in a series of articles on what he called the Modern History of China, which were published in the *Chinese Repository*. And here it may be worth while to mention, that the work of commencing and getting together and publishing that Repository during the twenty years of its existence, was done chiefly by Dr. Bridgman and myself. (Great applause.) The work was done at the Printing Office of which I had charge, without any outside help in the way of funds. The office supported itself by the works it printed, of which the Repository was one. The result so far as the Repository was concerned, was not encouraging from a pecuniary point of view. During the last 7 years of its existence there was an annual deficit of from $300 to $400. In the last year of its existence it had only 300 subscribers at $3 each, which hardly paid the workmen's wages. And so in 1851, having been continued 20 years, it was given up. But by that time other periodicals and newspapers had been commenced, so that the Repository was no longer needed.

The work of Foreign Missions, with which I was connected, was almost unknown by the Chinese at Canton in the years to which my remarks refer. Indeed, that work can hardly be said to have commenced till after the conclusion of the Treaty of Nankin. As I have said above, Dr. Morrison's preaching in Chinese was only to his own servants and a few others who came to the service, as it were by stealth. And when he died in 1834 two converts were all he was known to have made. The fear the Chinese had of being in any way identified with foreigners was, indeed, intense. So afraid were they of being accused of having assisted us to learn Chinese, that I remember that frequently there were Chinamen to whom I spoke Chinese and who knew perfectly well what I said, but who persisted in always replying to me in English. Mr. Thom talking freely with the Chinese who resorted to Messrs. Jardine's office did something to overcome this apprehension.

Residence in the Factories was exceedingly pleasant. We all lived together on the most friendly terms, probably because we were so close together, and the interchange of social courtesies was most agreeable. And then when the Tea season had passed, and the summer heats assailed us, we started for Macao where we could enjoy the sea and the cool breeze, and could get a little more room to stretch our legs. At Canton our range for pedestrian exercise was rather limited. We could sail on the river in boats, but on shore we could only walk round the City at very considerable risk of being robbed. I remember taking such a walk with Dr. Bridgman, Dr. Bradford, and his brother, and at one part of our walk we were stopped and robbed without ceremony. We had, however, half expected such a thing and had not taken any valuables with us. It was, indeed, no uncommon thing for those who ventured far into the back streets to be robbed; but no other violence was attempted. The country people were much afraid of us, but we always found that when we talked with them their fears were dispelled. But now when one looks back on the then state of things, he feels it difficult to understand how we should have been there so long and yet have known so little about the people, and been so little known by them. When Canton was thrown open to foreigners as late as 1858, some missionaries went into the City and found there Chinese who had never seen a foreigner; who had never heard that places for preaching had been opened by foreigners at Canton, and who did not think it possible that any foreigners could speak Chinese. And even at the present day at Pekin, though the foreign Legations have been there for over 10 years, there are districts in the City where the people have never seen a foreigner. For the Chinese, as a rule, are most unwilling to go beyond their accustomed bounds; and these people have never felt anything that made it necessary for them to go into the streets in which foreigners are likely to be met.

It is beyond the limits to which I have restricted myself in these remarks to speak of the changes effected in the life and trade of foreigners at Canton by the stirring events of 1841-42 and '48. I may simply say that, in 1842, a Chinese mob burnt the E. I. Co. Factories, which, however, were rebuilt in 1846. Those belonging to other nationalities were spared; but the whole of them were burned down by Governor-General Yeh in 1856. I was in Canton three days before this last fire took place, and Yeh then assured the foreigners that he would do no harm to them or their property; but it is quite certain that he had by that time determined on working the mischief that followed,—had, in fact, planned to set the Factories on fire. In this fire all the works on hand previously printed at my Press were destroyed, amounting to less than 7,000 volumes. Still there is no doubt that the work done in Canton prior to 1841-42 was a good preliminary to what was to follow; and as we now look back on the course events have taken, I think it will be generally admitted that the gradualness with which the country has been opened has been best for both parties. It was above all things necessary that the dense ignorance which prevailed among the Chinese, of foreigners and every thing connected with them, needed to be dispelled by a growing acquaintance with them and their ways. More especially it was necessary that their minds should be disabused of the idea that, though commerce and friendship might be our pretence, the real object at which we ultimately aimed was conquest. This was a very natural fear on the part of the Manchu rulers of China, for it was only supposing that we would serve them the same trick as they had served the Ming dynasty in 1644. I think that that fear may now be regarded as dispelled.

But when I came to Canton, such a fear had not yet been dreamed of. England, Spain, and Holland were still regarded as the insignificant States which they appeared to be as represented on Chinese maps; while, on the same notable evidence, they either believed that America did not exist, because it did not appear in their maps, or that, at all events, having no king, no fear need be felt as to anything she could do. But when, in 1841, the English fleet and forces proceeded up the coast, and Chusan, Ningpo and Shanghai, Chinkiang and Nankin fell, and Taku was reached, then the fear of conquest, suggested by their own history, became dominant in the breasts of the Manchu rulers, and they were forced to admit, at least to themselves, that foreigners were more powerful than they had supposed, and in their great ignorance they must have been at their wits' end what to do. But the experience gained by such leading men among the Chinese as Lin, Kishen, Keying, Ilipu, and others who had dealings with Elliot and Pottinger, must have been a kind of education not only to them, but to many others; and, as I review the growth of this knowledge from the time that the English Government began to deal directly with the Chinese Government in 1834, up to the present time, I feel convinced that this gradual development of the intercourse of China with foreign nations has been for her a source of safety and benefit.

No doubt Captain Elliot could easily have destroyed Canton in 1841; but he probably acted wisely in ransoming it. For many things had to be considered. First of all, the entire trade in tea was centred there and would have been paralysed for years had that emporium been destroyed. And then it was felt, besides, that the controversy was not with the Chinese people, but with the Chinese Government. And so long as the latter felt their own immediate interests secure, they would have cared as little for the ruin of so distant a place as Canton, as they now care for the sack and pillage of towns by the Panthays of Yunnan or the Mohammedans of Kansuh. But by proceeding along the coast, the British Navy became the pioneer of British trade, alike by the knowledge it gained and diffused of the navigation of the coast and the sources and trade of the country, as well as by the new and imposing views of foreign power and enterprise, which it made known over wide regions of China, where foreigners hitherto had almost never been heard of. When Admiral Parker took Amoy, in 1841 the people fled out of the place and were paralysed by fear; but when Dr. Abeel and Bishop Boone, both of whom spoke their dialect,—the one having learned it in Siam, the other in Batavia—went over to talk to them, the people came crowding round them wishing to know what the English wanted. And when they, evidently for the first time, heard the nature of the difficulty; they gradually came back to get particulars of the affair and its causes and no further difficulty was experienced with either people or officials. It was plain that it was only this ignorance that had made them unfriendly: as soon as they knew what our real wishes and objects were, all that passed away. It was immediately thereafter that Dr. Cumming established his Hospital there, which did much to re-assure and attract them, and nowhere in China have the people been more uniformly friendly to foreigners than Amoy. But where no such opportunities were enjoyed, of knowing what foreigners really are and wish for, we need not wonder that we are misunderstood, feared and hated, and that mistakes have been made and very serious ones too.

In these desultory remarks, which might be indefinitely prolonged, I have endeavoured to give some idea of the position which foreigners held in Canton up to the war of 1841 and to recall those features of their social life which have most strongly impressed themselves on my recollection. And before sitting down I would re-iterate my conviction that one great safeguard of our intercourse with China has been the gradualness of its development. I have no doubt the opening of the Five Ports in 1843 was better than the opening of the whole country would then have been, filled as the minds of both people and rulers were with wrong ideas regarding us. And my hope is that as our intercourse continues gradually to become more close and general, it may continue to be for the general advantage of all concerned. (Applause).

Mr. Medhurst said:—I have been asked by the Chairman to make a few remarks and I have great pleasure in doing so. My experience in China goes back to about the end of the period which Dr. Williams has made the subject of his Lecture to-night. I landed in China for the first time on the night of the day, on which the Chinese attempted to strangle in front of the Foreign Factories, a poor wretch who was found guilty of having dealt in opium but were prevented from dong so by the foreigners. That was in fact my first sight in China, and I regard it as the first step made by foreigners to contest the assumption of supremacy by the Chinese, which startled the Chinese into some idea of the strength of foreigners. Since that time great strides have been made in extending and strengthening our relations with China, and if the foreigners of whose life at Canton Dr. Williams has just been giving us such a graphic sketch could have seen the state of things at which we have now arrived, they would have been as startled as our remote ancestors would be, could they but see the manifold agencies of railways and telegraphs in full operation. And yet though important progress has been made in many directions, there is one important point on which we have been stationary, a point which we see looming in the distance indistinctly yet essentially, when we are told of petitions carried to the Oil-Gate in the days of Old Canton, and kept there the livelong day waiting, and sometimes in vain—for transmission. Of course, I refer to the Audience Question. The assumption of supremacy by the Chinese is still our difficulty. It is, however, to be hoped that the present year will see the solution of that difficulty also, and then there will be nothing more left us to hope for, but a more extended intercourse with the Chinese and the consolidation of our friendship with them. And now in proposing a vote of thanks to Dr. Williams for his graphic description of foreign society in Canton prior to 1840, I would ask you to remember that Dr. Williams has been one of the ablest pioneers of our intercourse with China alike as a missionary, a diplomatist and a scholar. In this last capacity he has left us that solid "foot print on the sands of time"--the *Chinese Repository*, which I regard as still our best authority in matters Chinese. I have, therefore, great pleasure in proposing that the thanks of this meeting be accorded to Dr. Williams. (much applanse.)

Dr. MACGOWAN said: We have great reason to felicitate ourselves that we still have among us a Chinese Repository—a living Repository of all that is known by foreigners regarding China. Nestor, we are told, was able to give instruction to men of 3 generations. But our Nestor can impart information to 6 generations of men, that is. according as generations of foreign residents are counted in China. Dr. Williams had referred to the formation of two institutions, with only one of which, present residents in China have an opportunity of becoming acquainted. That is the Medical Missionary Society of Canton, of the continued prosperity and usefulness of which we have pleasing evidence every year. The other institution was the Morrison Education Society; and though that is no longer in existence its beneficial influence is still felt. It is to it we owe the Chinese Educational Mission which has recently sent forth a goodly array of Chinese youth to be instructed in Western learning and science in America, and will probably ere long send similar bands of youth to the schools of Europe. For the leading spirit, the organising mind of the Mission, was a pupil of the Morrison Society School. It would be a work of supererogation in me to attempt to follow our friend further in his remarks, as I belong rather to the new era, not having come to China till the clouds began to disappear at the beginning of 1843. Still I have sufficient knowledge of Chinese matters to be able to appreciate the varied information that Dr. Williams has to-night so kindly conveyed to us. Before sitting down I should like to make one remark suggested by the previous speaker, Mr. Consul Medhurst, who, if I mistake not, is, next to Dr. Williams, our oldest resident* in China. In his recently published work, he has strenuously and ably advocated those favorable views of Chinese character which have pervaded Dr. Williams's lecture. Now that two such men, with such long and varied experience in dealing with Chinamen, and so thoroughly conversant with the Chinese language, should be so thoroughly at one in their favorable estimate of the Chinese character, is, I hold, a more powerful testimony in favor of the Chinese than could be given by a whole congress of ethnologists. (Great applause.)

The CHAIRMAN having in fitting terms conveyed to Dr. Williams the thanks of the meeting, the sitting closed.

---

* Mr. Gideon Nye of Canton arrived in China a few months after I did, six years before Medhurst.

CIRCULAR.

Since the death of the late venerable Dr. Morrison, suggestions relative to a Society to bear his name, have been circulated among his friends in Canton and Macao; twenty-two signatures have been obtained, and a subscription of $4860 collected. With a view to promote the object in question, by increasing the subscription, and making inquiries as to the best method of carrying into effect the proposed plan of education, the undersigned gentlemen have engaged to act as a provisional committee, until a general meeting of the subscribers in China shall be convened by public notice to form a board of trustees; which meeting shall be held on or before the first Wednesday in March, 1836.

If we except the pastors and teachers who visited Formosa with the Dutch, about two centuries ago, Dr. Morrison was the first Protestant missionary who ever reached the Chinese empire. Chiefly by his labors the Sacred Scriptures have been translated into the Chinese language, and a foundation laid for diffusing, among one fourth of the human family, that true religion which is one day to pervade the whole earth. Though his chief object was to benefit the people of China, yet the good which he has conferred on others, especially on those who speak the English language, demands of them a tribute of grateful acknowledgment, and urges them to "go and do likewise."

As a knowledge of the Chinese language has been of great advantage to foreigners, so an acquaintance with the English will be of equal or greater advantage to the people of this empire. For the purpose of conveying this benefit to the Chinese, and of aiding the great work which Dr. Morrison commenced, it is proposed to erect, in an institution characteristic of the object to which he devoted his life, a testimonial, more enduring than marble or brass, to be called the Morrison Education Society. The object of this institution shall be to establish and support schools in China, in which native youth shall be taught, in connection with their own, to read and write the English, language; and through this medium, to bring within their reach all the varied learning of the western world. The Bible and books on Christianity shall be read in the schools.

Already a Chinese, educated at the Anglochinese college in Malacca, has been advanced to the station of governmental interpreter at Peking. And our posterity, if not ourselves, may see the Chinese, at no very distant day, not only visiting Europe and America, for commercial, literary, and political purposes; but, having thrown away their antipathies, their superstitions, and their idolatries, joining with the multitudes of Christendom in acknowledging and worshiping the true God.

As the small contributions which our limited community in China can be expected to afford, must be utterly inadequate to the object in view, we look to the enlightened and liberal in other countries to coöperate with us.

PROVISIONAL COMMITTEE.

SIR GEORGE B. ROBINSON, BART.
WILLIAM JARDINE, ESQ.
D. W. C. OLYPHANT, ESQ.
LAUNCELOT DENT, ESQ.
J. ROBT. MORRISON, ESQ.
REV. E. C. BRIDGMAN.

N. B. At the request of the committee, Messrs. Jardine, Matheson, & Co. have engaged to act as Treasurers, and Mr. Bridgman, as Corresponding Secretary, until the Board of trustees is formed.

Subscriptions will be received by Messrs. Dent & Co., Jardine, Matheson, & Co., and Olyphant & Co., *Canton;* B. Baretto, Esq. *Macao;* R. Wilkinson, Esq., and Messrs. Lyell, Matheson, & Co., *Calcutta:* W. A. Hankey, Esq. *London;* Rev. J. Clunie, LL. D., *Manchester;* Frederic Leo, Esq. *Paris;* H. Hill, Esq. *Boston;* Messrs. Talbot, Olyphant, & Co., *New York;* F. A. Packard, Esq. *Philadelphia.*

Canton, February 25th, 1835.

NAMES OF SUBSCRIBERS.	RESIDENCE.	AMOUNT.

天保八年

米船モリソン号渡来の研究

相原良一著

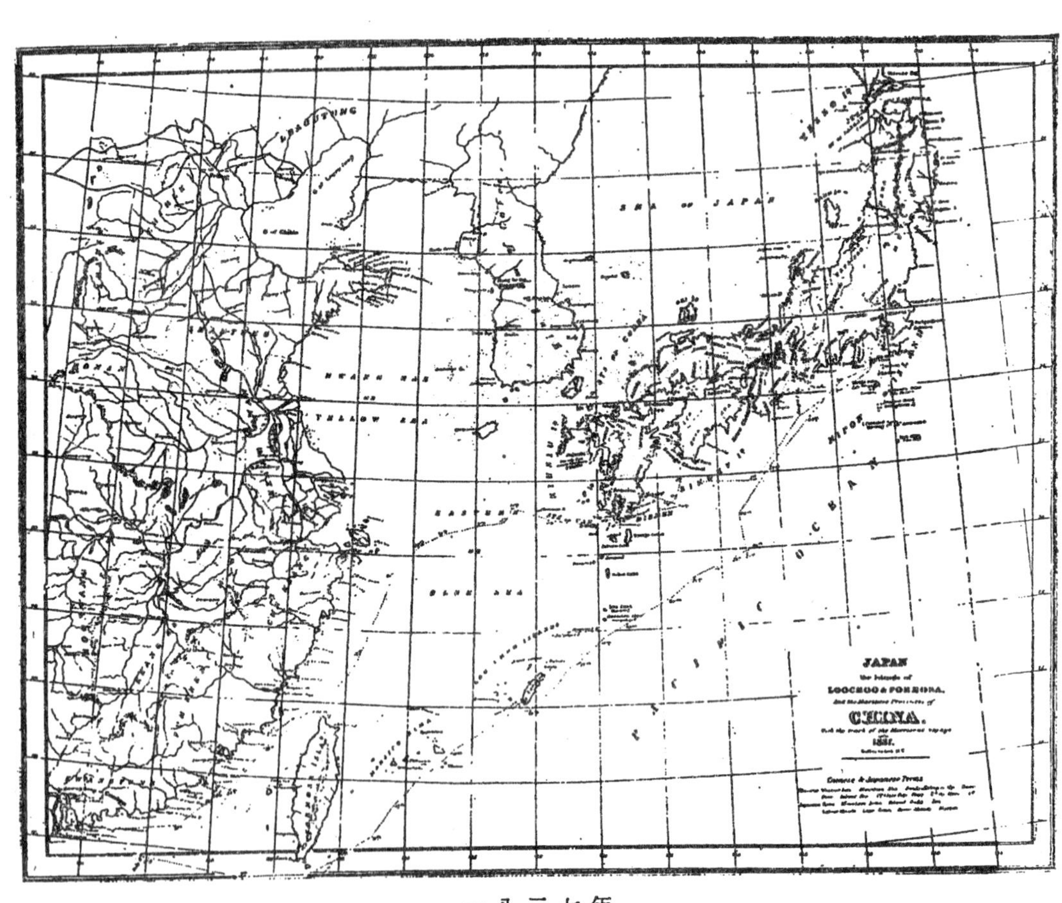

一八三七年

モリソン号来航の直後に作成され、キングの航海記に添付せられたる海図

第三章　航海の経過

以下の文中（P）はパーカーの航海記、（K）はキングの航海記、（W）はウイリアムズの航海記の略号

一八三七年七月三日、一行はマカオを出発し、夕刻碇泊地にあるモリソン号に乗船した（P）。モリソン号は五百六十四噸の強力な快速帆船である。[1] 乗員は一行四名に日本人漂民七名及び船員を加えて全部で三十八名、之に後からグッラフ師が加わつた（K）。船長はD・インガソル（W）。

七月四日[2]、朝出帆、この日は合衆国独立紀念日であつたが、一行はコスモポリタンであり、且つ備砲を取去つてきたので祝砲は放たず、ただ祖国の自由と繁栄と名誉のために神に感謝したのみ（K）。此の日も次の日も快晴無風、大陽が真上より直射して暑く、寒暖計は日蔭で九十度を示した。パーカー博士は一行の何名かに種痘を行つたが、初め興味をもつて之を眺めていた日本人達は、自分達の番になると好奇心も消え失せ、自分達は皆疱瘡をしたから種痘の必要はないと主張し

た。彼等のうち二名には疱瘡のあとがあつた（K）。

七月五日、夕刻より風が出て、六日には更に強まつた。我々は中国海岸に沿つて北上するか、バシー海峡を通過して太平洋へ出るかを検討した。台湾南端を廻つて太平洋へ出る方が、南東風を利用出来て都合がよいので後者に決定した。そこでバシー海峡を通過するならば、我々はボテル・トバゴ島及び台湾東海岸の数ヶ所に立寄りたいと考えた。それは、ボテル・トバコシマはその「シマ」という名が示す如く日本の勢力範囲にあり、台湾南端の他の島々と共に風俗・言語等に日本との通交の影響が見られるであろうと考えたからである。これ等の島々に日本の影響のあることは、次の四つの事実、即ち偶然的植民、計画的植民、民間の事業及び政治的要求の影響から説明することが出来る。

㈠は中国、呂宋、及びアメリカへ風によつて漂着した人々[3]、㈡はオランダ人以前に台湾西海岸のゼーランダに日本人が植民した事実[4]、㈢は二、三世紀前既に日本人はベンガルからマニラに到るまでの凡ゆる港に通交を行つており、アカプルコに於てすら相当数の日本人が見出されること[5]、また日本人がオランダやスペインの植民官によつて最上の補充兵と考えられ、暹羅の王のために宛も古代ローマの近衛兵の様な役目を果して居り、一五八〇年には実際に武器をとつた事実等[6]。㈣は日本北方の蝦夷（松前）、樺太の一部、千島列島の二、三の島々への発展[7]、朝鮮の侵略、琉球の征服、フ

イリッピン総督への敬意を表明したことなどに見出される[8]。そこで幸び我々は日本人を同行しているので之等の島々に対する日本の影響を調査したいと望んだのであるが、この時晴雨計が次第に降りはじめたので、船長の意見に従つて上陸を中止した[9]（K）。

七月八日、ボテル・トバゴの東方十五哩の地点を通過。船の動揺はげしく、船酔のため読書不能（K）。

七月十日、夜半マジコ島群島[10]に接近、翌朝同群島中の最大の島と連絡する準備を整えた（K）。この群島はその名の示す如く八つの小島からなり、その最大の島で一七九七年、英国の航海者ブロートンが難破した[11]（K）。ブロートンの航海記は今我々の手許にはないが、太平山の住民は彼を親切に遇し、彼に協力して難破したプロヴィデンス号から新に一隻のスクーナーを建造し、それによつて彼は琉球（或はマカオ）へ往き、更に探検航海を続行することが出来た（K）。

七月十一日、午前六時頃マジコシマを遠望（W）。午前九時北方に陸地を認め、それをウキマ島だと考えたが、間もなく船が夜の間に強い北東へ流れる潮流に影響されてゐて、前方の陸地は太平山であることが明らかになつた[12]（K）。我々の海図にある島の位置はホールズバラの海図[13]と十八哩違つて居り、この差異と強い潮流のため我々は八哩以上島に近づくことが出来ず、勿論島の人々と連絡することも叶はなかつた（K）。この群島は北緯二十四度と二十五度、東径百二十三度と百二十五度

の間にあり、琉球からは百八十哩の距離にあつて、ほとんど人に知られていない（W）。船中の日本人達はこの群島を知つており、その語るところによると住民は日本語を話し、人数は極めて少く、日本とは殆んど交通が無いとのことであつた（W）[14]。此の朝は天候が気象観測に適していたので、キング氏は島の正しい位置を確める事を希望し、我々はまた中国語で書いた宗教冊子を配布して住民が伝道者の来住を承諾するか否かを知りたいと思つたが、南西風のため上陸出来なかつた。村落は見えなかつたが、僅かな斜面には森や耕地が見られた（P）。我々は太平山の南方四哩の地点を通過した。太平山は緩やかな傾斜をなし、大体の輪廓は平坦である。海岸は急で白色を呈し、珊瑚礁によつて囲まれていた。また高地には樹木があるが、ボートも耕地も見られなかつた（W）。風が強く、而も相当の距離があるのでボートの来ることは期待出来なかつた。また我々の望遠鏡では土地がよく耕作されているか否かを決定出来なかつた。太平山を我々が一番近くから眺めた時は、南東の低い地点から次第に高くなつて約四百呎に達し、そこから稍々急な傾斜をなして北へ下つて居り、その沖合にブロートンの難破した珊瑚礁があり大波が砕けていた（K）。

七月十二日、午前六時頃東北東に大琉球島の西南端を望見（W）。船はバシー海峡を通過して以来北東へ流れる強い潮流に乗つていて、順風を受けて陸地に向つて進航を続けた。（W）。午前九時大琉球の南端二、三哩の地点に到達した（K）。この興味深い島に近づいたとき我々は土地の耕作状況

に就いて（語つて、互に）大いに意見を異にした。事実この様な場合に、森や草原の間の天然の区別を、高度に耕作された土地と判別することは甚だ困難なことである。崇高なマニラ湾に入る際に南岸の浜辺を庭園だと想像して感嘆し、また甲板から眺めて高度に耕作されていると思つた土地が、後に通つてみると彼のレガスピの[15]一行が初めて見たときと同様な荒地であるのを知つた人には、この事が理解できる筈である。ただ琉球の場合には、島の広い地域が初め見たときにまるで丘原（downs）か入会地（commons）位にしか思えなかつた。それは夏季に当つて土地が乾燥しているためなのか、収穫が済んだ後である故か、それとも元来土地が痩せている故か、どちらとも明瞭でない（K）。琉球の南端を通過して更に北方に進航を続けたが、過去五日間続いた不愉快な天候が尚続き、固定望遠鏡を使用することが出来ず、風が弱いのに陸に近づいても舷側の船錨材が水面に届くほどに横揺れした（K）。海岸全体に珊瑚礁があり、波が砕けていて、陸上に数人の漁夫が見え、別に二、三人の漁夫が丸木舟に乗つていたが、彼等はビーチイ船長の時と異り、我々の船を訪ねてくることもなく、また我々の釣鈎に魚をつけてくれることもなかつた（W）。北西にキラマ諸島[16]がはつきりと見えて来た。この島は琉球よりは嶮岨であるが、高さは同じ位であつた。那覇港に近づくにつれて樹木が多くなり、景色が変化に富み、はじめに遠望したときはロード・アイランドに似て単調であつたが、それに近づくにつれて全く異つた趣きを示してきた。円く或は尖つて突出してい

38

る高地の中で、特に前に訪問した人々によつて woody point と名づけられた山が目立つて居り、高さは明らかに二百呎あつた（K）。那覇港が見えたとき、一隻の大きな中国のジャンク（タイタウ行の[17]）が港を出て行つた。また船中の日本人が指さす方向に九隻の日本のジャンクが並んで碇泊していた（P）。午前十一時、アベー・ポイント[18]を廻つて那覇港に投錨した（K）（W）[19]。投錨地周辺の丘の上には見物人の無数の集団が見られたけれども、一時間たつても本船に近づき訪ねてくる者は一人もいなかつた。十年前にブラッサム号が[20]〔この島を〕訪ねた際には、船は見物の群集で一杯になつたとのことであるが、我々の船へ一名の訪問者もないのは、異国船に対する彼等の好奇心が前回既に充分に満足された為であろうか。或は十年の間に外国との交渉を禁止する命令が出た為であろうか（K）。午後三時岸から二隻の小船が近づいて来た。大きい方は長さが二十五呎程あり、十二人の半裸の土人が櫂で漕ぎ、船中に幾人かの人物がいた。役人であることは彼等に対して払われる尊敬によつて直に分つた。彼等は骨を折つて我々の船へ上つて来たが、袖の広い裕やかな着物を着て、腰に煙管と煙草入を挿していた。長い黒髪は油をつけ、頭の上で束ねてあつた。二本のピン、即ちカメシャシュとオーメシャシュを挿していたが、この簪は普通真鍮又は白銅で出来て居り、前者は四角で、髪を留めるスクリュウと、六弁の花に似た頭がついて居た。また後者は長さが八吋あつて、形は骨髄を抄ひ出す狭長な匙マアロー・スプーンに似ていた（W）[21]。甲板へ上るや否や彼等は中

39

国式に低く頭を下げて挨拶した。その中の主立つた者が我々に対して「中国語を話すか」と尋ねたので、「話す」と答えた。そこで一同着席したが、机の上には紙と鉛筆が用意してあつた。彼等は続いて「琉球へは何の用件で来たか」と尋ねた（W）。会談は不規則に数時間も、主立つた二、三人の者に対して行われたが、中国語であつた為めに、我々の方は完全には意を通ずることができなかつた（K）。通訳の中にアニアが[22]居たが、この時は四十歳に達して英語が非常に下手になり、僅に五・六語のブロークン・イングリッシュを話しただけである。何年かの間英語を使はなかつたから無理もないことである（K）。如何なる用件で琉球へ来たかという問に対しては、我々は数日間港に碇泊し、土地の人々に会ひ、飲食物を得るために来たと答えた。すると彼等の中の一人が懐から書物を取り出して一寸見ていたが、ブロークン・イングリッシュで「この船はアメリカの船か」と訊ねた。そうだと答えると、「人数は」というので「二十八名」[23]と応じた。「大勢だな、砲を備えているか」と言うので、「備えていない、之は商船だ」と答えると「人数も砲数も多い！[24]予はマンダリンに報告する」と言つて腰を下し、仲間の者達と相談をはじめた（W）。続いて主だつた人物が船の大きさ、航海の里程、アメリカから直接来たか否か、船長及び船客の姓名等を訊ね、答を全部書留めて置くように命じた。甲板に居たキング夫人に対しても色々質問してその答を書取つていたが、彼等の態度は中国の場合と違つて極めて鄭重であつた。彼等の話では、五日前に颱風があつて、果樹は全滅

40

し、莫大な被害があつたとのことである。この話によつて我々が琉球へ来る途中で経験した北へ向う大きな波のうねりの原因が分つた。彼等の話では颱風は毎年四月から九月までに発生し、猛威を振うとのことである。この時一隻の中国のジャンクが港を出て行つたので、何処へ向うのであろうかと訊ねると、その船は琉球のジャンクで砂糖を積みタイタウ[25]へ往くとのことであつた。船の船尾には「順風〇〇」（Shun Fung seang sung）[26]と書いてあつた（W）。アニアは我々が英語で話合うのを聞いて、再び我々が英国人ではないかと訊くので、「アメリカは元は英国から人が移住して出来た国である。今は独立国であり、英国とは大洋を距てて何千哩も離れて居る。アメリカ人は多数の商船を有し、琉球人の友である。」と語り、地図を示して説明したけれども、アニアは納得しない様子であつた（W）。彼等が船中を隅なく見て廻るので、我々は船中の日本人達と之等の人を会せないようにした。しかし間もなく彼等は互に相手を認めあひ、非常に熱心に二、三語を交すのを見た（K）。彼等はパーカー博士の用意して行つた外科手術の絵を見て驚いて、「病人は治つたのか」と訊ねたので、治つたと答えると満足した様子であつた。そこで琉球に於いても我々は同様な手術を行う用意があり、また病人を連れてくれば診療するということを伝えた（W）。かくて彼等は我々に飲食物供給の手筈を定め、それを翌日持参することを約束し、上機嫌で帰つて行つた（P）。この間、嘗てビイ船長の耳にしたという船歌は聞こえなかつた（W）[27]。

41

別に取極めがなかつたので我々は自由行動をとることにした。食事を済ました後、艦載ボートに乗り、キング夫妻、ウィリアムズ氏、インガソル船長と共に普通の上陸地点から遠く離れアベ・ポイントに接する砂浜に上陸した(P)。[28] 土地の者が大勢集まつて来たが、その中に四、五名の役人が居て(約二十名の下役人が息せき切つて馳けつけ—P)我々に船へ戻つて貰いたいと要求した。我々は静かに岬の岩の方へ歩いて行き、同時に一人の水夫をして附近の家へ水を一杯貰いにやつた。彼は一人の老婦人を伴つて来た(W)。前に琉球を訪れたものの記録に、琉球ではほとんど婦人を見掛けないとあつたので、我々はこの婦人を歓迎し、特にキング夫人は鄭重に挨拶を交し、一同その家へ案内された(K)。その婦人の手の甲には既婚者の印である文身がしてあつた(W)(P)。我々はボートへ戻り、湾を廻つて那覇の入江の方へ向つたが、この入江は船の碇泊に安全な内湾で、日本のジャンク八隻、大型の琉球ジャンク三隻、小型四隻、約百隻のサンパンが碇泊していた。日本のジャンクを見たのは之が初めてである。二百噸程の船で、中部と船尾が広く、船首は長く突き出て尖つている(K)。[29] 琉球のジャンクは見たところ、型が日本のジャンクよりも中国のものに近かつた。我々は予て那覇港はジャンクや小舟で賑わうということを読んでいたので、それらがほとんど皆船という名に価しないのを見て失望した(K)。

上陸地点へ往くと、今朝来訪した人達が、群集と共にそこにいたので挨拶を交して船へ戻つた

(W)。

七月十三日、早朝、ポッン[30]に上陸し、村へ入つたが何等の妨害も受けなかつた。森の茂つた丘を登つて頂上につくと、眺望甚だ好く、右手遥かの洋上にはキラマ諸島が見え、南には那覇があつて、その港の中に吹流しを掲げた船が碇泊していた。東には首府首里の独特の家屋が立ち並び、足下にはポッンの村が望見される。北方は見渡す限り耕地と丘の連続である。景色を賞していると、我々を眺めていた群集の中から一人の若い者が、筆記用具と二冊の書を持つてやつて来た。一冊は漢字で書かれており、他の一冊は漢字に平仮名で傍訓してあつた。後者は前者を説明したものに違いない。この若者は学問をしていると言つていたが、中国語は僅に数語を話し得るに過ぎなかつた。群集の中によい服装の人物数名が混じつていて、我々に対し、頻りに船に戻るように言い立てた。我々は暑さがひどいので引き返えすことにした。之を見た彼等は恐らく自分達の努力が成功したと考えたであろう(W)。中国から琉球へ来て意外に感じたことが二つある、即ち町の街路を大声で奴鳴りながら食糧品その他を売り歩く呼売人や、町角に物を並べて売る者のいないことと、犬の吠えるのを聞かなかつたことである(W)。

午前九時に役人達が塩、卵、瓜、水を持つて来た(P)。十一時、アニアが同僚と共に、予て依頼しておいた品をほんの少し持つて船へ訪ねてきた。一同が席につくとアニアは「二日前に一艘の外国

船が那覇へ来て、やがて西北の方へ立ち去つた」と語り、その船は我々の船ではなかつたのかと訊ねた。我々が「そうではない。それは恐らく我々が琉球で会うことになつている英国スループ艦ローレイ号に相違ない」と答えると、それを切掛けに次々と質問が発せられた。「何の為にローレイ号を待つのか」と訊いた。「ローレイ号は英国の軍艦で、我々と一緒に日本へ往く友人(グッラフ)を乗せてくるのだ」と答えた。すると彼等は明らかに不安の色を現して長い間相談していた。我々は琉球人に対しては、ローレイ号来航のことと、我々の目的地に就いて万一にも日本へわかるといけないと考え、ローレイ号の到着するまではそれを知らせないことにしていた。然し彼等がローレイ号の大きさ、備砲の数、滞在の予定日数等を知りたがるので「やむを得ず」それを教えてやつた。しかし何故那覇が外国船二艘の会合地に選ばれたのかとの理由を説明する訳にいかなかつたので、前に我々がアメリカ人であると言つたことに対し疑念をもつたようである(W)。この会見を了るに先だち、彼等から更めて質問が発せられた、「その人達は日本人か」、「あなた方は彼等を故国へ連れてゆく積りか」。之に対し我々は「彼等は漂民であり、故国へ送還するのだ」と答えた(K)。後で判つたことであるが、琉球人達は彼等漂民に対して言葉を盡して、モリソン号を離れ彼等の船で鹿児島へ往くように説いたということである(K)。

この時パーカー博士はピアソン博士の種痘論を取り出し、船にいる者に対し種痘をしようと申出

た。アニアが書を読みながらその目的を説明すると、最後にタカラ[31]と称する首長の一人が種痘を受けることを承認し、腕の三ヶ所にそれを受けた。疑い深いアニアは我々に関することは万事独占しようとして、琉球人は三才になる前に疱瘡を植えてしまうから、之以上他の者に試みることは不要だと言つていた。彼は我々と琉球の住民との直接の交渉を妨げ得る場合には、彼自身が何を言おうと平気だつたことがこれまでに何度もあつた(W)。

我々は乗馬をしたいから馬を何とかして都合してくれと頼んだ。前にビーチイ船長が馬を貸与して貰つたことがあると話すと、「奉行の命令によつて諸君は上陸を禁ぜられている。ビーチイ船長はこの命令を知らなかつたのだ。それは間違いで、諸君は皆礼儀を心得ているから上陸を希望しまい」と答えた。「訪問を受けて答礼しないのは、返つて礼儀に反するから」と言うと、「土地の法律だから、上陸してはならない」とのことであつた。そこで「我々はただ健康上散歩を希望し、その地方を見物したいのだ」と告げた。するとアニアは話題を変えて「何故日本へ往くのか、何故友人が日本へ行くのを待ち合せているのか」と訊ねた。この点に就いては、之等の上役達が事情を知らない筈はなかつた。彼等は船へ来るや否や、その中の数人が漂民の所へ行つて盛んに談話を交へ、時々テーブルについている同僚の所へ来ては話していたからである。そこで我々の来航の目的はただ漂民を故国へ送還するだけだと伝え、更に必要な食糧品のリストを差出すと彼等は間もなく帰つて行

つた。彼等は前日ほど友好的ではなかつたが、それは二艘の外国船が格別寄港する用件もないのに、那覇を会合の地に選んだことを知つて心配になつたからである(W)。

午後、一隻の日本のジャンクが砂糖二百ピクルを積んで薩摩へ向け出港した(W)。砂糖は報告によればこの島の主要輸出品であつて、輸出額は年に十七万五千ピクルに達するとのことである(P)。ジャンクは珊瑚礁に乗り上げたが、別に破損しなかつたらしく、間もなく離礁した(W)。船の船尾には「宝山丸」と書かれており、船首には〔浜〕としてあつた。更に別のジャンクには「凪」の文字があり、第三のジャンクには「余」印しがあつた[32](P)。

七月十四日、今朝もまた那覇市の桟橋から上陸した。行ける処まで歩いてゆく積りでいたが、岸へ上るや否や忽ち阻止され、濡れた石の上に坐れというので、「礼儀に反する」と抗議した。那覇市内に通ずる道路を無理にも進もうとしたが、役人達は狭い道路に立ち塞り、我々の腕や着物を捉えて附近の寺院へ往くように要求した。事を荒立てることを好まなかつたので、言われる儘に寺院へ行き境内を見物した。境内の建物は総括して中国使節のホールと称ばれ、ガウピル神父が曾て之に言及したことがあり、レポジトリの七月号にはチーンゼカンとして記されてある[33]。全体が荒れ果て大部分は空家で珊瑚壁によつて囲まれてゐる。海に面した方は、鋸壁(バトルメント)を施した防壁によつて護られていて、琉球としては大きい建物である。現在の有様から考えると、最近は中国使節が宿泊した

ことはないのではなかろうか(W)。我々は再びボートに乗つて那覇へ向つて漕ぎ出すと、役人達は之を見て直ちに櫓を操つて追かけて来た。静かに碇泊している幾艘かのジャンクの間を通り過ぎ、やがて或る入江へ入つた。入江に面して那覇の町がある。入江のはずれの小川まで来るとボートは泥土の中へ乗り入れた。丁度干潮だつたので、住民達が水の中をじやぶじやぶ歩き廻つていた。背後には所々に耕作地のある丘がそびえ、北側には那覇から首里へつづく道路に家が建ちならんでいて、穏和な感じを与えた。湾へ戻ると住民が大勢立ちならんでいた。その中の背の高い比較的立派な人物が扇を開いて我々に湾の外へ出て行くように合図をしたが、それに構わずに船を漕いで桟橋に到着した。役人達が追い附いて来たので、我々が入江を溯つたのは町を見物する為だつたのだと説明した(W)。

我々は湾へもどり、キャプスタン・ロック[34]の麓に上陸し、丘上の寺院を訪門した。頂上の建物は荒れるにまかせ、本堂には数人の僧侶が居て、手入れが行届き、大きな樹々にかこまれていて、奇妙に枝を曲げたバンヤン樹が涼しい日蔭をつくつていた(W)。この寺院には「護国寺」と書いて掲げてあつた(P)。祭壇には約百個の貨幣が上つていたが、クラプロット訳の「三国志」に les petites pieces japonaises en cuivre とある日本銅貨である。これは琉球唯一の通貨で、我々はその幾つかを貰つたが、クラプロットにある通り「寛永通宝」と刻まれてある(K)[35]。寺院を出て墓地へ行きア

ルセスト号の乗組員が此辺に埋葬したという海軍少尉候補生の墓を捜したが、役人達はその所在を教えようとしなかつたので、遂に発見できなかつた[36]。墓は中国のものに似ているが碑銘がない。琉球人は生前の住居よりも、死後の安息の場所に関心と努力を示すらしい。山へ登ると那覇とボッンの中間地帯が一望に眺められたが、犬が吠えるので困つた。琉球滞在中に犬の吠えるのを聞いたのはこの時だけである。寺院へ戻つて、茶をすすりながら、建物の構造を見、経典を見せて貰つた。その数冊を買い求めようとしたが、分けてくれなかつた。群集から離れて一団の婦人がいたが、彼等は男達と一緒にいることを恐れているらしかつた。我々は屡々、婦人達が手荒な取扱いを受けるのを見たので、男達を怖れるのは当然だと思つた(W)。

朝食後、パーカー博士は種痘の書を返えして貰いに再び村へ行つた。親切に迎えられ、中国使節のホールに案内されたが、そこに大きな眼鏡をかけた老人がいて、種痘論を全部写しとり、種痘のやり方に就いてもつと知りたいというたので、彼自身の腕に種痘して、彼及び廻りの人々にそれを教えてやつた。彼に幾本かのランセットを与えた。それは、種痘を説明した書物と共に将来この老医師を琉球人の恩人たらしめるであろうし、種痘に対する関心と書物による精しい説明とは、種痘が琉球全島に普く行われるようになるだろうとの希望を我々に抱かせた(W)。

種痘を取扱つたこのパンフレットは、広東の東印度会社の外科医アレクサンダア・ピアソン博士

が著し、種痘術が初めて中国にもたらされた一八〇三年に、ジョージ・ストーントン卿がそれを華訳したのである[37]。種痘は日本では既に蘭館の医師によつて行われていることと思うが、琉球では未だその様子がない。この琉球の老人が、種痘術の説明と、与えられた種痘菌とを琉球人の為に役立てることを希望する。来訪者の多くは疱瘡のあとがあり、広く流行しているとのことである(K)。

(この老人に関しPは次の様に述べている)「私は種痘を施すべき小児はいないかと訊ねたが、いないとのことであり、更に種痘を習得して貰う医師はと訊ねると、之も居ないとの返事であつた。間もなく、半白の顎髯を生やした一人の老人が種痘書の完全な写しを携えてやつて来た。それには幾つかの文字に符箋がつけられていて、これを説明して貰いたいとの事であつた。彼は、子供の時に牛痘を植えた者は年をとつてから疱瘡にかかることはないのか、種痘書に書かれていることは真実なのかと質問した。この時私はこの老人を医師だと思つた。誰も私にそう言つたものはないが私は今でもそう信じている」(P)。

次に役人達は皮膚病にかかつた友人の診断を依頼したが、私は我々の滞在期間の短いのを残念とした。若しもつと滞在出来れば、その日一日病人の診療が出来たのである。更に数名の患者を診療し、船から薬が送られた(P)。

モリソン号へ戻ると間もなく、アニアその他の役人達が見事な三頭の豚と二頭の山羊、飲料水数

稀を携えて来訪した。老医師その他数人の診察を希望するものも来たので、経験のない彼等にも安全だと思われる薬を与えたが、彼等は用心して、説明書の内容を完全に話して貰いたいと要求した。音吉の助力によつて、すべての疑念が晴れると、彼等は薬を丁寧に包んで煙草入れの中へ収めた。パーカー博士が解剖図と外科手術の絵を見せると、老人は興味深くそれを調べ、手術の仕方について色々好い質問をした。我々はこの老人に興味をひかれ、彼がもつと早く訪ねて来なかつたことを残念に思つたのであるが、この人物がビーチィの来航した際に部下の病人を診察した人物と同一人物であるかどうかは確めることが出来なかつた。彼は辞去する前に英国の地図を一枚貰いたいと申し出たが、残念ながら我々はその持合せがなかつた(W)。

ローレイ号に関して更に二、三の質問が行われた。役人達は今日は寧ろ日本人漂民と話したい様子であつた。我々の航海に関して何度も質問し、漂民達の之までいた所は何処か等と訊ねた。但し彼等は中国の地理について深い知識はないらしく、マカオを漢字で書いて示したが誰も知つている者はなかつた。タカラとアニアに対し、一枚の紙に我々の来航の意図を書いて示し、住民と友好関係を促進したい希望を告げて、彼等の取扱いは此の我々の意図に添つていないと言うと、彼等はその事実を認め、それ以上は何も言わなかつた。我々は彼等を船室へ案内して饗応した。コロン水を一人の手の中へ注いでやると、幾人かの者が、味を試したり、香を嗅いだりしてその用法を訊ねて

いるうちに、蒸発してしまつたので吃驚していた。また何故手が冷く感ずるのか分らず、更に頭へふりかけると、香が芳くて涼しいので、大悦びでその壜を受取つた。盲人の手術をしているカンッヂ博士の版画を見せて、医師に説明すると、しばらく眺めていたが、所望したのでそれを贈与した。役人達が下にいる間に一般の人達に更紗（printed calico）を与えると、大悦びでその派手な色合に満足していた。下にいた役人達が甲板へ上つて来たので、彼等の持参した食料品の値段を訊ね、一握りの弗貨を差出したところ、アニアは、「琉球には金貨も銀貨も銅貨もないから受取るわけにいかない。つまらぬ品を少しばかり差上げはするが、売買することは出来ない」と答えた(W)。

琉球人は自国の事情の法律に関する情報を提供しようとしないし、外国船に対して出来る限りの飲食物を供給はするが報酬は受取らない。彼等は金を持たないのだから、金は不要だというのである。之は恐らく琉球の港を外国船の会合の場所にしたくないという政策の故であろう(P)。

正午にアニア及びその一行と、最後の会見が行われたが、彼等は山羊、豚、薩摩芋、塩等約二十弗の価格の品物を持参した。牛は未だ貧弱で役に立たぬし、果物は颶風のために駄目になつてしまつたとの話である。が、つまりはこの食物調達者達が此の世の結構な品の余剰を多く持つていないので、外国の客人達を、出来るだけ安上りに逐い払う算段だつたのであろう。我々が貧弱な提供品に対して弗を支払うように申出でると、アニアは「我々の国では銀貨を用いない」と答えた。そこ

で更紗木綿や酒をボートへ運ばせようとしたのだが、それをも断つた。彼等が拒絶したのは品物が欲しくないからではない。上述の商品やその他の品物の見本を前に差出した時には大悦びで受取つて、ゆるい袖口から日本服の開いた懐ろへすべり込ませたことから考えると、之等の物は大いに尊重され、高く評価されているに相違ない。ぴかぴか光る真新しいアメリカの五仙貨を配ると、一層悦びその代償として彼等の袴の裾から棒縞や格子縞のラミー布を切り取ることを許した。この布地は、白地又は青地に黒、濃青、薄茶色の縞模様を施した、琉球人一般の用いているものである。膝では地の粗い捺染をした木綿を見たが、琉球人は中国人と同様に今も粗末な版木捺染法を行つているらしい。既に幾世紀にも亘つて、紙にインクを施す場合に木型を用いている国民が、布の色をプリントするのに大した進歩を示していないのは不思議である(K)。

会談に疲れたので、我々は一杯の葡萄酒と菓子を出した。かかる場合、一杯の薄いフランス葡萄酒が出されたのは儀礼的にして或はまた好奇心を満足させるためであるが、款待の方法としては葡萄酒の方が煙草を出すよりは害が少くて、効果に変りがないからまだましである。泥酔という文明の悪徳によつて質樸粗野な人々を誘惑する程批難すべきことはない。我々をして最初に琉球人に関して興味を起させた話の中に、酒のことが屢々出てくるのは残念なことである。同時に煙草についても、之は西洋が東洋へ贈つた最悪の贈り物であり、今日ではすべての善良な人々は、かかる「害

草」の使用を許容すべきではない。少くとも、之まで東印度会社の勅許状の及んでいた範囲内に於ては許されてはならないのである(K)。[38]

役人達が我々の船を辞去しようとしたときにローレイ号が南方にその姿を現した(K)。

日本人漂民をはじめ一同が歓呼の声を挙げたので、琉球人達は何事であろうと狼狽して舷側へ走つていつた。アニアのみは平然として、「待つていた英国船というのはあれではないか。あの船も一緒に日本へ行くのか」と訊ねた。我々は前に述べた通りに答え、明日出帆する由を話すと、彼等はそれを聞いて非常に悦んだ(W)。

ここで我々は再び食糧品の代価を支払うためにハンケチを数枚提供した。ハンケチは琉球で使用されている紙製のものよりも上等であるし、之は食糧品の支払いではなく、贈り物なのだからと説いたが、タカラは「それは結局売買と同じだから」と言つて拒絶した。更に他の品物を提供しようと申出たが、それも受け取ろうとしなかつた。アニアは「外国人と取引するのは、我が国の法律に違反することになるから、僅かな品物でも受け取る訳けにはいかない」と答えた。しかし実際にはアニアはポケット辞典を受け取り、その他の者も更紗の見本を取めた。彼等が斯の如く引続いて拒絶し続けた理由は、来訪者がすべて主だつた人物（chiefs）であつて、誰か一人が品物を受ければ全部の者に知れてしまい、結局所有者が迷惑することになるし、品物が新奇な物であるだけに、人に

見せたり使用したりすることが安全には出来ないからであろう。アメリカの旗を贈ると、まだ見たことがないとのことであつた(W)。

琉球に対する我々の観察を、琉球へ来た他の人々の観たところと比較すれば、琉球の人々は外国船に対して既に好奇心を感じなくなつたものと察せられる。また琉球政府の現在の政策は、外国船が来航した場合、飲食物を供給する為の接待の役人を任命し、之にその取扱の一切を任せ、来航者が住民に近づくことを禁じ、その上陸を制限して、出来るだけ速に退去せしむることにあつたようである。こうして、琉球へ来航した外国人を如何に取扱うのが最もよいかを知り、それによつて太平洋の多くの島々の外国人との交渉を特徴づけている行き過ぎを避けようとするものである。この点では、琉球人は恵まれておると言わなければならない。琉球の位置は太平洋の通常の航路を外れており、外国船の来航に制限を設けている中国や日本に近いために、彼等の対抗し得ない外国人の訪問を受けずに済んできたからである。毎日我々の船へは、多少の例外はあるが、同じ役人が来訪し、ローレイ号に対してもその同じ役人が出張した。然るに陸上でははとんどそれ等の役人の訪問を受けない。船に於いても陸に於いても彼等はその地位を表示するものを身につけていない。ただ従者の使用する扇、小さな竹、又は籐によつてそれと知れるのみである。政府の内政及び諸機関は中国をモデルにしたものであるとチャウ・ファン[33]は述べたが、今日では明らかに日本の習慣と勢力

54

の方が強く影響している、ルソンに漂着した西九州出身の四名の漂民の語るところによれば、琉球は薩摩の領主が支配し、その貿易を独占しているとのことである(W)。

那覇周辺の一般住民は生活程度が大体同様で、一般に農業に励むことによつて日常の必需品をととのえ、中国に見られるような極端な貧富の差がない。乞食ははとんど見かけなかつた。人の大勢集まつている場所でも、病人ははとんど見当らなかつたし、不具の者は全然いなかつた。彼等の体格はこの国民が重労働をしていないことを示している。衣食は自国で生産するもので足り、それに日本及び中国から来る僅かなものを加えるだけで必要は満され、それ以上外国の贅沢品を見せられても、別にそれを得ようと努力する気にもならないらしい。従つて事業を起す必要も感じないわけである。もし彼等が知識を広めるならば、それにつれて欲望が増し、活動も盛んになつて、彼等の勢力や重要性も増してくることになる。彼等は質樸であり、所謂「幸福なる無知」に恵まれていると同時に、偶像崇拝によつて品位を落し、酒によつて阿呆てしまつている。この夢魔が取り除かれるまでは、如何に事業欲を刺激しても、文明国と呼ばれる程度に立ち上ることはあるまい。もし彼等が基督教の影響を受けるならば、彼等の楽しみも、彼等の地位も現在の何千倍にも高められ、墓の彼方へまでも悦びと平和がもたらされることであろう(W)。

農業は中国と同様に主として手で耕され、田畠は小さく、二種類のミレット、粟、甘藷、米等が

55

主たる産物である。野菜類は大抵のものが獲れ、瓜その他多くの果実類を産する。砂糖は主たる輸出品であり、着物は綿類も豊富であるが大部分はラミー布を用いている。茶と絹はこの島では生産しないと聞いていたが、それは恐らく誤りであろう。肥料にするために海草が採集され、到る処に堆肥の山が見られた。灌水は中国よりは遥かに劣つている。農耕器具は数も少く簡単なもので、主に鍬、鉈、鎌、耙を用いている。我々の見る限り、工芸(mechanical arts)はすべて簡単なもののみであり、武器類では刀も火縄銃もナイフも見掛けなかつた。之は恐らく、彼等の主人である日本人達が、ヘブライ人を支配したフィリスタイン人の如く、彼等から武器を取り上げ、その使用を禁止した為めであろう。金属の使用は少く、簪、煙管、急須、台所用具等は日本及び中国からもたらされたものらしい。琉球は家畜の少いことが目立つている。日本や中国にいる種類は、知られていたが数が少い。我々が見たのは、一匹の白い小犬と数頭の豚、牛、山羊だけである。その外に馬、驢馬、猫がいると聞いた。家禽も稀で、之等の家庭生活を聯想させるものがいないために、混雑した町の街路さえも、何となく空虚な感じがした。博物学上では、ブラッサム号の人々の観察に付け加えるものは何もなかつた。植物も花も木も種類が限られていて、貝類、珊瑚、昆虫、魚類は、標本にする価値のあるものは殆んどなく、土地の人の持つて来たものは一つもない。自然界の産物、特に昆虫と魚はかなり多くの種類が居ることと思われるが、それを調べるには此の国に住まわなくて

56

ならない(W)。

琉球の取引は物々交換によつて行われるらしく、チャウ・ファン(註39参照)の輸出品のリストから判断して、周囲の国と盛んに貿易が行われたようである。この中国使節の古い記事は今日では余り信頼出来ないが、このリストの書かれた頃の大部分の商品の量はリストにのせる程のものでなかつたらしい。数隻の琉球ジャンクが中国へ往来するが、その一隻が数年前航路を外れて澳門へ着いた。グッラフ師の語るところによれば、ローレイ号で福州へ赴いた際に、琉球のジャンクにも乗つたとのことである。乾隆帝が琉球へ与えたジャンク建造の雛形は忠実に取り入れられた。それは日本のものよりも勝つていることが明らかである。琉球が中国や日本の近くにあり、両国の船がその港に来航出来ることは、之等両国に対する我々の交渉を深める上に特別の便宜を与えるものである。もし、那覇が自由港となるならば、満州とルソン島の中間に介在する港から、その生産物を積出し、外国の繊維類を持ち帰るためにジャンクが蝟集することであろう。那覇は現在中国と日本のジャンクが両国以外の国に於いて会合し得る唯一の港であり、此処ではお互いに恐れることなく交わることが出来、親しみを加え、取引を増すことによつて次第に反感と偏見とが消え去ることであろう。外国人もまた此の港を商品の置場とし、中国の茶と絹、日本の金属や陶磁器と交換することによつて、永い間、諸外国に対して門戸を閉じている両国の資源を開発し、その活動を正しく導くことが出来

57

る。高い代価を払つて経験して生じた猜疑と偏見とは、之等両国と諸外国とを距てる大きな障害であり、両国が港を閉すに至つたのは諸外国の人々の誤つた行為によるものであるから、公正な態度によつて彼等の猜忌を解くのも同じ諸外国人でなければならない。貿易の自由は思想交換の自由を生み、商品の進出はそれと共に文明と基督教とを伸展せしめる。世界解放の源たる福音から閉め出されていた之等の国々へも、この港を通じて近づくことが出来るようになり、聖書や宗教書がこの港を通じて、遠く中国や日本の奥地へまでも行き渡るようになるのである。かかる計画は果して夢であろうか。それにはシンガポールがよい例である。我々は那覇を以て、東太平洋の偉大なる島々に於ける第二のシンガポールにすべきである。我々は、この闇に包まれた国の為に微力を惜しまぬ人々に、これ等の島々が更に一層注目せられることを希望するものである(W)。

琉球の地名に関しては、その綴り方が人によつて区々である。例えば琉球は Lewkew, Lewchew, Loochoo, Liqueo, Licou, Kicou, Lequeyo, Liquio, Rio Kio, Riuku, Doo Choo である。最後のものは土地の人の呼び方である。首里は Showle, Tseuli, Tchoole, Shoody（土地の人の呼び方）, Cheudi, Shoomi, Sheni となつている。Kin-tching 又は Kin ching とあるのは、「黄金の市」の意で、首里の城壁内にある宮殿の名称であり、首都そのものの別名ではない。那覇は Napa, Napa foo（＝district of Napa), Napa ching（＝city of Napa）とあり、多くの場合 Napa keang 即ち「那覇の

入江」と称ばれている。これは那覇の面する入江（inlet）によつたのである。之等の幾通りもの綴りの中、どれを採つたらよいかを決定するのは、仲々困難なことであるが、大体に於て中国式の発音に従うのがよいのではあるまいか。Pootsung に対して、タカラは Pō tsun 即ち village of Po がよいと言ひ、ポート・メルビルに在る Oonting（運天）は Hwanteen とし、アベ・ポイントはヤラサ Yalasah と称んでいる(W)[40]。

通訳達は取調べの為ローレイ号へ赴いたが、それが済むと、グッラフ氏が我々を訪ねてきて、指示に従うて、漂民の送還に関し、日本人自身の意見と希望とを訊ねることになつた。彼等は船室へ案内され、其処で故国へ帰る準備は出来ているか、またそれを希望するか否かを尋ねられた。之に対して彼等は極めて熱心に再び故国を見たい由を答えた。モリソン号で行くか、それとも、他の方法を選ぶかとの質問に対しては、同じ熱心さを以て、我々と共にモリソン号で行きたいと答え、日本へ到着の上は親切に迎えられることを確信すると述べた。一度難船した彼等は危険な日本のジャンクに身を任せることは心配だつたのであろう。そこで、之等の気の毒な流浪者達が、宗教上の疑ひの係り合ひになつて危害を蒙ることのないように、予の知らぬ間にモリソン号に積載されて来た宗教書をローレイ号へ移した。之で今はもうグッラフ氏の移乗を待つばかりとなつたが、同氏はローレイ号に於ける会議が済んで、船に必要な品々を積み了るまで、同船に留まらなければならなか

つた(K)。

七月十五日、朝、北風のため、モリソン号はセメタリ・ポイント[41]の沖にある岩礁を離れなければならなかつたので、那覇港の外湾へ移動したが、潮のために数哩南へ流され、ローレイ号の近くの位置を取戻すのにその日一日かかつた。その間にローレイ号のクイン艦長はグッラフ氏に移乗を命じた(K)。

グッラフ氏は午後三時に移つて来た。ローレイ号はそれから小笠原へ向つた(W)。

港としての那覇は延長は短いが、東風の時はよい港である。但し西風の時は、我々が入港の際に見た波のうねりに依つても分る如く、外にならぶ岩礁も安全な護りではない。飲食その他の必要品の補給地としては、那覇は余り高く評価できない。琉球人は貧しく、しかも彼等をして謝礼を拒絶せしめるだけの強い政治的理由が存在する以上、費用の掛らぬ水だけが、この港へ寄港する船の期待し得る唯一のものである。ビーチイ船長は琉球の水に就いて不満を述べているが、我々が供給を受けた水は何等不快なものではなくまた無害であつた。但し若し船が度々この港へ来航して長く滞在し、飲食物の供給を求めるならば、琉球人は今日の遣り方をそのまま続けはしないであろう。食糧品を売るのを許可するか、或はこの方が一層可能性が強いのであるが、一切供給を拒絶することであろう。僅かな英国織維品を熱心に求めるところから考えると、もし輸入が自由に許可されるな

らば、彼等ば経済力の許す限り外国品を買うであろう。しかし現在之と交易すべき物として唯砂糖があるばかりで、しかもその大部分が日本へ輸出されるから、彼等の交易能力は極めて小さいに相違ない。那覇市それ自身は貧しい家々の集りで、中国の四流の町に過ぎない。田舎の家は竹で造つた粗末なもので、屋根は茅葺であり、寺院や舟も家屋と同様に貧弱であつて、住民の大部分は「貧乏の衣」を纏うている。もし群集がぞろぞろ我々に付き纏ふことがなかつたならば、モリソン号を訪ねて来た僅かな小舟の模様から推察して、琉球人は既に外国人に飽きていると考えたかも知れないのだが、実際にはそうではなくて、一般住民は舟で岸を離れることを禁止されていたに違ひない。この禁令が何時出たものか確め得なかつたが、その結果モリソン号へ来る小舟の数は一日二、三隻に限られ、明るい朗かな気分は真面目くさつたものに変り、以前に渡来した人々が屢々耳にしたという船唄は全く聞かれなくなり、毎日モリソン号の側を往来するカヌーは招いても寄つて来なかつた。我々が短い滞在中に見聞したすべてのことは、クラプロットやゴロウニンその他が日本人から聞いたといふ説即ち琉球と中国との関係は唯だ名のみで、実際には琉球は日本の属領であるという事実を証明した。クルーゼンステルンは朝鮮及び琉球に対する日本の主張を単に「虚勢」に過ぎないとして、彼が六ケ月間長崎に滞在しておる間に之等の属領と称せられる朝鮮、琉球のいづれからも、唯の一隻の船も入港しなかつたと述べているが[42]、朝鮮に就いては我々はただ一五九八

年太閤の死後、東岸に僅かな砦をその手中に留めたのみで日本軍は引上げてしまつたという事実を知るのみである。その後、満州が勢力を得てからは、朝鮮の西部、寧ろ恐らくその大部分が中国の例に倣ひ、その命令に服しているらしい。同時に朝鮮の東岸は依然として日本の勢力下にあるということも証拠立てられて居る。しかもその僅かな交易は対馬侯の手中に握られ、朝鮮の船はすべて対馬にのみ来船を許されて居る状態であるから、クルーゼンステルンが対馬以外の港で朝鮮の船を見かけなかつたとしても別に不思議ではない。琉球に関しては、日本、琉球雙方の証明によつて、台湾南部のすべての島を日本が所有し、薩摩侯に直属することは疑いない所である。両国間の交易が行はれていたことは、那覇で見たジャンクの数や、我々がその後鹿児島に於いて二隻の日本のジャンクと一隻の琉球のジャンクが到着したのを目撃した事実によつても間違ひないことと考える。グッラフ氏はその「アムハースト卿航海記」[43]に於いて琉球を中国の属国とし、もし琉球が外国との交易の為にその港を開放することがあるとすれば、中国の例に倣うであろうと述べている。しかし今やグッラフ氏も琉球諸島は薩摩に属し、我々が今最も興味を抱いている点に関して、中国ではなく、日本の裁量に従うものであることを確認したであろう。日本人漂民の語る所によれば、一般住民のことは分らないが、船へ来訪した下役人は日本語を話し、琉球の王及び役人は日本で生れたものか、又は日本人を祖先とする者で、薩摩侯の配下であるとのことである。「三国志」によれば、

この主従関係は一六〇九年の征服に始まり[44]、爾来、琉球政府のすべての政策は日本の支配者の命令に従ひその例に倣つて行はれるに至つた。琉球が現在武装せぬに拘らず、外国人の来訪を許すとその支配者が立腹するだらうとの懸念をしながら、一方では之を逐ひ払ふ力を有たない事実は之によつて説明される。今日までこの琉球を枯死に導くやうな〔隣国との〕関係によつて苦しめられて来たのであるが、この関係も、琉球人自身が少し勇気を出すか、外国からほんの少しの援助を受けるならば断ち切ることは不可能ではない(K)。

那覇港を出て、最後に我々の目を楽しませたのは首里である。ホール船長はこの首都の住民と王宮に就いて述べている[45]。薩摩の大名に依存する琉球弱小国王はその辺に住んでいるのである。この森と家屋の散在する地方は、田舎と言つてよいのか、町と称んでよいのか、又丘の上にある平凡な建物が王宮であるのか、寺院であるのか、或は砦であるのかは明瞭でないし、〔それを識別するのは〕重要なことでもない。

北方へ進航することが不可能と知つて、我々は島の南端へ向ひ、夕方六時には那覇港は全く視界を去つた(K)。

七月十六日、昨夜琉球の南端を迂回し、本日未明東岸を去る十八乃至二十哩の位置に達し、それより微風を受けて岸沿ひに一路北東へ向つて進航した。この辺りの景色は別に取立てゝ言うものは

ない。たゞオノダケ(恩納岳)が、くつきりと聳え立つていた。

この日、談話の折にグッラフ氏が語つた所によれば、同氏は昨十五日朝早くローレイ号への必要品の積載を急がせるために上陸して那覇で愉快な経験をしたとのことである—これはその話の様子から判断すると、ポッンではないかと考えられるが、その町はポッンよりも遥かに長い—即ち、彼は幾人かの役人に附添はれて市中へ入つたときに、同行者と一緒に朝食の饗応を受けた。町の通りを歩いていると、首里の方から背に砂糖を荷うた小形の馬が下りて来るのに出会つた。附添ひの役人達は、しきりにモリソン号の行先やその性格、国籍を訊きたがり、又漂民達の離航の模様や之まで触れる機会のなかつた話題に就いて質問した。グッラフ氏は言葉が達者であつたから、躊躇を使はずに答えることが出来たが、彼等の言葉にはその好奇心に気のきいたひらめきがあつた。アニアを含めて、二、三の者は一八三一年のアムハースト卿来航に就いて、卿のことを覚えていたが、その時も、今度も滞在期間が短かつたので多くの知人を作ることは出来なかつたとのことである(W)[46]。

之に就いてKは次の如く述べている、「グッラフ氏の報告によると、我々が出発した後で、我々の性格や意図に就いて繰返えし質問したそうであるが、彼等の関心は、我々が琉球を訪問した最初のアメリカ船であるからではなく、船に日本人を乗せていたからであると思う」(K)。

我々は針路を江戸湾へ向けた。この江戸湾の北西側には現代日本帝国の首都がある。この都市は

一四五八年に建設され、一六一六年に完成したもので、面積は六十平方哩、人口は約百万ある。我我が江戸へ行くことに決定したのは、江戸が最高政府の所在地であり、従つて送還日本人の将来の安全が最高度に保証せられ、且つ他の仲介なくして直接にアメリカとの交通が決定せられるのみならず、江戸こそは旧来の慣例や地方的偏見に捉はれることなく、道理(principle)に基いて問題を解決し得る可能性の多い新地点であると考えたからである。予は日本に於ては凡ゆる猜疑と排他とが、宛も中国に於ける広東の如く、繼く長崎に向つて集中されるものと考えた。もし日本との交通が開けるとするならば、交渉のための規約は現在行われている如き偏狭なものに依らず、日本が江戸に於て初めて西欧人を受け入れた当時の自由な先例に従うべきであると考える。万一、我々の江戸へ近づくことが国法を犯すものであるというならば、それに対して我々は、外国貿易を長崎に限定するという日本の法律には我々(アメリカ人)は含まれていないから、我々が仮に長崎以外の何処の港へ入港しようとも、それによつて国法を犯すことにはならないと答えればよいのである。我我は日本人に対して、「個別に統治せよ divide et impera」という古い諺に従うことが大いに賢明であること、外国人達を互に親密にかつ不断に接触せしめて置くことによつて、かえつて彼等をして一致団結して日本に対し事を起させる結果を招くが如き規約を作るならば、彼等の外国人に対して抱く危惧の念はそれによつて寧ろ誤つた方向へ向うであろうことを知らせてやるのがよい(K)。

船は北東へ向つて進航を続けたが、風が弱くて余り速力が出なかつたので、数日間は琉球の東海岸を眺めつつ航行を続けた。十六日、丸太をくり抜いて造つた数艘の小さなカヌーが近づいて来た。岸から十哩も離れているのにこの貧弱な船の漁師達は別に距離を気にかける様子もなかつた。その中の一隻から目方一、二封度、深青色に一面に白い斑点のある楕円形の魚を貰つたが、この魚は背鰭を後へなでつけようとしても仲々そうならないが、その少し下にある小鰭に一寸手を触れるとたちまち平になるので、水夫達は之を「引金 trigger」と称した（K）。

七月十七日　北西に小さな高い島が望見されたが、この島は之までは航海者から見逃されていたらしい。もし之がウキド(釣)であるならば、その位置は我々の観測によれば海図に示されている位置よりも二十四哩も東に寄つていることになる。琉球を去るに当つて我々は、夏季この緯度に於て、太平洋から亜細亜大陸に向つて吹くと言はれる南東風を期待していたのであるが、毎日風の無い暑苦しい日が続くので、遂に我々はこの説に対する信頼を全く棄ててしまつた。然し兎に角、船が目指す港へ向つている限り、多少でも目的地へ近づいているには違いない。こんな遅々とした状態で二十五日まで進航を続けた。しかし時には鯨の「潮吹き」に出会つて愉快な思ひをし、或は長さ九呎四分一もある魚を捕えて、その死体解剖に午前の丸半日を費したこともあつた。この辺の航海に当つては船用羅針盤を屡々用いて観測を行つたが、偏差は西五度三十分乃至七度であつた。この事は

船の甲板に於ける観測に慣れて居り、船首又は船尾にある羅針盤の位置、船首の方向等が観測の結果に対して更に大なる差異を生ずることを知る者にとつては何でもないことである（K）。

七月二十五日、南西に向う強い潮流の圏内に入つた為に前日進航した航程が全部失はれたことを発見して新たに失望を感じた。翌日も同じ強さの潮流、毎時一哩二分一を感じたが、幸ひ二十七日にはこの影響は無くなつた。船中の日本人は、船がこの潮流の影響を早く逃れるため、陸地に接近して進むことを薦めた。彼等の語るところによれば、陸地に近い所では潮流が絶えず確実に北東に流れているとのことである。この指図に従うことにより我々は次の日、潮の流れに乗り、目的港に向つて二十四時間に五十三哩進航した（K）。

我々は今や目的地に近接し、気温が涼しくなつてきた。そこで直に我々の出発地及び来航の目的等を説明した中国語の書類を用意し、之に筆を加えた。之等の書類は結局その作成の目的を達しなかつたが、我々の来航の精神を明らかにし、我々の希望する通交（intercourse）の性格が恩恵的でないまでも少くとも無害なものであることを示すものである。次にその訳文を掲げる。

書類は予の署名した左の四通よりなる。

一　送還漂民の紹介

二　アメリカの説明

三　贈物の目録

四　積荷の目録

書類その一の訳文

アメリカ商人キングは謹んで陛下に対し、陛下の臣民にして難破せる七人の者の送還に関して申上げる。同人はカプ・シュイ・モンより今回モリソン号と称する三檣船により来航した。船長はインガソルといひ、外に医師一名、博物学者一名が同船している。

同人の送還し来つた漂流民の内、三名は尾張国知多郡小野浦の出身にして、名は Ewa（岩吉）三三歳、Kioko（久吉）二二歳、Oto（音吉）一九歳。之等の者は廻米船にて一八三〇年十一月江戸へ向けて尾張を出帆し、大風に遭ひ、檣を失ひ、船の位置の測定が不可能になつて、十四ケ月の間、行方も知らず大洋を漂流し、乗組員の中十一名は病死し、之等三名の者のみが生き残つて、コロンビアと呼ぶ地方へ打上げられた。この地方はアメリカに属し、一部には未開の人種が住んでいる。この地方の領師が彼等を世話して船で中国へ送り届け、ヒアン・シャン・ケン（香山県）と称する地で十九ケ月を過した。この地の善良な人が「漂流民を助けざるものは猿に等しい」という孟子の言葉を思ひ出して、之等の漂民が再び故郷へ帰る機会の来るまで世話を続けた。

他の四名の者は、九州肥村の出身者で、その名は Chiojo（庄蔵）二八歳、Yusaboroo（寿三郎）二五歳、Cumatoroo（熊太郎）二八歳、之等の者は一八三四年十二月長崎へ向けて天草島の港を出帆したが、暴風に吹き流されて、檣及び舵を失ひ、三十五日間漂流した後、タカロボと称する地方へ漂着した。此処から、この人の手でヒャ

ン・シャン・ケンへ送られ、上述の三名の漂民と会合した。

故て私は之等の人々の悲惨な状態を見て、之を故郷へ帰えし、年老いた親達に再会させるために連れ戻つてきた。私は謹んで本書を呈し、貴国が之等の人々を受入れるとともに、外国のニュースを聞き、予の船の登録を検査し、必要な品を供給し、且つ通商を許可せられんために官吏を派遣せられんことを請願する。尚、貴国にアメリカ人漂民が居るならば、予の帰国に際し、それ等の者を本国へ連れ帰るために御引渡しあらんことを請願する。

書類その二の訳文

アメリカは貴国の東方、航程二ケ月の所にあり、西部は未だ開けず未開の人種が住んでいる。我々は東部から来た者であるが、東部は開けていて広い大洋によつてイギリスやオランダと距てられている。従つてアメリカは孤立しており、日本国民に知られている如何なる国とも境を接していない。アメリカは国土は広大であるが人口はあまり多くない。二百年前にはまだ野蕃人のみが住んでいたが、イギリス、オランダ、その他の国民が渡来して殖民地を建設した。その子孫が次第に増加して、今から六十年前にワシントンと称ぶ最初の大統領を選んだ。この高い位は今第八代の大統領によつて占められている。この六十二年間にアメリカは二回侵略をうけたが、我が方から他国を侵略したことはなく、外国の領土を所有したこともない。アメリカの船は何処の国の船よりも速力が速く、凡ゆる国の凡ゆる通路に通じている。もし日本との交通が許されるならば、我々は常に最新の報導を提供する用意がある。

アメリカの法律は公正であり、刑罰はただ罪の確定したもののみに適用される。国民はすべて自己の良心に従つて神を崇拝し、如何なる宗教に対しても充分な寛容をもつて望む。我々自身は平和の神を崇ひ、長上を尊敬し、互に相和して暮している。我が国民は未だ貴国を訪問したことはないが、その昔、諸外国の商人がすべて貴国の港へ来ることを許可されたことは承知している。後に彼等は法律を犯した為に交通を制限せられ、或は放逐せられたが、我々アメリカ人としては今回の訪問が最初であり、未だ如何なる過失をも犯していないので、嘗て諸外国に許した如く、我々に友誼的交通を許可せられんことを請願する。

贈り物の目録は、ワシントンの肖像画、望遠鏡、手袋、百科辞典、アメリカ条約集、アメリカ史その他である。

国によつて言語を異にするが、オランダ語やポルトガル語よりも遙に広く行はれる我々の言語を、貴国では未だ御存知ないかも知れない。もし御存知なければ、御望みにより、我々一行のうち一名が一ケ年貴国に残つて御教授申上げる用意のあることを申添える。

本船に積載せる商品の目録を同封して置いたが、之はただ将来貴国の商人と自由に交易し得ることを願い、且つ将来貴国へ積送すべき商品が、すべての点で、日本の趣味に合うようにするためである。

(日本人の思想、偏見その他を熟知する人々は、之等の書状に於いて、或点には触れ、或点は言及を避けた理由を了解せられるであろう)

以上の説明に対し、更にパーカー博士の持参した薬品に就いて「それらの薬品の驚くべき効力は之を用いる人の独特の技術と共に、ただ之を実際に経験することによつてのみ知ることが出来る」と附言しておいた(K)。

70

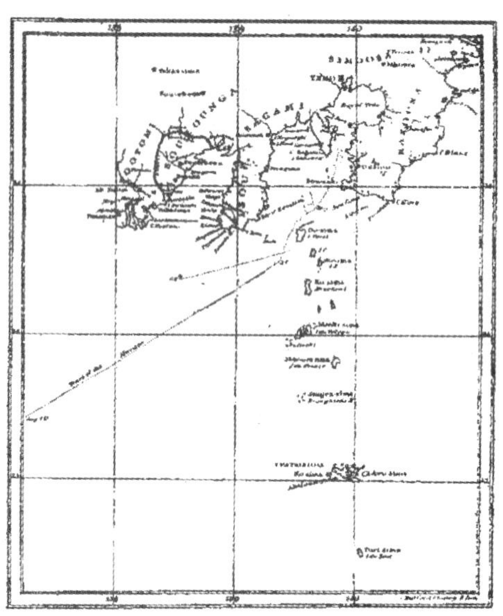

キングの航海記に添付せられたる江戸湾附近の海図

つた。この一連の島々は、或るものは僅かながら人の住む大きな島であり、また或るものは無人の小島で、その中間には多数の離れ岩が存在している。この一連の島々の南部には一般に最もよく知られている島の一つである八丈島がある。この島は謂はゞ日本のボタニ湾であり、将軍が好ましからざる貴族や厄介な有力者を島流しにした処で、之等の人々は各種の取引や技芸に従事せしめられ、主として、絹織物を朝廷へ供給したといはれる。八丈島と本土の中間にある島はフリース島(大島)とヂュ・ヴォルカン島(三宅島)とであり、共に火山があつて、その爆発は人畜財産に多大の危害を与えて来た。昔大島に起つた噴火のため住民は伊豆半島へのがれ、それ以来大島には定まつた住民が居ない。之等の島々の周辺の海は魚が豊富で小舟で漁業が盛んに行はれている。船の位置からは、低い島は見えないが、大島その他の見える島々は樹の茂つた箇所もあり、耕作も行われているらしい(W)。間もなく南西から北東へかけてブロークン島(式根島と神津島)とエイシャ(新島)が見え、午前十時本土の南端伊豆岬へ十二乃至十四哩以内に接近した(P)。江戸湾からジャンクの大船団が出てきたが、その大部分は西へ向つて行つた。その白い帆は無恰好な構造であつたが、中国の沿海を航行する船のマットに較べて美しく思われた。この日の中に約六十隻のジャンクが出て行つたが、いづれも、大きさは異なり、琉球のジャンクに酷似していた。それ等の船の中には我々に極めて接近して我々の針路を横切つたものもあつたが、乗組員は我々に対しては別に危惧

72

の念も示さなかつたし、訪ねて来ようとするものもなかつた(K)。

目の前にある日本の海岸は宛然堂々たる山々の連続する画廊である。険阻な凸凹した海岸にはじまつて次第に高まり行く峯を重ねて最後に富士山の頂が一万四千呎の高さに聳えている。この山は日本の物語でも有名であり、ケンペルも言う如く、「詩人も之を言ひ表はす言葉を見出せず、画家の技量と色彩も之を充分には表現出来ない」(W)。

午過ぎ我々は巨大な伊豆半島へ二、三哩以内に接近した。この半島の先端には半島と同名の伊豆岬が東側にあり、アガチエ岬が西側にある。半島は崇高な山々の集塊で、中央には日本に於ける最高峯の一である富士山が一万二千乃至一万五千呎の高さに聳え、傾斜せる両側と平らな頂上とで、大きな屋根の形をしている(K)。午後四時半富士山は北西にあり、雲が過ぎ去つた為、斜面に雪が現れた。この前から我々は雪が近くにあることを感じていたが、水銀柱は七十七度半を示していたにも拘らず、寒くて外套を着たい程であつた。四十八時間以内に八十四度から急に下つたのであるから、その差は一層はつきりと感ぜられた。富士山は高さ一万乃至一万二千呎の高さであり、この真夏に雪があるから、雪を一年中冠つていると推察される[4](P)。

伊豆の南端は、その長方形の半島型がグアチマラのユカタンによく似ていて、険阻な岬をなし、浜辺は灰の花崗岩の円錐形をなした峯即ち尖塔(aiguilles)をなしている。海岸にある無数の小さ

73

な入江は漁船が嵐の時避難する安全な場所を提供し、下田湾は広い便利な港として我々に指し示された（W）。

船が陸へ近づくと目に入るジャンクや小舟の数が増してきて、或る時は四、五十艘にも及び大部分は西へ向つて行つた。斯様な事には相当の権威者であり、江戸へ二十回も往つたことがあるという岩吉の説明によれば、之等の船は逆風のために湾内に閉ぢ込められて出られなかつたので、よくあることだという（W）。

北東風に阻げられながらもこれまでと同様潮の助けによつて我々は徐々に湾内へ進航した。夜湾を溯航していると、幾つかの高台に火が燃えているのを見たが、之は恐らく我々の接近を知つて首都へ知らせる手段なのであろう。南岸に沿つて突出した高台には毎夜船を導くために政府の手によつて灯がともされたことは聞いていたが、この場合の火は日本人達の之までに見たものとは異つて居り、その位置も違つていた（W）。

七名の漂民は再び祖国の海岸を見て非常に悦び、船首の斜檣に腰かけて熱心に祖国を見詰めながら、見慣れた陸の出鼻や島や山を見る毎に歓喜の声を上げ、間もなく、この世で最も親しい、しかも永い間別れていた人達に会えると考えて心も浮々していた。之が糠喜びに終り、僅か数日で牢獄へつながれる浮目を見るようなことのないようにというのが、口には出さなくとも、彼等の願いであり、兎に角親切に受入れらることを期待していた（P）。

七月三十日、朝日の登る頃、船はミサキ即ち相模の国の南端に位し、江戸湾の入口の西側に在るサガミ岬の南方程遠からぬ地点に到達した[50]（W）。

江戸湾はその名の示す如く大きな河口であり、入口は幅三十乃至四十哩あつて、北へ向つてミサキまでほとんど同じ幅で続いている。ミサキは小さな半島の南端で相模の国の一部をなし、河口に突出している。その西側には伊豆の海岸に向つて相模湾が横わつており、その入口の幅は約二十哩である。ミサキとスサキ（洲崎）は共に一際目立つた岬角で、ほぼ北東と南西に相対し、その距離は十二乃至十五哩、江戸湾の入口をなしている。この江戸湾の北端、洲ノ崎より四十哩の所に首都がある。前日まで晴天だつたのが今朝は霧雨が降り、加うるに向い風が吹いて一層不愉快さが加わり、隣接する海岸は全くかすんで見えなかつた。晴雨計が普通の高さであるのに、かかる不愉快な変化を生じたのは附近の高い山々が水蒸気を圧縮過充した甕の如く周囲に絶えず驟雨を降らせるからであろう。岸は険阻ではあるが余り高くはない。両岸は、我々がジグザグコースをとつて近づいて行くと、そのいずれの海岸も緑に覆れた山や谷の変化が美しかつた。山の頂には大きさや種類の異つた樹々が茂り、山腹には低い灌木が茂つて共に青々として、峨々たる伊豆の山とは全く異つた心持よい眺めであつた（W）。我々は山に囲まれた景色を見て中国の虎門の上流の珠江を憶い出し

た（P）。我々は右方にあつて岩の集まつたスサキの沖合に達した。此処は緑で覆れた所が殆どなく、余り高くもない。この地点から北にかけてオージオー（北条）に至る引込んだ箇所は一層低く平らであるが、サガミ岬の対岸の突出せる部分は再び険しくなり変化に豊んでいる。之に対してミサキから浦賀へ向つて北に延びる海岸には岩や丘が甚だ多く、色の濃い松が高地を被い、丘や谷を越えて長い列をなして続いている。之等の松で飾られた部分の間には深緑の広い畑があり、その注意深い耕作者達の住む小屋からは多くの煙が立ち上つていた（K）。

湾内へ進んで行くと沢山の覆いのない漁舟がおり、その乗組員達はほとんど我々に注意を向けず、又彼等の素頭に容赦なく降るひどい驟雨も同様に気に掛けていなかつた。この時一人が一、二回江戸の方角を指さすのを見たが、之は「あそこへ行つて交渉をまとめよ。事が決つたら我々は喜んで面会に行く」という意味であろうと解釈した[51]（K）。

十二時頃、初めて遠方に砲声が聞えたが、しばらくは霰と船の作業の音とではつきりとそれと分らなかつた。砲声はかなり間を置いて聞えたが、余りに意外な出来なので、之に対する各人の意見も区々で、日本人漂民達も之までの経験とは反対の出来事に満足な説明が与えられず、船に旗を掲げてはどうかと我々に提案した。この砲声は我々の進航を朝廷へ知らせるためのものだと考えた者もあるし、浦賀附近の役人は上司の命令なくして外国船を碇泊地へ通過せしめる自由を有しないと

考えたからであると推量した者もあり、船に対する礼砲であると考えた者もあつた。しかし空が晴れるや否やすべての疑は除かれ、我々は船の前方半哩の所に砲弾が落下するのを見た（W）。

我々は今やサガミ岬を通過して幅五乃至十哩の海峡に差かかつていた。この海峡は北方へ約十八哩続き、その先に江戸の内湾が拡つている。この内湾は周囲約六十哩あり、その大部分は浅いと言われている。両岸が高く聳え人の多く住んでいる美しい海峡を進んで行くと、東岸からの大砲に応えて反対側の浦賀の高地からも大砲が発射された。我々は湾内へ行く船が検閲を受け更に内湾へ進むために通航許可証を下附される最初の地点を通過することによつて、船内の日本人に累を及ぼすことを欲しなかつたので、浦賀へ碇泊する計画であつた。大型船はこの最初の地点で許可を受けると西岸に沿つて六乃至八哩進み、そこで再び碇泊するけれども、小型の船はそのまま十乃至十二哩進んで江戸へ往く。我々が予定の碇泊地から二哩程の地点へ来た時、西岸からの射撃は浦賀の入江を見下す丘の先端にある低い白亜の建物、即ち堡塁から行われていることがわかつた。砲弾は我々との中間に落下したが、之は我々を停止せしめんとするためのものであると見做して風下に転じて退避し、小湾即ち左側の海岸の湾曲部にある岩から一哩離れた水深十尋の地点に錨を投じた[52]。かかる譲歩をしたのは、若しそのまま進めば、我々が何等かの敵意を有し、無理に首都へ向つて進航を強行するものと誤解される惧れがあつたからである（K）。錨を下すと間もなく砲声は止んだ（W）。

我々が寄港しようとした浦賀の港は湾の西側にあり砲台の上手にあって江戸へ往くすべての船舶の寄港地である。此処に住む役人は内湾へ往く船舶の積荷目録と人員を調べて正確に符合するか否かを確め、船に女子が乗っていないことを確めた上、品川港へ往く許下証を与えるのがその役目である。もし女子のいることが判明した場合は乗組員全部が斬首刑に処せられるとのことであり、もし積荷目録の人員と乗組員とが一致しない場合は抑留せられて、面倒が起るとのことである。港の海岸には人家が建ち並び附近は人口稠密し、よく耕作されている。浦賀より十六里（原註、約三十三哩）上手に品川があり、検査の済んだ船はすべて其処に行き積荷の揚げ卸しをする。浦賀から先は広い海が続き、幅二十五哩に達する所もあって、絶えずジャンクや漁船が航行している。音吉の話では、一日の中に品川から七十乃至八十艘の船が発着するのを見たことがあり、碇泊する船の数は平素一千を下らないとのことである（W）。

我々が既に帆を巻き収めてしまった時、一艘の小舟が近づいて来たので本船へ来て貰った。応待にはグッラフ氏に当って貰い、日本人漂民達は見えないように下へ残して置いた。これはもし漂民達を日本人に会せれば、まづ本船へ最初に来る下役人達に質問された場合にその訊ねる事柄にすべて答えなければならないことになる。もしそれによって我々の来航に対する彼等の好奇心が満足されるならば、我々の書類は拒否されるのみならず、口頭による情報に基いて首都へ報告が行われる

78

ことになると予想したからに外ならない。我々の目的は、直接、上書によって皇帝の決裁を動かそうとするにあった（K）。

船内に日本人の居ることを知った場合彼等に如何なる影響を与えるか。また、漂民が当局の手に引取られるに至った場合、その安全な引取りに対し、今から前以て漂民のことを知られることがどの程度の影響を及ぼすかを知り得なかったので、少くとも最初の訪問者には会せない方がよいと考えた。役人が来たとき漂民自身に身の上を語らせ、引取られる前に予め充分の安全保障を日本政府から得て置かなければならない。同時に、もし外国船が水と食糧とを求めて日本帝国の港へ来航した場合、これに対して日本政府は果して如何なる処置をとるであろうか、それを知りたいと考えたのである（W）。

碇泊してしばらくすると、港のあちらこちらから漁舟が集まってきた。最初は仲々近寄らなかったが、我々が舷門へ招くと次第に近づいて来た。一艘の小舟が横づけになって、六十才ばかりの老人が腰をかがめて上って来た（P）。彼は手先が甲板へ届く程低身して挨拶し、周囲を見廻しながら次第に進んで来たが、忽ち仲間の者に呼び返えされた。しかし仲間の者達は彼から乗船しても何等差支えないという報告を聞くと、がやがやと上って来て甲板は忽ち日本人で一杯になってしまった。彼等は乗組の外国人に対しては別に関心を持たず、お互い同志で喋舌りあっていた。豚と鶩鳥

79

をじろじろ見ていたが、音吉の話では此の辺の日本人は豚や鶩鳥に就いては名を知っていてもそれを余り用いないとのことである（W）。彼等は船の大きさを測り、檣を見上げてぽかんとしていた。キング夫妻のいるラウンドハウスへ案内されたが、外国婦人を見ても大して好奇心を示さなかった（P）。飾のついたイギリス商品の見本、更紗木綿の残品、光ったアメリカの五仙貨幣を、甘い葡萄酒やビスケットと共に与えたが、どれも大歓迎で、貧民階級の幾人かはサキ（酒）の香を特に賞讃したものもあった（K）。彼等は何を貰ってもいちいち額に押載いて低頭した。酒を希望したものは少かったがパンは非常に欲しがり、一人の父親はその一片を受取ると、小舟へ行って十二才の娘を連れてまた貰いに来た。いづれもアテナイ人の如く珍しい物を熱心に欲しがったが、彼等自身の持物、例えば煙管や扇の如きものは仲々手離そうとしなかった。ウィリアムズ君は彼らが腰につけていて彼等の与えようとする唯一の持物たる矢立を得た。また、甚いリュウマチにかかった男と眼瞼の慢性粘液漏の者と皮膚病の者達を診療した。臼歯を抜いてくれというのも一人あった（P）。訪問者達はいづれも友好的で、最初は我々の所へ盛んに質問に来たが、言葉が通じないことが判るとグッラフ氏の所へ疑問を持込んだ。彼等は貰う物は何でも受取ったが、小魚の外は何一つ売る物を持参せず、僅かな衣類すら手離そうとしなかった（W）。

恐らく浦賀の役人は此の場に来ず、大切な我が身を我々の手中に委ねる前に、先づ之等非公式の

80

訪問者の報告を待っていたのではなかろうか。我々は之等の訪問者達が戻って、役人達に対して我々の好意あることゝ、武装を持たないことゝを報告するものと信じ、辛抱強く役人又はせめて通訳の来てくれるのを待っていた。来訪者の中で比較的よい服装をした人々に、我々が友好的なアメリカ人であること、及び我々と交渉するために役人を一人派遣して貰いたい旨を記したカードを一枚づゝ渡し、同時に船に旗を掲揚した。

配布したカードは中国語で書かれたが、うち数枚はグッラフ氏が日本語で認め、我々の国の名及び上奏書を皇帝に進達して貰いたい由を記した。之は我々の使命を誰よりも先に皇帝に知って貰ひたかったからである(53)（P）。小舟の群は——その中の数隻には婦人の顔も見られたが——夜に到るまで引続き船を取り巻いていたが、終に一人の役人も来なかった。但し想像した通り、一隻の他より比較的大型の船が本船の周囲を漕ぎ廻り、その中の一人が我々を偵察していたが、本船へは来なかった（K）。恐らく彼等は浦賀から来たスパイであろう（P）。

やがて薩の役人の廻し者と思われる一人の役人らしい男が、鹿爪らしい様子で甲板へ上って来た。彼は人を馬鹿にした態度で周辺を見廻していたが、多少驚いた様子である。最初は馬鹿にした態度を示した彼も、飲食物をとってからは少し友好的になり、且つ上機嫌になった。この男の乗つ

81

できた舟は他の舟より大きく、土地の者が一杯に乗つていたが、誰も船へ上つて来ず、件の役人風の男が船や乗組員を見廻し、役人の来訪を求める書付を受取つて漸く舟へ戻ると、湾の上手のもと来た方角へ戻つていつた。我々は此の小舟が少々気になつたので望遠鏡で跡を追うと、その小舟の着いた浜辺には多数の人々が集つていてこちらを見て居り、文字を書いた四、五枚の赤い四角な板が地に立てゝあつた。其の辺には幾艘もの小舟が見え、我々を訪ねて来た舟のうちの幾艘かは其の方へ戻つて行つた。群集は恐らく、その先の蔭になつて見えない地方から、珍しい船を見物する為に集つて来たのであろう（W）。

日本人漂民に、役人はどこで分るのか、彼等は有名な二本の刀の外に何か印をつけているのかと訊ねたところ「船へ来てぶるぶる震えている者があれば、それが役人だ」という答であつた（K）。

午後はひどい雨が降り続いた。我々としても船を離れて上陸するわけにいかなかつたし、役人達にとつても来訪を翌朝に延ばすのに都合のよい雨であつた。それに何処の国でも偉い人は目下の者を待たせることを好むものである。しかし日本の役人は昔から好奇心の強いことで有名であるから、好奇心を満足させるだけのためでも必ず来ることは間違ないと考えた。彼等の来た場合に、その訊問に対して一々書類を指し示して答え、書類を首都へ伝達してくれるよう依頼することにした。そうなれば我々の説明は漂民の受取りと将来交渉を開く特権とに関して日本政府の決定に影響

82

を与へることが出来て、我々の目的は達成されるわけである。之まで外国船が来航すると必ずその周囲に見張りの舟が集まつて来たので、今度もそのようにして陸との連絡を絶たれるのではないかと察したので、そうならない前に、夜が明けると同時に上陸して、少くとも一度は巡視してみようと準備を整えた（K）。午後七時には最後の小舟が船を退去し、この日の訪問者は全部で二百人以上に達した（W）。

七月三十一日、時折驟雨はあつたが、夜の間に天候は多少回復した。午前四時、二、三艘の小舟が上手から海岸に沿つて下つて来るのが見え、やがて漁民の小屋の附近で停ると、乗つて来た者は上陸して浜辺の近くの円い丘に集結した。しかし我々はこの行動に就いて別に気にもしていなかつた（W）。夜明直前にひどい驟雨があり、半時間程天候の模様をみていると、夜の間に我々に気の付かぬようにこつそりと船に一番近い箇所に据え付けられた二門乃至四門の大砲から突然射撃を受けた（K）。一弾が唸りを生じて船の上を過ぎ、続いて三発が、小舟から上陸した一行の集結している丘の上の四門の大砲から発射された。不意の出来事だつたので我々はその意図が分らず、当惑してまず旗を揚げ、やがて白旗を揚げて陸からの来訪を求め、その理由を説明して貰うことにした。しかし我々の合図は一顧も与えられずして砲撃が続いたので錨を上げ、帆を張ることにした。退去する意図を示すために後斜桁帆（スパンカー）を上げたが砲撃は益々劇しくなり、遂に一弾は舷檣に命中し甲

83

板をすり抜けた。然し別にそれ以上の損傷はなかつた（W）。船は左舷が砲台の方を向き、舵が砲火に曝された（K）。もし砲撃の目的が単に侵入者を逐い払うだけのためならば、退去する希望と意図を示せばそれで充分な筈である。しかし事実はそうではなかつた。船が錨を揚げ、微かな風の動きによつて除々に砲撃圏外に立退くまで丸半時間砲撃が続き、砲弾の落下地点が遠のいて本船の通つた航跡に次々に落下するようになり、既に危険を脱したと我々が明瞭に覚るまで続いたのである。船に命中した一弾は先づ前部の錨と主鎖との間の舷窓を突き抜け、甲板の板三枚を破り、はね上つてロングボートの舷側板に当り再びバウンドして海中に落下した（K）。舷門のすぐ後の綱では幾人かの者が作業をして居り、二人の日本人漂客は弾の命中した箇所から僅に数呎の所に立つて居たのである[32]（P）。

弾の音に慣れず、しかも我々自身が標的になつているので、我々の神経に対する砲撃の影響はとても筆紙に尽し難く、決して忘れることの出来ない一瞬であつた（P）。綱が六十尋も出て居り、錨を巻き上げ、帆を上げる作業に従事出来る人手は僅かに十六人しかないので、一時間も砲撃に曝されている間に一人も負傷者を出さなかつたのは神の庇護によるものである。大砲の操縦は下手で、弾丸は或いは頭上を超え、或は船と陸の中間に落下したが、砲弾が通過する時非常に大きな唸りを立てたのは弾の製造が粗雑な為であろう（W）。しかし、日本人は、弾丸を込めるのにブリーチピ

84

ンを抜き出すと言つたクルーゼンステルンの時代から思うと戦技が幾分進歩したというのが我々の意見であつた。即ち弾丸の装塡にはそのような遅滞がなく迅速に射撃が行われたので、もし彼等がヨーロッパの火薬を持つていたならば、我々に非常な損害を与えたことであろう（P）。退去に際して、船の近くの断崖から海に向つて一条の砕け波のあることが引潮のため判明したが、幸い風向がよかつた為にその上手を通過し、間もなく弾丸と岩の危険はなくなつた。この時早朝見た砲艦が岸を離れて我々を追つて来たが、どれも各一隻に三、四十人の者が乗り組んでおり、旗を掲げていた。砲が賞讃すべき動作で我々を狙い、旋回発射された。かなりの距離を退避して停船し、彼等の近づくのを待つたが、やがて引返えして行つた（W）。港外は波が高く強い風が吹いていた。港を出てくる時、中国語で、役人の来訪を求め、水を欲する旨を認めた一枚のカンバスを海中に投下した（P）。一艘の小舟が之を拾い上げたが、此方へは来ずにそのまま陸の方へ入つて行つてしまつた[33]（W）。

以上述べた所により日本の役人が我々に対し出来得る限りの危害を加えようとしたことは明らかである。船とその乗員が重大な危害を免れ得たのは、彼等に望遠鏡が無かつたこと、及び大砲を操縦する訓練が下手であつたからに外ならない。この欺瞞的な攻撃に対して我々の間に憤怒の情が起つたのは当然である。もし甲板に大砲を備えていたならば、我慢出来なかつたかも知れないし、我

85

擾したならば、定めし船中に不満を生じたことであろう（K）。

ひとたび敵の手の届かぬ所へ来てしまうと、次にはこちらからは何もしないのに斯の如き処置を受けたことに対して説明を要求しようという気持が当然起つてきた。しかし之は容易なことではなく、我方から人を指向けることは適当でないと考えた。砲台のほかに数隻の警備船が浦賀の上陸地点の沖合に配備されていた。その砲弾は我々の所まで届かなかつたが、更に角砲撃に参加して居り、我々に対して敵対心を有していることは明らかであるから、もしボートで人を指向ければ、再び船へ戻るまでに戦を交えなければならず、捕虜になる惧れがあつたのである（K）。

我々を砲撃の射程外に脱れさせてくれた微風が再び吹きはじめたので、之以上江戸湾に留まるべきか否かを決定しなければならなくなつた。斯様に簡単に逐い払われてしまうのは決して愉快なことではないし、この儘退去する理由もなかつたが、一方、たつた今我々に砲撃を加えたばかりの者達が之から先我々の船へ来て、みすみす我々の手中に陥いるとも考えられないし、その上今交渉に応ずる準備も全く出来ていない。どちら側の海岸に碇泊しても数時間で砲台に制圧されてしまうし、今は既に北方の浅瀬を調査する機会もなく、天候は定まらず、南からは大きな波のうねりが押寄せて来ていたので、かかる状況では寧ろ何処か他の場所で新たに交渉をし直す方がよいと考え、多少心残りではあつたが、前日あれ程の楽しい期待をもつて入港した湾を遂に立去つた。船中の日

本人達の希望と祈りも我々の決意と同じで、彼等は砲撃に遭つて驚き且つ恐れ、斯の如き野蛮な乱暴を敢てする役人達の所へは仮令どんなことがあつても上陸しないと断言した。可哀そうに、彼等の恐怖は失望に劣らず大きかつた。長い間他所へ行つているとよくあるように、彼等は時の経過に従つて必ず起る荒廃のことを考えず、専制政府の省共が彼等を如何に迎えるであろうかを予見せずに、前日まで温い希望に浸つていたのである。彼等のうち二人の妻帯者岩吉と庄蔵は妻との再会を待ち侘び、他の者も皆年老いた親達のもとへ戻る仕合せを期待していたのである。さて今後我々の航海の第一の目的を確実に達成するには一体どうしたらよいのか。どうすれば今後尚彼等を安全に上陸させることが出来るのか。浦賀に於ては彼等の素性は知れなかつたし、人に会うこともなかつた。昔彼等を知つていた僅かの人達の外は今や彼等のことを夢みる者は一人も居ないし、それら少数の知人すらも今ではもう彼等が大洋の底に埋もれてしまつたと考えているに相違ない。そこで我々は彼等を湾の外で日本のジャンクの一隻に移乗させるか、人の居ない海岸にそつと上陸させるか、或は更に西に往いて再び交渉を試みるかに就いて相談してみた。第一の提案に対して漂民は「日本に於いても琉球に於けると同様、ジャンクの乗組員はすべて登録されて居り、船中で死んだ場合でも、船が帰港した際、その死体をその他の役人に示し、船出した時の人数に変化を来たしたことを、途中で死んだと称して法律の規定を避けることのないようにしてあるから駄目だ」と答えた。

日本人が国外へ行くことを禁ずる法律は、外国人の渡来を禁ずる法律と同様に厳しく行われたのである。第二の提案の人目につかないように上陸することに就いては、彼等が故郷へ戻れば勿論知れるし、仔細を尋ねられ、結局役人の不興に身を曝して、ひどい刑罰を受けるに相違ないからと言つて反対した。結局、江戸の西の砦のない港へ行つて再び交渉してみる方が望ましいとのことで、彼等は幾つかの城のない地点を挙げた。彼等の指図に従ひ、何処にせよ、彼等が同意する地点以外には上陸させないと保証して、我々はもと来た道を引返し海へ出た（K）。

かくて我々は漸くこの日の出来事を反省し、かくの如き敵対行為を受けた理由を検討する余裕を得たのであるが、一体何故に我々は砲撃を受けたのであろうか。それは最高政府の許可に基いて行われたものなのか、それとも浦賀の出先官憲が国内一般に出された命令に従ひ自己の責任に於て行つたものであるのか。この疑問に対しては結局明確な結論には達し得なかつたが、我々の船は三十日の夜明には彼等によつて望見され、その報告は直に北に向つて駅から駅へ伝えられ首都にまで達していた筈である。正午には最初の砲声が聞かれ、午後三時には船は国旗を掲げて碇泊地へ近づいたのである。午後四時に土地の人々が乗船し来り、我々の国籍、上役人と交渉したいという希望、船には砲を備えていないこと、婦人が居ること等が一時間後には陸上の役人に判つていた筈である。浦賀から江戸までは海路二十哩、陸路二十五哩であつて、翌朝午前五時には大砲を移動して来

て砲撃を開始したのであるが、それまでに委細の報告が宮廷に伝達され、命令がもたらされていたに相違ない。もしそうであるとすれば、砲撃は、我々が非武装の好意的アメリカ人であることを承知の上で、しかも政府の許可を得てなされたことになる。もし報告されなかつたものとすれば——之はありそうもないことであるが——、或はまた我々がその朝到着した時に直に砲撃されたのであつたならば、浦賀の役人はただ一般的指示に基いて砲撃を行つたのであつて、それは殊更にアメリカの国旗に対してなされたものではない。それとも、之までに日本の東海岸に於てアメリカの捕鯨船が掠奪を行い、その為に、宛もゴロウニンがチ・ストフの乱暴の贖いをさせられたように[96]、我々の頭上に彼等の犯罪の報いがやつて来たのであろうか（K）。

ここで我々は一八一七年ゴルドン船長の試みた例に倣ひ[97]、湾の入口にある多数の都市のいづれかひとつに寄港して、来訪者があり次第我々の書類を渡して陸の役人に届けて貰い、返事を待つているからと伝えて江戸へ送つて貰うことにしようかと考えた。しかし我々が江戸湾の閉された海を突破しようとして撃退されたニュースは既に燎原の火の如く拡まつているであろうから、下役人はかかる役目は引受けないであろう。また中国に於ては責任のなすり合いが多くの有害な結果を生じているが、日本政府の場合も同様で、我々が書類を陸へ届けて貰つた場合、役人は自己の責任を免れるために先ず書類を受取り之を進達する前に、江戸からの許可を求めるであろう。我々は水深と風

波に曝されているために船の今まで居た位置を保つことが出来なかつた。即ちその場所は防波堤のない碇泊所と同様であり、水深は十五乃至三十尋で底には石が多く、潮は水門のように劇しく流れていた。それに相手は極めて封建的な日本政府であり、地位の低い諸侯は何事をなすにもその主君の命に服従し、同輩に対しては猜疑心が強く、自分の行為が江戸へ報告されて不利益を蒙ることのない様に用心して居る。従つてこれ以上交渉することは止めて首都を立去ろうという意見が強く、我々もすべてそう感じたので、先に岩吉外二名の者が船出して離船した志摩の国鳥羽へ向うことに決定した（W）。

日本人漂民達は親切にしてくれたキング氏やグッラフ氏が斯の如き非道な取扱いを受けたことに対して、失望に劣らぬ憤慨を感じ、出来れば皇帝に対して出先役人の卑劣な行為を告げて死刑に処して貰いたいと望んだ。但し上陸すれば必ず死ぬのだからと言つて敢えて上陸しようとはしなかつた。この時の光景は如何に頑な心をも動かしたであろう。前日故郷の山河を見た時の喜びと両親や知己に会える悦び、希望、不安の入り交つた感情は今や外国に流浪するという憂鬱な予想と変つてしまい、彼等は落胆して頭を垂れ、口も利かなかつた。岩吉は最初のショックの後で、もしもう一度両親に会うことが出来、自分や仲間の運命を知つて貰うことが出来さえすれば、日本の習わしに従つて腹を切つて死んでもよいとさえ言つた（P）。

90

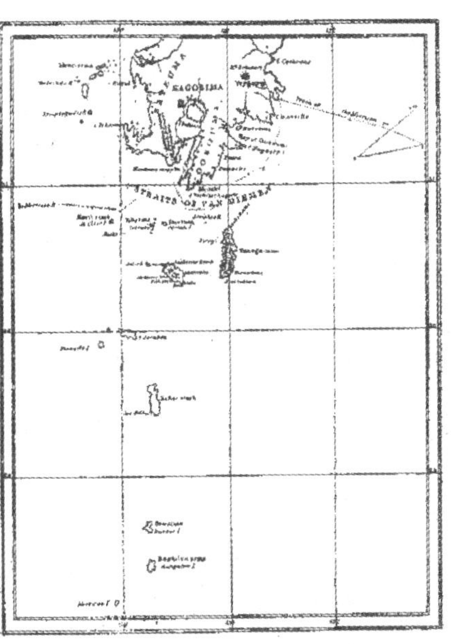

キングの航海記に添付せられたる鹿児島湾附近の海図

江戸の港（浦賀港）を出帆した時は強い北東風が吹いていたが、そのお蔭で毎時二、三ノットの逆流——この潮流は我々が同湾へ入る際は我々を助けてくれたのだが、今度は我々の邪魔になつた——を克服して毎時五哩の速度で進航することが出来た。三十一日夕刻、イヅ岬（石廊崎）を通過し、この岬と日本の南端の中間にある港のひとつに向つて進航した。但し、ヨシド（吉田即ち今の豊橋）、トバ（鳥羽）、シグ（新宮）等、城のある都市は避けることにした。この季節には日本の南海岸は霧群に覆われるものらしいが、我々はこの霧群を後にし、晴れた温い地方へ入つてきた。然し鹿児島に至るまで終始逆流に阻まれ続け、その為に毎時一哩半乃至三哩四分一づつ船脚が遅れた。この強い潮流の原因、力、方向に関しては巻尾の気象観測の中で更めて言及する（K）。

八月一日、鳥羽を過ぎ、紀伊の国の潮岬へ向つたが、再び風に遮られて薩摩の国の鹿児島へ向うことに決した。此処はポルトガル人が初めて上陸した地であり、且つかのザヴィエルが布教活動を始めた所である（W）。

この時風が海岸の方から吹いて逆風になつたので、之に逆つて時間を費すよりは、もつと西方の地点で第二の交渉を試みる方がよいということになつた。漂民達が相談の結果、次の交渉地としては、九州南部の薩摩の首都であり諸大名の中で最も強力にして他に依存することの少い大名の居る鹿児島が最もよいということに意見が一致した[53]（K）。

91

K原註—クルーゼンステルンの日記はこの港と居城をカグル岬とチェメ岬の中間の湾内で、九州の南西にある半島の西側に置いているが、之は誤りである。しかし我々の用いている彼の海図では鹿児島は首都であるという印を付して、南の湾内の正しい位置に記入してある所から見ると、クルーゼンステルン自身も、その「日記」を出版後間もなく前述の位置の誤りであることが分つたのであろう（K）。

さきに九州から台湾に至る南の島々全体にその権威の及んでいることは疑いないと言つたのは此の君主（プリンス）のことである。此の地方の政府ならびに住民が海国的色彩を有するのは、之等の諸島を領有し之と通商することによるものと想像される。此処へは支那のジャンクが来航するとのことであるが、それは長崎を出帆した後、残りの積荷を密貿易するためで、数年来オランダの商品を当地へ輸入する取極めが出来たという事実もあるから、我々が鹿児島を選んだ理由である。鹿児島へ到着した際に提出するため我々は薩摩の藩主に宛てて前に述べた上書と共に一通の書面を用意した。前の時と同様の理由で次にその訳文を掲げる（K）。

薩摩藩主に宛てた書面の訳文

下名の者は添付せる書面に述べられた目的を以て、他の者の作成せる海図により、七月三十日江戸港へ入港した。

諸船の碇泊地たる浦賀港に近接するや本船は砲撃を受けたので、無理に通過することを欲せず、そのまま投錨

92

したところ、一般住民が来船したので之に書面を渡して役人の来訪を求めた。然し我々の正しい請願は拒否され、翌朝下名著自身上陸して敬意を表そうとしたとき、本船は再び砲撃せられた。

斯の如く好意に報ゆるに敵意を以てせられたので本船は出帆して当鹿児島を訪問した。願くは書類を御取調べの上、陛下に御進達下されたい。武装せざる友好的なる本船を、前に御取調べもなく砲撃されたのは、恐らく陛下の御許しによるものではないと推察せられるので右再度御依頼申上ぐる次第である。前の如き御取扱いはただ外国との戦に日本を捲き込む結果になるものと愚考する。

薩摩の御領主は皇帝に対して大なる勢力を有せられることを承知して居るので、御領主の御仲介により、祖国へ帰還せる漂流民達が安全に上陸できるのは確実だと存ずる次第である。

更に若し御同意下さるならば、アメリカの商人はオランダ人が長崎へ来航する如く貴国の港へ来航すべく、閣前の御領主に対し永年許されたる特権は必ず閣下にも与えられるものと確信する。

アメリカの商人等は、尊敬に値いし、平和を愛するものにして、その船は速力が速く、最も豊富にして変化に富める各種の積荷を供給し得るが故に、彼等と通商することにより必ずや御領主の栄光は増し、臣民の福祉は増進せられるであろう。

浦賀に於いて砲撃せられた次第を述べることは我々の好まぬ所であるが、後日、この事が判明して、船中の日本人が不測の禍を蒙ることのないように、如何なる場合にも真実を語ることが最上策なりと信ずる次第である(K)。

93

八月四日、七月三十一日江戸湾を出発以来三日間続いた風のため我々は薩摩への距離の四分の三を進んだ(P)。しかし四日には風が止み、潮の流れが強くて六十哩走つて僅に二十哩進んだに過ぎなかつた。六日は情況が更に悪化し前日進んだ以上の距離を失い、翌日もこの距離を取り戻すことが出来なかつた。一日七十哩に達したこの速い潮流は全く我々の予期しなかつたもので、毎日怠らず観測をつづけなかつたならば遂には危険に陥つたことであろう。かかる水域を航海日誌によつて航海する船乗りは、宛も自分の位置を世間的な事物の関係や、周囲の尺度との比較からのみ判断するモラリストと同様に、己の進路から遥に逸れてしまう惧れがある(K)。

八月八日、朝早く西方に九州の陸地が先ず望見され、エイゴグ岬[59]の辺りを南西に望んで進んだが、やがて再び日本のジャンクが陸地の風下に見られた(P)。

正午、九州東岸のダンヴィル岬[60]に隣接する陸地が望見され、夕刻には三、四哩の距離に近ずいた(K)。

八日に至つて九州のコクレン岬[61]に達した(W)。

正午、我々は「鯨の餌」と称ばれる広大な層を見たが、水中にあつて宛も凝固せる血液の如く見え、幅は八乃至十呎、長さは一哩に及んだ。バケツで掬つてみた所が、卵から成つて居り、更に検微鏡で調べたところ、直経は二ラインあつた(P)。

94

海岸に沿つて航行しているとき各種の海鳥が船の周囲に飛んで来たがその数は限られていた。多数の魚の群が見られ、浮石と海草が流れていつたが、各種の海草はその形が繊細優美であるのが目をひいた。(W)。

午後三時、陸に接近したとき、多数の漁船が見られたが、いずれも近ずいて来ようとしなかつた(P)。

村落は殆んど見えず、コクレン岬附近を除いては、小舟やジャンクの数は江戸附近よりも遥に尠かつた。やがて一、二艘の舟が、我々の船を近くから見物しようとするかの如く近ずいて来たので船へ来るように繰返し頼んだが、どうしても来ようとせず、ただ薩摩の舟だと答えたのみである[62](W)。

夕方ダンヴィル岬の南数哩にあるミウウラ(有明湾)にいくつかの灯火が見えた[63](P)。之等の舟に出遭つたダンヴィル岬とコクレン岬の間の浜辺には僅かながら村落があつたが、それより南の海岸には人家もなく、耕作された形跡もなく、また小舟も見えなかつた(W)。

八月九日、夜の間にナガエフ岬(火崎)を通過し、今朝はオスローミ(大隅)の海岸に沿つて、岸から二哩の距離を進んだが、北東にはチチャゴフ岬(佐多岬)[64]があり、南東には種子島が在つた(P)。

95

午後一時、岩層の勾配が見える程チチャゴフ岬へ接近した。午後は穏かな順風が吹いていたが夕刻止んでしまつた。この時檣頭監視人が北西に砕け波のあることを報じたが、その場所は全く平穏なので、斯かる幻想を起したのは不思議であるが、恐らく少々うねりがあり水に夕月の映るのが砕け波のように見えたのであろう。船は二、三ノットで走つていたが、突然風が無くなり海は鏡の如くなり、宛も静かな湖水に映る林の如く美しい景色を水に写していた。この時南西から大波が寄せ来り、満潮の海は堂々とうねりはじめた。その上有難いことには順風を伴つたので、船は我々の思う通りになり、順調にコースを進んで行つた。さもなければ船は陸の方へ流されて行くところであつた。日が暮れてから陸地にはたゞ一つの火を見たゞけである(P)。

夕刻から次第に九州と種ケ島の間にあるファン・ディメン海峡(大隅海峡)が目の前にひらけてきて、遠方には薩摩と琉球の中間にある島々の一部が見られた(W)。

八月十日、未明に鹿児島湾を望む所へ到着した[65](K)。

ここえは二百九十五年以前、はじめて葡萄牙人が着いた。また使徒ザヴィエル以下多くの基督教徒達も上陸した(K)。

右手には半哩離れて大隅の海岸が真北に続き、目の届く限り険阻な緑の崖が切れ目なく続いている。シオノミサキ(チチャゴフ岬=佐多岬)から三哩入つた所に小さな湾があり、海岸は浜砂利で

96

ここに佐多浦の村がある。その後方は次第に高くなつて山の峯に続き、その間山腹には緑の小山が重なり、多くの穀物畠があつて今までにない美事な眺めであつた。小山と小山の中間には二、三の平たいよく耕された高台があり、特にその一つは周囲の小山が頂上まで段階に切り開かれて宛も大きな庭園の如くであつた。湾の入口の真北二十哩の処に榎島があり、その正反対の北西岸に首都鹿児島がある。湾の西側は距離が遠くて様子がよく分らなかつたが、たゞ正円錐形の開聞岳（ピーク・ホーナー）が海岸に近く千二百乃至二千呎の高さに聳え立つていた[66]（W）。

東海岸は丘や山の背が水辺にまで達していて田島を耕し、人の住む余地は残つていない。内湾の一部を占めている円い土地が北方の眺望を遮ぎり、その中央の高い峯はミタケ山即ち「眺望の山」と称ばれている。反対の西側には鹿児島市に至る水路を距てゝ、更に別の高い山があり、之は高さも形も全くオカイモンと同様である。この水路の入口はミアバナ（宮浜）の小村の真後にある断崖の沖の小島によつて遮られている。此処（山川）は内陸へ向うジャンクの碇泊地で、いわば鹿児島湾の浦賀である。予は直にミアバナに向つて進航することを提案したのであるが、船中の日本人漂民は前に受けた取扱いが忘れられず、もつと用心深く近ずくことを望んだ。彼等漂民の希望によつてボートが降され、その中の二人（庄蔵と寿三郎）が岩の近くの漁舟に近ずいてそれに移乗し、エサセケ（佐多浦）の小さな村に向つた[67]（K）。

彼等が岸へ着くと住民は我々の不意の出現に大騒ぎした。役人達は防備をはじめていたが、船の一行が近ずいたので中止し、一行を取り巻いて頻に質問を発し、我々の来航の目的を質した（W）。日本人漂民二人の説明は、我々の近接によつて生じた驚きを直に取除いた。その話は人の心を動かすものであつたので、婦人や子供達は涙を流し、村の役人達は直に我々の船へ来て相談するように仲間の一人を代理として船へ派遣してよこした。その中年の役人は穏かな而も風彩の立派な人物で、別に当惑した様子もなかつた。腰にはその地位と役目の標識である二本の刀即ちサーベルと脇刀を差していたが、孰れも少し反つていて刀身は黒い鞘に納り、柄には紐が巻いてあつて狭い鐔で保護されている。我々は之等二本の神聖な武器の長い方を引抜いて彼等に軽い不興を与えたが、間もなくかかる好奇心は全く不都合なものであることを知つた。この来訪者は青い上衣に薩摩の定紋をつけていた。この定紋は白い丸の中に白い四角があり、外側の輪の直径は一吋半、白い角は四隅が白い輪の内側に接し、青い地色の四個の小さな部分を残していた。この定紋によつて鹿児島湾の東側は海図の上では大隅と呼ばれているが、湾の西側と同様に薩摩藩主の領土であるという此の役人の言葉が確実に証明された。この点に就いて得心がいつたので、予て準備しておいた書類の包を渡したところ、彼は直ちに之を領主に進達すると約束した（K）。

彼の語る所によると彼等は我々の突然の出現に非常に驚き、海賊と考えて砲撃の準備を整えたと

のことであり、また我々の来航したことは既に首都へ報告されたということであつた。彼は部下二、三名を船に残して戻ることになつたが、之より湾内へは岩があつて危険だから進入しないようにと言い、間もなく水先案内をよこして船を安全な場所へ誘導すると約束した（W）。

彼はその希望によつて我々のボートで陸へ戻つたので、二人の日本人（岩吉と庄蔵—W）が、再び長い間離れていた故国の土を踏む機会を得た。之等二人によつて、その艱難辛苦、流浪中に受けた取扱い、その送還に関する我々の希望等の説明が繰り返えされ、彼等はこれらの説明を首都へ進達するため全部書き取つた（K）。

船に残された水先案内人の語るところによれば、大隅は現在農作物の不作のため食糧の不足に悩み、住民はシラタ樹を喰べている程だとのことであつた。模様入りのハンケチその他些細な品を与えた処、悦んで受取つたが、彼等の持物は何一つ呉れようとはしなかつた。また何を見ても欲しがらず、たゞ塩漬のビーフとビスケットだけは悦んで喰べた。そして何も用事が無いので正午に帰つていつた。午後になると一艘の小舟が大きな水桶に一杯水を持つて来た。之は佐多浦の役人がよこしたもので、折角持つては来たが我々の船が動いているのと波が荒いので、縛り縄を差出すことが出来ず、風下へ流されてそのまま帰つてしまつた。水を運んで来たのは、この朝役人と会談の際特に水と新鮮な食糧の不足を強調しておいたからで、折角約束を守つて直に水を運んで来てくれたの

にすぐに受取らず、一見彼の心遣いを無にしたようなことになつたのは残念であつた。住民達は浦賀の場合と同様大勢見物にやつて来たが、売る品物は持参せず、見物を済ますと直に帰つていつた。彼等の中には灸や鍼のあとのあるものが幾人も居たが、鍼は両肩の間か腰部か又は大部分は腹に七、八度うつてあつた。浦賀に於ても、薩摩に於ても、身体に多数の創痕のあるものが見られ、また船を訪ねて来た者には大部分疱瘡の穴があつた。中には随分穴の深い者もあり、漂民達一同の語る所によれば日本では疱瘡が流行し、時には多くの死者が出るとのことであつた（W）。

佐多浦では来訪者の外見や衣服は浦賀よりも勝れていたが、人数は余り多くなかつた。恐らく船までの距離が遠いのと波が荒かつた故であろう。彼等の興味が艢の高さや豚と鵞鳥に向けられたのは前と同様であるが、質問の内容は琉球人より劣つていた（W）。

午後二時、岩吉と庄蔵が三名の役人と共に戻つてきた。之等の役人は皆二本の刀を帯びていたが、その他の点では他の従者と異つた所はなかつた。役人の中に頭髪も髯も半白の老人が居た。船の動揺に酔つて、甲板へ上つて来ることが出来ず、ボートの中にすつかりへこたれて横になつていた。役人達は我々が至急伝達を依頼した書類を未開封のまゝ持ち帰つた。彼等の話によれば、佐多浦の上司は、鹿児島への進達を拒否し、その代りに委細の報告を送つたから、恐らく鹿児島から高官が書類及び漂民を受取りに来訪するであろうとのことであつた。役人の同伴した水先案内は我々

の船を西岸の安全な碇泊所へ移す命令を受けて居り、我々は其処で三日間奉行所よりの返事を待たなければならなかつた。尚翌日は多数のボートが来船して船を湾内の更に安全な場所へ案内し、食糧も充分に供給するとのことであつた(W)。

水先案内に二、三の指図をした後、役人は船を退去し、我々は西岸へ向つた。氣の毒にも斯くて急に外人達と直接接触することになつた水先案内は非常に不愉快な地位に置かれることになつた。彼は自ら船を操縦することは出来ず、而も船を誘導するように命令された碇泊地は風や波のうねりに直接曝されて何等の保護施設もない吹き曝しの錨地である。彼は諸所に危険な岩や洲が在ると称して盛んに我々の恐怖心をかき立てるに努力したが、斯る危険は何処にも見当らず、鉛測深は十五乃至二十尋を報じていた。我々が彼の危険だと称する方向へ向うと、彼は最初危険だと言つた地点を別の場所と変えた。予定の錨地に近ずくと宮浜までは危険な箇所はないと言つたが、氣の毒に彼は自分の今居る位置も、自分が何を言つているのかも分らない程面喰つているのだ。船の士官が水底の調査に派遣された結果、安全な碇泊地であるという報告があつたので、海岸から四分の三哩の水深六尋の地点に投錨した。船が錨を下すや否や水先案内は大急ぎで帰つて行つた。間もなく一艘の小舟が船に横付けになつたが、之は見張船の中の一隻で、一人の役人が乗つて居り、甲板へ登つて来た。彼はグッラフ氏の質問に対しては一言も答えず船を点検する恰好で甲板を意気揚々と練り

歩いて居た。その様子は外国船の見張りの役に任命された日本の役人の例の一種独得の得意な態度で、その滑稽な様子は我々を楽しませてくれた。彼はやがて帰つていつたが、彼が最後の訪問者で、その後は船に上つてくる者はなかつた。日が暮れると対岸の児ヶ水には灯がともされ、湾外の無数の漁船にも灯がついた(W)。

午前中に上陸した者が船に戻つてきたとき、上陸して役人から如何なる取扱いを受けたかを質ねたところ、岩吉の話では役人も住民も非常に親切に迎えてくれたとのことであつた。庄蔵は幸いに難船当時のジャンクの乗員名簿を失わずに保存していたので、最初に佐多浦へ上陸した際に携行していつたが、之が彼の物語る話に非常に役立つたとのことである。二人は集つた村民の面前で役人に対し、委細を語り、漂流せる七名の名、年令、原住所、出船の日時、数項目に亘る冒険の経過、外国人より受けた待遇などを述べたところ、役人はそれを悉く書き取り、又モリソン号の平和的な性格を説明した際には、最初に船へ訪ねて来た役人達が大いに協力してくれたという。斯くて鹿児島へ進達するため之等の口書が封緘されると、主立つた役人は「その外国人達は実に人間より秀れた何者かに相違ない」と感嘆し、書類を進達することは承知しなかつたが、我々が好意を以つて迎えられ、漂民達も間もなく故郷へ帰されることは疑いないと述べたとの事である。彼は漂民達に向い「日本は目下食糧不足に悩んでいるのに、中国で充分に米を得られるならば、何故日本へ帰つて

来たのか」と訊ねたそうである。また、前に船へ来訪した役人が「日本の飢饉」に就いて述べたので、もし日本政府が許可するならば、我々は必要とするだけの米を外国から持参すると話した由である(当時の日本の飢饉に就いては註70参照)。まわりの村民達は息を殺して漂民の物語りに耳を傾け、役人達と共に口を揃えて彼等に「甘い言葉」をかけた。岩吉は自分達が好意を以つて迎えられることは間違いないと確信し、船へ戻ると船のまわりの小舟を一艘雇つて首都へ行きたいと希望した。彼は更に友人達に会つた後で江戸へ往き浦賀で非道な攻撃を加えた「かの残忍無情な役人共」を裁いて貰うように努力すると申し出た。庄蔵も故郷へ帰つて妻や友人に会えるというのですつかり朗らかになつていたが、何と言つても岩吉が一番元気で、嬉しがつてじつとしていられない様子であつた(W)。

岩吉は我々の江戸に於ける失敗は岩吉等七人の漂民を日本人に会わせなかつた為だと言つた(P)漂民が聞いた話によると、日本は今叛乱状態にあり、江戸では盛んに斬首が行われ、日本で第三の都会である大阪は謀反人の為にほとんど灰燼に帰してしまつたとのことであるが、恐らく何かそういつた事実があつたに相違ない[68](P)。

之を聞いたグッラフ氏は之等の話を全く信用したが、自分は全然否定することは出来ないまでも余り当にはならないと思つた(K)。

我々の前面にあるチュゲムツェ[69](児ヶ水)の小さな村は海面から四、五十呎の狭い崖の上にあり、更にその四、五十呎上には小さな森や果樹園の点在する豊かな耕地が北と西に向つて数哩続いている(K)。

錨を下すと間もなく一艘のボートが来て、翌日上役人が来訪する旨を告げ、我々をより安全な碇泊地へ連れてゆくとのことであつた。との知らせと共に、前に渡した書類の包が未開封のまま戻されたが、残念なことに我々の識らぬ間にそうされたのでどうすることも出来なかつた(K)。

予て必需品の供給を依頼しておいたので、蓋のない大きな水桶を真中にすえた小舟が一艘水を運んで来た。水以外の食物に就いては、去年は嵐が十三日も続いて穀物の収穫が悪かつたので、一般に食物が不足して困つていると前置きして、たゞ持つて来る約束をしただけである。之に就いては食物の不足を示すような実例を実際に見ることが出来た。偶々船尾を見下していると、一団の飢えた連中が船の若者達の用意した一籠のパンと大きな鉢へ入れた糖蜜を囲んで座つていたが、此の時程ヤンキーの軽便食が思う存分に賞味される有様を、ニューイングランドでは嘗つて見たことがない[70](K)。

児ヶ水では村との通信連絡は明らかに制限されていて、役人を乗せた小舟以外は全然来訪せず、岸近くの三隻の小舟もただ我々を監視するためのものであることは明らかであつた(K)。

八月十一日、船に旗を揚げると、一艘の小舟がその理由を確めにやつて来た。小舟に乗つてきたのは昨夕甲板を闊歩した役人であつた。我々は彼に船が外国の港に入港したときは国旗を掲揚する慣わしであると説明した所が、彼は外国の船を見たことがないので理由が分らなかつたと答えた。飲食物の供給をして貰いたいことと、天候が悪化する模様なので若し嵐にでもなれば岸へ打上げられるかも知れないので、至急安全な碇泊地へ案内して貰いたいと申入れた所、水は直ちに届けるが、小舟の派遣は鹿児島からの高官の到着を待たなくてはならないとの事であつた。之では前日と話が違うと考えたが、この程度の地位の役人では上司の意向に従う外仕方がないのであろう。彼が退去すると、一艘の小舟が水を一桶持つて来たが、その乗組員は一人も甲板へ上つて来なかつた。恐らく役人によつてすべての交渉を禁ぜられているに相違ない（W）。

インガソル船長は水先案内の小舟が来そうもないので、風に備えて錨を更に二本用意し、船のひきずりを防ぐすべての処置をとつた。住民との交渉がないので周囲の地勢を調べる余裕が出来たが、この辺は高い山が隣接して、江戸湾の周囲と同様緑に覆われ水蒸気が凝縮してたちこめている。浜の形も江戸湾と同様に緩い線をなして両端が岩石に終り、松の木で覆われている。南端には監視の役人が居り、堤防によつて風波から完全に護られている。然し浜の湾曲部以外には浦賀と異り、土堤は急で、小山と小山の間の二、三哩の間に馬の登れる箇所がただ一箇所あるのみである。

105

ある箇所は五十呎の高さがあり固い粘土から成つていて所々岩層が露出している。土堤から先は概して緩い傾斜で、高さも特に高いという程ではなく、多くの小山と樹木によつて変化に富み高度に耕作されていた。階段式耕作は頂上にまで及び浦賀の場合以上で、中間では之程の高さに達しているものは見掛けなかつた。中でも特に目立つているのはカイモンダキ（開聞岳）で、山腹は松の木が茂り、山頂はいつも雲を戴いている。附近には之に匹敵する山がなく、その為に一層美しさが引立ち、形の正しい点から言つて mons 風に数えてよいものである。一連の山々が北方に連なり、九州を従走する山脈の一部をなしている。その中の高い峯の一にウジュ山（雲仙）[九]があり、燃える硫黄泉と天主教迫害の際に教徒に対して加えられた迫害によつて有名である。この山から三哩の距離にある島原で生れた熊太郎の話によれば、此の辺は人口が少く、温泉の多くは熱くて有害であるが、中にはぬるくて皮膚病に効くものがあり、ケンペルがとの温泉場は病人のために出来たものであると書いているのと一致する。頂上には一年中雪が積つているとのことである（W）。

湾曲部の端にある小山の向うは見渡す限り耕地が続き、小山のすぐ沖に鋭い円錐形の岩があつて眺望を遮り、水際に艦載ボートがやつと通れる程の穴があいている。反対の端にある小山は海に向つて赤岩が突出して平坦になつて居り、打寄せる波のために多数の穴があいていた。小山から四分の三哩の距離にある土堤の唯一の登り道をなす谷間の附近に墓地があるが、灰色の墓石が西洋式に

106

幾列にも直立し、那覇の馬蹄型の墓とは非常に違つている。墓地には囲みがなかつたが、墓の周囲には無数の大樹が茂り、墓地にふさわしく奥まつていて感じがよかつた。この墓地から四分の一哩程先に児ヶ水の村があり、浜辺の凹所に納つている様子は宛も村を納めるために用意された龕に入れたような恰好である。即ち家の屋根は両側の堤と同じ高さで後の樹の茂みを背にして浮彫になつている。家は大部分が白く、村は清らかで家が建て込んで居り、浜から登り下りする道が作られている。道路を保護しその存在を示す並木が四方に通じて一種独得の眺めをなし、鹿児島湾周辺の眺めは全体として美しい。しかし壮大さと崇高さに於ては江戸湾に及ばない（W）。

水を運んで来た小舟が行つてしまつた後は誰も近ずいて来ないので、午後一時、青旗を掲げてみたが無駄であつた。ところが昼食後、士官が岩吉と共に艦載ボートで浜の水底調査に出掛けると、之を眺めた陸の人々の間に明らかに動揺が起り、一艘の小舟が来て艦載ボートに引返せと命じ、更に一艘の小舟が本船に近ずいて来た。之には役人が三人乗つていて本船に横ずけになると立上つて艦載ボートの派遣された理由を気持ちのよい態度で訊ねたので、天候が悪くなりそうなので船の周囲の水深を調査するためであると答えた。小舟の中で立上るのは不便であろうから甲板へ上つて来てはどうかと招いたところ、そうしたいが命令によつて禁止されているからといつて拒絶した。鹿児島から役人が来るのは何時頃か、約束した食糧と小舟は何時頃来るかと訊ねると、役人は未だ来

107

ないが間もなく到着するであろうと答えた。彼等のいうところでは、漂民は受入れられないであろうとのことであつたので、これには一同吃驚したが、特に漂民達は直ちに大声でその理由を質した。すると役人達は急に頑固になり、返答を避けてただ見張りを命ぜられているだけで、上司のすることの理由などは何も知らないという。そこで我々が当地へ来たのは数名の漂民を送還する為だから、若し薩摩侯が漂民の受取りを希望されないならば、代理の役人が来訪して説明せられたい。その上で我々は出帆することにすると告げた（W）。

この最後の訪問の際の役人の態度は、好意ある様子に見せかけようと努力しているにも拘わらず、前日ほど友好的なものではなかつた。恐らく厄介な昼夜を分たぬ見張りのため、また度々の驟雨にあいながら何時間も覆いのない小舟にじつとしている退屈さの為に不機嫌になつていたのであろう。もつとも日本の役人は斯る情況を極めて有りがちなことと思つているので、別にそれを口にしなかつた。個人的には彼等は好意を持つていたようであるが、仮令個人として我々の成功を願つても、職務上、下僚として上司の命令に従わざるを得ないと考えたのである。供の者達は前の時よりも服装がきちんとして居て、その多くは筋骨が逞しかつたが、目が小さくて斜になつている故か、顔に生気がなく人好きのする容貌ではなかつた。次々に現われる人々の中には周囲の珍しいものに非常な興味を感じたらしい若者も幾人か居た。役人はその態度や知的風貌が特に供の者に勝つてい

108

るわけではないので、腰に刀を差していなければそれと区別がつかない。役人達が退去すると間もなく艤装ボートが戻つて来たが、その報告によると浜から五ロッド以内は一様に五尋の水深で、浜は断崖の崩れた奇麗な砂地であるとのことであつた。間もなく日が暮れて天候が悪くなり、其夜は度々風と雨のスコールがあつた（W）。

八月十二日、今朝は雨降りでうすら寒い。岩吉は夜の間に役人が到着した徴候がありはしないかと見張りに出ていた（W）。しかし約束した高官は遂に来なかつた。昨夜はずつと静かであつたが、之は謂わば嵐の前の静けさで、日本人は最も友好的な時が最も危険なのだという言葉を更めて確めたのである。斯る時こそ日本人はその裏切り行為を実行する機会を狙つているのである（P）。

午前六時[72]、一艘の小舟が近ずいて来た。舟中に三人いたが[73]、本船が監視とその小舟との中程の位置まで来ると、我々に言葉をかけ、之から釣りに行くのだが、外国船との交渉は一切禁止されているので、ただ見物に来たと言つた。岩吉が鹿児島から役人が来たかと尋ねると、役人は来ないが、噂によると船は撃退される手筈になつており、当局は漂民を受入れないという。噂の出所は言わなかつたが、根拠のある話で間違いないといい「錨を上げて出帆した方がよいと思う」とのことであつた。約三十分間、漂民と話しをしていたが、その説明によつて、今までよりも遥によく事情が判明し、住民の我々に対する感情も知ることが出来た。村民達は最初我々が近ずいた時は非常に吃驚

109

したが、使命が分るにつれて好意を持つ様になつたという。また、我々を撃退するという噂は確実であると繰返えし述べ、之から湾外へ釣りに行くところであるが、帰りには魚を少し持つてきてくれるとのことであつた。然るに彼等は湾外へ往かず、沖から帰つてきたように見せるためにへさきに釣糸を垂れながら、我々の船の船首を廻つて岸へ戻つていつてしまつた。彼等が如何なる意図をもつてかかる行動を行つたかは知る由もないが、波の荒い悪天候の中を密に船に近ずいてくるのは容易なことではない。ただしかし彼等が如何にも躊躇するような不確実な態度であつたので、彼等の言う噂は充分あり得ることだとは思つたが、我々はそれによつて態度を決するまでに到らなかつた（W）。

彼等が行つてしまうと間もなく児ケ水の樹々の間に薩摩の定紋のついた幅の広い青と白の布が垣根のように張られ、住民達がこの幕と村との間を往来し、浜辺を只ならぬ様子で走り廻るのが見られた。之は怪しいと思つていると岩吉が口惜しそうな顔付きをしてやつてきて、幕が張られたのは戦の準備であり、恐らく力ずくで船を撃退せよという命令を鹿児島から伝えてきたに相違ないという。また、幾条かの幕は兵士を護るためのもので、四、五枚の厚いカンバスが少しづつ間隔を置いて重ねて張つてあり、布で出来た砲台というと滑稽に聞えるが、ゆるくはつた布の震動によりカーン砲の爆風を防ぎ、旋回砲の弾丸を喰い止めることが出来るのである。村民達はしばらくこの即席

110

の砦の周囲に集まつていたが、やがて何か号令が発せられたらしく、一斉に立退いて村の反対側の墓地へ向つて大部分は素足で浜や小山の山腹伝いに小径を駆けていつた。他に気に掛けることがなかつたならば、大勢の群衆が五、六十呎の高さの白い堤にくつきりと浮彫りになり、距離のために三分の二程に小さくなつて浜辺を駆けて行く有様は実に滑稽なものである。我々はヘロドトスの小人達が鶴との戦に出掛ける有様を憶い出した。彼等が墓地に着くと更に布の保塁が設けられ、多数の小旗が風になびき[74]、人々が集合してその中に白衣を着た者や馬を走らせる者の姿がはつきりと見られた（W）。

しかし之は何か大きな催しがある時に日本の砦の前面に張りめぐらされるとゴロウェンが書いている幔幕で、誰か偉い人物を迎えるための準備かも知れないと考え、現在の位置を立退く前に更に手掛りの得られるのを待つた。第二の陣地が出来上つたとき訝しく思つたのは、普通ならば見物の群集が村の周囲や高台の先へ出て来る筈なのに、木の間に身を隠して居たことである（K）。

之等の行動の目的がはつきりしないので、結局我々は退去するのが最上策であるということになり、七十五尋も出ている錨を揚げはじめた、帆を開かずに帆桁を揚げ、旗を掲げて合図をしたが何の答えもなかつた。陸の人々が最後に占めた位置は完全に本船を制圧する位置にあつたので、之だけの用心は必要であつた。もし彼等が我々を撃退しようと思えば、浦賀と同様の大砲を以つてすれ

111

ば充分我々を制圧することが出来、我々の位置は危険になるからである。旗を揚げると間もなく一艘の小舟が漕ぎ出して来たので、呼び掛けたが、一顧も与えず佐多浦へ向つて行つた。すると之に続いて小銃と大砲によつて射撃が開始され、大砲の弾は岸と船との中間に落下した。初めのうちは陸上の準備が手間どつているので、大騒ぎしているのは、我々を撃退する以外に何か目的があるのではないかとも考えた。この砲撃によつて日本政府が外国との交渉には依然として敵意を有し、漂民に対して二度目の追放を行う考えであることが明瞭になつたので、風が無く且つ満潮のため錨を揚げると湾の上手の風洞のある岩へ乗り上げる危険があつたが、出来るだけ手早く帆を揚げた。幾百人となく集つた陸上の兵士達が、我々の無防備であることを知つていたことは明らかである。彼等は平気で身を曝していたばかりでなく、住民達も隣接した小高い場所に群れ集つていて、砲手がやつと砲を操縦するだけの余裕しかない程であつた。随つて若し我々が葡萄弾一発を発射しても幾十人の人を殪すことが出来たであろうし、礫石の破片は更に多数の者を傷つけたことであろう（W）。

幸いにして砲台の大砲は浦賀のものよりも軽量で、打出す弾丸は何れも船まで届かず、遥かに手前の海中に落下したので、はじめしばらくは、此の欺瞞的な而も無能な仕草を面白く見物していた。然し遂に我々は、より強力な大砲が余り遠からぬ場所にあり、船が錨を上げて出て行く際、も

112

し現在居る碇泊地の北の海岸の彼等に非常に接近した場所を通らなければならないことを彼等が悟るならば、船に大危害を及ぼすことが出来るということに気がついた。この時風が非常に弱くなり、船は風圧や潮流からいつて、当然岩に向つて流されているので、全部の帆を上げボートを出して船を曳航させなければならなかつた。随つて敵の「軍人」が「水夫」に相談せず、風向や潮流のことを考えずに砲を据えたからよかつたものの、そうでなかつたら大変なことになつたのである（K）。船首を風下に転ずるために船尾に小錨を下し、[75]二艘のボートを船首につないで曳航することによつて、一時は船にとつて砲弾よりも危険な存在であつた岩を無事に避けることが出来た。この困難な状況から船が救われたのはすべてインガソル船長のお蔭である（W）。風は二時間程続き、船は七、八哩湾内へ向つてゆつくり溯航したが、江戸の場合の様に砲艦の追跡を受けることもなく、我々は白い清らかな家が建ちならぶミヤバマ（宮浜）の町とその周囲のよく耕された土地の眺めを楽しんだ。山から流れ下る川が町の下手の小さな入江に注ぎ、その堤の上にヤマガワ（山川）の大きな町が在る。ミヤバマは険阻な小山の麓にあり、大きさから判断して日本では中流の町であると思われる。湾の中から見た景色は実に美しく魅力があつて、自然の手で飾られたこの美しい土地を、斯の如き人間嫌いの国民が所有することは如何にしても残念であると思わずには居られない。時々来る驟雨の中を湾外へ向つて進航し、午後三時佐多浦へ来て、此処で大型の大砲二、三門

の砲撃を受けたが、弾丸は船へ届かず遥か手前に落下した。更に下つて元の碇泊地へ近ずくと、驟雨の合間にまだ砲撃を続けていた。車へ乗せた四門の大砲が小山を迂回して運んで来られ、海に向つて平たい土台の上に据えられて、我々が近ずくと砲撃を加えて来た。斯くて薩摩侯の忠実な臣民達はその命令を実行するために凡ゆる手段を尽し、全力を挙げて我々に危害を加えようと努めたのである（W）。

船中の日本人漂民達は、今や、長い間抱き続けてきた懐しい我が家へ帰り友人達に会えるという期待を棄てなければならないことが明らかとなつた。彼等としてはその計画が漸く成功したと思つた瞬間にそうなつたのであるから、その失望は一層悲惨である。浦賀に於ては彼等は人に接しなかつたから、砲撃は彼等が目標ではなく、我々が目標であつた。今度の場合は自国の人々に会つて身の上を話し、土地の人々からも同情を受けていたのであるから、政府も亦同情を寄せてくれるのは確実であると信じていたのである。しかし事ここに至つては凡ゆる帰国の機会を悉く断ち切られ、再び他国の人の保護に身を委ねることになつた。我々としても彼等に対してとられた卑劣な所置を隠したり取繕うことは出来ない。彼等を乗せた我々の船は公式に碇泊地に案内され、然るべき役人との交渉、必要とする物の供給が約束されたに拘わらず、その約束が未だ果されず、我々がそれを待つている間に、何等の警告もなく、而も友情の仮面に隠れ、夜の闇に紛れて、船を攻撃する（拿捕或

は遮断しないまでも）準備が行われたのである。我が方は帰航を望んで居り、ただ漂民受取りに対する返事を待つているのだという趣旨を申し送り、出航出来るように一刻も早く掛りの役人を差向けて貰いたいと頻に要請していたにも拘わらず攻撃が行われたのであるから、この攻撃が単に我々を追払うだけの目的でなされたものでないことは明白である。然らば何故に言葉によつて我々を退去せしめようとしなかつたのであろうか。何故に少くとも言葉では無効であることが明らかになるまで武力に訴えることを差し控えなかつたのであろうか。彼等の計画がこの未知の船を撃滅して、後日この話を人に伝える者の残らぬようにするにあつたとは信じられないし、また何等の危害も加えず、そのまま無事に逃がすことが役人の希望であつたとも信じられない。攻撃の命令を発した責任者に就いては、大砲の前に張られた布地に薩摩の定紋がついていたから疑問の余地がない（K）。

我々が前に碇泊していた場所に向つて、逆風と湾内へ流れ込む潮流に逆いつつ遅々として湾を横切つて帆走を繰り返えしていると、その度毎に新に砲撃を受け、大砲は開聞岳の麓の最先端まで下されて、勇敢な敵共は「花火」を打ちつづけた。午後はしばらくひどい驟雨が彼等の熱をさましたが、夕闇を通して閃めく光によつて、既に敵の姿は見えず、猛烈に発射される大砲の音も我々の耳へは届かなかつたが、戦が依然として続いていることは明らかであつた。容易にかち得た勝利に歓喜する勝誇つた攻撃者達を後にして、予は最後の寄港地として船を長崎へ向けるように命じた。長

崎へ着いても港外に留まつて錨を下さず、既に用意されている書面に一通の抗議書を添えてボートで送り、返事の来るまで二十四時間待つことにした。若し船内の日本人に満足のいくような保証が得られないならば、澳門へ帰る予定であつた（K）。

しかし我々の漂客にとつては、クルーゼンステルンが長崎へ送還した漂民達のような取扱いを受けることは余り有難いことではない。その時の漂民達はロシア使節が長崎に滞在している間六ケ月も監禁され、使節が出発するに当つて初めて日本側へ受入れられたのである。[76]それに我々に第三の試みをなすことを躊躇せしめる理由が幾つかあつた。即ち佐多浦へ上陸した人々の話を綜合してみると、我々の来航の目的、国籍、船の性格等に関しては充分な説明が役人に対してなされて居り、従つて岩吉はじめ漂民達は我々の計画を部分的にしか知らなかつたとはいえ、その説明は此の度の航海の主たる性格を役人達に充分に伝えている筈である。説明を聞いた役人達は勿論委細を上司に報告したであろうし、船が入つて来るという噂さは更に広く話を弘めたであろう。従つて多くの港で一包の書面を渡してあるくよりも遥かに広く人々の間にその事実が弘まつたことと思われる。しかし乍ら今や故郷の人々に会える望みを無慘に打ち砕かれた漂民達は、之以上何処の港へ赴いても取調の結果によつて受入れられる望みは殆んどないし、といつてこつそり潜入することの出来ないのも明らかである。なる程彼等の家族は各方面から彼等の無事であつたことを聞き、更に友人達は

既に大洋の藻屑と消えたと思つていた彼等が無事でいることを知るであろうし、また庄蔵は佐多浦に於て父に宛てた手紙を手渡し、必ず届けるとの約束を得た。しかし一方彼等漂民が自分達の身の上をすつかり話したのでは、返つて彼等が何処へ往つても直にそれと知られる結果になり、取調べを受けて結局は罰せられるのは明らかである。政府が受入れない以上、何人も彼等を安全に引取ることは出来ない。同様にジャンクに乗つて上陸し、或は本土を離れた島に上つて通り掛りの船で人の居ない場所へ連れていつて貰うことにしても、結果は同じことである。彼等は確かに受入れられるという固い信念があつた為に委細を説明したが、それは返つて自ら帰国の道を塞いでしまつたのである。之は漂民自身の見解であるが、我々としても中国政府が同様な場合にとつた態度を知つているので、之はあり得ないことではないと思つた。その上漂民達は、仮令長崎奉行が彼等の安全を保証すると約束しても、それに随う意志は無いし、長崎奉行としても今回の撃退の事実を知れば、漂民を敢えて受取ることはしまいとの意見であつた。更に我々としても此の上長崎へ赴いて、既に貿易を独占し、外国人を閉出そうとしているオランダ人の疑惑を起すことを欲しなかつた。以上の理由により我々は澳門へ戻り、日本の閉された門戸を開くために之までとられた処置の結果をすべて神の手に任せることにした(W)。

八月十三日、昨日の午後、我々が薩摩を後にした時、琉球から来た一艘のジャンクが湾内へ入つ

117

て行くのに出遭つた。夕方我々は砲撃を続ける敵に別れを告げた。彼等は夕闇のために見えなくなる迄砲撃をつづけた。夜は余り進航しなかつたが、今朝は開聞岳が全容を現わした(W)。

今朝になつても未だ我々が二度と見たくないと考える場所が見えていた。前に船を急いで湾外へ出す為に中錨のケーブルを切断したが、この錨を取り戻すために一艘のボートが刀やピストルを用意して派遣された。しかし本船は浜や岩から距離を保つために全員を必要としたので、幸いボートは余り行かぬ内に呼び戻された。もしその儘進んで錨を取戻す際に、日本の兵士に妨害されたならば、日本の処置に憤激していた乗組員達は必ず自衛のために流血の惨事を引き起したに違いない。何故ならばボートに乗つていた士官は流血の場面は初めてではなく、乗組員達も非常に昂奮して、危険に身を曝すことを物ともせず、先を争つて行きたがつたからである(P)。

此の朝早く気の毒な日本人漂民達を集めて、オランダ船に対して正式に開かれている長崎港へ往つて、もう一度受入れの保証を得るよう努力してみることを提案したが、彼等は今更役人の手に引き渡されるよりは死んだ方がましであると答え、再び中国へ送り還して貰いたいと懇願した。特に長崎で或る役人の召使をしていた一人は仲間の者に向つて長崎へ往くことの危険を強調した。此の者の説明を俟つまでもなく、彼等一同はたとえ如何なる約束がなされようとも長崎へは上陸しないと拒否したので、長崎へ往くことは諦めなければならなかつた。切角彼等のために受入れを依頼し

118

てその許可を得ても、彼等自身が承知しないのでは我々が立場に困るし、その上ただ単に憤激した抗議書を渡す目的のみのために長崎へ往くことは、アメリカ政府がより賢明に且つ強力に行い得ることをわざわざ自分の手に引受けることになる。更にアメリカと日本との交渉に最後の手段をとる場合は、現在通商を長崎に制限し、その貿易を圧迫している法令を、ただ遠くから眺めることに依つて生ずる偏見のために判断を歪められてはならないのである。合衆国は仮令如何に身分の低い市民であろうとも、その国民を第二の出島に委ねることは敢えてしないであろう(K)。

ここで少し気に掛つたのは、漂民達が澳門へ帰ることを希望するのは、グッラフ氏の家に世話になつていた折の呑気な生活を憶い出したからではあるまいかということであつた。そこで彼等自身のためを思つて、この点に関して明瞭な説明を要求し、祖国を棄てたからにはその瞬間から自分の手で食を得なければならないがそれでよいかと質した所、この立ち入つた質問に対して彼等は「仮に祖国へ帰つても現在のような窮乏の際では、自分のため又恐らくは飢えている家族のために働かずに居られましようか」と答えた(K)。

浦賀から撃退されたとき、不幸な漂民達は「友達に手紙を送つて、自分達が未だ生きて居り、親切な人達の手に保護されているのを知らせることが出来ればそれで満足だ」と話し合つて居たが、今や彼等は全く希望を失つてしまつた。なかでもアメリカ海岸へ漂着した三人の漂民は、祖国を棄

119

て去つたことを言葉よりも強く表現するために頭髪を剃つて甲板へ現われた[77](K)。

この日は一日中九州の沖合にある島々が我々の目をひいた。種子島には幾つかの町があつて、果実と木材を取引して居り、その北端はシオノミサキの南東二十五哩の距離にあたり、長さ二十哩幅八哩あつてよく耕作されている様子である。種子島の西方十五哩、開聞岳の真南四十哩には屋久島があつて、面積は四、五十平方哩あり良質の木材を産するので有名である。夜はこの二つの島の間を進航したが、潮流は種子島に向つて流れた。無風のため潮に流されて低い浜辺から一哩以内の距離にまで流されたが、五十尋でもまだ底に達しなかつた。しかし風が出て来たので我々は黄海に向うため北西の方へ進んだ[78](W)。

八月十四日、午後アポラス島(硫黄島)から数哩以内の地点を通過した。この島は森がなくて、少しばかりの芝生に覆われ、東端に近い頂上には孤立した一群の木立があつた(P)。

屋久島の東にはタカシマ(volcano Island)エウォシマ(Apollo Island)コロシマ(St Clair Island)がある。クルーゼンステルンの名付けたジュリ、セリフォス両島に対しては土地の原名が得られなかつた。タカ島の横を過ぎるとき中腹から幾条もの煙が立ちのぼり、頂上に到つて雲をなし、そのため一日中頂上は見えなかつた[79](K)。

この島々の間を通過して、クルーゼンステルンの海図が全く正確であることを確認した。我々と

120

してはただ之にタカ島とコロ島の沖合にある数個の岩山を附加し得たに過ぎない（K）。

八月十五日、コロ島を十四日の夜通過し、午前五時海図に示されていない一塊の岩石よりなる一小島を発見し、差し当り「モリソン岩礁」と名付けた。之等の岩山は勿論日本には知れていたであろうし、恐らくオランダ人にもわかつていたであろう。我々は風の方向によつて西へ向うことを余儀なくされたので、往航に通つた航路、即ち南方に続く一連の島々に沿つて進み、マジコ島を訪ね台湾の北西端へ立寄るという計画を放棄して、日本の属領に別れをつげ、中国に寄港地と飲食物を求めて進航を続けた（K）。

十八日—二十二日、黄海を通過の際は北へ向う逆流に出遭つたが、日本の南岸で経験したものよりは弱かつた。一日か二日の間海は前に九州の東方で見掛けたように色のまだらな縞で覆われたが、その中にバリステ魚を主とする魚群が居たので、それが魚の餌であることが一層確実になつた。この辺の海は中国の大河から流されてくる良質の淤泥が充満し、交流する潮流のため常に海水に溶解した状態にある。海岸に近ずくに従つて鉛測は三十尋から二十尋の水深を示し、測量の際鉛は糸に続く革の部分まで幾时も良質の泥の中へ入り込んだ。福建の海岸で二、三艘の漁船が近ずいたが、大盤のセピア即ち烏賊を甲板で干して作つたするめだけしか持つていなかつた（W）。

中国沿岸を望みながら台湾海峡を進んでいるとき、ナモアの附近で数人の漁夫と言葉を交した。

一艘の小舟が来て更紗木綿（サラサ）を買いたいと希望しスペイン弗を差出した。彼等は非常に友好的でグッラフ氏の与えた中国語で書いた本を心よく受取つた。之は今回の航海中に魂の言葉を弘めることの出来た唯一の機会であつた（P）。

順風に乗つて台湾海峡をアモイに下り、(80) その後風と逆流のため数日間遅延はしたが八月二十九日の夕刻マカオ碇泊地に投錨した（W）。

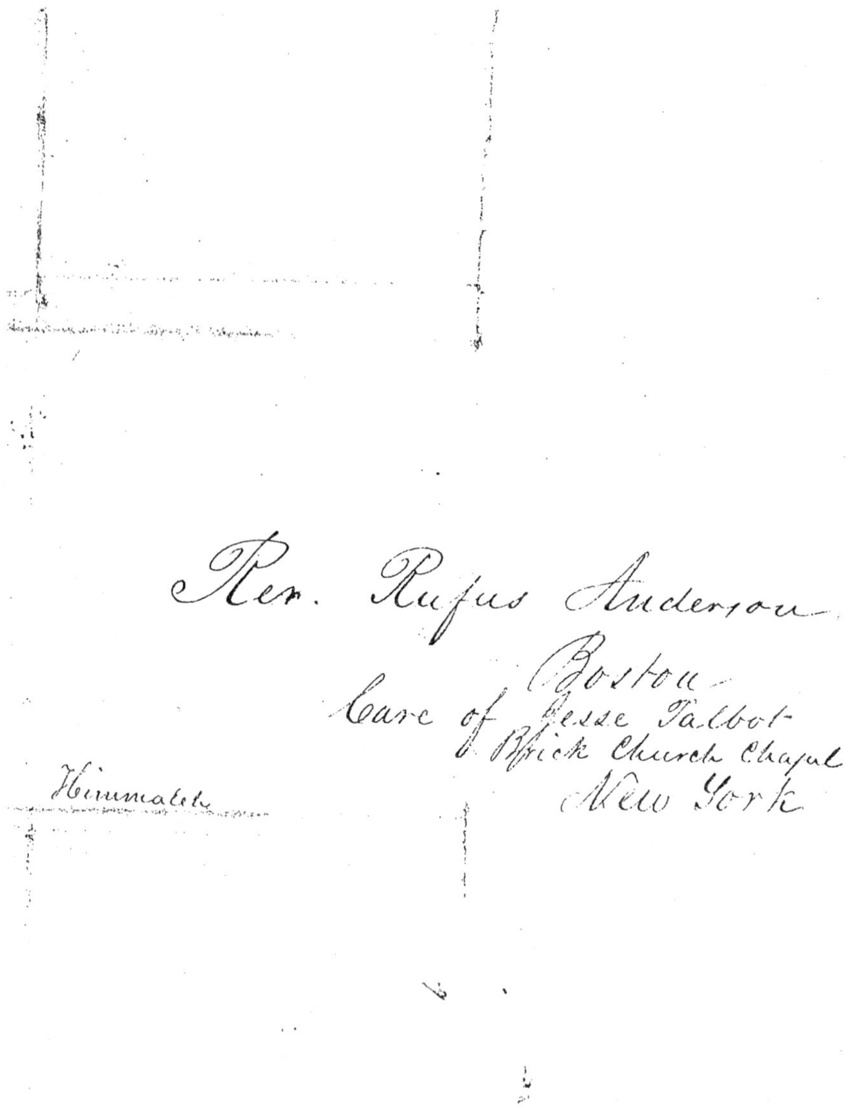

Rev. Rufus Anderson
Boston
Care of Jesse Talbot
Brick Church Chapel
New York

Himmaleh

Per Himmaleh

Canton, Sept. 10. 1837.

Rev. R Anderson

Dear Brother,

I write you a line in order to inform you of the return of the ship Morrison from her cruise to Japan. You were, I believe, informed by Dr Parker of the object of the expedition, which was to return to their homes seven shipwrecked Japanese, and by so doing endeavor to open some communication with that people.

The voyage was planned by Mr. King, and had for its ultimate object the extension of civilization & Christianity. He was accompanied by his lady, and a female servant. Dr. Parker, provided with a large stock of medicines and instruments, and myself, were also attached to the party. We set sail from Macao on the 4th of July, and on the 12th, anchored in the harbor of Napakiang, a port on the S.W. side of the island of Lewchew, the same that was visi-

2

ted by Captains Hall & Beechy. We remained in the harbor three days, during which time we had much pleasant intercourse with the inhabitants, going on shore daily, and receiving visits from the officers on board ship. The intercourse was somewhat restrained on account of the slowness of communicating with each other, which was chiefly by means of the Chinese character. This, when written was legible by both parties. Many of the educated persons whom we saw, could converse in the mandarin dialect, which made the exchange of ideas easier; and in our visits on shore we usually met with a sufficient number of persons who could talk in short in this dialect to obviate the use of a pencil.

This group of islands is supposed to contain about 20.000 inhabitants, and numbers nearly 50 islands, some of which are ~~nothing but~~ mere barren rocks. The largest is 60 miles long by 15 broad; & some of the others are ~~of~~ capable of supporting a sparse population. They are under the control of the Japanese, who monopolize many of the offices, and exercise a vigilant supervision over the whole. The language of the people is Japanese,

3

with perhaps a dialectical variation. Our Japanese could make themselves perfectly understood; and there were seven junks of that nation in port. We saw no Chinese, nor were there any Chinese junks in ~~port~~. When we asked the officers what they would say to a foreigner coming to live among them, & learn their language; they said that they could not permit the least trade with foreigners: how much more then could they not allow one to reside among them. So decided were they not to trade, that we could not force them to take the money in payment for the provisions they had given us. The country is probably under Japanese influence more entirely at the present time, than ever before; & consequently it would be a very doubtful experiment for ~~a~~ one ~~should~~ to attempt to settle himself down among them.

After having taken Mr. Gützlaff on board H. B. M. ship "Raleigh" we set sail for Yedo, the capital of the Japanese empire. We came in sight of the bay at the top of which Yedo is situated on the 28th of July, and were obliged to beat up against a northeasterly wind for 60 miles. The number of fishing smacks and junks in sight was very great, and they gave notice of our approach, ~~a~~ to the officers ~~at~~ of the

4
several villages lying on the sides of the bay; and probably also information was carried to the capital. During the night of the 29th we had penetrated about 40 miles up the bay of Yedo, with much difficulty making the course on account of the darkness and fog. The morning was so misty that we could hardly discern the banks, but we could hear the firing of cannon far ahead of us, although the weather was too thick for the men on shore to see the ship. About noon, it broke away, and we could see the shot falling about 3/4 of a mile ahead of us, being fired from a fort situated on a hill near the anchorage of Uraga, which we wished to gain. On seeing the shot, we came to about 4 miles below the fort, casting anchor a mile and a fourth from the shore.

As soon as we had anchored, several fishing-boats laden with natives came on board, curious to see so unusual a sight. Mr. Gutzlaff conversed with them freely, requesting them when they returned on shore to tell the mandarins that we wished to see them. Nothing was brot off to sell, every one coming from mere curiosity;

yet they were friendly and talkative, inviting us to come on shore, and ramble about. This we promised to do as soon as was practicable.

During the night, we observed no intimation of any hostility; but as soon as the morning broke we were surprised by shot falling about us, ~~from~~ which were fired from four guns that had been brought down from the fort at Ouragawa, and placed on the bank directly opposite the ship. As soon as we saw these manifest indications of hostility we weighed anchor and left the bay, as we judged that after such a commitment on the part of the government they would not enter into any communication. The firing was continued long after we had weighed anchor; and one shot struck the vessel, but did no damage. Several gun boats were sent out, ~~against~~ ~~us~~, who fired at us ~~from~~ with small guns. We endeavored, but unsuccessfully, to induce some fisherman in the small boats that were in the bay to come on board, ~~but they would not come~~ in order to give them a paper to hand to the mandarins on shore stating our nation, character, & object.

Still Desirous of ~~still~~ executing the object of our voyage we bore away for some port on the southern shore of Japan; and arrived on the 10th of August at the bay of Kagosima in the principality of Satzuma. As soon as we reached the entrance of the bay, two of our Japanese were put on shore in order to find an officer with whom we could communicate, and bring him on board. After an hour's absence, they returned bringing a petty officer, who declared that the inhabitants of his village were so terrified at our approach, that they should have fired on us, if the Japanese we sent had not come to explain. This officer soon left us, with two others of our men, in order to give their deposition before a higher magistrate farther up the bay at Miabara. After an absence of three or four hours, they returned highly delighted with their reception, and at the "sweet words" which they had heard. Their deposition was very minute, and was delivered in the presence of several hundreds of natives, all of whom joined in praising the "benevolent foreigners." After it had been taken down in writing, it was sealed & sent to Kagosima the capital; and they were directed to tell us to come to anchor where the pilot sent should direct us, and wait three days for an answer. to come. Every one who heard the deposition, (as we were told,) were of the opinion that our message would be received, and that a high officer from court would be dispatched to take our papers & the shipwrecked men.

We accordingly came to anchor, tho' the situation was not a very desirable one, and waited from the evening of Thursday until Saturday morning for a messenger from Kagosima. Nothing was brought off to us, in comp although we repeatedly requested some water, fruit & provisions, except a cask of water. None of the common people were permitted to come on board after we anchored; and a guard was stationed to watch our movements, & prevent our landing. The Japanese on board were also strictly confined to the ship.

About 7 o'clock on Saturday morning, we observed the people on shore much excited, running in all directions, and mustering in little parties on the eminences near the stone beach. Soon after we saw several strips of cloth, blue & white in bars, stretched across from trees, among the stones of a graveyard. Behind the cloth, were many persons having flags, and guns, assembled, and officers on horseback were seen hastening to & fro all betokening some hostile operations. As soon as our Japanese saw the canvass, bearing the arms of the Prince of Satzuma, they said that a messenger had probably come from the capital, & that his orders were to drive us away. Our suspicions of an attack were strong, and we accordingly began to weigh anchor, though in such a manner as not to excite the notice of those on shore. Before we ~~could~~ showed any sails on the ship, the party behind the canvass battery began to fire at us with musquetry, the shot falling about half way to the vessel. Altho' there was no wind, we concluded it best to make sail, and get beyond their reach, before any cannon should be brought to bear on us. In doing so, we narrowly escaped ~~going on~~ getting foul of a rock towards which the tide was drifting us; and we were carried five or six miles farther up the bay than we had ~~before gone~~ yet been, before the wind arose. As we came out, which was very slowly, cannon were fired at us from the opposite side of the bay; but we were cautious in approaching the coast, and none of the shot hit us. The firing was continued from both sides of the bay until dark.

7

No attempt was made to come on board by any one after the firing was commenced, altho' we had repeatedly told the officers that we woul depart at the first intimation of their unwillin ness to receive the men. Perhaps however the execution of our rejection was committed to other hands than the guard who had been stationed over us.

After leaving the bay, we concluded that there was little prospect of being received at any other port; and our men declared that their lives would be in jeopardy if they should be received at any other port, or if they should attempt to steal ashore under cover of night. The risk of detection in the latter case was greatly increased by the minuteness of the deposition they had given at Miabara. Their disappointment was great, for their expectations had been raised to the highest pitch; and three of them shaved their heads like a Budhist priest in order that the hair might grow equally, thereby showing their determination to live among foreigners. All of them agreed in quietly going back & becoming perpetual exiles.

After a pleasant passage down the coast

10

of China, we reached Macao on the 29th ult. thankful that we had been preserved from all dangers. Mrs. King was somewhat indisposed during the voyage from the ~~great~~ heat and reflection from the surface of the water; but otherwise all enjoyed excellent health.

Our semiannual meeting will be held in a few days, and we shall then probably send you a fuller statement concerning the voyage. Dr. Parker has his journal nearly ready to send, and it will probably accompany the general letter. We are somewhat desirous of receiving a line from the Rooms; for it is now more than a year since we had a letter. Our funds are also rather low, as we have been obliged to send [about] £1200 to Singapore in order to print Bibles & Tracts.

The news from America is rather disheartening, and that in these regions is not very encouraging. Br. Wolff, who accompanied the Himmaleh died in Mindanao.

Yet God reigns, & his kingdom will come & his will be done, and all the steps in its progressive advancement will be done in the best possible manner. Only let us pray more fervently, & grow more in humility & grace

Affect'y Yours

S. Wells Williams

敬啟者
米利堅國水師提督現管本國事務暫駐中華
咖呢恭札知會
大憲近日聞有
欽差大臣數位來同英吉利領事咨議貿易各樣之
事待數日想必到粵省矣兼聞漢英兩國之大
臣互相會議定立一貿易之約只指英吉利國之
商人並不關別國商人之事本水師提督心情緊
急懇恩
大憲奏聞
大皇帝察識此事且我米利堅國貿易每年算不得稀少
故敢請
朝廷施恩惠顧商人貿易容其買賣即同別國商人一樣
現今本水師提督故不敢催迫此事于今亦欲靠着
漢與米利堅兩國和好往來並憶歷年恭順通商之
意特此顯言明白兹本提督粗率無文統求原諒兼請
崇安不備
上
兩廣總督大人 察正

現駐中華米利堅國兵船咖呢謹啟
壬寅九月初七日寄

太子少保兵部尚書兩廣總督部堂祁　為覆知事
頃接來函均已閱悉各國商稅事宜總要畫一辦理方
免偏枯凡稅課之應增應減規費之應留應革現與
暎咭唎公平商酌
貴國應有所閑俟
欽差到來定議具奏後即當通行各國一體照辦必不使
暎咭唎一國得利而各國仍不免受累也至各省如福
州寧波上海等處新立馬頭已奉
大皇帝諭旨准令暎咭唎通商貿易其各國是否一例
前往本部堂未便擅定須俟
欽差據情代奏請
旨遵行所云立定盟約一節固係
貴國和好美意惟中國與各國通商二百年來從無互
換和約之事近因與暎咭唎用兵連年彼此不能相信是
以議立和約以釋嫌疑乃係因不睦而起若我兩國照常
通商本來和好自無庸更立盟約徒多一番周折祈
貴帶兵官熟思之至咪唎㗯商人應追贓銀仍當飭催
洋行按數措繳四月之期轉瞬即至想亦不至推延也此覆
咪唎㗯貴帶兵官查照

道光二十三年三月　十七　日

第3部分

远征琉球与日本

（1）琉球

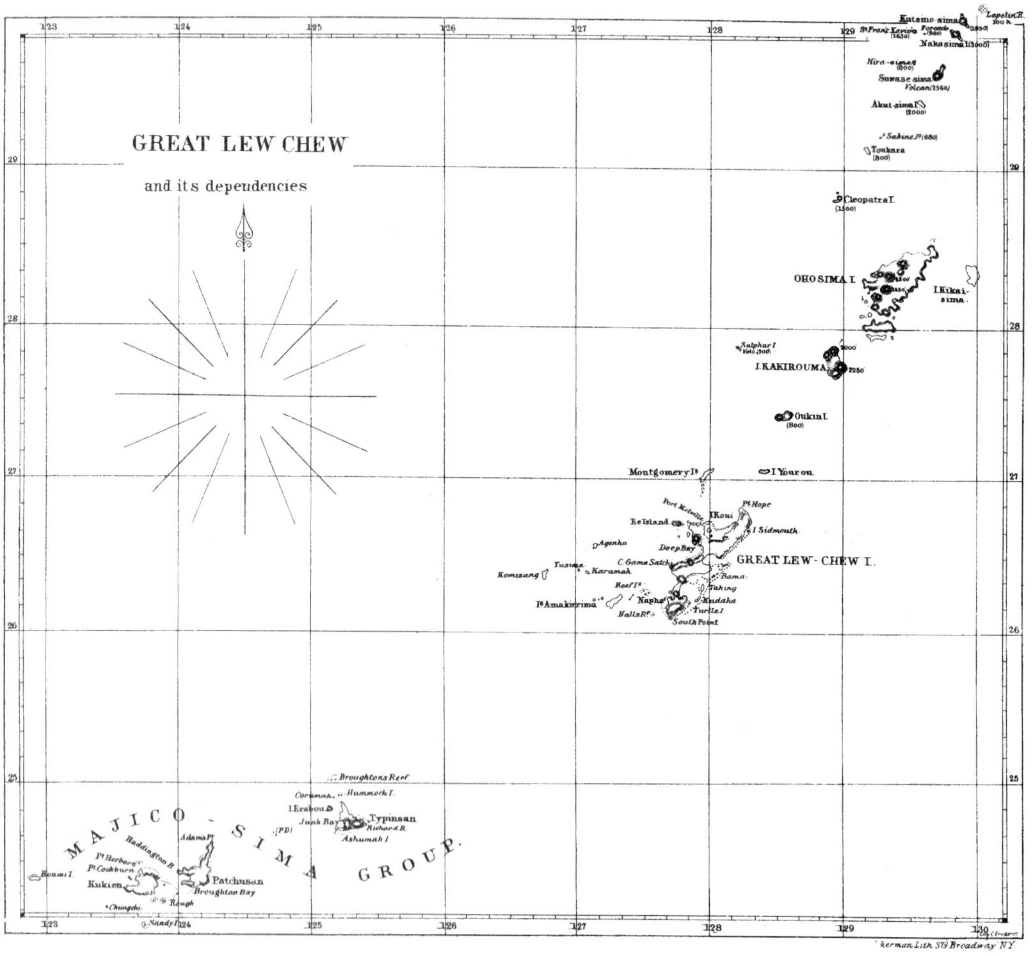

GREAT LEW CHEW

and its dependencies

kerman Lith 3?? Broadway N.Y.

NAPHA FROM THE SEA.

ANCIENT CASTLE OF NA-GA-GUS-KO, LEW CHEW

MARKET PLACE AT NAPHA.

琉球の墳墓

REGENT OF LEW CHEW

COURT INTERPRETER SHIN
Lew Chew

CHIEF MAGISTRATE OF NAPHA
Lew Chew

COM: PERRY'S VISIT TO SHUI, LEW CHEW

RECEPTION AT THE CASTLE OF SHUI.

日本への門戸、キリスト教伝道の拠点

琉球宣教に命をかけた男

バナード・ベッテルハイム
ロジャー・バンダム画伯によるペン書き肖像

To His Excellency the Tsung li Kwan of the Kingdom of Lew Chew.

Sir

The Commander in Chief of the U.S Naval Forces in the East India, China and Japan Seas having returned to this Port from Japan is about sailing for China, and before leaving is desirous of communicating to His Excellency the Tsung li Kwan a few observations having reference to the intercourse of persons under his command with the authorities and people of Lew Chew.

The Commander in Chief while he thanks the officers of the Lew Chewan Govern-ment for the services which they have already rendered in furnishing a few supplies to the Ships of the Squadron cannot see the necessity of enforcing against Strangers a System of restriction which is altogether at variance with the customs and practices of all civilized nations, and which cannot at the present day be recognized as just or proper.-

The Commander in Chief is especially desirous of remaining on the most friendly terms with the Government of Lew Chew, and of contributing all in his power to the prosperity and happiness of the people, and he claims that the Officers and men under his command shall be received upon the same footing as are those who arrive from China and Japan.

Kwan

That they shall have the privilege of purchasing in the market and shops whatever they may need, and for which they will pay the prices demanded by the Sellers. That the inhabitants particularly the women and children shall not fly from us as if we were their greatest enemies; and finally that our officers and men shall not be watched and followed by low officials acting as spies. He declares that if this system of espionage is persisted in he will on his return to Lew Chew take the necessary steps to stop it.

It is repugnant to the American character to submit to such a course of unhospitable discourtesy — and though the citizens of the United States when abroad are always regardful of, and obedient to the laws of the country in which they may happen to be, provided they are founded upon international comity ~~and rights~~, yet they never can ~~recognise~~ admit of the propriety or justice of those of Lew Chew which bear so injuriously upon the ~~privileges~~ rights and comforts of strangers resorting to the Island with the most friendly and peaceful intentions.

~~With all due Consideration~~
With The Highest Consideration

琉球王国の総理官閣下に呈す

拝啓　東インド、中国および日本海域における合衆国海軍司令長官は、日本より当港に帰航し、まもなく中国に向けて出帆するところでありますが、出発の前に、総理官閣下に対し、指揮下の者たちと琉球当局および琉球人民との交際に関して、2、3の意見を伝えたいと思います。

司令長官は、艦隊所属の艦船へのいくつかの物資の供給に際して果たされた、琉球政府の役人の助力に感謝いたしますが、すべての文明国の慣行や習慣とまったく相容れない制限制度を、外国人に強制する必要があるとは思われません。このような制度は現代においては正当とも適切とも認めることはできません。

司令長官は、とくに琉球政府ときわめて友好な関係を続け、自己の権限内のすべてをあげ、琉球人民の繁栄と幸福に役立ちたいと心から願い、以下のことを要求いたします。すなわち、指揮下にある士官および兵士が中国および日本から訪れる人々と同様の処遇を受けること。彼らは自分が必要としているいかなる物品も市場および商店で購入する権限を持つべきであり、その商品に対しては、売り手の要求する価格を彼らが支払うこととする。住民、とくに女性と子供が、われわれを見てまるで極悪人のように逃げ去ることがないように、そして最後に、わが士官と兵士が下級役人や密偵によって監視され、尾行されることがないようにすること。この密偵制度がいつまでも続くならば、司令長官は次に琉球に帰った折に、これを中止させるために必要な措置を講ずることを声明します。

このような一連の不快な非礼に屈することは、アメリカ人の性格には耐えがたいものであり、合衆国市民は、どこの国にいるときでも、訪れた国の法律が国際礼譲に基づくものであれば常に尊重し、遵守しますが、琉球の法律を妥当で正当なものと認めることはできません。琉球の法律は、きわめて友好的で平和な意図をもってこの島を訪れる外国人の権利と慰安をはなはだ不当に圧迫するものであります。

敬具

東インド、中国および日本海域における合衆国海軍司令長官

M.C.ペリー

亜美理駕國船現泊那覇一船之主並但奉

欽差大臣兼水師提督總管本國戰船來中國日本國等海大臣彼理之命

轉咨地方官鄭長烈為覆事我等船到此各海相恐留數年亦有到那覇

海不少往來所以同　貴國官民務相和睦我心實在構惜必厚相

待我先失相凌官民必以禮待我以為國船來務相和悦必望

貴國收留船到此地必要上水兼要各款食物民間採買到船交銀

欽差轉諭地方官差一委員開寫各食物之價兼辦買收各船之銀或在船

上或在別處至繁相償一二間屋在岸因為船內之官兵上岸散步無

定處所　貴國無嚴店或遇風雨抑或夜間不能回船無處住腳兇開進

百姓屋船內之人不識　貴國話若欲一杯水亦不可得屋或要一二間或別

有使用因此和睦亦無別事但此屋必要用處至現在船人現賃往個間地

方官請見公館如有別問先行指明亦能按出照

貴國官議一斷但不已要其屋一二間近此屋要馬四六匹雜轉但全預備

應用之價給足此數日預定本月二十日已刻

欽差大臣兼同隨從船上昇去宮殿首里回拜

總理大臣早祝地方官務要備具籍傍公用轎馬等能前去以事緊要

所無失望亦我為此致備

咸豐三年四月二十六日

具稟琉球國中山府總理大臣尚大謨為瀝情稟請事本月二十一日奉

大人鈞諭本月二十日巳刻意要到京城鳴謝等因嗣于二十六日據地方官鄭長烈詳稱奉

大人憲箚內云預定三十日巳刻去宮殿首里回拜總理大臣等因理合詳明等由前來切

查敝國京城與中國省城大異只有王宮另無衙署市店從古以來未有他國人員

進入宮中詎前年十二月有英國總兵捧國書來到即要入宮中交授大臣隨即瀝

情再三懇請在別處交授不肯聽從竟入宮中此時上自幼君國母下至官民人等皆

懷驚怕魂不付体國母從此染成積病至于近日其病沉重侍醫奉進湯藥尚未

見效現今諸官正在憂慮之秋傳聞

貴國主寬洪惻怛常以仁慈為重懇乞　大人仰体

國主仁慈愛人之至意俯察國母與病之實情停止入宮鳴謝之舉若必要鳴謝而不已

仍請駕到太子宮向會鳴謝又據地方官詳稱賃屋寄居一款于本月二十四日

陳由請辭二十六日奉

大人憲札內云船內之官兵上岸散步無定處所貴國無歇店或遇風雨抑或夜間不

能回船無處歇腳免闖進百姓屋內船內之人不識貴國話欲想一杯水亦不可得屋

一二間或別有使用因此和睦亦無別事但此屋必要用處至現在船人現賃住個

間地方官話是公館如有別間先行指明亦能換出照貴國官議一斷等因查

現所寓公館乃係官役會議公務之所茲求可居之屋有一間聖現寺實船泊

此之間可以寄居祈飭搬到此寺暫居則君臣上下共戴

鴻仁于無既矣切稟

琉球

咸豐三年四月二十七日

國　印

具禀琉球國中山府總理大臣尚大謨爲奉命求請事本月二十日奉
大人鈞諭三十日已刻要入王宫鳴謝等因即將國母染成積病療治未痊已准
到太子宫鳴謝等情昨天渡伯德令上船轉請乃奉
大人鈞諭我未見太子不便入其宫中且前年英國總兵亦入王宫我亦要入宫
等因奉此卑職具禀奏明奉
國主諭曰英官入宫以來國母染成積病未見痊可若有
大人駕入宫中深恐其病益重難以得痊懇宜安爲休歇務其期不入宫中爲要緣
此切念本職也受國恩矣我同休戚宜當竭力辭拒使君無憂心乃臣子之
職也且前年英官入宫之時國母無恙迨後病今已年病未愈則時勢比前不
同況且奉命任身理應冒死再瀆伏乞
大人俯賜憐憫恩准到卑職衙署以行謝禮倘仍不蒙允准則不得再見國主
而復命卑職之死生專在
大人准與不准也仍祈
大人上察國母患病之實俯下憐卑職須臾之隙及格外垂念准其所請則
上下一統頂祝千秋切禀

琉　球
咸豐三年四月二十八日
國　印

亜美理駕欽差大臣兼水師提督晉本國戰船天竺
中國日本國等海大臣彼理　　為
照會事昨日本欽差與僚上到臺司拜
貴總理大臣早秉閲時通知其寬慰候二三日此
船暫時去或十日返鎖那覇海則涓便日恭請
總理布政等官越見各船可也本欽差多蒙
貴大臣數日有使委員付食物到各船而今請轉
飭此委員完數收價因為余必不宜受食物一
款無還銀亦此後要委員每七日之尾與各船
之買辦清數或
貴國之牛是少農夫耕牛不便賣則未帶来就是
因不要助耕田之事也各船官兵上岸散步之
時每見各街市上下之人時時隱從跟隨之似
窺探行止蓋本船官兵已預早吩咐上岸行時
於民間秋毫無犯以是不用窺探本國人見女人
無不禮貌恭敬他又無人曉傳達說話或見在
街上忽相語船此婦人心内已不欲諱話無庸
走避無使怕此事嚴定章程無有人敢行不礼
之事矣本國
政愛同萬國和睦往来所以本欽差想越日本
國與該國立和約故以本欽差一幇船到来務
相和悦諒無推辭肅此　　敬候崇安
琉球國中山府總理大臣
咸豐三年五月初一日

具禀琉球國中山府總理大臣尚宏勲布政大夫馬良才等為禀

請事昨日聞得華人二名搬到伯德令所寓寺院佔住隨即委員訪

問其由據伯德令口称近因有人坐駕英船到来替我交代故英官先

以通事華人二名搭駕来國船隻来此等語查伯德令逗遛以来雖經欲施

醫術復要傳

耶穌教然國人不肯信服雖再有人交代要施這樣之術尚屬無益且伯德令由

此已及八年之久士民為備其供應甚致勞苦若正在等候其回之間乃使華

人来此逗遛原係英官所令然因搭駕 貴國船隻而来故敢冒瀆伏乞

大人迅賜体照着將該華人坐駕原船一同率回則感戴無既矣切禀

咸豐三年五月二十四日

琉球

國印

亞美理駕欽差大臣兼管本國兵船現在天竺中國
日本國海水師提督大臣被理為照會事今由日
本國回來到此處而俟數日開船去中國但未離
要通達
貴大人明知其意至於船官兵等與
貴官民等交友知何本欽差知悉
貴官各等助給少食物與船用亦要眞謝此先費
在西域各國但有兩友國人來往常時兩伴准交
好此莫禁彼彼莫須此且有旅人就
貴國豈有此樣拘束他而違各國之例俗乎然後
必無容此例是正義之法而
貴官更改除之讓旅民隨意相交也查知有由中
國日本國人船到了能買賣無禁之亦本欽差要
問　貴官待其船官同知諠二國之船人若他能
買東西出店市交易支平價錢若他散步男女兒
不怕不走知見惡敵若他行路無小役常從探窺
之何故此兩樣乎本欽差眞要與
貴政官立定好和意保益百姓萬福但不早止此
孽障罪今傳
貴官明知船回錨此處必設計自己停止之本國
人入別界常問其律法若有者則順之不悅別國
人待其嫌疎交之貌而不肯吃虧奚旅人眞有分
所當然本國良人不許
貴國應當設此不宜義之法所以急除改各不友
之俗然不使心悵為此照會者肅此
敬候崇安
琉球國總理大臣尚宏勲

咸豐三年　六月　廿二日

亞美理駕合衆國、欽差大臣兼管本国師船、天竺中華日本等海水師提督大臣被理　爲覆照會事、前經接到稟覆文函、內具情由、已得查知、但此後須照稟覆情由切實行事、毋得口是而心非、如今本大臣先往日本公幹、此後回来、祈爲照前稟覆行事、本大臣即便篤信于　貴国之誠實而無疑矣、如今准于明日啟行、但于前者到宮殿內、所議金銀銅錢與本国須要彼此平換、是以即將金銀銅錢當時交下、此必要換了交與泊村管理之人收入可也、今現留下本国幾人在泊村屋內、該　貴国官員総宜以禮待他、他若有不法之事、亦必要將其人品、于本大臣回来之日啟知、本國自有法律在也、右此照　會

中山府総理官

甲寅年正月　初八　日

具禀琉球國中山府総理大臣尚宏勳、布政大夫馬良才等、爲稟覆事、前有繙譯官屢説將度佳喇金銀與亞國金銀對重相換等語、隨即回覆、敝国雖與度佳喇貿易、只有以雜物兑換、而無用金銀、国人所戴簪子、在中國購來金銀、聊倫其用、前日又有　提督大人在王宮發出金銀、囑以對重相換、本職等即着官役細問度佳喇人商、該據商人口稱、夾帶金銀交通他國、原係日本嚴禁、若有犯禁、即罹重罪、故無帶來等語、今已如此、不能兑換金銀、理合稟覆、統祈　大人垂念小邦、俯賜體諒、切稟

咸豐四年正月　初八　日

亞美理駕合衆國欽差大臣兼總管本國師船天竺中華日本等海水師提督大臣彼理

照會

貴國總理大臣等，為表陳弊端，請速改易事。今因本國兵船火船
寄泊于那霸地方海邊數月，各官兵、各水手或時上岸行遊散步，
均要遵循道理行事。至若與貴國買食物，係時時俱有錢銀交給，
斷不容一毫苟且。但因貴國規條總不妥善，特此指陳于下：
一、於貴國之官等待我外國人總不以朋誼為重，亦不以真意相
交，此一端也。一、官教百姓離遠奔走，看我人如仇敵，以致彼此貿
易不通，此一弊端也。供應食物又不按數與足，此一弊端也。一、
貴国互相議約，總不留心，亦有反口識，有措閒慢之意，此一端也。
夫大臣原至此，乃必要公道之事待人。今貴國總不留心着
意，實以本国之名而輕賤矣。且本大臣又係操持威柄者，豈
可以此而失體面乎？今本大臣以慈謙厚待，彼此皆視同朋友一
般，是以遏止威嚴而不作令行。貴国總理大臣等即要改移
數端之弊，即要出示准從百姓買賣食物，又要兩國人彼此和
好如友，不准允本大臣到來京城查閲，此事有何難也。審之慎之，
此宜兩国不失和好，免生事端可也。右此照會

中山府總理官尚

甲寅年正月 初四 日

具稟琉球國中山府總理大臣尚宏勲布政大夫馬良才等為稟覆事昨日奉

提督大人憲劄內開

一於貴國之官等待我外国人總不以朋誼為重亦不以真意相交竊查

本職等從前概飭屬僚於接待

貴國官兵衷禮敬待勿得怠慢今蒙

大人憲示甚懷驚惶嗣後仍飭遵行勿違

一官教百姓離遠奔走看我人如仇敵以致彼此貿易不通供應

食物又不撥數與足本職等前經催飭小民人等種見

丞客勿得失禮奔走但市上小民恐其威勢自避而走嗣後仍飭

小民使之不蹈前轍且在市上買賣者皆是婦人而所賣物件亦僅

少耒以米穀雜項互為交易而無銀子通用

丞客供應物件不能在市自買是以着令官役人等為之承辦又

敝国僻處海隅土瘠地薄產物無幾況且客歲四月以來

貴国船隻絡繹往來灣泊日久所需物件亦及冗繁現令官役人等差

人四方百般搜求所以備辦於其難辦者無奈之何或減省其數然嗣

後仍飭官役其力堪辦者可以承應

一貴国相會議約總不留心亦有反口誠有簡慢之意前日

大人所示議約本應遵不違但事難應者雖經備由冒瀆何敢懷簡

慢之意伏念

大人寬洪惻怛極貧容遇常以仁慈為重曷勝仰慕敝国

大人分訖示諭陳情稟覆統乞

仁憲大人垂憐小邦俯賜

體諒則感戴鴻慈于無既矣切稟

咸豐四年正月 初五日

1854 Jan 5

亞美理駕合衆國管理本國師船現泊中華日本天竺等海欽差大
臣彼理
為照会事、前因本大臣由此處往日本、與日本欽差各大臣結
深交睦往來、先時未往日本之時、留下亞人幾名此處地方
官也曾應允厚待之、所以本大臣之心甚安、今回時甚不悦
聞得不厚待亞国之人、本大臣聞知前時亞人到街、被人驅
逐、及又咾嘆亞人被殺之事、該官又不辯明其多事、又不曾
呈献兇手、何也、豈官員自上至下、不能明晰何人為兇者、
而作此極惡之事乎、倘若不呈兇手、本大臣則不悦與各官
相見、所以拿得兇手、亞国遣官員幾人從旁觀看審判兇
手、須照琉球事例公道審判辦理可也、亦毋問要照亞
國之例焉、夫按琉球官員每言地小而不欺人、則何今而又
殺亞人之命、以此思之、前按官員所言者、僅是一口兩面而已、而
今明白告説總理各官知悉、該因未能秉公查察清明兇手
之事、本大臣則不與往來、若秉公清了其事、則能和睦往來、
也、所以今日本大臣不至公館、則遣大官一位到爾公館定
必要立刻回音對答、務要兩邊公平、悦得兩國民心、或彼此俱
有罪、亦要聲明也、若得你回答、本大臣自知事體之是非曲
直、自有權而辦此事矣、毋違凛之、

敬啓者本月十一日據
貴客尊札內云本月初十日必報先生水手一人行
路之時、約有土民二十名把石拋搥、將擊二亞等語、
查土民人等逢有亞客過行、務必讓路迴避勿得輕
慢等因、屢經飭示在案、且夫小國人民敬畏大國人
員者、乃理勢之當然也、是以土民老幼從前每逢亞
客之行讓路肅避、不敢輕慢、豈有特意把石拋打亞
客者乎、竊念小孩人等、或有羣集以迴礫為戲者、想
必亞客見其石轉過于前、却認其要把石打身歟、嗣
後飭行國中除確禁小孩人等把石為戲、外逢有亞
客之行、愈行肅讓少莫失禮萬望
貴客據情體照切勿留怒于心幸甚幸甚茲修寸啓
謹覆順候
鴻安不宣、

咸豐四年四月二十一日那霸地方官毛玉麟敬覆

敬啓者本月十八日接據
貴官尊札內云昨晚本船一人名味連破耳的在那覇遇死了本官察看死人頭面帶被打傷身上亦有受強之踪跡該人因悪手而遭殤本官今日擇定数發撆審司細細追究該人受死來歷專要究出其實早可看出該人受死原由等因畢職即着屬官審問據稱亜船水手三名經過那覇侵入个家搮取燒酒過量飲醉走到各處或踰墻垣或破門户侵入人家驚動老弱二名轉到市上醉臥一名一步一倒不知去處暫時有土船水手等經過海邉目擊其溺跳水捞之命脉既絶等由據此據其所稱情詞已悉且從前屢飭小民每逢亜客行路之時務必肅避勿得失禮況遇其醉狂愈加敬怕不敢輕慢豈有毒打加害使其失命哉今以二名醉臥市上之情状推之則該一名莫非顛倒失足淹死水中伏乞
貴官據情
體諒茲修寸啓謹覆順候
近祉不宣

咸豐四年五月十九日中山府總理大臣尚宏勲敬覆

亞美理駕合衆國欽差大臣兼管水師提督被理　為批覆事、

緣亞國兵船水梢一名破耳的歷闖累由深悅　貴國官員當

得公平、今已知水梢果是爲惡、但不宜集党投石擊之以致

殞命、今　貴大臣遵我所欲、即將渡慶次帶至火船、本大

臣已照亞国法度閒明、已知得　貴國是真心辦事矣、故將

該人交返批覆辦理、是警將來、若别名不法者、亦宜秉公

辦理、乃後不失和睦之道也、右此批　覆

琉球國官中山府總理大臣

甲寅年六月　十七　日行

具稟琉球國中山府總理大臣尚宏勳、布政大夫馬良才等為
瀝情懇乞大垂
仁慈妥為照料、携帶留國伯德令、冒耳敦等一同還藉、以恤小邦事、
切查敝國蕞爾區疆、土瘦地薄、所屬諸島、亦俱褊小、素無金銀
銅鐵、復無絲斤綢緞、更兼物產無幾、不可稱國、前明以來、叨列
中朝屏藩、世膺王爵、代修貢職、凡係國家大事者、無不奏聞、又
每逢入貢之期、購買絲斤綢緞、以成上下冠服、採買藥材諸物、
以備國家需用、猶為未足、乃通度佳喇島、僭結隣國之交、將所
產黑糖、燒酒、蕉布等項、兑買貢物納款
中朝、凡國中所需米穀、木料、鉄鍋、棉花、茶葉、烟草、菜油、器具等物、
亦求自該島、聊得濟用、更兼五穀不裕、人民常用番薯、以供
日食、家無升斗之儲、每逢風旱、稼穡不登、嗷嗷殘黎、無物可食、

穀食鉄樹、猶未充飢、乃借米穀于該島、那保殘喘、且在市店
貿易者、不過茶葉烟草黄蠟菜油草鞋蕃薯蔬菜棉布並
布古衣並日用微物、是皆婦女所為、不可與他國一律論也、奈
近年以來、屢有西土船隻到來、其所需日用物件、紛紛不一、不能
在市收買充數、即着官民群集那霸、或遣各處買辦、或賦
諸郡調辦、上有糜餉之費、下有農業之荒、甚至窮阨、乃于道
光甲辰丙午等年、又有佛朗西人員及嘆咭唎伯德令携帶
妻子到國寄居、每日供應物件、甚苦難辦、業經每逢咈嘆
船到來、屢陳情由、懇請帶回、至其咈人知敝國之苦情、于
戊申年接回故土、自時厥後、未曾再來、該伯德令依舊逗
遛不去、至于今般、乃有胃耳數要代伯德令率同眷屬來
國居住、民無安息、國益困疲、今知
大人管理中華、日本、天竺等海、凡西域諸國船隻、涉行他國、

亦無不督理、爲此歷陳苦情、仰乞

大人大垂仁慈、准俟寶船返棹、將該伯德仝併冒耳敦等、一同

携回、則舉國官民、皆感

憲恩于無既、頂祝千秋矣、切禀

咸豐四年六月　十六日

琉 第一号

琉球國
米國

條約書

一 此後合衆國人民到琉球須要以禮厚待和睦相交其國人要買求物雖官雖民亦能以所有之物而賣之官員無得設例阻禁百姓凡一支一收須要兩邊公平相換

Hereafter, whenever Citizens of the United States come to Lew Chew, they shall be treated with great courtesy and friendship. Whatever Articles these persons ask for, whether from the Officers or people, which the Country can furnish, shall be sold to them; nor shall the authorities interpose any prohibitory regulations to the people selling, and whatever either party may wish to buy, shall be exchanged at reasonable prices.

一 合衆國船或到琉球各港內須要供給其薪水而亦公道價錢支之至若該船欲買什物則宜於那霸而買

Whenever Ships of the United States shall come into any harbor in Lew Chew, they shall be supplied with Wood and Water at reasonable prices but if they wish to get other Articles they shall be purchaseable only at Napa.

追隨之窺探之但或闖入人家或妨婦女或强買物件又別有不法之事則宜地官拿縛該人不可打之然後往報船主自能執責

or having Officials sent to follow them, or to spy what they do; but if they violently go into houses, or trifle with women, or force people to sell them things, or do other such like illegal acts, they shall be arrested by the local Officers, but not maltreated, and shall be reported to the Captain of the Ship to which they belong for punishment by him.

一於泊村以一地為亞國之墳所倘或埋葬則宜保護毋毀壞其墳

At Tumai is a burial ground for the Citizens of the United States, where their graves and tombs shall not be molested.

一要琉球國政常養善知水路者以為引水之用使其

The Government of Lew Chew shall appoint skillful pilots who shall be on the lookout for Ships

一合衆國倘或被風颶漂壞船於琉球或琉球之屬洲俱要地方官遣人救命救貨至岸保護相安俟該國船到以人貨附還之而難人之費用幾何亦能向該國船取還於琉球

If Ships of the United States are wrecked on Great Lew Chew or on Islands under the jurisdiction of the Royal Government of Lew Chew, the local authorities shall dispatch persons to assist in saving life and property, and preserve what can be brought ashore till the Ships of that Nation shall come to take away all that may have been saved; and the expenses incurred in rescuing these unfortunate persons shall be refunded by the Nation they belong to.

一合衆國人民上岸俱要任從其遊行各處毋得遣差

Whenever persons from Ships of the United States come ashore in Lew Chew, they shall be at liberty to ramble where they please without hindrance

合衆國全權欽差大臣兼水師提督被理以洋書漢書立字
琉球國中山府 總理大臣尚宏勲 布政大夫馬良才 應遵執據
紀年一千八百五十四年七月十一日
咸豐四年六月十七日在那霸公館立

Signed in the English and Chinese languages by Commodore Matthew C. Perry, Commander in Chief of the U.S. Naval Forces, in the East India China and Japan Seas, and Special Envoy to Japan, for the United States; and by Sho Fu-fing, Superintendent of Affairs (Tsu-li-Kwan) in Lew Chew, and Ba Rio-si, Treasurer of Lew Chew at Shui, for the Government of Lew Chew; and Copies exchanged, this 11th day of July 1854, or the reign Hien-fung, 4th Year, 6th moon, 17th day, at the Town hall of Napa.

M. C. Perry

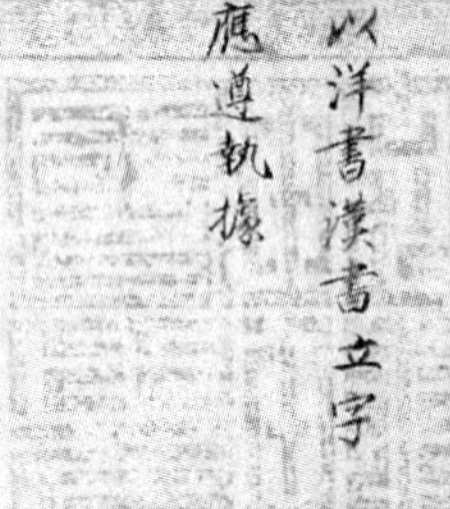

採望海外倘有外國船將入那霸港須以好小舟出於沙灘之外迎引其船入港使知安穩之處而泊船該船主應以洋銀五員而謝引水之人倘或出港亦要引出沙灘外亦謝洋銀五員

appearing off the Island, and if one is seen coming towards Napa, they shall go out in good boats beyond the reefs to conduct her in to a secure anchorage, for which service the Captain shall pay the Pilot Five dollars, and the same for going out of the harbor beyond the reefs.

一此後有船到琉球港內須要地方官供給薪水薪每壹千觔價錢叁仟陸伯文水每一千觔工價六百文凡以中大之玭杷桶六個即裁水千觔

Whenever Ships anchor at Napa, the Officers shall furnish them with Wood at the rate of [illegible] per thousand catties; and with Water, at the rate of 600 Copper Cash (43 cents) for one thousand catties, or Six barrels full, each containing 30 American Gallons.

（2）横滨

FIRST LANDING AT GORAHAMA

DELIVERY OF THE PRESIDENTS LETTER

COMMO: PERRY MEETING THE IMPERIAL COMMISSIONERS AT YOKUHAMA

CHIEF INTERPRETER MORYAMO YENOSKI
AND TAKO JURO INTERPRETER

Drawn by E. Brown, Jr. T. Sinclair's lith. Phila

TATSNOSKI, SECOND INTERPRETER.

WRESTLERS AT YOKUHAMA.

DELIVERING OF THE AMERICAN PRESENTS AT YOKUHAMA

DINNER GIVEN TO THE JAPANESE COMMISSIONERS ON BOARD U.S.S.F. POWHATAN.

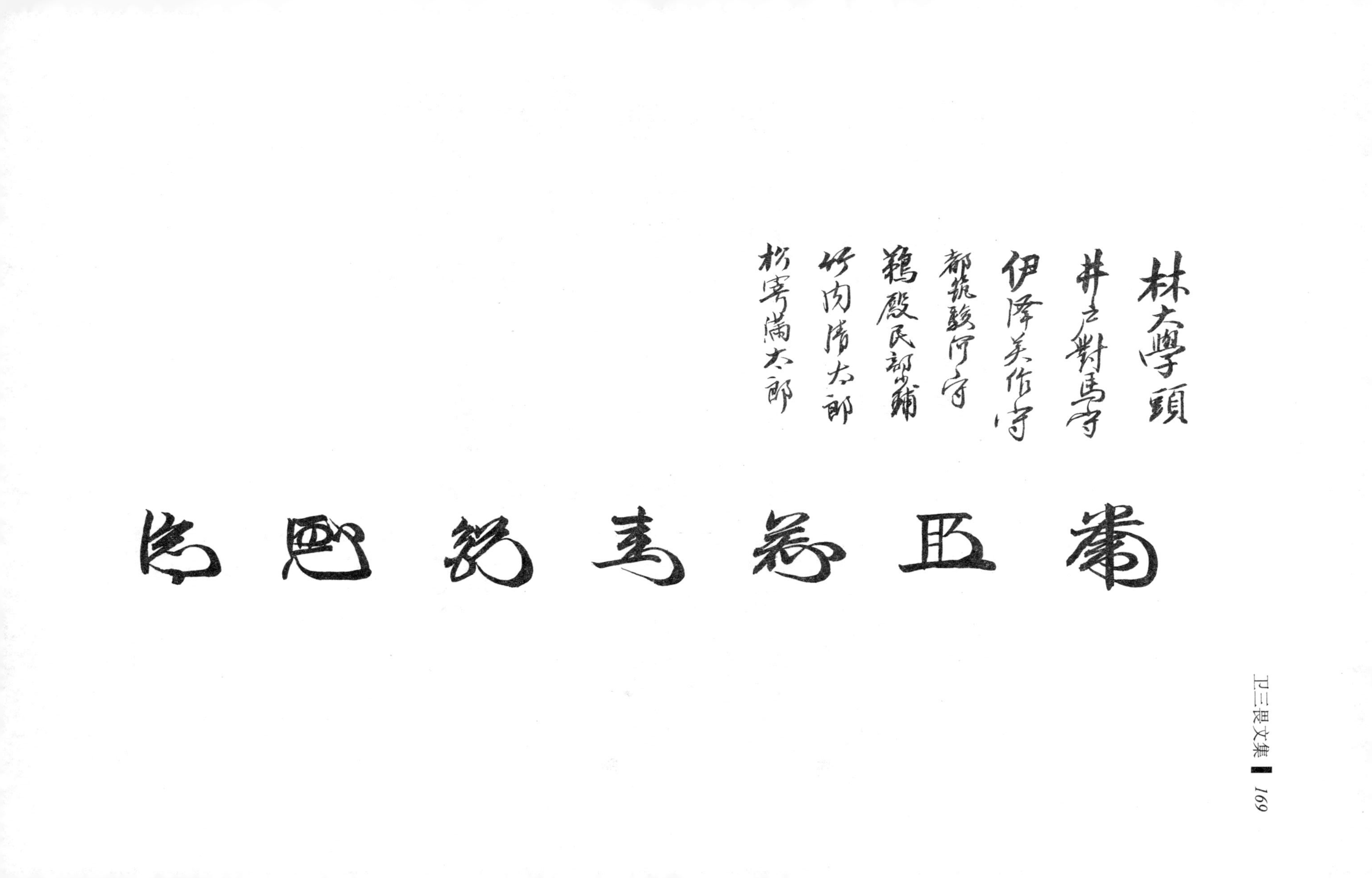

林大學頭

井戶對馬守

伊澤美作守

都筑駿河守

鵜殿民部少輔

竹內清太郎

松崎滿太郎

衛[illegible][illegible][illegible][illegible][illegible][illegible]

EMPEROR

HAYASHI, CHIEF COMMISSR

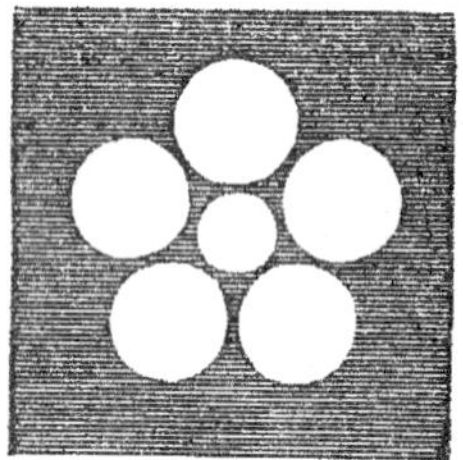

IDO, PRINCE OF TSUS-SIMA
SECOND COMMR

ISAWA, PRINCE OF MIMASAKA
THIRD COMMISSR

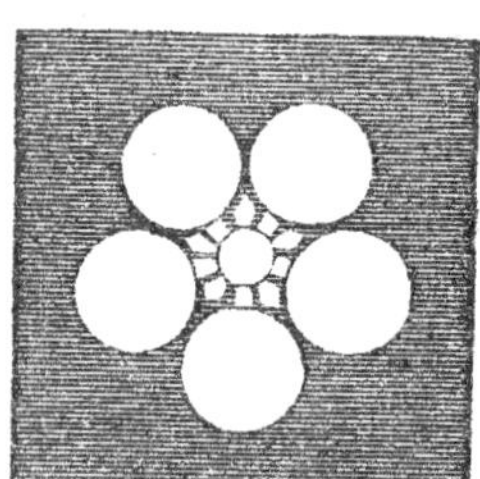

TSUDZUKI, PRINCE OF SURUGA
FOURTH COMMISSR

UDONO, MEMBER B'D REVENUE
FIFTH COMMISSIONER

TAKE-NO-UCHI SHEÏTARO,
SIXTH COMMISSR

MATSUSAKI MICHITARO,
SEVENTH COMMR

LEW — CHEW

茫々堪與之際、孰非天地帝
之赤子、惟宜以禮讓信義
相交、以兄弟同抱之情也、如夫
貪利以逐錐頭之末則凡人
所應羞而不言者也、且講
武練兵、則誅暴戡乱之要務、
宜講、日夜講究而不置耳、

Kenzhiro's note

Chinese caligraphy

Writer unknown (Presumably a Japanese)

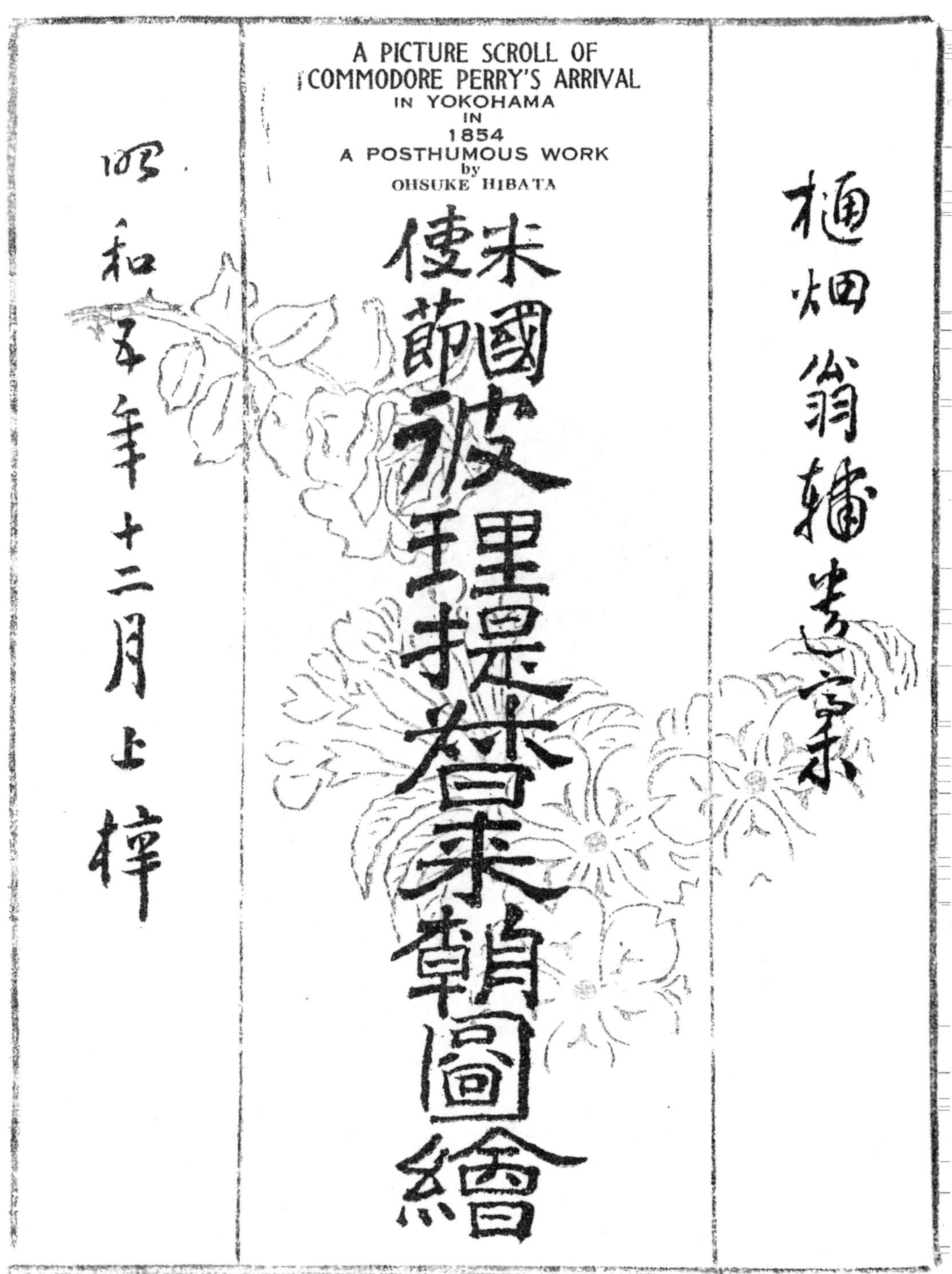
A PICTURE SCROLL OF
COMMODORE PERRY'S ARRIVAL
IN YOKOHAMA
IN
1854
A POSTHUMOUS WORK
by
OHSUKE HIBATA
米國使節彼理提督來朝圖繪
樋畑翁輔遺稿
昭和年十二月上梓

嚴考壽像題詞

嚴考諱清房通稱翁輔彌立志以文化十年五月十日生於江戶深川世仕松代藩考亦歷仕大暎感應文聽三公賞曾學猿樂大鼓于葛野九郎兵衛極其奥大先年井直弼公聞之召為師厚賜呂五人口少時學畫歌川國芳号寫樂齋又好能歌藝雜屋三團風集永六年外舶之來于浦賀世海防尤嚴矣考奉藩命闌軍樂及皷術于江川坦菴元治元年致仕傳闌於兒爾來客思風月遊於信越間以俳歌與謠曲自樂焉執弟子禮者百五十人矣明治三年十二月朔已病發于松代寓居齡五十有八矣臨終泰然詠辭世命兒畫像兒俯泣援筆固愚劣耳今茲二十七年祭祀謹改寫焉旹明治廿九年十二月一日也

雪湖樋畑正圖

Ohsuke Hibata.

緒言

(一) 此の彼理(ペルリ)來朝繪卷稿本は安政二年二月即ち西紀千八百五十四年三月八日(日本二月十日)米國水師提督(ペルリはカピテンでアドミラルではない、代將官こ譯すべきだが暫く慣稱による)彼理が使節こして横濱に上陸したる時の光景を實寫したものに係り、其の筆者は先考樋畑翁輔が高川文筌こ共に當時横濱御警衛に當られた所の松代藩主眞田幸教公の内命によりて墨斗の筆によりて寫生せしものである。

(二) 當時應接塲内に於て其の光景を寫生する如きは取締上容易に成し得べきものではなかつた然るに文筌は松代藩の醫師にして畫は文晁に學んだ所の餘技、先考は同藩の能役者にして歌川國芳に學んだ是亦餘技であつた、そして當時調役助こして警衛中に出役してゐた。そして文筌は浦賀奉行伊澤政義の醫師に先考は其の藥籠持に變裝して其構内にあり、應接掛林大學頭了解の下にあつたが故に其のスケッチをするに何等支障を生じなかつたこいふ事である。而して世上流布する所の本件の繪畫は多く此の圖に基きしものあるを認む、錦繪其他の杜撰にして其の信を置き難き所以のものは外邊より窺ふ所の想像から着圖せしものに過ぎぬ。

(三) 此の畫稿は安政三年江戸深川小松町の自宅に於て海嘯の爲めに家屋倒潰し浸水の厄に遇ひしを蒐集して保存せしもの、隨つて幾分の散逸せしものなきを保せず。而して先考の描きし畫卷は幕府の紅葉山文庫を始めこして諸侯の需に應じて描きしもの多きよしを聞けご今は眞田伯爵家松代の寶庫中に其一部を存するのみにして他にあるを聞かず。

(四) 此の畫稿は畏くも明治四十五年五月　大正天皇が皇太子にましますこき遞信省に行啓あらせられ、時の遞信大臣林董伯の御説明により親しく台覽に入りたるの光榮を有す。其他通俗教育映畫、桑港博覽會出品畫の史料として屢々文部省より又維新史料編纂係、帝國大學史料編纂係、横濱開港記念展覧會等幾多の公開場に出品或は他の著書にも引用せしものありき。

（五）書稿中の解說は專ら彼理日本遠征記、横濱開港五十年史及同七十年記念横濱史料展覧會出品物の解說等を參考して不肖自ら記述せしものなり。

（六）劈頭に掲げたる文筌の『横濱記事』の文稿は先考の書稿と離るべからざる當時のよき文獻であるが、それが偶然にも益友石井研堂氏の所有であつた事である。氏は先考の書稿に對して此の文稿を割愛して余に贈られたのは麗はしき友情のあらはれてある。玆に深厚感謝の意を表す。

（七）此の書稿は米使來朝に關する根本史料の一たるべく信ずるが故に他日の參考に資せんとし是を剞劂に縮刷して縁りある諸彥に贈呈せんと企圖した所以である。

昭和五年十二月一日

先考長逝の忌辰にあたりて

男　樋畑雪湖誌

CONTENTS

目次

The "Manuscripts of Yokohama Notes" by Bunsen Takagawa in the beginning of this book is an inseparable piece of literature as regards my father's Picture Scroll on these subjects. This short, but invaluable piece of literature was once in the possession of a very dear friend of mine, Mr. Kendo Ishii. On this occasion I wish to express my hearty thanks to Mr. Ishii for so kindly giving me the Bunsen literature for the purpose of enabling me to complete my father's Picture Scroll.

In venturing to now publish this Scroll in book form and to present it to any parties interested in it, it is hoped that it will be treated as one of the basic historical materials to Commodore Perry's arrival in Yokohama in 1854.

Sekko Hibata.

December 1st, Fifth Year of Showa:

The Anniversary of my Father's Death.

physician in the Uraga magistracy, and my father disguised himself as Bunsen's medicine bearer, and it is said that they were thus able to make sketches of everything about the Treaty Hall without difficulty under a clear and friendly understanding with Hayashi Daigaku no Kami, the chief of the Japanese Commissioners.

All pictures in circulation throughout the country are, with rare exceptions, derived from the present work. There are, however, a great many nishikiye painted only from the artists' imaginations.

There is ample cause for fear that some of these pictures have lost owing to their having been injured in a great tidal wave which occurred in the third year of Ansei, in which my father's residence was completely swept away. It has come to my ears that there exist many picture scrolls of my late father's drawn in compliance with the request of the Shogun Momijiyama's librarian and of many other lords, as well as Count Sanada, former Lord of Matsushiro, in whose treasure house some of these scroll's are still kept.

The present scroll has had the honour of being inspected by the late Emperor Taisho when Crown Prince, the same being explained by Count Hayashi, Minister of Communications. In addition to this, it has been exhibited, or referred to in various exhibitions or publications, such as the Jubilee Exhibition of the opening of the port of Yokohama, the Panama Pacific Exhibition at San Francisco, or in popular educational films, etc., all at the request of the Department of Education, the Bureau of Historical Relics of the Restoration period, and of the official historians of the Imperial University at Tokyo.

The explanations of the pictures were written by myself mainly according to the "Narrative of the Expedition of an American Squadron to the China Seas and Japan under the Command of Commondore M. C. Perry, U. S. Navy, by order of the Government of the United States," "Fifty Years' History of the opening of the port of Yokohama," and "Explanatory Notes on the Exhibits of the Historical Relics Exhibition of the opening of Yokohama."

A PICTURE SCROLL
OF
COMMODORE PERRY'S ARRIVAL
IN
YOKOHAMA
IN
1854

A POSTHUMOUS WORK

by

OHSUKE HIBATA

PREFACE

The present work, "A Picture Scroll of Commodore Perry's Arrival in Yokohama" in February of the second year of Ansei (March 8th, 1854), is a collection of actual sketches made by my father, the late Mr. Ohsuke Hibata, and the late Bunsen Takagawa, at the official command of the Lord of Matsushiro, Yukinori Sanada, who was a member of one of the clans guarding the place where the negotiations were carried out, in connection with the Clan of Ogasawara.

It was, indeed, an exceedingly difficult task to make sketches of the various scenes, owing to the strict police vigilence around and inside the Treaty Hall at the time. Fortunately, however, Bunsen, a physician to the Lord of Matsushiro, had taken lessons in painting under Buncho Tani, while my father, a "No" performer (a kind of Japanese classical drama) in the employ of Lord Sanada, was also skilled in ukiyoye painting, having received instruction in the art from Kuniyoshi Utagawa, and he also was one of those guarding the Treaty House in Sanada's force. In order to carry out Lord Sanada's order, Bunsen obtained the position of Lord M. Yanagisawa's

○浦賀鎮臺伊澤君は浦賀奉行伊澤美作守政義、
○吾公感應は眞田信濃守幸貫にして樂翁公の二男幸教の祖父なり
○應接掛は儒者林大學頭煒
○町奉行井戸對馬守學弘
○目付鵜殿民部少輔長鋭
○儒者松崎滿太郎の四人なり
二月己卯の會見第六圖七圖を參照を要す

横濱紀事

YOKOHAMA NOTES

by Bunsen Takagawa

高川文筌 文稿 家藏

嘉永七年歳在甲寅春正月某日亞美利賀使節某来乞國書之報蓋去歳夏呈書乞通商且假地也於是碇泊於我横濱洋火船三隻軍艦五隻幕府議既定有司與彼應接吾公奉命警衛之衆士往陣於横濱浦賀鎮臺伊沢君幹理衷事君與吾公感應有莅故假文貝匿負文是以得與亞客接察其情態矣新造旅館別有内席三方皆設床席之以紅氈前有机覆之以花紋之紅綃外席亦同之而定上下之別其上者在於紫幔内其下者各有差焉大學頭林君對馬守井戸君並預其事民部少輔鵜殿君爲監察松崎君某佐林君而伊沢君獨管内外焉二月己卯五君及官吏會於横濱以待亞客既而海面浮小艇都廿有八隻運其械也恰如天魚游水中一時皆着岸各揚一小旗一艇全白者即使節某所乘也紅羽冠者先上陸率銃隊數百直接劔指揮而列之於場左鼓吹者十有五人化其背是水軍也次鳥[illegible]冠者上陸同指揮銃隊而列之於右鼓吹者十有六人又化其背是陸軍也水陸兩隊相對而後隊長各擲之時鼓吹勃然起其節甚鄙其曲甚俚以錣

○第八圖饗宴の光景參照
寫眞像第一圖參照
○廣東人羅林は第九圖中の清國人參照

使節上陸也次黒装金飾之一隊先揚五曜紋之小旗中行而來就中一人容貌優偉正面不顧者使節提督彼理也從者五人躰殊長大肉色黧煤是為銃卒步々如有節而入館内焉彼理以下凡三十有六人矣堂之上邊我五君立而迎之更人列下邊相对揖之譯官森山某通辞彼我既而五君南面倚床彼亦北面着床先饗以茶菓及煙五君入而後延彼理以下五人於内席一則副使某一則彼理之嗣子一則通蘭語者一則通國語者也少焉我五君又出對群客此時張笠章紫幔以隔内外幕即伊沢君家物也雖官吏管其事者不敢許入外席茶菓已終而後更勸酒肴彼曰此酒不能飲乞賜餅釀蓋懼其猛烈也乃飲以養老美酒各適口欣然彼皆向杯盤先把刀匙喰食一人有把箸喰食者皆争倣之是亦足見彼好新奇矣惟恨雖珍羞尽其美不適彼嗜千菜萬魚殆如塵芥矣文時在床傍採筆摸圖画彼作悟之皆來乞寫己之肖像為寫與數枚皆喜其肖而藏之於胸中握文之手以如謝之者席末有廣東羅森字向喬者頗解画文以解試問曰儞何故在此船曰避朱氏之乱顧彼或有罪科潜逃寄身於此船者欤蓋

耕云逵臺粟

詰之遂言他聞前年夏齋圖層時作漢文者出於彼之手云今日上陸凡四
百四十六人在其小艇者凡二百人雖銃隊之外皆腰間帶短銃乃一箇六發者
也然所攜之長短銃皆實彈藥知是備其變者援目睹肉席事稍整猶
期後會而無能皆來艇去後數會事漸整彼所欲和親之約成乃水薪石炭
等之物其授受之處豆之下田比與之管館定為碇泊之處其他禁之二月戊
戌彼理欲饗我五君迎於火船及軍艦文亦從焉此日東北風烈波浪頗急故
以漁船之大者侵巨浪而行舟師等厲精力勢尤強俱言對妾奴莫見笑其
拙忽近彼舶腥之氣穿鼻或有惡心欲嘔者奴然濤激鐵壁我舟不敢近彼
忽投一條索依而得近我衆皆屬心跳身以攀船梯殆免躋只然我五君特
在於船頭彼先令銃卒調煉且為接戰船防之手段各揮劍鎗臨艦而突
空乃是禦欲上船者也或以龍吐水澆檣頭乃鎮撲火者也其上索梯也恰
如猿走藤蘿次降曲梯一段即是演礟場也置鉄礟各十口當船之頭尾各置
一口殊長大隊長曰附器而一聲指揮之則百餘之銃卒雷同以各列於礟傍恰
如一人所為作應声一發起於左邊而連之及於右邊一声未竭又一声二十之

所云條滌誤

所云輟輟誤

吐烟捲没船形人或雖暫耳聾猶不及江山霹靂震動也當此時雖悪心者
皆蕩滌胸中鬱氣乍下降壯心快然而船少不動搖彼言祝我五君來臨也
且此船軍艦中最極佳麗名者也彼理先下而乘於白艇尊我五君々々
即與彼同艇此時扈從之人為以恐有変然五君泰然不為意我舟続而到
於鮑舟火船而風波未平也延五君於其室先進茶菓而後有酒肉之饗宴
余頃日屢與彼會於横濱故知面者多乍迎握余手接一語然彼我共解
半言耳且知文 画手引文 於蒸氣器根元幽暗之處指其功極處以要写之
文不能曉其理而不能下筆肴收筆以謝之次至於銅壁之処中有小道左右
各如画方二間前後共有三口以燒石炭艖頭之車輪各分其根脚而有中道
可連行若欲左回則輟左輪而任右輪之力左右惟如意也時車輪乍有声船
進百歩許又退百歩而止是総出於一人之手矣知今朝頻揚烟者即欲
示此進退以誇其巧也此間之製造都以銅鉄或作碧緑或有金銀之光耀
其洪大者愈大其精密者愈密目不可窮口不可説四方上下皆以鉄板
雖半寸間不敢露木理此中火気塡満如炎晴疑是墮落於所謂地獄中

致。

放，漸至其尽處，上鉄梯凡三段，而出於明處，恍有風波声，身始寒矣。當船尾之一
方，擁幃幔以設杯盤之席，中置大机各二，以使居曲机外，悉置床几，而與雞
倚先領杯觴，各一磁盆，一刀匕一，具其肉魚豕牛及菜菓之類，畢々於几上，其
間処々置磁瓶，盛以桃花李，及橘花，是昨所乞於我者也。至牛豕，乃以一股肉全
雞，乃以其全肉，盛之於大磁盆，切領之於各盆，其欲尽則稍露筋骨，亦不忍
視而喰之也。至其〻酒，各種稍帶酸味而不可一。一種号葡萄者，味尤美且豫非
和蘭列〻酒之比，言是非尋常之物，極其〻精醸者，獨彼本不知美及豆豉之
味，故獨以海鹽調百味，其〻調也，先取肉以入一箇器，焼而蒸之，我衆陪賓傾觴未
敢下，〻刀匕於肉，彼諭曰是牛豕雞也，何為不下匕，然猶訝為何等之肉，各先試加
刀匕於雞之一股肉，切而喰之，味頗佳，故略及外肉，未尽，又取一片以加各盆，更勧
杯觴，彼我共〻醺然入佳興焉。時一人勃然一声，群声應和之，亦只不一音，始有一
節而和之者也，或仰而投冐，又取之各〻人亦為之，而喜色満顔，美訳者云此合
声以饗我衆也，我衆亦以和之，彼殊增喜色，幔外鼓吹者，自始連〻不歇
此時彼理之室中，殊極珍羞，有牛舌及菜菓之各品，五君亦不

嚼嗜各肉，且醉各酒，既而杯盤狼籍，彼忽命其部下，以奏弦歌。若
塗面以朱，染唇以（脂），以獸毛作髭鬚，各服花紋衣，共九人矣。連而倚床几，以四
或如阮咸物，或鼓笛鐃鈸之類，而和倡歌，其調略類清樂。或作金音，或作鈴唱
其急忽作斷曲，兩人相見有辭，知其滑稽俚語。或作異形之面，開口閉目而
吐舌，亦惟墨面朱口，兩人作抛其器，立而相對，以脚頭漫舞，或時翹一足飛走
其疾如亂蝶，而皆合節者也。彼理者，喜怒常不見色也。此時拍手大笑，頗極
歡樂矣。其曲其情何等之滑稽乎，未可察，只大噱欲解頤耳，不知至
此戲曲殆愚弄我者歟。相共提刀起以謝之，下移於我舟。時風落波靜，腥
氣始相忘，日暮還於金川之旅館矣。

〇甲寅春三月　〇松代　高川惟文識

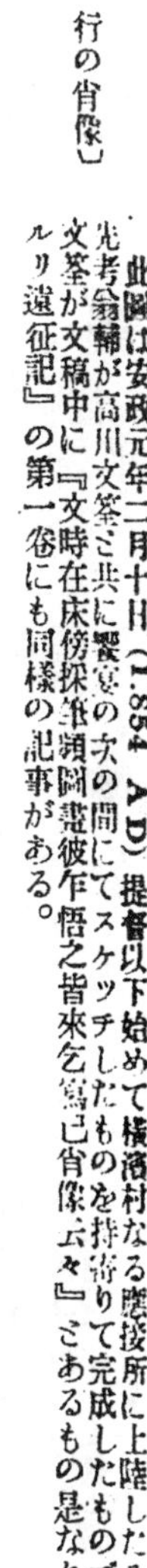
【第一圖】（使節一行の肖像）

此圖は安政元年二月十日（1.854 AD）提督以下始めて横濱村なる應接所に上陸したるとき先考翁輔が高川文筌と共に饗宴の次の間にてスケッチしたものを持歸りて完成したものである文筌が文稿中に『文時在床傍探筆頭圖畫彼乍悟之皆來乞寫己肖像云々』とあるもの是なり『ペルリ遠征記』の第一卷にも同様の記事がある。

Commander Adams.

Commodore M. C. Perry.

ヘルリ之子

Mr. Perry, the son of Commodore M. C. Perry.

Captain Abbott.

Mr. Williams, Japanese Interpreter. Mr, Portman, Duch Interpreter.

第二圖

一行中の士官より贈られた釦と銀貨

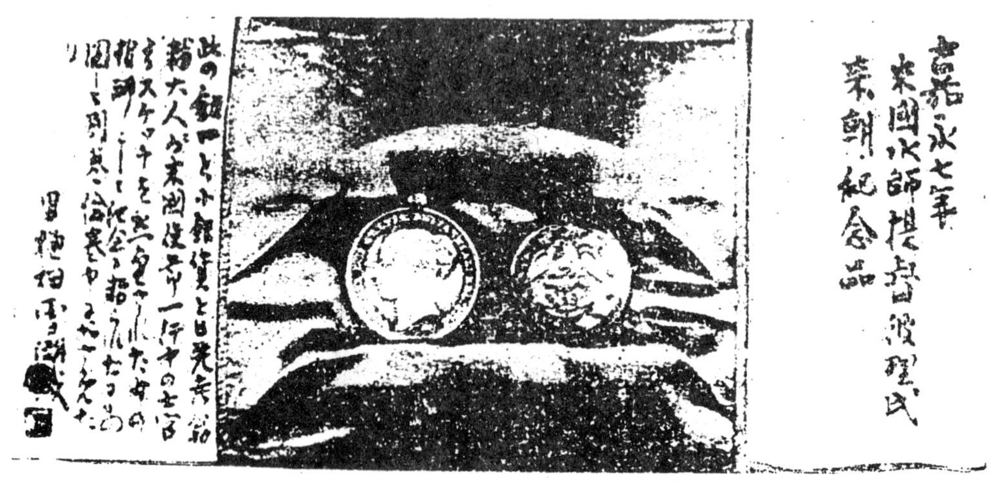

Silver Coin and Button presented to my father by an officer of U. S. Navy.

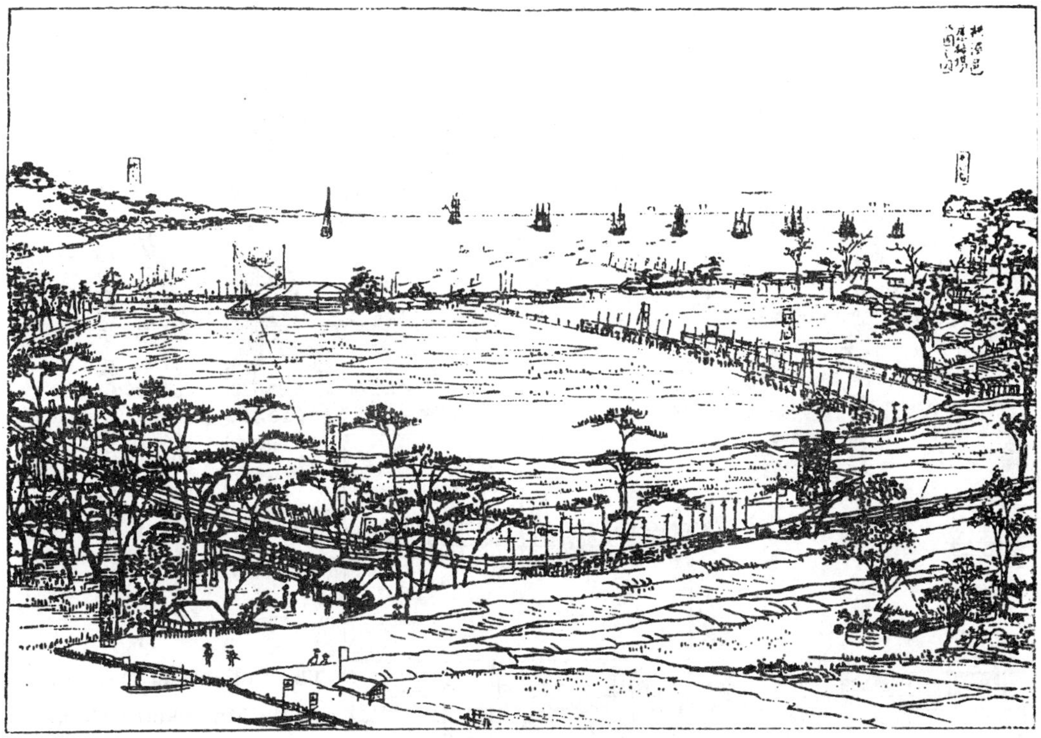

A Part of Yokohama where the Imperial Commissioners received Commodoer Perry, 1854.

【第三圖】

〔横濱村應接場警固の光景〕

嘉永六年浦賀に乘込んだ米艦七隻は始め小柴沖に碇泊したり翌安政元年二月朔日には八隻となりて次第に神奈川沖に近づき來つて錨を下した。それは圖中上方に見ゆる八隻の黑船がそれである。

中央の濱邊にある建物は字駒形といふ所に浦賀から移され二月二日、三日の間に急速に建造された談判の應接場である其位置は後の英領事館邊であるとの事。此の建物と前方民家の間に一線を描きあるのは米國から幕府に贈つた電信機實驗の爲めに架設した電線である、即ち應接所と洲干辨天前の民家吉右衛門宅の二ヶ所にして今の燈臺局邊であらう。而して此の時に使用した電信機二座は東京帝國大學に傳はり今は遞信博物館に陳列されてある。

應接場を中心に左右の警固幕張を描いてある、其の幕張の陣地左は小倉藩の固にして海岸から今の馬車道を辨天通角迄に。又右は松代藩の固にして海岸から薩摩町筋辨天通角迄を互に取圍んで警戒長さ々々怠りなかつたといふ事である。

左前にある『野毛渡場』とあるのは其時代の里路て今の櫻木町停車場附近辨天橋邊大岡川を渡つたのであらう。

桑海の變横濱の今昔を語つてゐるものである。

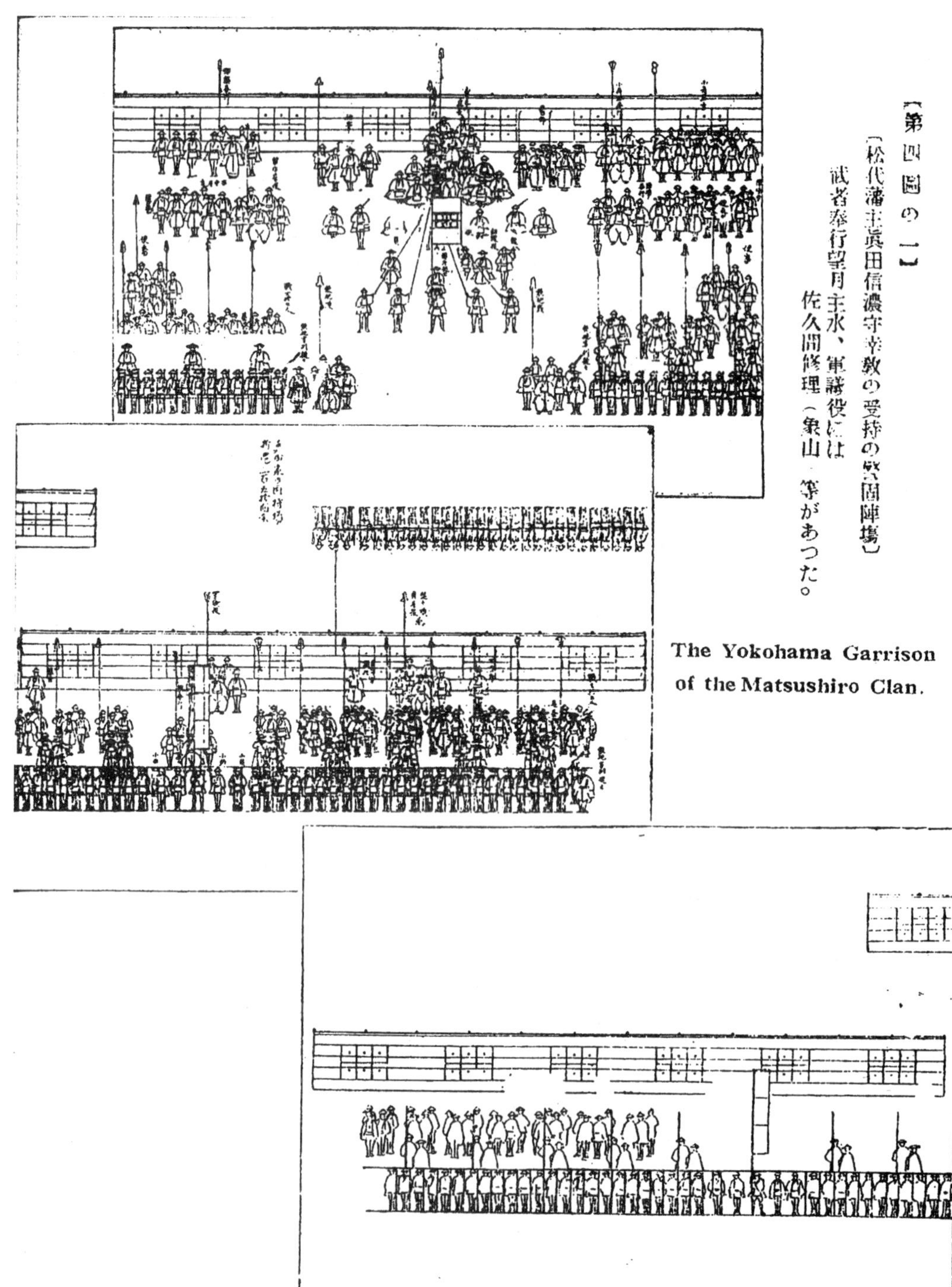

【第四圖の一】

〔松代藩主眞田信濃守幸敎の受持の警固陣場〕

武者奉行望月主水、軍議役には佐久間修理（象山）等があつた。

The Yokohama Garrison of the Matsushiro Clan.

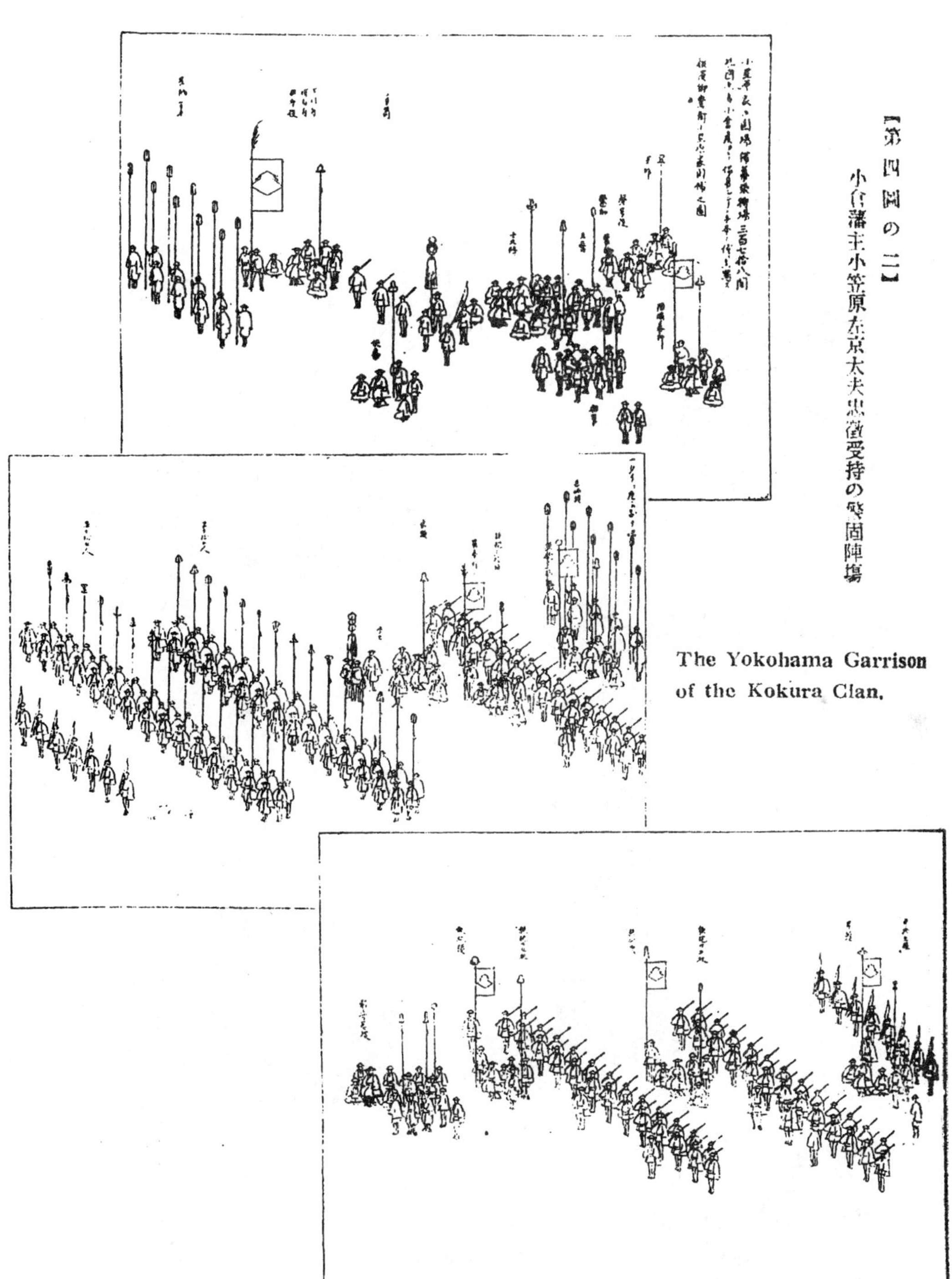

【第四図の二】

小倉藩主小笠原左京大夫忠徵受持の警固陣場

The Yokohama Garrison of the Kokura Clan.

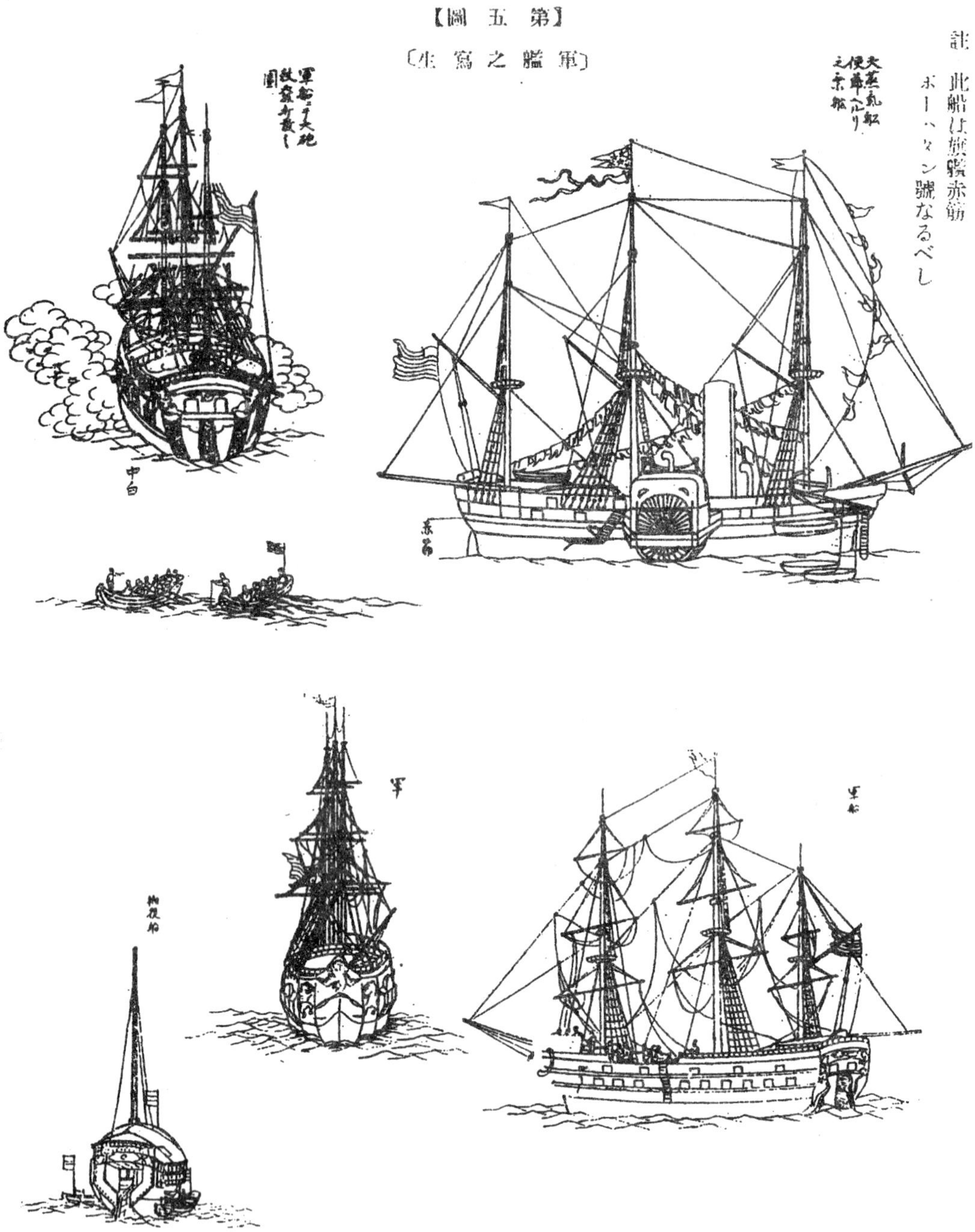

【第五圖】

〔軍艦之寫生〕

註 此船は旗艦赤筋
ポーハタン號なるべし

Sketches of U. S. Ships and a Japanese Government Junk.

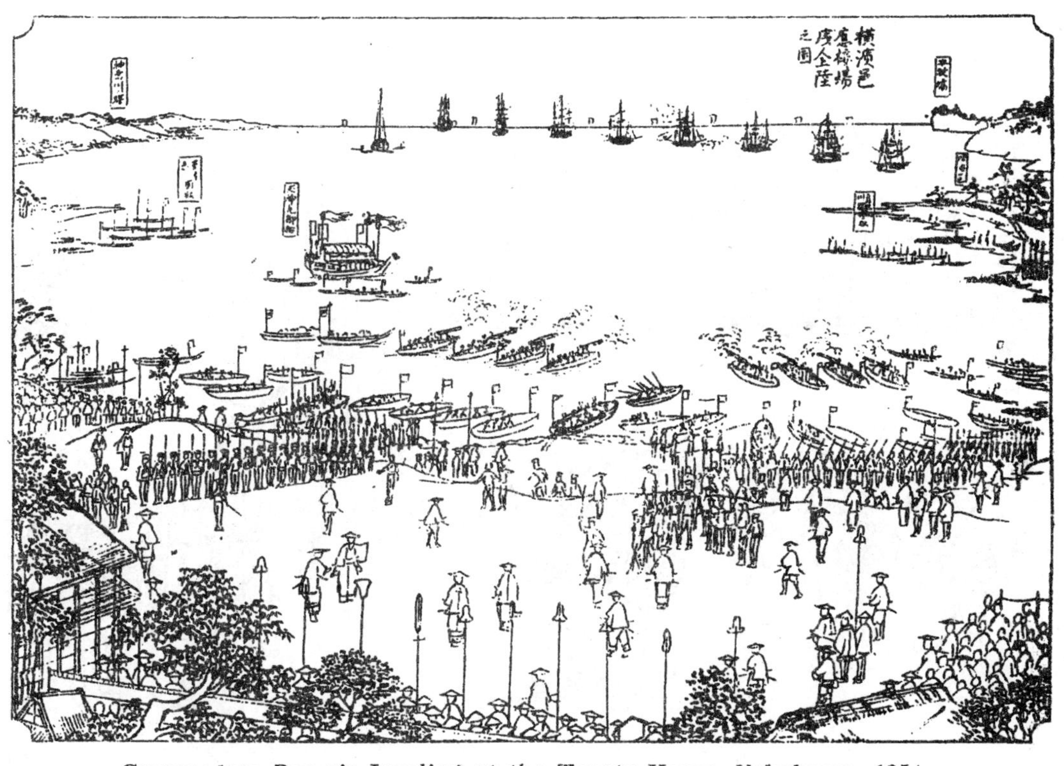

Commodore Perry's Landing at the Treaty House, Yokohama, 1854.

【第　六　圖】

〔ペルリ提督横濱村應接所へ上陸の光景〕

二月十日米艦八隻の乗込員中より總人員四百四十六人、短艇二十八隻に分乗して禮砲發射中に提督を護して上陸した所の光景である、左端にあるものが應接所の建物にして其左右には眞田小笠原兩藩の兵士が警固の任に當つてゐる。

灣上右方が本牧の鼻にして左方に見ゆるのが東海道神奈川の宿驛である。

幾旒かの吹流の船印を海風に飜し朱塗の船艦に紫地に葵紋を染拔きたる幔幕を張り廻したるは幕府の軍船天神丸なり其の左方にある小舟に小旗をたてたるは會津及忍藩の固船又右方横濱の出崎にある番船は彦根及川越藩の固船である沖の方八隻の米艦は左の順序であらう。右の方本牧方面より

一　レキシントン　帆　船
二　サスクハナ　汽　船
三、ポーハタン　仝
四　マセドニア　帆　船
五　ミシシツピー　汽　船
六　ヴアンダリヤ　帆　船
七　サラトガ　仝
八　サウザンプトン　仝

外に運送船サツプライ號壹隻

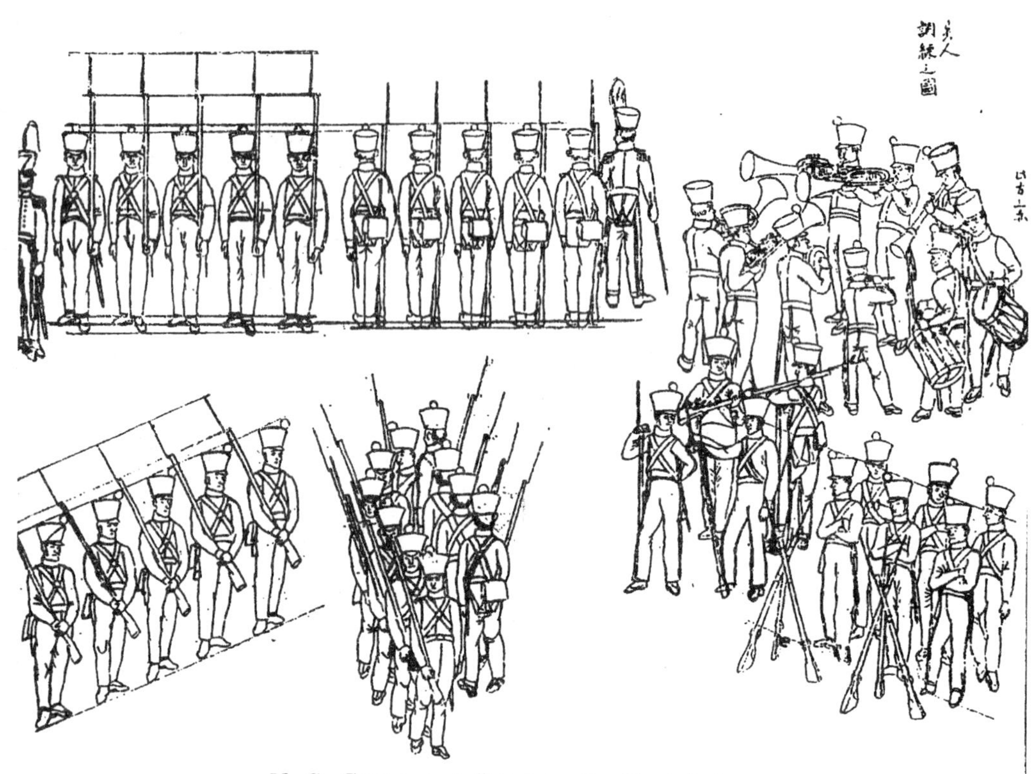

U. S. Crews and Band under Training.

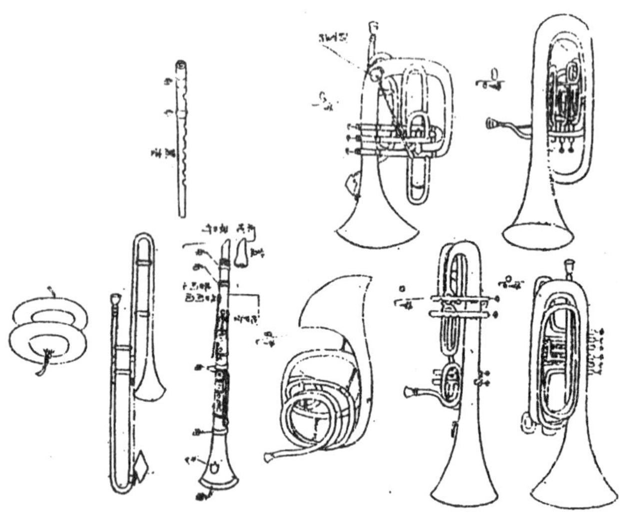

Their Musical Instrument.

【第七图】上陆兵の操練こ樂器の寫生

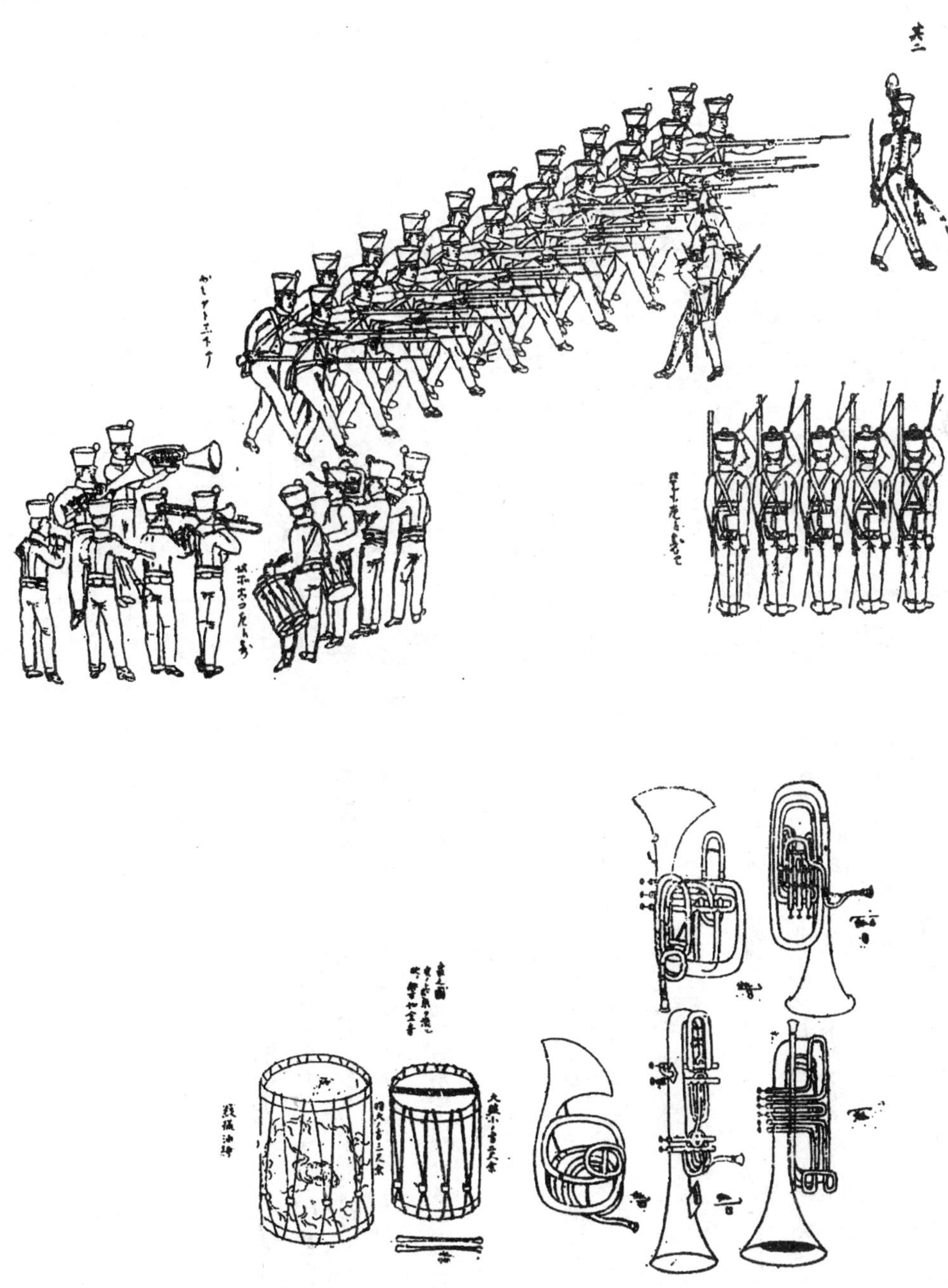

【第 八 圖】

〔横濱村應接場米使饗應の光景〕

二月十日ペルリ提督以下上陸應接所に入り應接掛林大學頭始め五人と外交談判が開かれたのであつたが終つて幕府よりの饗應があた時の光景である。此圖は高川文筌と先考翁輔が内命によりて宴席の次室に於て第一圖と共に描きしものに係れり、世間流布する所の本圖は多く文筌及先考の描きたるものを原圖とする如し、如何となれば此の宴席を瞥見するといふ事は充分の警戒を爲してあつたから餘人の猥りに入るを得なかつたのである、文筌の描きしものと大同小違であるが、後方の菓子皿をさしあげて、二人が品評し合ふ圖あるものは先考の原本から描きしものにはあらざる乎。

此圖は最初茶菓を供する光景なるべく。次に長熨斗、銚子盃から酒三獻、取肴、本膳、二ノ膳等純日本料理にして江戸日本橋浮世小路料亭百川の仕出であつたと傳えてゐる客席前列右より提督ペルリ、アボット、アダムス以下の面々なるべく、饗應掛は右より林大學頭煒（御儒者　井戸對

Commodore Perry and Suite being entertained at the Treaty House.

馬守覺弘（江戸町奉行）伊澤美作守政義（下田奉行）鵜殿民部少輔長鋭（大目付）一席離れて松崎滿太郎（御儒者）が羽織小袴にて腰をかけ何れも太刀持を後方に控へさせてゐる。

前後に張廻した紫の幔幕には伊澤の定紋なる三ツ笹の丸を附してある。

【第九圖】

米艦上陸者の風俗

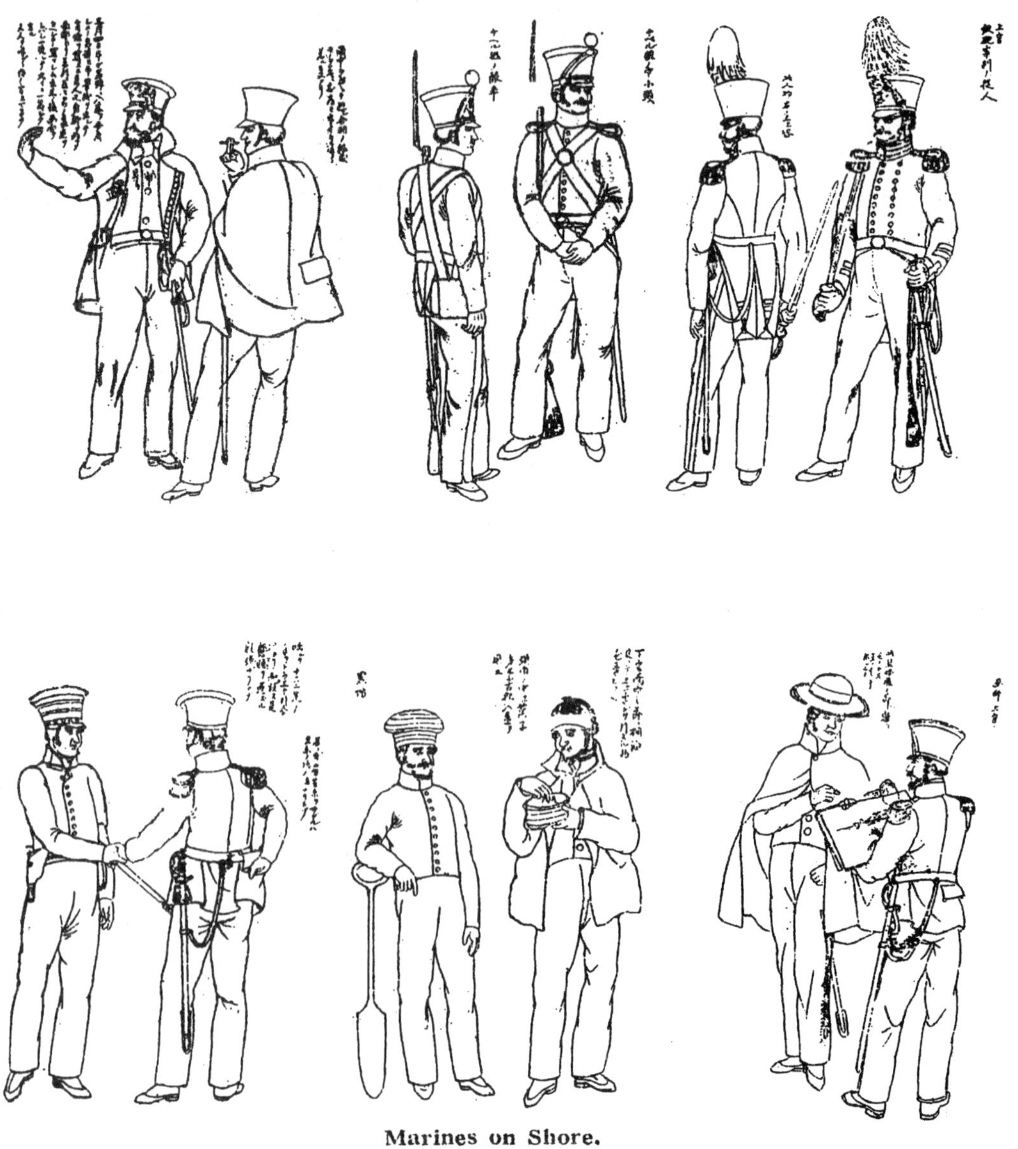

Marines on Shore.

（註）文案の記事第二頁中にある廣東人羅森なるべし。

（註）玆に大小貨幣の圖ありしものと思はるれど存せず剝落せしならん。

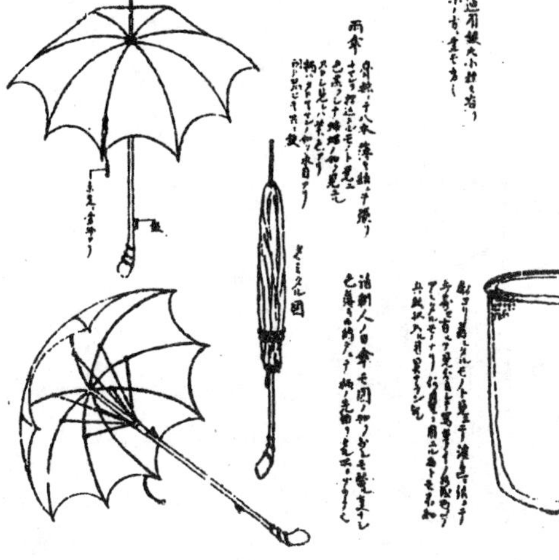

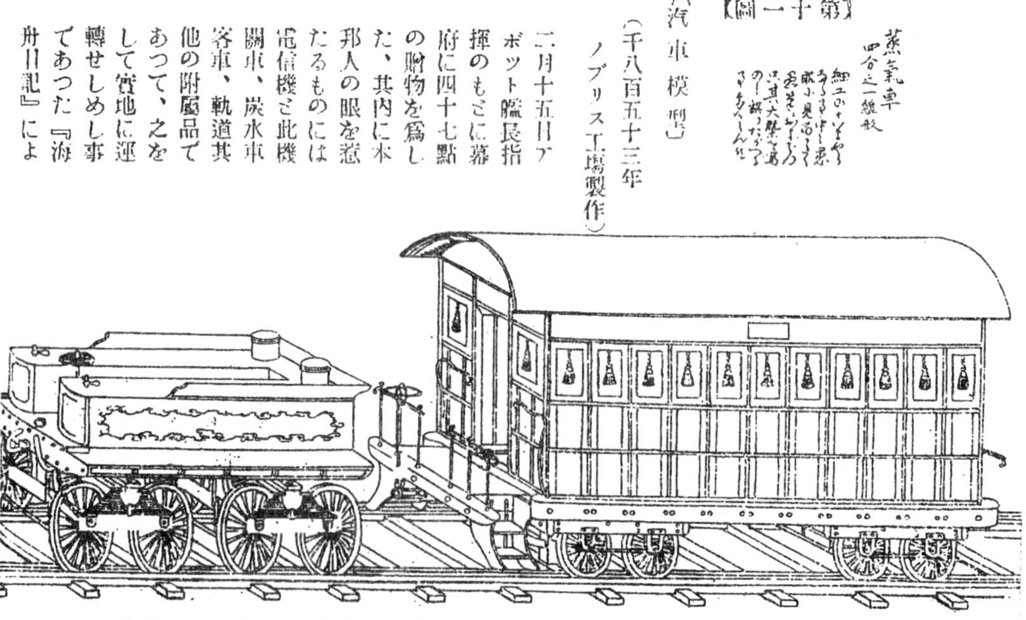

【第十一圖】
〔汽車模型〕
（千八百五十三年
ノブリス工場製作）
二月十五日アボット艦長指揮のもとに幕府に四十七點の附物を爲した、其内に本邦人の眼を惹たるものには電信機と此機關車、炭水車、客車、軌道其他の附屬品であつて、之をして實地に運轉せしめし事であつた『海舟日記』によ

A Locomotive and Cars, donated by the American Government.

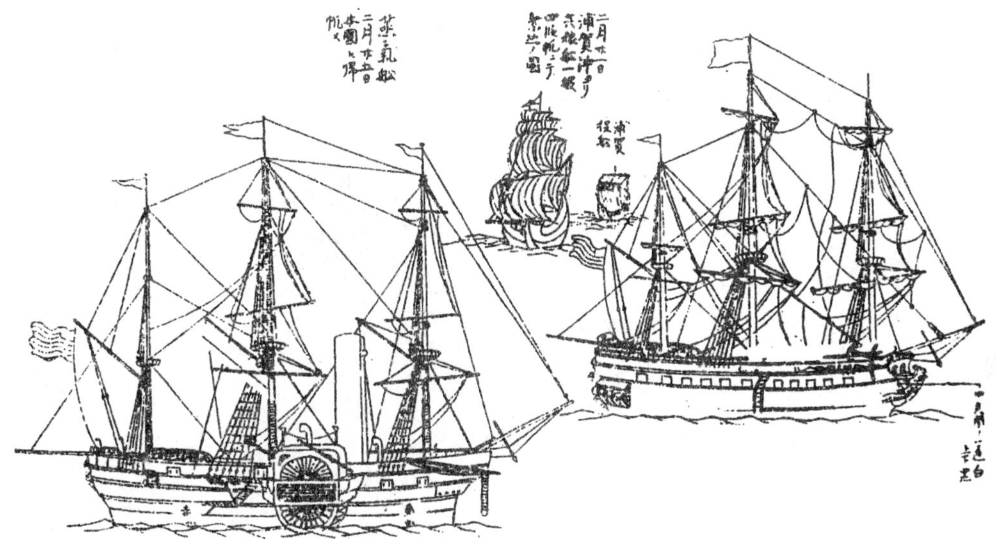

Commodore Perry's Squadron off Yokohama.

れば此の模型幕府の海軍所に於て焼失せりといふ惜むべし。

【第拾貳圖】【提督が日本委員招待の餘興舞踊】

Dancing on board the U. S. S. F. "Powhatan" in entertainment of the Japaneses Commissioners, 1854.

二月十九日提督は日本委員並に其の屬僚をポーハタン號の午餐に招待した、其の餘興として滑稽なる水兵の黑んぼ踊を見せた、是れ今いふ所のジャズバンドであつたのであらう。ペルリの『遠征記』によれば眞面目の林大學頭も破顏一笑した事や、日本人の大食の事や、委員松崎滿太郎が醉機嫌で提督の頸を抱しめて『日米同心』を繰返した事などが書いてある。

【第十三圖】（幕府米使への贈物運搬に力士を使用す）

Wrestler "Koyanagi"

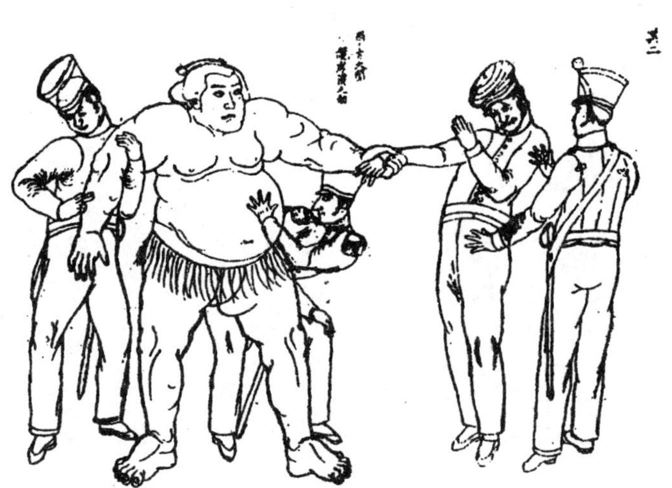

Wrestler "Kagamiyama"

二月廿六日、幕府より米使へ答禮として種々の贈物あり、其内船員一同へ米二百俵を遣すに方り江戸の力士東の大關小柳常吉、同西の大關鏡岩濱之助以下九十三人をして一人に二俵乃至は三俵を兩手にさゝへて之を運ばしめ、以て其の腕力を誇り、終て應接場の前庭に角力の技を演ぜしめたといふ。

ペルリの遠征記には其の肉體が動物の如く發達したには驚きしこと、及ペルリ提督は日本官憲が饗應の爲に催した所の此の殘忍な餘興を冷評し、其の自分のもたらした電信、鐵道諸機械に對照して其の文明を誇つてゐる。

The Funeral Service of a Crew of the American Squadron at Yokohama, 1854.

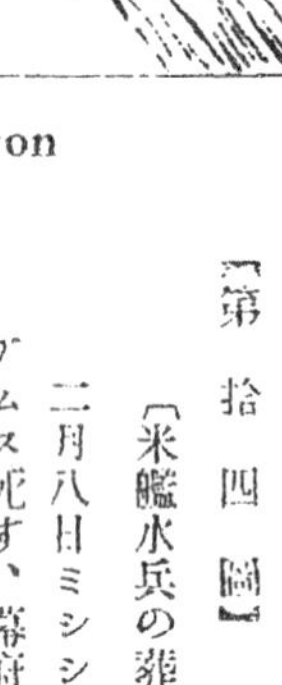

【第拾四圖】

〔米艦水兵の葬式と墓標〕

二月八日ミシシッピー乗組ロバート・ウィリアムス死す、幕府の承諾を得て同月十一日横濱村山下なる增德院境内に葬りたる時の葬儀行列と墓標との寫生である、後下田港附近柿崎村玉泉寺に改葬して今猶ほ存すといふ。

左方の寺は增德院にして警衛松代藩の宿營であつた。

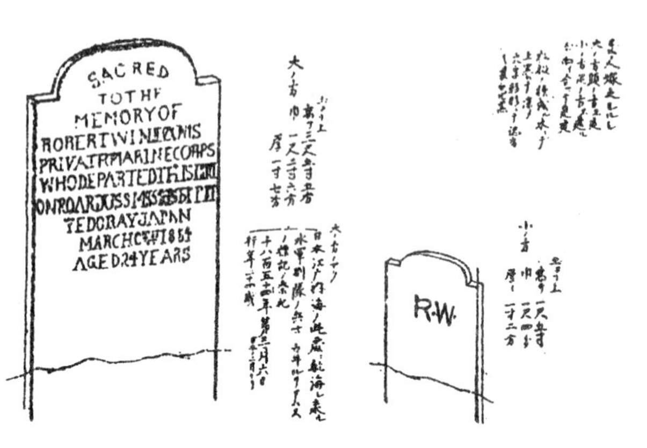

【正　　　誤】

◇英文緒言第一頁の最後の行
Lord M. Yanagisawa's は
Governor M. Izawa's の誤

◇『第十三圖』の
Wrestler "Kagamiyama" は
Wrestler "Kagamiiwa"の誤

◇和　　文
第八圖解說三行目『あ』の上『が』は衍

昭和六年二月十一日印　刷
昭和六年二月十八日發　行

『不許複製』

編　者　　樋畑雪湖
發行者　　吉田一郎
東京、目白、高田町三六〇〇
印刷者　　吉田一郎
東京、目白、高田町三六〇〇
印刷所　　日本郵券倶樂部印刷部
東京、目白、高田町三六〇〇

非賣品

July 14th

The squadron was full of bustle this morning, getting arms burnished, boats ready, steam up, men dressed, and making all the preparations necessary to go ashore, and be prepared for any alternative. About 7½ o'clk, the steamers were under weigh, and soon opened the beach around the point, and disclosed the preparation made to receive the letters from Pres. Fillmore. The officials, in their boats, were lying off the "Susquehanna" waiting to see the flag hoisted, and about the time our anchor was down, they were alongside. There were two boats carrying six officials dressed in full costume, who when seated on deck presented a most singularly grotesque & piebald appearance blended with a certain degree of richness from the gay colors they wore. The 2d officer was a conspicuous member of this party, he not having been aboard before since the first day; his dark face & sharp features contrasting with his yellow robe, and his black socks, hairy bare legs, and short trowsers, all showing out from the overalls of his uniform made him rather an attractive object. I cannot describe the dresses of these men, minutely, but the effect was not unpleasant, tho' in most of them no harmony of colors was aimed at in the uniforms. They all seemed to be in good spirits, and amused themselves looking at the officers in their uniforms, & other objects.—

By 10 o'clk. the boats had left the steamer, and under the lead of the natives were pretty much landed before 11 o'clk on the beach at 久里濱 Hori-hama, opposite the shed erected for our reception, & surrounded with striped curtains; Com. Perry left under a salute & found the escort ready when he landed to conduct him

83

July 14th

to the house prepared for his audience. There were 15 boats in all, containing about 300 people, say 112 marines, 40 musicians 40 officers, and a hundred or more sailors. Every one was armed with a ~~sword~~ sword, a pistol or a musket, & most of the fire-arms were loaded; I borrowed a coat & sword so as to appear like the rest, but my uniform would hardly bear inspection or classification. A jetty had been made of bundles of straw covered with sand, and facilitated the landing very greatly. The precaution of bringing down the two steamers to cover the place of meeting made it easy to land from them without exposure to the sun; the bay near shore was deep but full of seaweed growing in long leaves to near the surface, and doubtless full of marine productions.

The place appointed for receiving these letters was a hut set up on the beach, having two small ones behind it, the whole inclosed by white & blue striped curtains hanging from poles; a screen was in front, concealing the front of the room, and a large opening at each end of it, between that and the side curtains, which were prolonged along the beach on each ~~side~~ hand for nearly half a mile. The village was in the south of the cove, near the corner from whence the "Morrison" was fired at, a poor hamlet of 200 thatched huts, mostly concealed from our view by the curtains and the crowd. The hills rose behind, partly cultivated and looking exceedingly fresh and green, inviting us in vain to explore their slopes, for the ridiculous laws interfere to pre

July 14th.

vent our trespassing on them. Truly, laws which prevent such things must have been brought about by a hard & dear experience, for it is against nature thus to prohibit intercourse between man & man.

The Japanese had placed a row of armed boats near the ends of the curtains, and detachments of troops were stationed before the curtains in close array, standing to their arms, their pennons flying from the curtains, and gradually bending down to meet the boats at each end. Some of these troops were dressed in dirty white in a manner similar to the troops in Egypt, with full breeches & tight stockings; others resembled Chinese troops, and many were in a tightly-fitting habit. Horsemen were placed behind one or two curtains, who wore brass cuirasses and metallic helmets or something like it. Their horses were large animals, far beyond the Chinese beasts I have seen in size, and looking like another race than the little Lewchewan ponies. All these troops, (numbering about 5000 men as one of the Japanese told me,) maintained the utmost order, nor did the populace intrude beyond the guard. A few miserable field pieces stood in front, not over 4th or 5th cr I should think; many files had muskets with bayonets, others had spears, and most I could not see. Crowds of women were noticed by some near the markee, but I suspect they were not numerous. Altogether, the Japanese had taken great pains to receive us in style, while each side had provided against

85

July 14th.

surprise from the other, and prepared against every contingency.

As soon as Comre Perry landed, all fell into procession; Capt. Buchanan, who was the first man ashore, had arranged all in their places, so that no hindrance took place. The marines headed by Major Zeilen led off, he going ahead with a drawn sword; then half of the sailors, with one band playing between the two parties. Two tall blacks heavily armed, supported as tall a standard bearer, carrying a Commodore's pennant, went next before two boys carrying the President's letter & the Full Powers in their boxes covered with red baize. The Commodore, supported by Capt. Adams & Lt. Contee, each wearing chapeaux, then advanced; the interpreters & secretary came next, succeeded by Capt. Buchanan & the gay-appearing file of officers, whose epaulettes, buttons &c. shone brightly in the sun. A file of sailors & the band, with marines under Captain Slack, finished this remarkable escort. The escort of Von Resanoff at Nagasaki of seven men was denied a landing until they had been stripped of almost everything belonging to a guard of honor; here, 50 years after, a strongly armed escort of 300 Americans does honor to their President's letter at the other end of the empire, the Japanese being anxious only to know the size and arrangement of what they felt themselves powerless to resist. There were fully a thousand charges of ball in the escort,

July 14th.

besides the contents of the cartridge-boxes. Any treachery on their part would have met a serious revenge.
On reaching the front of the markee, the two envoys were seen seated on camp-stools, on the left side of a room, 20 ft. square or so, matted & covered with red felt; four camp stools were ranged on the right side, and a red lackered box between them. The chief envoy, 戸田伊豆守 Toda, Idzu no kami, (Toda, prince of Idzu) and his coadjutor, 井戸石見守 Ido, Iwami no kami (Ido, prince of Iwami) rose as the Commodore entered, & the two parties made ~~a~~ slight bows to each other. The boys laid the boxes on the floor, & the two blacks came in to open them. They were taken out and opened upon the lackered box, and the packet containing the copies and translations presented by Mr Contee. Tatsnoske and Yezaimon were both on the floor, and the former commenced the interview by asking if the letters were ready to be delivered. When he made known the reply, he put his head nearly to the floor in speaking to Yezaimon, who on his knees informed the envoy in a whisper. The receipt for them in Dutch & Japanese was then delivered to Mr Portman; and the originals themselves opened out in the boxes as they lay. Soon after, Com. Perry said that in two or three days he intended to leave for Lewchew & ~~Japan~~ China; and would take any letters, &c., for the envoys. This produced no acknowledgement on their part; and he then added that there was a revolution in China

87

July 14th

by insurgents, who had taken Nanking & Amoy, and wished to introduce a new religion. "It will be better not to talk about revolutions at this time," was the significant reply; and proper one too, for I thought it very mal-apropos to bring in such a topic. Yet one might regard it with interest as ominous of the ~~ecstasy of~~ important changes which might now be coming on the Japanese, & of which this interview was a good commencement.

Conversation being thus stopped, & no signs of any refreshment appearing, there was nothing else to do than to go. The contrast between its interlocutors was very striking. In the front was a group of foreign officers and behind them the picturesque-looking shaven-pated Japanese in relief against the checked screen; on the left a row of full-dressed officers, with swords, epaulettes &c. all in full lustre; on the right the two envoys and a secretary, with two more plainly dressed men on their knees between the two rows. To describe the robes of these two envoys is difficult. The upper mantilla was a slate col'd brocade kind of silk, made stiff at the shoulders so as to stick out squarely; the girdle a brown color, & the overall trowsers of purplish silk; the swords were not very rich-looking. The coat of arms was conspicuous on the sleeves, & some of the under garments appearing, gave a peculiarly harlequin-like look to his dress, to which the other envoy was accordant. They were immovable & never stirred or hardly spoke during the whole

July 14th

interview; and one who tarried a little as we came out, said that they relaxed in their stiffness as soon as we had gone, apparently glad that all was over. I got the impression that the two high men had pursed themselves up to an attitude, and had taken on this demure look as part of it, but others looked on it as a subdued manner, as if afraid. The reëmbarkation took place gradually, no one being in much of a hurry, & I began to talk to the people, and invited two of them on board to see the steamer & a revolver. One man wished to know if the women in America were white; another, how he could learn strategy, to wh I replied, "only by your going abroad or letting us come here." I asked him why there was no music, to which he answered that it was very poor. Considerable curiosity was manifested in comparing swords, & some exchanges were proposed; altogether this part of the interview was far the pleasantest to both parties, and I suspect the Japanese were sorry to see the show end so soon. Many picked up shells & pebbles to remember the spot, & by 1 o'clk, every body was back to his place.

Two boats full of people came alongside soon after, and stayed on board while we steamed back to Uraga. Yezaimon especially, took much interest in seeing the working of such stupendous machinery, and inquiring into the manner of turning the wheels. All was made as plain as we could explain it, tho' I fear the ideas were very crudely expressed, for I did not know their language well enough, & Portman seemed not to know the machine well enough.

89

浦賀與力應接掛
中島三郎助

佐倉桐太郎

Sasakura Töötaro

Toriki Ööshets' gakari
Card of N. Saboroske

Signature of a military officer at Uraga.

Copy of seal of Prince of Iwami, Ido.

Copy of seal or Signature of prince of Idzu, Toda.

Their sec'y was 辻茂右衛門 Tsuzhimo Uyemon.

One of our visitors was the military commander of Uraga, an open faced pleasant man, who wished to learn something of tactics, and the construction of revolvers. One of the pistols was fired off by Capt. Buchanan to gratify him & Saboroske, and they had many measurements to take of the cannon on deck; the latter greatly [illegible]used us by going thro' the manual with a gun he took off [illegible] stand, his face pursed up as if he was a valiant hero. This [illegible]an is altogether the most froward, disagreeable officer we have

July 14th

had on board, and shows badly among the generally polite men we have hitherto had, prying round into everything and turning over all he saw. At our request the party remained on board while we steamed up to Uraga, and then bid us good-bye, having made themselves conspicuous in every part of the ship by their particolored dresses. Some refreshments were given them in the cabin, and they went off in good humor.
The receipt given by the two envoys was to this purport: "According to Japanese law it is illegal for any paper to be received from foreign countries except at Nagasaki, but as the Commodore has taken much trouble to bring the letter of the President here, it is notwithstanding received. No conversation can be allowed, and as soon as the documents and the copy are handed over, you will leave." The Japanese original is written on very thick paper, made from the mulberry (Broussonetia); the last sentence of it intimated they were to make sail immediately.
The four ships now stood up the bay, and anchored about where the "Mississippi" had sounded, some 12 miles above Uraga. Erelong Yezaimon appeared along-side, looking sour enough at this his third visit to the "Susquehanna" to-day. His object was soon explained, and we endeavored to ease his mind in respect to surveying the harbor, telling him that we had told him we were not going to sail immediately, but to go about the bay, & seek a better anchorage than that off Uraga for placing our ships next year.

91

July 14th

The extent of the time we should stay could not be stated, but not likely to exceed four days; we would not land, nor would there be any trouble if the Japanese made none, for our boats were strictly ordered to abstain from this. I think he himself was satisfied of our intentions, but his superiors were probably alarmed at the risk, and sent him to do what he could to prevent further progress. The interview was rather tedious from its being a struggle, and I suspect the interlocutors were all pleased when it was over. Others from the boat came on board, & walked through the ship, and I wish there were more who could have seen her. At this visit and the one earlier in the afternoon, many things were shown our visitors, such as engravings, daguerreotypes, & curiosities of various sorts which tended to relieve the monotony of the visit, as well as instruct them a little. I have now learned more fluency by my practice, & did considerable side talking.

At eventide we were left alone, & thus closed this eventful day, one which will be a day to be noted in the history of Japan, one on which the key was put into the lock, and a beginning made to do away with the long seclusion of this nation, for I incline to think that the reception of such a letter in such a public manner involves its consideration if not its acceptance; at least the prestige of determined seclusion on her part is gone, after the meeting at Gori-hama.

July 15th

The "Saratoga" & "Plymouth" came up to-day from the anchorage off Uraga in Lat. 35°15' N. Long 139°49' E. to join the two steamers at the "American Anchorage" in 35°23 N. 139°41' E, off a thinly inhabited coast. The shores were much more wooded here than off Uraga, and steeper. North of us on a low projecting point were seen many pennons and increasing crowds of people, perhaps many of them soldiers brought or attracted from Kanagawa & the interjacent country to see us. No signs nor words could attract any of the numerous boats to draw even within fair speaking distance. The surveying boats went up in the morning almost out of sight, & in the afternoon, the Commodore ~~went up~~ proceeded in the Mississippi over the same & some new ground. The town of ~~Kanagawa~~ Kawasaki stretched along the north bank of the ~~river~~ Taba gawa, a well placed & populous town. We tho't at the time that this was Kanagawa, but by Siebold's map that town lies south, & on no stream a little inland not far from our "Am" Anchorage," and the people who come on board seem so chary of telling the name of a single place, that one cannot feel confident they tell it right when they do give it. There were many vessels entering, & more at anchor in the river, which seemed a wide stream near the town. Nothing of Yedo could be distinguished, but a long serried row of masts seemed to indicate the position of Shinagawa the suburb port of the capital. A singular shaped struc-

Webster Island or Natsu
Japan
April 1854

Commo. Perry
U.S.N.

被理将军的名片

孔夫子像并讚

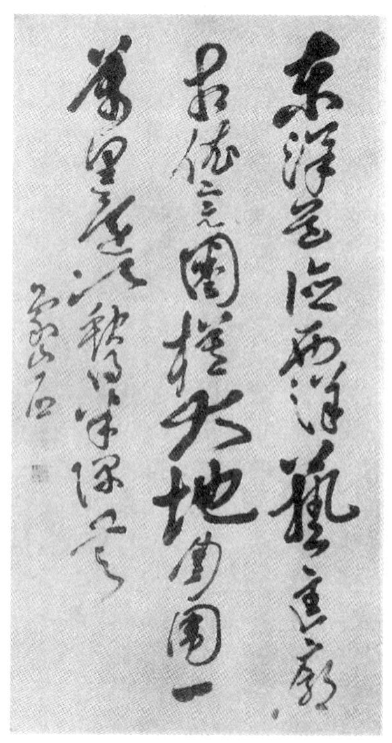

書幅「東洋道徳　西洋藝術」

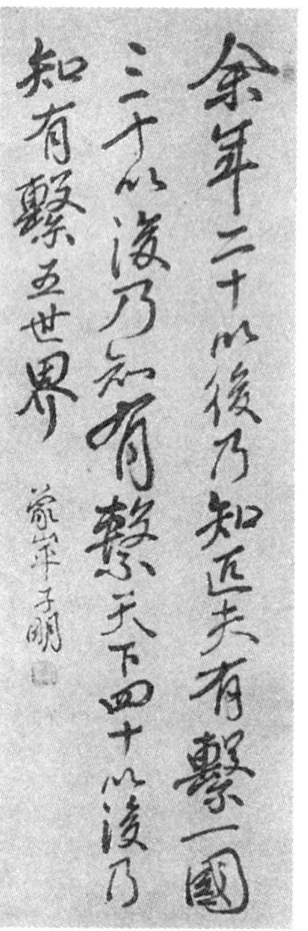

省諐録中語

象山先生碑

贈正四位佐久間象山先生碑
元帥陸軍大將正二位大勲位功二級侯爵山縣有朋題額
勅選議員正四位勲三等文學博士重野安繹撰
予視於百餘年來儒流得先見之士二人焉一爲仙臺林子平一則松代佐久間象山子平以寬政癸丑殁當
其時天下乂安四海無虞士大夫卑狃宴安而子平獨論邊防慷慨著書以此獲罪禁錮終身象山後子平四
十餘年夙憂外事究時務而迂違轍軔終罹於奇禍二子洞觀時勢其言皆有驗乎所謂先天下之憂而憂
者君子避其志識而歎其不遇而象山之事最可悲矣初天保中英人致我漂流民乞互市幕府拒而不納彼
修海防令諸藩爲之備象山深於儒學兼通海外兵制乃獻言當路指陳大勢幕府未之信也迨嘉永癸丑米
艦果入浦賀幕吏始服其先見之明米艦遂要求通商貿易期以明年幕府下議諸藩問和戰利害象山又款
時務十策言皆天下大計而幕府不能用也安政甲寅米艦再來申前約促開港幕府擬以伊豆下田而米艦
繫在横濱象山聞之曰下田僻遠且有天城曰金之險緩急難應不若宜以横濱之爲愈也其洞見利害如此
當是時四方志士爭倡鎖國攘夷陰攝朝紳而迫幕府象山注意大局其所主在立自強不敗之地以擴開國
進取之計長州志士吉田松陰深服其言欲航海外以探事情象山賦詩送之事露下獄象山連坐尋各幽於
其藩象山已廢而時事益非憂世之念不能自禁竊託人進說朝紳會　朝廷　勅諸藩上意見象山受藩命
草上書索滔滔數萬言聳動天下耳目其名隱然重於朝野元治甲子春大將軍家茂公在京師辟象山人咸
危之象山曰國事方急微軀何足惜是志士效力之秋也四月至京師屢進謀議周旋　朝廷幕府之間而其
所說非開國貿易則公武合體顧爲時人所忌遂殞命兇手實是年七月十一日也年五十四葬京師妙心寺
往時鄂羅之擾北疆外事初動而衆人未知其可憂子平乃大聲疾呼以警醒之迨英米出沒東海外患既迫
上下洶洶不知禁所出象山講之方略爲之措置如燭照而數計竟定他日之國是蓋二子學該識明通達内
外故先天下之憂而憂而命運不至不得後天下之樂而樂可勝慨夫象山卒之後四年　王室中興海宇一
變遂致今日之盛推其所淵源二子之功寧可沒哉於是　朝廷旌襃並有贈位典死者而有知可以瞑矣象
山名啓字子明信濃埴科郡人世仕松代侯真田氏以其生象山麓故自號象山云屬鄉人謀建碑山顛徵文
於予方今兒女猶識象山何待敍述乃特表其大節係以銘銘曰
東洋道德　西洋藝術　精粗弗遺　表裏兼該　因澤民物　以報國恩　卓哉斯語　百世可師
爰揭爰示　以代銘辭　象山之顛　有此豐碑
明治三十五年歲在壬寅七月　正五位日下部東作書　田鶴年鐫

象山先生顕彰碑

條約

條約

現今亞美理駕合衆國謀與日本
國人交相親睦將依此意以定後
來久守之章程是以
合衆國大統領差全權被理到於
日本
日本國大君差全權林大學頭井
戸對馬守伊澤美作守鵜殿民部
少輔相與遵奉　勅諭立約如
左
一兩國之人嗣後當互相親睦不得
以其人之高下貴賤與所遇異地
而各別視之也
一日本國政府今定下田箱館兩港
做為合衆國船發薪水食料石炭
等諸缺乏物之現存者儘數給之
之地准其駕舶入港但下田港應
以鈐印約書之日為之始箱館應
以來年三月而始開其發給諸物
應自日本官吏講價報知而抵以
洋金洋銀也

一合衆國船漂到日本諸處海濱者應救恤周濟併其所携諸物具船送致之于下田或箱館附之該國人到港者其周濟漂民諸費項彼此所同兩國皆不用追支也

一漂民及到港合衆國人應同海外諸國之俗從容待之不得一處安置也但至日本正理之例合衆國人亦不得不甘心從順

一合衆國漂民及其他到港者兩港官吏不應倣長崎港置唐山和蘭諸國人之制而錮禁之也但下田港則其港內小島居中向四方能步遊七里若箱館港行步之規應俟日後量度較定

一或要覓必需諸物及其餘宜見允准之事應俟兩國議定

一合衆國船到兩港者准其以洋金洋銀及諸貨抵換必需諸物應謹守日本政府法制若其所發諸貨不中日本人之意而却之者合衆國人應甘心帶回

一其取薪水食料石炭及缺乏諸物皆應從該地官吏等斡辦凡一支一收皆不得私下相與也

一嗣後日本政府倘以今不相允於合衆國之事與他海外諸國相允則亦應同允之于合衆國毋庸遲

緩待議也

一兩港既開則合衆國人除猝遇風颶之外不得向別處恣意入港也

一倘兩國政府均有不得已之事情或應置合衆國總領于下田但置總領之事應以鈐印約書以来十八月後為期

一條約一定兩國各官民自應謹守且

合衆國大統領同長公會大臣議定允肯致書于

日本大君此事應以今後十八個月即將兩國　君上批准之條約互換

已上

約書如上兩國全權諸臣下印作證

嘉永七年甲寅三月三日即

紀年一千八百五十四年三月卅一日

在横濱村鈐蓋關防

松崎滿太郎（花押）

條約

現今亞美理駕合衆國謀與日本國人交相親睦將依此意以定後來久守之章程是以

合衆國大統領差全權被理到於日本

日本國大君差全權林大學頭井戶對馬守伊澤美作守鵜殿民部少輔相與遵奉　勅諭立約如左

一兩國之人嗣後當互相親睦不得以其人之高下貴賤與所遇異地而各別視之也

一日本國政府今定下田箱館兩港做為合衆國船發薪水食料石炭等諸缺乏之物現存者儘數給之之地准其駕船入港但下田港應以鈐印約書之日為之始箱館應以來年三月而始開其給發諸物應自日本官吏講價報知而抵以洋金洋銀也

一合衆國船漂到日本諸處海濱者應救恤周濟併其所携諸物具船送致之于下田或箱館附之該國人到港者其周濟漂民諸費

項彼此所同兩國皆不用追支也

一漂民及到港合衆國人應同海外諸國之俗從容待之不得一處安置也但至日本正理之例合衆國人亦不得不甘心從順

一合衆國漂民及其他到港者兩港官吏不應倣長崎港置唐山和蘭諸國人之制而錮禁之也但下田港則其港内小島居中向四方能步遊七里若箱館港行步之規應俟日後量度較定

一或要見必需諸物及其餘宜見允准之事應俟兩國議定

一合衆國船到兩港者准其以洋金洋銀及諸貨抵換必需諸物應謹守日本政府法制若其所發諸貨不中日本人之意而却之者合衆國人應甘心帶回

一其取薪水食料石炭及缺乏之諸物皆應從該地官吏等幹辦凡一支一收皆不得私下相與也

一嗣後日本政府倘以今不相允於合衆國之事與他海外諸國相允則亦應同允之于合衆國毋庸遲緩待議也

April 1. Off Kanagawa

In faith whereof, we, the respective plenipotentiaries of the U.S. of A. & the empire of Japan, aforesaid, have signed & sealed these presents. Done at Kanagawa, March 31. 1854, & Kayei, 7th year 3d month & 3d day.

一两港既開則合衆國人除猝遇風颶之外不得向別處
恣意入港也
一倘两國政府均有不得已之事情或應置合衆國総領
人於下田但置総領之事應以鈐印約書以来十八月
為期
一、條約一定两國各官民自應謹守且
合衆國大統領同長公會大臣議定允肯致書於
日本大君此事亦應以今後十八個月即將
两國君上批准之條約互換
已上
約書如上两國全權諸臣下印作證
嘉永七年甲寅三月　日即我主
耶穌基督後紀年之一千八百五十四年三月　日
在横濱村築館鈐盖関防

約條

約條

亜墨利加合衆國と帝國日本兩國
の人民誠實不朽の親睦を取結ひ
兩國人民の交親を旨とし向後可
守ヶ條相立ル為合衆國より全權
マテユカルブレトヘルリ 人名 を日本に差越し

日本君主よりハ全權林大學頭
井戸對馬守伊澤美作守鵜殿
民部少輔を差遣し勅諭を信し
て雙方左之通取極ル

第一ヶ条

一日本と合衆國とハ其人民永世不
朽の和親を取結ひ場所人柄の
差別無之事

第二ヶ条

一伊豆下田松前地箱館の両港ハ
日本政府に於て亜墨利加船薪
水食料石炭欠乏の品を日本

人にて調候丈を給候為免渡来之儀
差免し候 尤下田港を約條書
面調印之上即時相開き箱
館を来年三月より相始候事

一 給候品物直段書之儀を
日本役人より相渡可申右代料を
金銀銭を以て可相弁候事

第三ヶ条

一 合衆國の船日本海濵漂着之時扶助
致し其漂民を下田又は箱館に護送
致し本國の者受取可申所持の品物も同
様に可致候 尤漂民諸雑費を両國互に
同様之事故不及償候事

第四ヶ条

一 漂着或は渡来の人民取扱之儀を
他國同様緩優に有之閉籠候
儀致間敷乍併正直の法度には伏
従いたし候事

第五ヶ条

一 合衆國の漂民其他の者とも當分
下田箱館逗留中長崎に於て唐
和蘭人同様閉籠窮屈の取
扱無之下田港内の小島周り凡
七里の内は勝手に徘徊いたし箱

館港之儀ハ追て取極候ハん事

第六ヶ条

一 必用之品物其外可相叶事ハ雙方談判之上ニ而取極候事

第七ヶ条

一 合衆國之船右両港ニ渡来之時金銀錢并品物を以て入用之品相調候を差免し候尤日本政府の規定ニ相従ふへし且合衆國之船より差出候品物を日本人不好して差返候時ハ又受取候事

第八ヶ条

一 薪水食料石炭并欠乏之品を求る時ニハ其地の役人ニて之を取扱すへく私ニ取引すへからさる事

第九ヶ条

一 日本政府外國人江當節亜墨利加人江差免さゝる廉差免し候節ハ亜墨利加人江も同様差免可申右ニ付談判猶豫不致候事

第十ヶ条

一 合衆國之船若難風ニ逢さる時下田箱館港之外ニ渡来不致候事

第十一ヶ条

一 両國政府に於て無據儀有之候ハ模様により合衆國官吏之もの下田に差置候儀も可有之候尤約定調印より十八ヶ月後に無之候ては不及其儀候事

第十二ヶ条

一 今般之約條相定候上ハ両國の者堅く相守可申尤合衆國主に於て長公會大臣と評議一定之後書を日本大君に致し此事今より後十八ヶ月を過君上許容之約條取替し候事

右之條日本亜墨利加両國之全權調印せしむる者也

嘉永七年三月三日

林大學頭

井戸對馬守

伊澤美作守

鵜殿民部少輔

The United States of America, and the Empire of Japan, desiring to establish firm lasting and sincere friendship between the two Nations, have resolved to fix in a manner clear and positive, by means of a Treaty or general convention of peace and Amity, the rules which shall in future be mutually observed in the intercourse of their respective Countries; for which most desirable object, the President of the United States has conferred full powers on his Commissioner, Matthew Calbraith Perry, Special Ambassador of the United States to Japan: And the August Sovereign of Japan, has given similar full powers to his Commissioners, Hayashi, Dai-gaku no Kami; Ido, Prince of Tsus-Sima; Izawa, Prince of Mima-saki; and Udono, Member of the Board of Revenue. And the said Commissioners after having exchanged their said full powers, and duly considered the premises, have agreed to the following Articles.

Article I.

There shall be a perfect, permanent, and universal peace, and a sincere and cordial amity between the United States of America, on the one part, and the Empire of Japan on the other part; and between their people respectively, without exception of persons or places.

Article II.

The Port of Simoda in the princi-pality of Idzu, and the Port of Hako-dade, in the principality of Matsmai, are granted by the Japanese as ports for the reception of American Ships, where they can be supplied with Wood, Water, provisions, and Coal, and other articles their necessities may require as far as the Japanese have them. The time for opening the first named Port is im-mediately on Signing this Treaty; the last named Port is to be opened imme-diately after the same day in the ensuing Japanese Year.

Note. A tariff of prices shall be given by the Japanese Officers of the things which they can furnish, payment for which shall be made in Gold and Silver Coin.

Article III.

Whenever Ships of the United States are thrown or wrecked on the Coast of Japan, the Japanese vessels will assist them, and carry their Crews to Simoda, or Hakodade, and hand them over to their Countrymen appointed to receive them; whatever articles the Shipwrecked men may have preserved shall likewise be restored, and the expenses incurred in the rescue and support of Americans and Japanese who may thus be thrown upon the shores of either nation are not to be refunded.

p. 513

Article IV.

Those Shipwrecked persons and other Citizens of the United States shall be free as in other Countries, and not subjected to confinement, but shall be amenable to just laws.

Article V.

Shipwrecked men and other Citizens of the United States, temporarily living at Simoda and Hakodade shall not be subject to such restrictions and confinement as the Dutch and Chinese are at Nagasaki, but shall be free at Simoda to go where they please within the limits of Seven Japanese miles (or Ri.) from a small Island in the harbor of Simoda, marked on the accompanying Chart, hereto appended:— and shall in like manner be free to go where they please at Hakodade, within limits to be defined after the visit of the United States Squadron to that place.

Article VI

If there be any other sort of goods wanted, or any business which shall require to be arranged, there shall be careful deliberation between the parties in order to settle such matters.

Article VII.

It is agreed that Ships of the United States resorting to the ports open to them, shall be permitted to exchange Gold and Silver Coin and articles of goods for other articles of goods, under such regulations as shall be temporarily established by the Japanese Government for that purpose. It is stipulated however that the Ships of the United States shall be permitted to carry away whatever articles they are unwilling to exchange.

Article VIII.

Wood, water, provisions, Coal and goods required shall only be procured through the agency of Japanese Officers appointed for that purpose, and in no other manner.

Article IX.

It is agreed, that if at any future day the government of Japan shall grant to any other Nation or Nations privileges and advantages which are not herein granted to the United States, and the Citizens thereof, that these same privileges and advantages shall be granted likewise to the United States, and to the Citizens thereof, without any consultation or delay.

Article X.

Ships of the United States shall be permitted to resort to no other ports in Japan but Simoda and Hakodade unless in distress or forced by stress of weather.

Article XI.

There shall be appointed by the Government of the United States, Consuls or Agents to reside in Simoda at any time after the expiration of Eighteen months from the date of the Signing of this Treaty, provided that either of the two governments deem such arrangement necessary.

Article XII.

The present Convention having been concluded and duly signed, shall be obligatory and faithfully observed by the United States of America and Japan, and by the Citizens and Subjects of each respective power; and it is to be ratified and approved by the President of the United States, by and with the advice and consent of the Senate thereof, and by the August Sovereign of Japan, and the ratification shall be exchanged within eighteen months from the date of the Signature thereof, or sooner if practicable.

In faith whereof, we the respective plenipotentiaries of the United States of America and the Empire of Japan aforesaid have signed and sealed these presents.

Done at Kanagawa this thirty first day of March in the Year of our Lord Jesus Christ. One thousand eight hundred and fifty four. and of Kayei the Seventh Year, third month and Third day.

M. C. Perry

Dutch Translation of a treaty. United States & Japan. March 31. 1854.

De Vereenigde Staten van Amerika en het Keizerryk Japan wenschende te sluiten op-regte en duurzame vriendschap tusschen beide Natiën hebben besloten, door middel van een Verdrag op eene duidelyke en bepaalde wyze vast te stellen de regelen welke voortaan in den omgang van beide Natiën met elkander wederkeerig zullen worden in acht genomen; ten dien einde is onbepaalde volmagt verleend ge-worden door den President van de Vereenigde Staten aan Zynen Gevolmagtigde Matthew Cal-braith Perry, buitengewoon Afgezant naar Japan, en door den Doorluchtigen Heerscher van het Japansche Ryk aan Deszelfs Gevolmagtigden Hajasi Daigak-no-kami, Ido Tsoesima-no-kami, Isawa Mimasaka-no kami, en Oedono Minboe Sjojo.-

En gevolmagtigden voormeld, na elkanders geloofsbrieven te hebben gezien en goedgekeurd, zyn overeengekomen het navolgende:

Artikel Een.

Daar zal zyn volkomen, duurzame en algemeene vrede, en opregte vriendschap tus-schen de Vereenigde Staten en Japan, en tusschen de ingezetenen van beide landen, zon-der uitzondering van plaatsen of personen.-

Artikel Twee.

De haven van Simoda in het Vorstendom Idsu, en de haven van Hakodate in het Vorstendom Matsoemai worden door de Japansche Regering toegestaan als havens, waar Amerikaansche Schepen zullen kunnen binnen loopen, ter verkryging van hout, water levensbehoeften, Steenkool, en al wat nodig mogt zyn voor zoo ver zulks door de Japanezen kan worden geleverd.- De eerstgenoemde haven zal geopend zyn onmiddelyk na het onderteekenen van dit Verdrag, en de laatstgenoemde haven in de derde maand van het toekomende jaar.

Een tarief van pryzen zal door daartoe bevoegde Japansche beambten worden gegeven van al zoodanige voorwerpen, welke geleverd kunnen worden waarvoor in gouden en zilveren munt zal worden betaald.-

Artikel Drie.-

Wanneer schepen van de Vereenigde Staten op de Japansche kust geworpen worden of Schipbreuk lyden, zullen dezelve zoo veel mogelyk bystand genieten, en derzelver bemanning naar Simoda of Hakodate worden gebragt, om aldaar door hunne landgenoten te worden ontvangen; gelykerwyze zal aan hen worden teruggegeven wat hun mogt toebehoorenen, en zullen aan beide Regeringen de onkosten voor het redden en het onderhoud van Schipbreukelingen niet in rekening worden gebragt.-

Artikel Vier.

Schipbreukelingen en ingezetenen van de Vereenigde Staten zullen vry zyn als in andere landen, en niet opgesloten worden, doch deugdelyk onderworpen zyn aan regtvaardige wetten.-

Artikel Vyf.-

Schipbreukelingen en ingezetenen van de Vereenigde Staten tydelyk verblyf houdende in Simoda en Hakodate zullen niet onderworpen zyn aan opsluiting en beperkingen, zoo als de Nederlanders en Chinezen in Nagasaki, doch vry zich ongehinderd te bewegen binnen grenzen, welke by deze worden bepaald op zeven Japansche mylen (Ri) in alle rigtingen, uitgaande van het eiland in de haven van Simoda, als aangewezen op nevensgaande kaart by deze aangehecht, en voor Hakodate zullen de grenzen later bepaald worden.-

Artikel Zes.

Indien iets anders nodig mogt zyn, of eenige schikking te treffen viel, zal zulks in zorgvuldige overweging genomen en geregeld worden.-

Artikel Zeven.

In de voormelde havens welke schepen van de Vereenigde Staten mogen binnen loopen, zal het geoorloofd zyn goud en zilver geld en goederen te verruilen tegen waren en goederen, onder zoodanige bepalingen als by dezen door de Japansche Regering ten dien einde zullen worden vastgesteld. En is het verder bepaald, dat het vergund zal zyn om in Amerikaansche schepen terug te nemen en weg te voeren zoodanige goederen, welke de eigenaar daarvan niet heeft willen verruilen.-

Artikel Acht.

Hout, water, levensbehoeften, steenkool en alle goederen welke nodig mogten zyn, zullen alleen kunnen worden verkregen door tusschenkomst van bevoegde Japansche ambtenaren, en op geen andere wyze.-

Artikel Negen.

Indien in vervolg van tyd de Regering van Japan aan eenige andere Natie of Natiën verleenen mogt voorregten of privilegiën, welke nog niet zyn verleend geworden aan de Vereenigde Staten en derzelver ingezetenen, dat alsdan gelyke voorregten en privilegiën zullen worden verleend aan de Vereenigde Staten en derzelver ingezetenen, zonder verwyl, en zonder dat daarvoor verdere beraadslaging nodig zy.-

Artikel Tien.

Schepen van de Vereenigde Staten zullen geene andere havens in Japan dan Simoda en Hakodade mogen binnen loopen, tenzy in hoogen nood of door storm gedwongen.-

Artikel Elf.

Consuls of Agenten, om verblyf te houden in Simoda, zullen door de Regering van de Vereenigde Staten worden benoemd, wanneer zulks door een van beide Regeringen zal worden nodig geoordeeld, doch niet dan na achttien maanden van het onderteekenen van dit Verdrag.-

Artikel Twaalf.

Wanneer de tegenwoordige overeenkomst zal zyn gesloten, zal dezelve verbindend zyn voor, en getrouwelyk worden nagekomen door de Vereenigde Staten van Amerika en Japan en door iederen ingezetene en onderdaan van beide in het byzonder. Deze overeenkomst of Verdrag zal worden geratificeerd door den President van de Vereenigde Staten met den raad en de toestemming van den Senaat daarvan, en door den Doorluchtigen Heerscher van het Keizerryk Japan, en zullen de ratificatiën gewisseld worden binnen achttien maanden na den datum van het onderteekenen dezes.-

Ten blyke waarvan wy, de Gevolmagtigden van de Vereenigde Staten van Amerika, en het Keizerryk Japan voormeld, hetzelve hebben onderteekend, en ons zegel aangehecht.-

Gedaan en geteekend in Kanagawa den

een en dertegsten Maart in het jaar onzes Heeren
Jesus Christus achttien honderd (1800) vier en vyftig,
en Kaei Sitsinen Langoeats (Japansche tydrekening.
(Geteekend) M C Perry.-

a correct translation

A L C Portman.

Actg Dutch Interpreter. & Commodore's Clerk.

[1854 MAR 27]

List of the Presents received from the Japanese Commissioners on the 27th March, 1854.

1st. For the United States government from the Emperor of Japan

1 Gold Lacquered Writing Apparatus
1 Do. Do. Paper Box
1 Do. Do. Bookcase
1 Lacquered Writing Table
1 Bronze Censer on a stand, shaped like an ox with a silver flower on his back
1 set of two lacquered Trays
1 Lacquered Bamboo flower holder & stand
2 Braziers with silver tops
10 ps. fine red pongee
10 ps. white pongee
5 ps. figured crape
5 ps. red dyed flowered crape
2 Swords & 3 matchlocks

2d. For the United States' Government from Hayashi, First Japanese Commissioner

1 Lacquered writing Apparatus
1 Do. Paper box
1 box of flowered paper
5 " of stamped note paper
1 " of flowered note paper.
1 Lacquered chowchow Box
1 box of coral branch and "silver feather" of byssus
4 boxes 100 assorted kinds of sea-shells
1 box lacquered cups, three in a set
7 boxes of cups & spoons cut from conch shells.

3d. For the United States government from Ido, Prince of Tsus-sima, Second Japanese Commissioner

2 boxes lacquered waiters, two in each

2 boxes 20 paper Umbrellas
1 box 30 coir brooms.

4th For the United States' Government from Izawa, Prince of Mimasaki, third Japanese Commissioner
1 ps. red Pongee
1 ps. white pongee
8 boxes of 13 dolls
1 box bamboo articles
2 boxes bamboo low tables

5th For the United States' Government from Udono, member of Board of Revenue, fourth Japanese Commissioner
3 ps. striped crape
2 boxes 20 porcelain cups
1 ~ soy, 10 jars.

6th For the United States' Government from Matsusaki Michitaro, fifth Japanese Commissioner
3 boxes porcelain cups
1 box figured matting
35 bundles oak charcoal

7th For the United States' Government, from Abe, 1st Councilor of the Empire & Prince of Ishi
15 ps. striped & figured pongee or taffeta

8th – 12th For the United States' Government from each of the other five Imperial Councilors, viz. Matsudaira Prince of Iga, Matsudaira Prince of Idzumi, Makino, Prince of Bizen, Naito Prince of Ki, & Kuzhei Prince of Yamato.
10 ps. of striped & figured pongee or taffeta

For Kurokawa Kakeyoye
14 ps. striped & white cotton
Demijohn of Whiskey
1 Revolver
9 sorts of perfumery
Box of cherry-cordial

For Moriyama Yenoske. Chief Interpreter
Websters Dictionary
Revolver in a box
Box of Cotton goods
Box of cherry cordial
6 sorts of perfumery
Breaker of Whiskey

For M Tatsnoske. Second Interpreter
9 ps. Striped & White Cotton
5 galls Whiskey
1 Revolver
1 Hall's Rifle
6 kinds of perfumery

For Namura Gohachiro. Third Interpreter
9 ps Striped & White Cottons
5 galls Whiskey
1 Halls Rifle
6 kinds of perfumery

One sheet-iron stove
Six dozen Assorted perfumery, soaps, essences, pomatum &c
Catalogue of New York State Library
2 Mail bags with padlocks
Box of arms, containing 5 Halls Rifles, 3 Maynard's
Muskets, 12 Cavalry Swords, 6 Artillery Swords,
1 Carbine, & 20 Army Pistols

2^d. For the Empress
1 Flowered silk Embroidered Dress
1 Gilded Toilet dressing case
Six dozen assorted Perfumery, soaps, essences, oils, &c

3^d. For Abe, Prince of Ishi, 1st Councilor
One copper Life Boat
Kendall's plates of Mexican War & Ripley's History
One box of Champagne
Three boxes fine tea
One Clock
One Stove
One Rifle
One Sword
Fifty Gallons Whiskey
One Revolver & box of Powder & caps
4 yds. Scarlet Broadcloth
2 doz. Assorted Perfumery

4th For Makino, Prince of Bizen 2^d Councilor
Lossing's Field Book of the Revolution, 2 vols
Cabinet of Natural History of State of New York
Ten gallons of Whiskey
One dozen Assorted Perfumery
One Clock One Sword
One Revolver One Rifle
One large Lithograph

5th. For Matsudaira, Prince of Idzumi, 3d. Councilor
Owen's Architecture
Lithograph View of Washington City, with a plan
One Clock One Sword
One Rifle One Revolver
Ten Galls. of Whiskey
One dozen Assorted Perfumery

6th. For Matsudaira, Prince of Iga, 4th. Councilor
Documentary History of State of New York ~~2 vols~~
Lithograph of a Steamer
One dozen Assorted Perfumery
One Clock One Rifle
One Sword One Revolver
Ten galls. of Whiskey

7th. For Kuzhei, Prince of Yamato, 5th. Councilor
~~Downing's~~ County Houses
~~Owen's Geology~~ of ~~Minnesota~~ ~~& book of plans & fossils~~
Lithograph of ~~Georgetown, D.C.~~ San Francisco
Ten Gallons of Whiskey
One Clock One Rifle
One Sword One Revolver
Nine sorts of Perfumery

8th. For Naiito, Prince of Ki, 6th. Councilor
Owen's Geology of Minnesota & book of plans & fossils
Lithograph of Georgetown, D.C.
Ten galls of Whiskey
One Clock One rifle
One revolver One Sword
Nine sorts of perfumery

9th. For Hayashi, Dai-gaku no kami, member of Council and
Chief Commissioner
Audubon's Quadrupeds of America

One tea-set of fine chinaware
Fifty galls of Whiskey
Three boxes Fine Tea
4 yds. scarlet Broadcloth
One Clock One rifle
One Sword One Revolver & box of powder & caps
Box of Champagne
Two doz. Assorted Perfumery
One stove

10th For Ido, Prince of Tsus-sima, 2d Commissioner
Appleton's Dictionary 2 Vols.
Lithograph of New Orleans
5 galls. of Whiskey
Nine sorts of perfumery Brass Howitzer & carriage
One Sword One Rifle
One Revolver One clock
Box of Cherry Cordial

11th For Izawa, Prince of Mimasaki, 3d Commissioner
Model of a Life-boat 5 galls. Whiskey
Lithograph of Steamer "Atlantic"
1 Rifle One Clock One Sword One Revolver
Box of Cherry Cordial 9 sorts of Perfumery

12th For Udono, Member of Board of Revenue, 4th Commissioner
List of Post Offices - Lithograph of an Elephant
One Rifle One revolver One Sword One clock
5 galls of Whiskey Box of Cherry Cordial
9 Assorted perfumery

13th For Matsusaki Michitaro, 5th Commissioner
Lithograph of a steamer - 6 kinds of perfumery
One revolver - One Clock - One Sword
5 galls Whiskey - Box of Cherry Cordial

List of Presents given to the Emperor
of Japan and his high ministers by the U.S.
Government. March 13th 1854

1st For the Emperor
One 1/4 size miniature locomotive, tender, car & track
A Telegraph apparatus, with three miles of wire
One Francis Life Boat
One surf boat of copper
Collection of Agricultural Instruments, as per annexed list
Audubon's Birds of America, 9 Vols.
Natural History of the State of New York, 16 Vols.
Annals of Congress, 4 Vols.
Laws & Documents of the State of New York
Journal of the Senate & Assembly of New York
Lighthouse Reports, 2 vols.
Bancroft's History of the United States, 4 Vols.
Farmer's Guide, 2 Vols.
A full series of the United States' Coast Survey
Norris' Engineering
A dressing-case, bottles silver-topped
8 yds. fine scarlet Broadcloth
1 ps. scarlet Velvet
A series of U.S. standard weights, balances, gallon,
yard, bushel & gallon
One 1/4 cask of Madeira
One barrel of Whiskey Box of seeds
One hamper of champagne
One box of Cherry-cordial
One box of Maraschino
Three ten-catty Boxes of fine Tea
Maps of several of the different States
Four large Lithographs
One Brass Telescope & stand in box

13^t. For Commodore Perry from the Emperor of Japan
1 lacquered writing Apparatus
1 Do paper Box
3 ps. red pongee
2 ps. white pongee
2 ps. flowered crape
3 ps. dyed figured crape

14th. For Capt. H A Adams from the Japanese Commissioners
3 ps. plain red pongee
2 ps red dyed figured crape
24 lacquered cups & covers

15th-17th. For Mr. S W Williams, O H Perry & A Portman, each, from the Japanese commissioners
2 ps. red pongee
2 ps red dyed figured crape
10 lacquered cups & covers

18th-22d. For Messrs. Jesse Gay, R Danby, J. Morrow, J P Williams & W B Draper, each, from the Japanese Commissioners
1 ps dyed crape
10 lacquered cups & covers

23d. For the Squadron from the Emperor
300 fowls
200 bags of rice, each 160 lbs.

24th. For the U.S.A. from the prefect & Interpreters
5 ps figured crape.

一千八百五十四年十一月朔旦　第十一號

遐邇貫珍

香港英華書院印刷

遐邇貫珍

第拾一號目錄

CHINESE SERIAL.

Vol. II. No. 11.

1st November, 1854.

INDEX OF CONTENTS.

其子生卽活動、養之以乳、分有兩族、曰食菜者、曰尋常似鯨者、海牛及甲翅之生物、皆屬第一族、牙甚平厚、故便於食菜、常登岸以尋其食、第二族之所異於第一族者、以有一吹氣孔、故亦謂之吹氣者、其口極大、於其食時、水與之俱進、於此必當有以處之、故當水入鼻孔、卽轉入一囊、囊護以筋、頭項復有一小孔、卽上所謂吹氣孔、一舒其筋、水卽由此孔噴出矣、鯨魚江豚、皆屬此族。（下月附鳥之論）

日本日記

遐邇貫珍數號、每記花旗國與日本相立和約之事、至第十號、則載兩國所議定約條之大意、今有一唐人、爲余平素知已之友、去年搭花旗火船、遊至日本、與助立約之事、故將所見所聞、日逐詳記、編成一帙、歸而授余、玆特著于貫珍之中、以廣讀者之聞見、庶幾耳目爲之一新、但因限于篇幅、未便詳叙、此月祇印其三分之一、餘待後續。

合衆國金山、名驚拉寬、近今人多往彼貿易、洋面遠闊、欲設火船、而石煤不足、必于日本中步之區、添買煤炭、能設火船、便于來往、是故癸亥三月、合衆國火船于日本商議通商之事、未遽允依、是年十月二十二、有某友請予同往日本、共議條約、予卜之吉、十二月十五揚帆、十六予于火船默祝指示機宜、後在船上仰看雲氣、見南方之雲、如獅添翼、直騰天頂、北方雲氣低小、內藏殺氣、惟有小雲數簇而會于獅、獅之昇有氣、壓其小雲、不久而北方之殺氣俱滅、惟獅愈久而愈壯、予因對某友曰、此日之事、初恐不允、後必允成、天道已先兆矣、某友以言爲奇、且試驗之。越三日、火船直向東北而駛、出了臺灣之外、幾日不見天涯、是時北風大作、波浪冲天、火船亦甚飄蕩、而不能立、見有沙鷗隨風而逐浪心、直駛七日、漸見小山而到琉球、琉球一國、長闊一百七十五里、其國城、在地球圖、緯線赤道之北二十六度十四分、經線中華北京偏東十一度二十四分、自明以來、世封王爵、叨列藩籬、其處土產不過蔬菜、番薯、菜油、黑糖等類、人民束髻大袖、足穿草履、男女粧飾、頭上祇插一簪二簪爲別、故少年之男女、瞥目則無異、及其壯也、皆留鬚髯、故街上長鬚之人甚多、甲寅正月初一、予上岸遊玩、見街上兒童甚多、分以銅錢、各極歡喜、人民亦甚謙恭、民居間亦貼新春聯于門外、但不見有別等繁華之事、那覇有寺、寺內有園、是名家世宦之墳所、以石刊刻姓名年號于碑上、每日道人打掃、供奉生花樹葉于墓前、另有人家祖墳、與中國之明塚無異、峰巒之上、樹木多植、民房則以蠻石圍牆、內以茅草結屋而居、佳物椅棹俱無、惟以草蓆屈膝而坐、對火盆而吹煙、民間亦有識中國言語字墨者、不張舖店、惟有墟塲、男不貿易、婦女爲之、以貨易貨、而外方之金銀弗尙焉、然而百姓亦甚畏官長、飲食亦甚粗粕、甘守樸儉、不務奢華、亦鮮欺詐、板門紙窗、夜間亦不防竊、曾見途中撿物、亦能以返原人、公門之內、冷冷落落、並無案牘之煩、淳樸之風、畧有同于上古之世、我等外國之欲買什物、須言于官、官爲代辦、正月初六、提督彼理、衞廉士等、一班將官、布列威嚴、與予乘轎至王宮、總理大臣尙宏勳爲主席、布政大夫馬良才爲知客、享宴甚豐、食物多與中國無異、宴後、各官皆饋有紙扇、烟包、布帛、等項、是物雖粗、此亦世子之恭敬外國、故亞國亦以禮物而返贈之、世子王宮、離岸三里、在于山頂、是名守禮、將至其宮、一路亦有樹木石牌坊、宮室亦甚寬大幽雅、垣局可觀、其處多栽鳳尾草、森樹等類、以障陰、山邊田土、樹藝五穀、近海沙田、水漲之後、人收其沙以煎鹽、此時明月當圓、予覽山川、亦足見一方之風景。越二日、揚帆往日本、四日不覩天涯、海水共長天一色、偶見鯨魚四丈餘、在船頭噴逐水花、越片時而逝、經歷無人洲、兩日而造日本、共合火船兵船九隻、泊于橫濱、此時正月當春、予望橫濱、百里之遙、有尖峰高約八里、白雪迷之、其山勢龍脈、由此層層壘壘、起伏結構于江戶、江戶、即日本之京都也、其京城大君聞知亞國兵船火船至境、則命林大學頭、梯殿民部少輔、伊澤美作守、井戶對馬守等、以辦其事、初時兩國未曾相交、各有猜疑、日本官艇、亦有百數泊于遠岸、皆是布帆、而軍營器械、各亦准備、以防仁之不仁、次日有官艇二三隻來視火船、艇尾插一藍白旗、上寫御用二字、亞人招之上船、以禮待之、與其玩視船上之鐵炮輪機等物、各官喜悅、予見其官粧飾、則闊衣大袖、腰佩雙刀、束髮剃去腦信一方、足穿草履、以錦褌外

套至膝、不同言語、與其筆談、其亦叙邂逅相遇、景仰中國文物之邦云、予問其名、則曰山本文之助、曰掘達之助、曰合原操藏、曰名村五八郎、乃是日本之官也、因而各叙寒暄、次日其官饋來蘿蔔一艇、雞二十頭、蛋五百枚、柑數箱、葱數担、亞船受之、而答以物、因而與之酌議通商之事、其官返報大君、大君則築公館于橫濱、內結綾綿、屏障氈薦而相會、命林大學頭爲欽差、合衆國欽差大臣、駐中華日本天竺等海、權管本國師船提督被理、布列威嚴、上岸相會、衞廉士爲通理國師、呈以通好條約、各官于館內俱有饌盆餅食欵待、不過鮮魚、蠔、蜆、雞蛋、蘿蔔、黃酒、而已、其處人民、不畜牛羊豚豕、亦不宰生而食客、予見人家畜雞、至數年而不宰者、以言食物、則萬不及于中國矣、欽差接收條約、五日始有回音、自此每日俱有官至船、給來薪水雞蛋鮮魚等物、有平山謙二郎者、其

人純厚博學、趨而問予中國治亂之端、予將平日紀錄之事、及治安策視之、其付來一信曰、仁台文章煥發、議論正大、昨日賓會之事、未遑詳讀、願借册子携回一涉、下日完璧于橫濱公館云、予因與之、閱畢送返、亦答予書曰、

爾來契闊、未審起居、筆研清艮否、頃者被視南京紀事、及治安策二册子、熟讀數四、始審中國治亂之由、且知羅向喬之學術淳正、愛君憂國之志、流離顛沛、未嘗忘、亦未嘗不掩卷而嘆也、民情下鬱、下情不達、人牧失職、賄賂公行、古今季運之通病也、所以然者、何也、曰、利而已矣、嗚呼、利者、人之所共欲、而萬害所由胎也、予罕言利、常杜其源也、我祖宗絕交于外邦者、以其利以惑愚夫、究理之奇術以騙頑民、頑民相效、惟利是趨、惟奇是趨、駸駸乎至于忘忠孝廉耻、而無父無君之極也、原夫天道流行、發育萬物之

妙理、則茫茫堪輿之間、雖冰海夜國人、亦孰非天地之赤子、孰非相愛相友之人、所以聖人一視同仁、不分彼此也、全地球中、禮讓信義以相交焉、則太和流行、天地惠然之心見矣、若夫貿易競利以交焉、則爭狠獄訟所由起、寧不如無焉、是我祖宗所深慮者也、由是觀之、則交際一也、唯有無相通、患難相救、則天地自然之道、所謂太平和好之、眞者、而只逐錐頭之末、惟利是務、則人欲爭狠之由、不能始終其事者也、兩者相去一髮、無他、義與利之分而已、古往今來、千百萬年、治亂興廢、起戎出好、未嘗不決乎此也、凡萬國交際之道、宜首講此義也、次練兵講武、代天心以行天討、各國君王、所以不可一日而闕焉者也、昇平之久、忽之、則所由衰也、我邦有深省于此者、近頃練兵講武、演炮製艦、日就月將、不數年、馴致乎湯武之正兵、夫然而後

始可保萬年不朽之太平耳、不然則或奸臣巨盜、暴亂威刼、無以征之、全地球中、强幷弱、大吞小、殆庶幾乎虎狼之交矣、惟上帝鬼神、以父母之心、視其赤子之相欺相爭、寧不惻然乎、不憫然乎、全世界中、各國布棋、賢君英主、必不乏其人矣、先著鞭以奉行天道者誰也、方今世界形勢一變、各國君主、當爲天地立心、爲生民立命之秋也、向爾寓合衆國火船、而周遊乎四海、有親覩焉者乎、若不然、請足跡到處、必以此道說各國君主、是繼孔孟之志于千萬年後、以擴于全世界中者也、今因完附二册子錄、所當志以告諸羅向喬、並候崇安。

論銀事數條

屢聞亞美利加之秘魯、智利、及墨西哥數處、所出之銀、其銀色較于唐銀更勝、然於中國獨不得其益者、因市上貿易、時

價不一、譬有一人、於某日收入鷹銀十圓、斯時銀價適與唐銀無異、迨後銀價變易、每圓鷹銀減低三分五釐、則以所收入十圓而計、已虧去三錢五分矣、所謂鷹銀較勝於唐銀、勝于何有、似此不能言有益於中國也、然此皆因賣銀店與找換店、奸詐爲心、故低昂其價、變易靡常、以希圖射利而已、何能使人人獲其益哉。〇道光五年三月二十九日、粵東制臺、據縣憲禀請、特仰海關發示、各商工人兵丁與衆民等、自後所有鈎鏹之銀、不得復照每圓用少五分之例、祇每圓用少銅錢二文而已、其所以爲此者、因皇上命官下察銀件、見有鈎鏹之異如此、故曉諭各府州縣、一體遵行。〇道光十五年三月十四日、少傅兩廣總督盧、出示曉諭、命將鷹銀較於唐銀、果如上段所云、惟有波蘿銀、值多於唐銀一文錢之六毫、杖銀値多於四文錢零四毫、故令百姓得以此銀通用、每圓

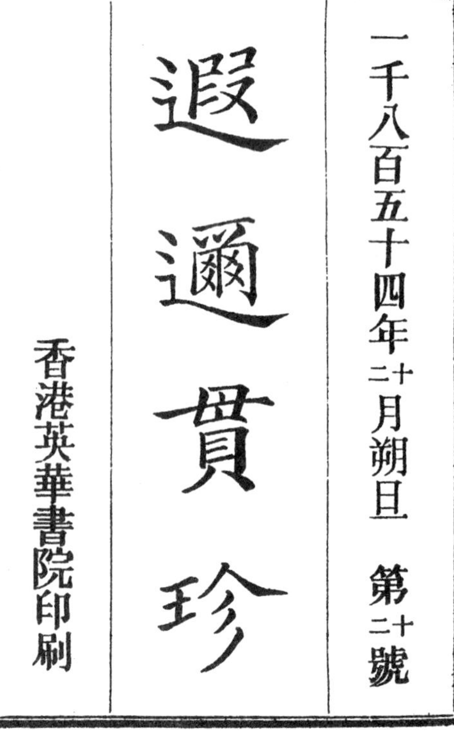

第拾二號目錄

遐邇貫珍

CHINESE SERIAL.

Vol. II. No. 12.

1st *December*, 1854.

INDEX OF CONTENTS.

間有膜以裹連之、所以甚利於泅、頸長於足、實鳥中所僅見者、蓋所以助其於浮水之際、能抵水之深處、以尋其食也、分有四家、野鶩企鵝之類、皆屬第一家、其翼不甚長、海鵠鷗鳥、海燕之類、皆屬第二家、翼長而健、淘河、鵜鶘之類、皆屬第三家、足趾全爲膜所裹連、鳧、鷖、鴻鵠、鵞鴈之類、皆屬第四家、其喙扁平、水爲此等鳥之居、且常於水尋其食、間有恆居於水、其所食者、小魚及凡浮游於涯涘之間者、間亦食水菜水虫之類。下號方附虫魚論

續日本日記

三月初旬、提督再會林大學頭于公館、其時公館之旁、有茶花數叢、燦爛鮮紅、天氣嚴寒、林大學頭以粟米數百包、每約二百餘重、遣肥人九十餘名、俱裸體、一夫獲舉二三包、不一時、而數百包之粟米、盡遷于海畔、再後復使肥人清服赤體、

以武力角于公館之墀、勝者賞酒三巵、予在公館、閱覩數刻、亦足見日本之多勇力人也。合原操藏是浦賀府之官、予問其國取士之方、稱說文武藝身言皆取、而詩不以舉官、所讀者、亦以孔孟之書、而諸子百家、亦復不少、所謂讀書而稱士者、皆佩雙劍、殆尚文而兼尚武歟。日本人民、自從葡萄牙滋事、立法拒之、至今二百餘年、未曾得見外方人面、故多酷愛中國文字詩詞、予或到公館、每每多人請予錄扇、一月之間、從其所請、不下五百餘柄。三月廿五、林大學頭相議條約之事已成、則允准箱館下田二港、以爲亞國取給薪水、食料、石炭之處、由是兩國和好、各釋猜疑、過日提督請林大學頭于火船宴會、船上結綵奏樂、日本官員數十、于火船大宴、有詩爲証、

兩國橫濱會、驩虞一類同、解冠稱禮義、佩劍羨英雄、樂奏

巴人謳、歌陳太古風、和幾番悅意、立約告成功。
宴罷、于船歌舞、日暮方終、次日、亞國以火輪車、浮浪艇、電理機、日影像、耕農具、等物、贈其大君、即于橫濱之郊、築一圜路、燒試火車、旋轉極快、人多稱奇、電理機、是用銅線通于遠處、能以此之音信、立刻傳達于彼、其應如響、日影像、以鏡向日繪照成像、毋庸筆描、歷久不變、浮浪艇、內有風箱、或風壞船、則以此能浮生保命、耕農具、是亞國奇巧耕具、不勞而穫者、大君得收各物、亦以漆器、瓷器、綢縐、等物還禮、官士明篤以

元旦試筆錄以覩子曰、
斗轉年還改、書生世事灰、空懷宗慤志、終乏武侯才、詩就聊揮筆、憂多復舉杯、依依門外柳、青眼為誰開。

玉斧僧居中以新陰咏以覩子曰、
昨夜惜花窓下詠、今朝愛緣苑中吟、人間何識天公意、已

遐邇貫珍 七

變紅林作碧林。

子亦咏詩以返之、
遙看春色偶為吟、日本山川雪盡侵、古徑茶花紅滿綫、鞏岡松樹翠成陰、沙鷗冒雨浮波面、海鳥隨風逐浪心、岸側軍營烟漠漠、灣中戰艦霧沉沉、橫濱築館應非遠、江戶樓臺望轉深、未識人家何處是、泛舟搖漾到前林。

是日子遊橫濱、見郊外祇有龍神古廟、以木為之、內懸鏡像、儼若興雲致雨之意、有店燒瓦、其瓦堅實、灰色而厚、不同中國之式、再行二三里、則有人居、屋亦或灰或草結蓋、屋外多以紙符貼于門上、女長見外方之人、予在橫濱、祇見一婦人而已、越數日、事畢、火船由橫濱一日而至下田、下田之港、乍地球圖緯線赤道之北、三十四度三十九分、經線中華北京偏東二十二度二十九分、其處有山水灌溉、澤邊膏腴肥潤、以此名曰下田、下田港心、有一小石島居中、以為該處之水口、船隻泊入于內、但見山環海繞、垣局稠密、雖有颶風、亦甚堅穩、其時火船寄泊島邊、一望四圍之山、俱有大石盤腳、而波浪故不撼塌之、山上樹木蔚茂、亦有雉雞、麻鷹、烏鴉、水鴨、果狸之類、次日、提督上岸、館于法順山了仙寺、其寺有僧、名日淨、小徒二名、內有佛殿、殿旁墳所、各家信士信女之墓也、墓以石為墳塔、僧人時時掃淨、供奉名花、寺後有石亭、小魚池、花果等類、是日在此烹茶、男女千百入寺觀看、以物賞之、女亦不羞趨避、衣長委地、腰後有裙、以紅綢束其髻、顏色亦多美艷、少年則朱唇皓齒、及至生育子女後、則以五棓粉染黑其牙、再日往遊街市、見鋪屋或編以茅草、或乘以灰瓦、比鄰而居、屋內通連、故曾入門見其人、再入別屋、而亦見其人也、女人過家過巷、男女不分、雖于途間、招之亦至、婦人多有

遐邇貫珍 八

裸裎、傭工者、稠人廣衆、男不羞見下體、女看淫畫為平常、竟有洗身屋、男女同沐于一室之中、而不嫌避者、每見外方人、男女則趨而爭看、雙刀人至、則走離兩旁、其街則有大工町、伊勢町、店之町、池之町、新町、各等町十餘條、循海濱過橋里許、名柿崎、則有玉泉寺、寺外蒼松陰翳、門向石島遮攔外洋汫湃之勢、茲于寺旁准以一地為亞國之墳所、其處人民俱重拜佛、雖山邊海旁、多以石刻置佛像、墳墓石碑、多刻南無妙法蓮華經、予至大安寺見人拜佛、不設香燭、拜後、放錢數文于箱、名曰放生錢、寺有僧人二名、以紙求予書、予觀山景則書峰廻水遶四字與之、其亦題詩曰、
一丈方庵玉座同、寸餘硯石白雲通、黃金畢竟塵中物、不省明朝炊米空。
同坐之間、適有女人拜寺、但見朱唇皓齒退嬌姿、雲鬢斜釵淡掃眉、半面新粧郎絕妙、恰如明

月掛梅枝、

是日天氣太暖、在寺烹茶、其處之茶味、畧帶甘甜、似同于西樵茶味、步出寺外一箭之地、有山溪、砂石、流泉、水光澈底、堪以濯纓、池之町、有一廟、內製偶像、身帶弓矢、廟牆每懸一鏡、畫一船、大抵人家行洋、托賴平安、酬愿之意、亦有髮髻數十枚、掛于牆上、亦是酬恩者、此日本之大畧風俗然也、其處山嶺、杜鵑花甚盛、而各花亦復不少、衞廉士曾採名花數百種、壓乾以備考覽、所謂多識于鳥獸草木之名歟、夫一方斯有一方之善政、以日本雖國小于中華、然而搶掠暴刼之風、亦未嘗見、彼其屋門、雖以紙糊、亦無有鼠竊狗偷之弊、此見致治之畧、各有其能矣、是日遊山、不識路、得遇僧人引步、行逾五里、有人村、名洲崎、適遇菊池森之助、談間亞國所遵何教、予曰、其所奉者獨一神、神卽造化之主宰、所謂昭事上帝、事

懷多福、其明徵歟、因在途間、言雖悉遠、遂作別于松陰之下、步至海旁、多見大鮑魚、是下田之土產也、同于町店買物、則以漆器瓷器爲佳、所揀物品、則書名于物上記價、然後店人送到御用所、交價于官、官者、海關之吏也、近藤艮次主之、御用所、卽其處之海關也、設官數名、而司買物之事、每洋銀一圓、作錢一千六百文、其日本則有當百之大錢、亦有純金一分、亦有純金小判、亦有黃金大判、亦有一分銀、亦有二朱金、二朱則表金而裏銀、世間乃通用、可易當百八枚、一分銀、可易當百十六枚、四分銀、可易一小判、黃金大判、則以分銀百餘方按時價而兌換、行歷下田七里之遙、未曾見一羊一豕、馬則多有以負物、牛則間有以耕田、女人織布、與中國無異、打鐵做木、亦與中國畧同、而女工之顧繡、未曾親也、男人女子、俱尚扇、予于下田一月之間、所寫其扇、不下千餘柄矣、黑川嘉兵衛、是主理下田事務之官、掘達之助、森山榮之助、中臺信太郎等、是行事之官、其以扇請書、付詩一首、

避亂夷船亦一奇、吳中鼙鼓不聞知、翻將萬里東來色、快覩芙蓉絕世姿、　關研次詩曰、橫濱相遇豈無因、和議皆安仰賴君、遠方駃舌今朝會、幸覩同文對語人、　合原猪三郎、其於臨別贈予墨盒一詩一曰、樹外雨收鶯語流、聲聲啼近旅人舟、不知黃帽金衣客、似解轉蓬飄絮愁、

水不尅火論

嘗考唐人經典內說五行之理、爲事物之基、然其生尅之道、不能無疑、余茲各舉其說、以證其謬、試先卽水能尅火之道而論之、如曰水能尅火、則火在水內、其火必爲水所滅、不能復由水中而出、乃以雷火而觀、有時劈燒人間房屋、此時雲行雨施、其雷火卽從空中之水而出、若恐其劈燒人物、用法

引其火瀉於別處、法當有雷電之時、將風箏一隻、在其頂上放鑼石一片、用銅線放之、可高一百尺、此時、雷火卽從銅線尾射出、光芒數尺、人或動著其線尾、卽被劈死、或撲地下、若將銅線引落深坎地中、其患可免、夫雷乃火物、竟與雲雨並行不悖、然則空中之火、其水又安得而尅之、又考南阿墨利加比拉拉司徒等、水中常有雷鱔、其身長約六尺、有雷電之火勢、遇有人馬等物、偶涉其間、卽挾其火勢、劈死人物、人欲引出其身內之火、法用馬牛、送與擊搏至倦、用銅鍊繫其身、其火自出於銅鍊內、若將鍊尾墊著火藥、亦能著火、夫鱔乃水族、其火若是、而在水中、亦能遂性、以此知地中之水、又不能尅火者矣、且以一甌水、能息一爐火、其說維何、此是水蓋火氣、火故息了、使用別物蓋住、其火亦息、然則水能尅火、其說安在哉、博雅君子、思以答之、夫西國之道、有五十五行、各

一千八百五十五年正月朔日　第壹號

遐邇貫珍

香港英華書院印刷

CHINESE SERIAL.

VOL. III. No. 1.

1st January, 1855.

INDEX OF CONTENTS.

第壹號目錄

續日本日記終

四月十六、火船啟行、五日至箱館、在地球圖緯線赤道之北、四十一度四十九分、經線中華北京偏東、二十四度十九分、天氣寒熱、與盛京同、惟此處僻土偏壤、地多沙漠、生物不毛、故民之食貨、恒取給于別埠、此港為船隻運貨往來之區、因號其名曰箱館、其港垣局寬曠、海闊山朝、時當五月、尚有白雪于山巔、房屋較下田而壯麗、衣冠人物、似富盛于下田、婦女羞見外方人、深閨屋內、而不出頭露面、風俗尚正、人民鮮說淫辭、其處有護國山、山有一寺、畫棟雕梁、寺中器皿鮮明、牆懸佛家偶像、寺旁亦有墳墓之所、提督遣人于此繪照日影像、以贈各官、松前大夫、勘解由之公館、幽雅潔淨、貼近海濱、登樓眺望、用千里鏡窺看、微茫之際、見有人村甚多、遙山遠水、如看畫圖、予同辨地衞廉士等、入而晤之、款接甚恭、人品醇善、遠籐又左衞門是參議、石塚官藏奉町行、工籐茂五郎是縣令、關央老子次郎是近書、代島剛平、籐原主馬是司事、相議于港行步之規、共說必俟江戶君王之命、乃能議定、往遊町上、百姓卑躬敬畏官長、人民肅

穆、膝跪路旁、不見一婦人面、舖戶多閉、因亞國船初至此、人民不知何故、是先逃于遠鄉者過半、蓋以溫語安撫百姓、乃敢還港貿易、街上驢馬數百、多負食物于遠方、此處舖店、亦用紙糊、多稱野屋龜屋、與下田無異、此處店內綢縐亦多、但不及中土、惟描金漆器極佳、人多愛之、三日間、于店上品漆器、沽之竭矣、此處土產、鹿皮、魴魚、昆布、白糖、茶葉等項、食物豐美于下田、越數日、平山謙二郎、與安閒純之進等、由江戶前來、約返下田、與林大學頭以定箱館行步之規、予將臨別、謙二郎以唐詩錄扇贈予曰、

渭城朝雨浥輕塵、客舍青青柳色新、勸君更盡一杯酒、西出陽關無故人。

予答其詩曰、火船飛出粵之東、此日揚帆碧鏡中、歷覽螺蜂情不盡、遙瞻蛟室興無窮、雙輪撥浪如奔馬、一舵分流若耿虹、漫道騎鯨冲巨浪、休誇跨鶴振長風、琉球乍別雲方散、日本初臨雪正融、暫寄一身天地外、知音聊與訴離衷。

是日遠籐贈予畫二幅、所繪亦與中國無異、大夫贈書數卷、其書字板勝於中土、予各以香珠答之、即于五月初九揚帆、其官用艇送出山外、火船行五日回下田、次日將官一班、布列威儀上岸、與林大學頭宴會于了仙寺、午後亞國官兵、排列隊伍、歷遊各町、男女人民、觀者如堵、伊澤氏之侍兒桂正敏年紀雖小、身佩雙劍、志氣昂昂、善于應答、復能于公堂之上、描繪亞國各官之像、聰明俊秀、人多悅之、太醫文筌問予中國取士之方、予曰、中國讀孔孟書、伸明孔孟之理、以文字分為八股、謂之文章、文章之外另咏一詩、雖小試會試、亦復如是、越日、有官至船、贈予詩曰、

君產廣東我沽津、相逢萍水亦天緣、火船直擘鯨濤至、看破五湖無限邊。

復遇明篤筆談曰、予乃中國之士、何歸鴃舌之門、孟子所謂下喬木而入幽谷者非歟、予因寓意、吟成七律一首以示之、

日本遨遊話舊因、不通言語倍傷神、雖題未識雲中鳳、鑿齒焉知世上麟、璧號連城須遇主、珠稱照乘必依人、東夷習禮終無侶、南國多才自有真、從古英雄猶佩劍、當今豪傑亦埋輪、乘風破浪平生願、萬里遙遙若比隣。

夏五念二日、林大學頭、都筑駿河守等、會議附錄條約十三款、彼此恪遵永久、并准箱館步遊五里之遙、明年通商貿易、提督是日請各官于火船宴會、另演火船戰法與之看、適雨而回、予聞下田雲松裔善口筆、請其書畫十餘本、但其字多大草、仍有龍飛鳳舞之勢、人罕識之、季夏朔日、亞國火船返港、各官泛舟送行、越六日、還琉球、其官饋來食料、亞船受之、望後一日、總理大臣尚宏勳布政大夫馬良才、請提督各官詣那霸公館宴會、享設甚豐、相議和好章程、務祈遵守罔替、總理大臣書字一幅贈予、是程明道先賢詩也、六日念五日、予到那霸海旁、于岡脊上見有醫館、英國伯德令在此居住、予入其館、則寬曠幽雅、時當盛暑、海風徐來、胸懷頓覺爽快、是日提督傳琉球官將器皿什物陳設公館、以備亞人採買、其物不過烟包、烟草、花布、蕉布、粗漆器、瓦器等類而已、每銀一圓、准錢一千四百文、外國洋船所取薪水、每千觔亦議定價、在條約內、以垂久遠、越三日、各船返埠、提督在美士摇被先回香港、予同衞廉士在鉋了丹火船往浙江寧波、船泊于虎蹟山外、予上鎮海入縣城、用四工銀貿絲價畧低于粵

省、其時寧波土人、與西洋爭鬧、亞國排難解紛、而免滋事、七月初二、火船駛至福州、其處水淺、船泊于洋外、是晚風颶、隔日以小舟棹入一百八十里、是乃府城、七夕火船駛至厦門、是時厦門土匪、經清兵蕩平、該處人民紛紛貿易矣、七月十四火船還香港、始知粵省各處之亂、內治安冊二十一欵、後願表陳諸君子。

續生物總論 虫魚類

爬虫乃第一類生物之第三種、令人瞻之、則駭且厭、第傷人者少、其色多斑、爬虫心肺之部位、有與禽獸不同、其血不能盡經于肺、所經者不承天氣之化、如哺乳及禽鳥之全備、是故其血本寒、性質遲慢、及四肢愚鈍也、其爲物也、雖無食無氣、亦能久全、若於寒方隆冬之際、常伏不出、即其身偶有受傷、比之獸之温血者、尤忘其苦、時或失去一體、或肢或目、亦能再萌、其子由卵以生、不用殷勤乎之、其子難長、既長則常久不死。○爬虫分爲四等、曰龜、曰龍子、曰蛇、曰蛙。第一等曰龜、如脚魚等亦入此等、均有二硬殼、一在背上、一在腹下、其背上殼、

乃脊骨及脅骨所連生、其腹下殼、乃胸骨之開張耳、龜無齒、惟頰硬如角以代之、居於陸者、背殼甚厚而駝、足趾幾盡相連、其所食乃樹根、百菓小虫等、有居於澤者、其背比陸居者畧平、其趾四開、而爪尤長、有居於熱地之海中者、其足善於游泳、多食海藻、及藻中小虫以生、此族即脚魚類。○爬虫之第二等曰龍子類、其身圓長、其尾前大後小、以漸而尖、四足趾爪多長、鱗甲方、圓、大、小、不同、頰有多齒甚鋭、故能噬而不能嚼、居於水者極多、故恒名之爲水陸之物、但在水中不能吸噴、必收蓄其氣、待呼吸時、則昂首水面而爲之、分爲六家。首家乃鱷魚、舌纖而柔、左右貼連下頷、鼻孔內有二皮、能開閉、以制其氣之出入、眼蓋三層、其項難左右轉動、前二足有五趾、後足四趾。二家乃守宮、其爲物也、靈變無毒、其舌分岐而出、前後之足、均有五趾。第三家乃蛤蚧、下頷有囊、背脊有鱗一串、如牙突起。第四家乃雷公蛇、雖平滑之處、亦能倒懸而行、其背向下、若青蠅。然第五家乃石龍子、此物時變其色、蓋因血之行於皮有多寡也。第六家乃蜥蜴、或爲物所驚、轉瞬能穴入沙內。○爬虫之第三等乃蛇類、其所以異於別

東京帝國大學文科大學史料編纂掛編纂

大日本古文書

幕末外國關係文書附錄之一

東京帝國大學藏版

濕灑貫珎ニ日米條約締結ノコトヲ識ス

日本ニ於テ石炭ヲ求ムル必要

九　米國使節隨行清國人羅森日本日記

（嘉永六年十二月十五日より安政元年七月十四日に至る　米國使節應接の模樣其他日本に於て見聞の件）

○此日記ハ、香港英華書院發行遐邇貫珍ニ載セタルモノナリ、今原本ヲ獲ル能ハザルヲ以テ、向山篤ノ録鈔ニカヽル謄録一冊及ビ中村不能齋筆記ニ收ムル所ニ據ル、

日本日記

日本日記

遐邇貫珍數號、每記花旗國與日本相立和約之事、至第十號、則載兩國所議定約條之大意、今有一唐人、爲余平素知己之友、去年搭花旗火船、遊至日本、與助立約之事、故將所見所聞、日逐詳記、編成一帙、歸而授余、玆特著于貫珍之中、以廣讀者之聞見、庶幾耳目爲之一新、但因限于篇幅、未便詳叙、此月祇印其三分之一、餘待後續、

合衆國金山名爲拉寃、近今人多往彼貿易、洋西而遠、(注六)欲設火船、而石煤不足、必于日本中歩之區、添買煤炭、能設火船、便于來往、是故癸亥三月、合衆國火船于日

出帆

琉球ニ到ル

琉球ノ風俗

本、商議通商之事、未達允、依是年十月二十二(注二七)、有某友、請予同往日本共議條約、予卜之吉、十二月十五、揚帆、十六、予于火船默觀、指示機宜、後在船上、仰看雲氣、見南方之雲如獅添翼、直騰天頂、北方雲氣低小、内藏殺氣、惟有小雲數簇、而會于獅々之鼻有氣、嘘共小雲、不久而北方之殺氣俱滅、惟獅愈久而愈壯、予因對某友曰、此日之事、初恐不允、後必允成、天道已先兆矣、某友以言爲奇、且試驗之、越三日、火船直向東北而駛、出了臺灣之外、幾日不見天涯、是時北風大作、波濤沖天、火船亦甚顛簸、而不能立、見有沙鷗隨風而逐浪心、直駛七日、漸見小山、而到琉球、々々一國長圍一百七十五里、其國城在地球圍緯線赤道之北二十六度十四分、經線中華北京偏東十一度二十四分、自明以來、世封王爵、叨列藩籬、其處土產、不過蕃薯菜油黑糖等類、人民束髻大袖、足穿草履、男女難辨、頭上祇插一簪、二簪爲別、故少年之男女、皆目觀無異、及其壯也、皆留鬚髯、故街上長鬚之人甚多、甲寅正月初一、予上岸遊玩、見街上兒童甚多、分以銅錢、各極歡喜、人民亦甚纖嗇、民居門亦貼新春聯于門外、但不見有別等繁華之事、那覇有寺、々内有園、是名家世官之墳所、以石刊刻姓名年號于碑上、每日道人打掃、供奉生花樹葉于墓前、另有人家祖墳、與中國之明塚無異、峰巒之上、樹木多植、民房則以巒石圍墻、内以茅草結屋、而居

淳樸ノ風上古ノ世ニ同ジ

提督ペリー王宮ヲ訪フ

琉球ヲ發シテ日本ニ向フ

横濱ニ碇泊ス

林大學頭等應接

住物椅棹俱無、惟以草薦席膝而坐、對火盆而吹煙、民間亦有識中國言語字墨者、不張鋪店、惟有墟場、男不貿易、婦女爲之、以貨易貨、而外方之金銀弗惰焉、然而百姓亦甚畏官長、飯食亦甚粗糲、甘守樸儉、不務奢華、亦鮮欺詐、板門紙窓、夜間亦不防竊、會見途中拾物、亦能以返原人、公門之内、冷々落々、並無案牘之煩、淳樸之風略有同于上古之世、我等外國之欲買什物、須言于官、々爲代辦、正月初六、提督被理衛廉士等、一班將官、布列威嚴、與予乘轎至王宮、總理大臣備宴勸爲主席、布政大夫馬貢才爲知客、享宴甚豐、食物多與中國無異、宴後各官皆饋、有紙扇煙包布烏等項、是物雖粗、此亦世子之崇敬外國、故亞國亦以禮物而返贈之、世子王宮離岸三里、在于山頂、是名守禮、將至其宮、一路亦有樹木石牌坊、宮室亦甚寬大幽雅、垣局可觀、其處多栽鳳尾草松樹等類、以障陰、山邊田土、樹藝五穀、近海沙田水漲之後、人收其沙以煎鹽、此時明月當圓、予覧山川、亦足見一方之風景、越二日、揚帆往日本、四日不觀(注二八)天涯、海水共長天一色、偶見鯨魚四丈餘、在船頭噴逐水花、越片時而進、經歷無人洲、兩日而遣日本、共合火船兵船九隻、泊于横濱、此時正月當春、予望横濱、百里之遙、有尖峯高約八里、白雲迷之、其山勢龍豚、由此層々疊々起伏、結搆于江戶、江戶即日本之京都、其京城大君開知亞國兵船至境、則命林大學頭

應接吏米船訪問
日本人ノ扮裝
横濱ニ應接場ヲ造ル
使節上陸
平山謙二郎清國爭亂ノコトヲ問フ

鵜殿民部少輔伊澤美作守井戸、對馬等、以辦其事、初時兩國未曾相交、各有猜疑、日本官艇亦有百數、泊于遠岸、皆是布帆、而軍營器械各亦准備、以防人之不仁、次日、有官艇二三隻、來視火船、艇尾揷一藍白旗、上寫御用二字、亞人招之上船、以礼待之、與其玩視船上之鐵炮輪機等物、各官喜悅、予見其官粧飾、則闊衣大袖、腰佩双刀、束髮(髮カ)剃去腦信一方、足穿草履、以錦褲外套至腰、不同言語、與其筆談、其亦叙邂逅相遇、景仰中國文物之邦云、予問其名、則曰、山本文之助、曰、堀達之助、曰、合原操藏、曰、名村五八郎、乃是日本之官也、因而各叙寒暄、次日、其官饋來蘿蔔一艇、鷄二十頭、蛋五百枚、柑數箱、葱數担、亞船受之、而荅以物、因而與之酌議通商之事、其官返報大君、大君則築公館于横濱、內結綾綢屛障氈蓆而相會、命林大學頭爲欽差、合衆國欽差大臣駐中華日本天竺等海權官本國師船提督被理、布列威嚴、上岸相會、衞廉士爲通理國師、星以通好條約、各官于館內、俱有饌盃餅食、欵待不過鮮魚蠔蜆鷄蛋蘿蔔黃酒而已、其處人民不畜牛羊豚豕、亦不宰生而食、客予見人家畜鷄至數年而不宰者、以言食物、則万不及于中國矣、欽差接收條約、五日、始有回音、自此每日俱有官至船、給來薪水鷄蛋鮮魚等物、有平山謙二郎者、其人純厚博學、趨而問予中國治乱之端、予將平日紀錄之事、及治安策視之、其付來一信曰、

平山ノ書翰
我祖宗ノ外交ヲ絕ツ所以
萬國ノ交際ハ宜シク義ヲ以テスベシ利ヲ以テ

仁台文章煥發、議論正大、昨日實會之事、未遑詳讀、願借册子、携回一涉、下日完璧于横濱公館云、予因與之、閱畢送返、亦答予書曰、

爾來契闊、未審起居、筆硯清貝否、頃者被視南京紀事及治安策二册子、熟讀數四、始審中國治乱之由、且知羅向喬之學術淳正、愛君憂國之志、流離顚沛未嘗忘、亦未嘗不捲卷而嘆也、民情下欝、下情不達、人牧失職、賄賂公行、古今季運之通病也、所以然者何也、曰利而已矣、嗚呼、利者人之所共欲、而万害所由胎也、子罕言利、常杜其源也、我祖宗絕交于外邦者、以其利以惑愚夫、究理之奇術以騙頑民、頑民相競、唯利是趣、唯奇是趣、駸々乎至于忘忠孝廉耻、而無父無君之極也、原夫天道流行、發育万物之妙理、則茫々堪輿之間、雖氷海夜國人、亦孰非天地之赤子、孰非相愛相友之人、所以聖人一視同仁、不分彼是也、全地球之中、礼讓信義以相交焉、則大和流行、天地惠然之心見矣、若夫貿易競利以交焉、則爭狠獄訟所由起、寧不如無焉、是我祖宗所深慮者也、由是觀之、則交際一也、唯有無相通、患難相救、則天地自然之道、所謂太平和好之眞者、只逐錐頭之末、惟利是務、則人欲爭狠之由、不能始終其事者也、兩者相去一髮、無他、義與利之分而已、古往今來、千百万年、治乱興廢、起戎出好、未嘗不决乎此也、凡萬國交際之道、

スベカラズ
我邦近時大ニ武備ヲ脩ム
相撲ヲシテ米ヲ運搬セシム

宜首講此義也、次練兵講武、代天心以行天討、各國君王、所以不可一日而闕焉者也、昇平之久、忽之則所由衰也、我邦有深省于此者、近頃練兵講武、演炮製艦、日就月將、不數年馴致乎湯武之正兵、夫然而後始可保万年不朽之太平耳、不然則或奸臣巨盜、暴乱威刧、無以征之、全地球中强并弱、大吞小、殆庶幾乎虎狼之交矣、惟上帝鬼神以父母之心、視其赤子之相欺相爭、寧不惻然乎、不憫然乎、全世界中各國布棋、賢君英主、必不乏其人矣、先著鞭以奉行天道者誰也、方今世界形勢一變、各國君主、當爲天地立心、爲生民立命之秋也、向喬寓合衆國火船、而周遊乎四海、有親觀焉者乎、若不然、請足跡到處、必以此道說各國君主、是繼孔孟之志于千万年後、以擴于全世界中者也、今因完附二册子、錄所當志、以告諸羅向喬、並候崇安、(千八百五十四年十一月、〇コヽニ向喬トアルハ、羅森ノ號ナラン、第四卷第五六五頁ニ、向喬ト署名セル羅森ノ詩ヲ收メタリ、參看スベシ、)

續日本日記

(二)

三月初旬、提督再會林大學頭于公館、其時公館之旁、有茶花數簇、燦爛鮮紅、天氣嚴寒、林大學頭(饋脫カ)以粟米數百苞、每包約二百余斤重、遣肥人九十餘名、俱裸體、一夫獲擧二三包、不一時而數百包之粟米、盡遷于海畔、再後、復使肥人淸服赤体、以武

日本士ヲ取ル方法、
扇面ニ書ヲ請フモノ多シ
箱館下田ヲ開ク
獻上品

力角于公館之墀、勝者賞酒三巵、予在公館、閱視數刻、亦足見日本之多勇力人也、合原操藏、是浦賀府之官、予問其國取士之方、稱說、文武藝身言皆取、而詩不以擧官、所讀者亦以孔孟之書、而諸子百家亦復不少、所謂讀書而稱士者、皆佩雙劒、殆尙文而兼尙武歟、日本人民、自從葡萄牙滋事、立法拒之、至今二百余年、未曾得見外方人面、故多酷愛中國文字詩詞、予或到公館、每々多人請予錄扇、一月之間、從其所請、不下五百余柄、三月廿五、林大學頭相議條約之事、已成則允準箱館下田二港、以爲亞國取給薪水食料石炭之處、由是兩國和好、各釋猜疑、過日、提督請林大學頭、于火船宴會、船上綵奏樂、日本官員數十、于火船上大宴、有詩爲証、

兩國橫濱會、驪虞一類同、解冠稱礼義、佩劒羨英雄、樂奏巴人調、殺陳大古風、幾番和悅意、立約告成功、

宴罷、于船歌舞、日暮方終、次日、亞國以火輪車、浮浪艇、電理機、日影像、耕農具等物、贈其大君、卽于橫濱之郊、築一圓路、燒試火車、旋轉極快、人多稱奇、電理機、是用銅線通于遠處、能以此之音信、立刻傳達于彼、其應如響、日影像、以鏡向日、繪照成像、毋庸筆描、歷久不變、浮浪艇、內有風箱、或風壞船、則以此能浮、生保命、耕農具、是亞國奇巧耕具、未勞而穫者、大君得收各物、亦以漆器瓷器綢緞等物還礼、官士明篤

以、

元旦試筆錄以視予、曰

斗轉年還改、書生世事灰、空懷宗慤志、終乏武侯才、詩就聊揮筆、憂多復舉杯、依々門外柳、青眼爲誰開、　玉斧、僧居中以新陰咏視予、曰、

昨夜惜華窓下詠、今朝愛綠苑中吟、人間何識天公意、已變紅林作碧林、

予亦咏詩以返之、

遙見春色偶爲吟、日本山川雪尽侵、古徑茶花紅滿簇、羣岡松樹翠爲陰、沙鷗冒雨浮波面、海鳥隨風逐浪心、岸側軍營烟漠々、灣中戰艦霧沉々、橫濱築館應非遠、江戶樓臺望轉深、未識人家何處是、泛舟搖漾到前林、

橫濱附近ヲ遊覽ス

是日予遊橫濱、見郊外祗有龍神古廟、以木爲之、內懸鏡像、儼若興雲致雨之意、有店燒瓦、其瓦堅實灰色而厚、不同中國之式、再行二三里、則有人居屋、亦或灰或草結蓋屋外、多以紙符貼于門上、女畏見外方之人、予橫濱祗見一婦人而已、越數日、

下田ニ赴ク

事畢、火船由橫濱一日而至下田、下田之港在地球圖緯線赤道之北三十四度三十九分、經線中華北京偏東二十二度二十九分、其處有山水灌溉澤邊、膏腴肥潤、以此名曰下田、下田港心有一小石島、居中以爲該處之水口、船隻泊入于內、但見

山環海繞、垣局稠密、雖有颶風亦甚堅穩、其時火船寄泊島邊、一望四圍之山、俱有大石盤脚、波浪故不撼搨之、山上樹木蔚茂、亦有雉鷄雁鷹鴉水鴨猓狸之類、次日、

提督了仙寺ニ館ス

提督上岸、館于法順山了仙寺、其寺有僧、名日淨、小徒二名、內有佛殿、々旁墳所、各家信士信女之墓也、墓以石爲墳塔、僧人時々掃除、供奉名花、寺陵有石亭小魚池花果等類、是日、在此烹茶、男女千百、入寺觀看、以物賞之、女亦不羞避、衣長委地、腰

下田ノ風俗

後有裙、以紅綢束其髻、顏色亦多美艷、少年則朱唇皓齒、及至生育子女後、則以五倍粉染黑其牙、再日、往遊街市、見舖屋、或編以茅草、或乘以灰瓦、比鄰而居、屋內通連、故曾入門見其人、再入別屋、而亦見其人也、女人過家過巷、男女不分、雖于途間招之亦至、婦人多有裸裎傭工者、稠人廣衆、男不羞見下体、女看淫畫爲平常、竟有洗身屋、男女同浴于一室之中而不嫌避者、每見外方人、男女則趨而爭看、雙刀人至、則走離兩旁、其街則有大工町伊勢町店之町池之町新町各等町十余條、循海

玉泉寺ヲ觀ル

濱過橋里許、名柿崎、則有玉泉寺、々外蒼松陰翳、門向石島、遮攔外洋泙湃之勢、茲于寺旁、准以一地爲亞國之墳所、其處人民俱重拜佛、雖山邊海旁、多以石刻置佛像、墳墓石碑、多刻南無妙法蓮華經、予至大安寺、見人拜佛、不設香燭、拜後放錢數文于箱、名曰放生錢、寺有僧二名、以紙求予書、予觀山景、則書峰廻水遶四字與之、

某亦題詩曰、

一丈方庵玉座同、寸餘硯石白雲通、黃金畢竟塵中物、不省明朝炊米空、

同座之間、適有女人拜寺、但見、

朱唇皓齒逞嬌姿、雲髻斜釵淡掃眉、半面新粧却絕妙、恰如明月掛梅枝、

是日、天氣太暖、在寺烹茶、其處之茶味、略帶甘甜、似同于西樵茶味、步出寺門、（外ノ本）一箭之地、有山溪、砂石流泉、水光徹底、堪以濯纓、池之町有一廟、內制偶像、身帶弓矢、廟墻每懸一鏡、画一船、大抵人家行洋、托賴平安酬恩之意、亦有髮髻數十枚、掛于牆上、亦是酬恩者、此日本之大略風俗然也、其處山嶺、杜鵑花甚盛、而各花亦復不少、

日本政俗ノ善ヲ稱ス

衞廉士曾採名花數百種、壓乾以備考覽、所謂多識鳥獸草木之名歟、夫一方斯有一方之善政、日本雖國小于中華、然而搶掠暴却之風、亦未嘗見破其屋、門雖以紙糊、亦無有鼠竊狗偸之弊、此見致治之略各有其能矣、是日、遊山不識路、得遇僧人、引步行、遶五里、有人村、名洲崎、適遇菊地森之助談、問亞國所遵何教、予曰、其所奉者獨一神、々卽造化之主宰、所謂昭事上帝、聿懷多福、其明徵歟、因在途間、言難悉述、遂作別于松陰之下、步至海旁、多見大鮑魚、是下田之土產也、回于町店買物、則

御用所

以漆器瓷器爲佳、所揀（陳カ）物品、則書名于物上記價、然後店人送到御用所、交價于官、

日本ノ貨幣

々者海關之吏也、近藤良次主之、御用所卽其處之海關也、設官數名、而司買物之事、每洋銀一圓、作錢一千六百文、其日本則有當百之大錢、亦有純金一分、亦有純金大判、亦有一分銀、亦有二朱金、二朱則表金而裏銀也、世間乃通用、可易當百八枚、一分銀可易當百十六枚、四分銀可易一小判、黃金大判則以分銀百余方、按時價而兌換、行歷下田七里之遙、未曾見一羊一豕、馬則多有以負物、牛則間有以耕田、女人織布、與中國無異、打鐵倣木、亦與中國略同、而女工之顧繡未曾覩也、男人

扇面ニ書ヲ請フモノ多シ

女子俱倘扇、予于下田、一月之間、所寫其扇不下千余柄矣、黑川嘉兵衞是主理下田事務之官、堀達之助、森山榮之助、中臺信太郎等、是行事之官、共以扇請書、付詩一首、○大槻清崇詩文集寧靜閣三集ニ收ムル所ノ昨夢詩曆ニ、贈清人羅森トシテ、此詩ヲ載セタリ、但夷ヲ蠻トシ、鼙ヲ戰トシ、色ヲ眼トスルヲ異ニスルノミ、

避亂夷船亦一奇、呉中鼙鼓不聞知、縱將萬里東來色、快覩芙蓉絕世姿、

關研次詩曰、

橫濱相遇豈無因、和議皆安仰賴君、遠方缺舌今朝會、幸觀同文對語人、

合原猪三郎、其於臨別、贈予墨盒一詩一、曰、

樹外雨收鶯語流、聲々啼送旅人舟、不知黃帽金衣客、得解轉蓬飄泊愁、

續日本日記終

箱館ニ赴ク

四月十六、火船啓行、五日至箱館、在地球圖緯線、赤道之北四十一度四十九分、經線、中華北京偏東二十四度十九分、天氣寒熱與盛京同、惟此處僻土偏壤、地多沙漠、生物不毛、故民之食貨、恆取給于別埠、此港爲船隻運貨往來之區、因號其名曰箱館、其港垣局寬曠、海闊山朝、時當五月、尚有白雪于山巔、房屋較下田而壯麗、衣冠人物、似富盛于下田、婦女羞見外方人、深閨屋內、而不出頭露面、風俗尚正、人民鮮説淫辭、其處有護國山、々有一寺、畫棟雕梁、寺中器皿鮮明、牆懸佛家偶像、寺旁亦墳墓之所、提督遣人于此、繪照日影像、以贈各官、松前大夫勘解由之公館、(松前)幽雅潔淨、貼近海濱、登樓眺望、用千里鏡、窺看微茫之際、見有人村甚多、遙山遠水、如看畫圖、予同辨地衞廉士等、入而晤之、欵接甚恭、人品醇善、遠藤又左衞門是參議、石塚官藏町奉行、工藤茂五郎是縣令、關央、老(蛯)子次郎是近書、代島剛平藤原主馬是司事、相議于港行步之規、共説必俟江戸君主之命、乃能議定、往遊町上、百姓畁躬、敬畏官長、人民肅穆、膝跪路旁、不見一婦人面、舖戸多閉、因亞國船初至此、人民不知何故、是先逃于遠鄉者過半、蓋以温語安撫百姓、乃敢還港貿易、街上驢馬數百、多負食物于遠方、此處舖店亦用紙糊、多稱野屋龜屋、與下田無異、此處店內綢縐

箱館ノ風俗

松前大夫ノ公館ヲ訪フ

米船ノ至ルヲ見テ遠鄉ニ逃ル、者多シ

亦多、但不及中土、惟描金漆器極佳、人多愛之、三日間、于店上品漆器沽之竭矣、此處土產鹿皮鮑魚昆布白糖茶葉等項、食物豐美于下田、越數日、平山謙二郎與安間純之進等、由江戸前來、約返下田與林大學頭、以定箱館行步之規、予將臨別、謙二郎以唐詩錄扇贈予曰、

平山安間江戸ヨリ來ル

渭城朝雨浥輕塵、客舍青々柳色新、勸君更盡一杯酒、西出陽關無故人、

予答其詩曰、

火船飛出粵之東、此日揚帆碧(鏡一本)海中、歷覽螺峰情不盡、遙瞻蜃室與無窮、双輪撥浪如奔馬、一舵分流若耿虹、漫道騎鯨冲巨浪、休誇跨鶴振長風、琉球乍到雲方散、日本初臨雪正融、暫寄一身天地外、知音聊與訴離衷、

是日、遠藤贈予画二幅、所繪亦與中國無異、大夫贈書數卷、其書字板勝於中土、予各以香珠答之、卽于五月初九揚帆、其官用艇送出山外、火船行五日、回下田、次日將官一班、布列威儀上岸、與林大學頭宴會于了仙寺、午後亞國官兵、排列隊伍、歷遊各町、男女人民觀者如堵、伊澤氏之侍兒桂正敏、年紀雖小、身佩双劍、志氣昂々、善于應答、復能于公堂之上、描繪亞國各官之像、聰明俊秀、人多悦之、大醫文荃問予中國取士之方、予曰、中國讀孔孟書、伸明孔孟之理、以文字分爲八股、謂之文章、

下田ニ回ル

使節上陸

文章之外、別詠一詩、雖小試會試亦復如此、越日、有官至船、贈予詩曰、

君產廣東我沽津、相逢萍水亦天緣、火船直擘鯨濤至、看破五湖無限邊、

復遇明篤筆談、曰、子乃中國之士、何歸鴃舌之門、孟子所謂下喬木而入幽谷者非歟、予因寓意、吟成七律一首、以示之、曰、

日本遨遊話舊因、不通言語倍傷神、雕題未識雲中鳳、鑿齒焉知世上麟、璧號連城須遇主、珠稱照乘必依人、東夷習礼終無侶、南國多才自有眞、從古英雄猶佩劍、當今豪傑亦埋輪、乘風破浪平生願、萬里遙々若比隣、

夏五念二日、林大學頭都筑駿河守等、會議附錄條約十三款、彼此恪遵永久、幷准箱館步遊五里之遙、明年通商貿易、提督是日請各官于火船宴會、別演火船戰法、與之看、遇雨而回、予聞下田雲松窩善口筆、請其書畫十餘本、但其字多大草、仍有龍飛鳳舞之勢、人罕識之、季夏朔日、亞國火船返港、各官泛舟送行、越六日、還琉球、其官饋來食料、亞船受之、望後一日、總理大臣尚宏勳、布政大夫馬良才、請提督各官、詣那覇公館宴會、享設甚豐、相議和好章程、務祈遵守罔替、總理大臣書字一幅贈予、是程明道先賢詩也、六月念五日、予到那覇海、旁于岡脊山、見有醫館、英國伯德令在此居住、予入其館、則寬曠幽雅、時當盛暑、海風徐來、胸懷頓覺爽快、是日、提

條約附錄

米船ノ饗應

下田ヲ發シテ琉球ニ還ル

和好章程ヲ議ス

督傳琉球官、將器皿什物、陳設公館、以備亞人採買、其物不過烟包煙草花布蕉布粗漆器瓦器等類而已、每銀一圓、准錢一千四百文、外國洋船所取薪水、每千觔亦議定價、在條約內、以垂久遠、越三日、各船返埠、提督在美士攝被、先回香港、予同衞廉士、在鮑了丹火船、往浙江寧波、船泊于虎靖山外、予上鎭海入縣城、用四工錢貿綵、價略低于粵省、其時寧波土人、與西洋爭鬪、亞國排難解紛、而免滋事、七月初二、火船駛至福州、其處水淺、船泊于洋外、是晚風颶、隔日、以小舟棹入一百八十里、是乃府城、七夕、火船駛至厦門、是時厦門土匪、經清兵蕩平、該處人民、紛々貿易矣、七月十四、火船還香港、始知粵省各處之乱、內治安冊二十一欵、後願表陳諸君子、（千八百五十五年正月、）

寧波ノ土人西洋人ト爭鬪ス

香港ニ還リテ粵省各處ノ亂ヲ知ル

日本日记

·罗　森·

《走向世界丛书》编者按：罗森《日本日记》，原载一八五四年十一月号、十二月号和一八五五年一月号的《遐迩贯珍》月刊（香港英华书院发行），今据日本小岛晋治教授提供的日本辑印本（汉文）排印。

日本辑印本题为：

米国使节随行清国人罗森日本日记

（嘉永六年十二月十五日至安政元年七月十四日）

题后并有一小注，略云：《遐迩贯珍》原本不易获得，此系据向山笃《蠹馀一得》及中村《不能斋笔记》所录重印。

英华书院（英文名"Anglo－Chinese College"）由第一个来华的基督教（新教）教士罗伯特·马礼逊（Robert Morrison）于一八一八年创办于马六甲，一八四二年迁至香港。《遐迩贯珍》（英文名"Chinese Serial"）系以英华书院名义发行之中文月刊，创刊于咸丰三年（一八五三年），由麦都思（W·H·Medhurst）为主笔；次年，由奚礼尔（C·B·Hiller）继任；咸丰六年（一八五六年）改由理雅各（J·Legge）为主笔，旋即停刊。

《遐迩贯珍》编者按：《遐迩贯珍》数号，每记花旗国与日本相立和约之事。至第十号，则载两国所议定约条之大意。今有一唐人，为余平素知己之友，去年搭花旗火船游至日本，以助立约之事；故将所见所闻，日逐详记，编成一帙，归而授余。兹特著于《贯珍》之中，以广读者之闻见，庶几耳目为之一新。但因限于篇幅，未便详叙，此月只印其三分之一，馀待后续。

合众国火船往日本

合众国①金山名驾拉宽②，近今人多往彼贸易。洋西面辽阔，欲设火船，而石煤不足；必于日本中步之区，添买煤炭，能设火船，便于来往。是故癸丑③三月，合众国火船于日本商议通商之事，未遽允依。是年十月二十二，有某友请予同往日本，共议条约。予卜之吉，十二月十五扬帆。

十六，予于火船默祝指示机宜。后在船上仰看云气，见南方之云如狮添翼，直腾天顶；北方云气低小，内藏杀气，惟有小云数簇而会于狮；狮之鼻有气压其小云，不久而北方之杀气俱灭，惟狮愈久而愈壮。予因对某友曰，此日之事：初恐不允，后必允成，天道已先兆矣。某友以言为奇，且试验之。

①合众国：美国。 ②驾拉宽：加利福尼亚。 ③癸丑：公元1853年，清咸丰三年，日本嘉永六年。

28

越三日，火船直向东北而驶，出了台湾之外，几日不见天涯。是时，北风大作，波浪冲天，火船亦甚飘荡，而不能立。见有沙鸥，随风而逐浪心。直驶七日，渐见小山，而到琉球。

琉球一国，长阔一百七十五里，其国城在地球图纬线赤道之北二十六度十四分，经线中华北京偏东十一度二十四分。自明以来，世封王爵，叨列藩篱。其处土产，不过蔬菜、番薯、菜油、黑糖等类。人民束髻大袖，足穿草履。男女妆饰，头上只插一簪二簪为别；故少年之男女，瞥目则无异。及其壮也，皆留鬚髯，故街上长鬚之人甚多。

琉球一瞥

甲寅① 正月初一，予上岸游玩，见街上儿童甚多。分以铜钱，各极欢喜。人民亦甚谦恭。民居间亦贴新春联于门外，但不见有别等繁华之事。那霸有寺，寺内有园，是名家世官之坟所，以石刊刻姓名、年号于碑上。每日道人打扫，供奉生花树叶于墓前。另有人家祖坟，与中国之明冢无异。峰峦之上，树木多植。民房则以峦石围墙，内以茅草结屋而居。住物椅桌俱无，惟以草席屈膝而坐，对火盆而吹烟。民间亦有识中国言语字墨者。不张铺店，惟有墟场。男不贸易，妇女为之，以货易货，而外方之金银弗尚焉。然而百姓亦甚畏官长。饭食亦甚粗粕，甘守朴俭，不务奢华，亦鲜欺

那霸风俗

①甲寅：咸丰四年（1854年），日本安政元年。

诈。板门纸窗，夜间亦不防窃。会见途中拾物，亦能以返原人。公门之内，冷冷落落，并无案牍之烦。淳朴之风，略有同于上古之世。我等外国之欲买什物，须言于官，官为代办。

随被里访琉球王宫

正月初六，提督被里①、卫廉士等一班将官，布列威严，与予乘轿至王宫。总理大臣尚宏勋为主席，布政大夫马良才为知客，享宴甚丰，食物多与中国无异。宴后，各官皆馈，有纸扇、烟包、布帛等项。是物虽粗，此亦世子之恭敬外国，故亚国②亦以礼物而返赠之。世子王宫离岸三里，在于山顶，是名守礼。将至其宫，一路亦有树木、石牌坊。宫室亦甚宽大幽雅，垣局可观。其处多栽凤尾草、森树等类以障阴。山边田土，树艺五谷。近海沙田，水涨之后，人收其沙以煎盐。此时明月当圆，予览山川，亦足见一方之风景。

火船兵船共九只

越二日，扬帆往日本。四日不观天涯，海水共长天一色。偶见鲸鱼四丈馀，在船头喷逐水花，越片时而逝。经历无人洲，两日而造日本。共合火船、兵船九只，泊于横滨。

此时正月当春，予望横滨，百里之遥，有尖峰，高约八里，白云迷之。其山势龙脉，由此层层叠叠起伏，结搆于江户③。江户即日本之京都，其京城大君④闻知亚国兵

①被里：M·C·Perry，又译作柏利、培理，美国海军准将，时任东印度舰队司令。　②亚国：亚美利亚国之简称，即美国。　③江户：现东京。　④京城大君：此指江户的幕府大将军。

船至境，则命林大学头鹈殿、民部少辅伊泽美作守、井大对马等，以办其事。初事，两国未曾相交，各有猜疑。日本官艇亦有百数泊于远岸，皆是布帆，而军营器械各亦准备，以防人之不仁。次日，有官艇二三只来视火船。艇尾插一蓝白旗，上写“御用”二字。亚人招之上船，以礼待之，与其玩视船上之铁炮、轮机等物，各官喜悦。

日本官艇来视火船

予见其官妆饰，则阔衣大袖，腰佩双刀，束发，剃去脑信一方，足穿草履，以锦裤外套至腰。不同言语，与其笔谈，其亦叙邂逅相遇，景仰中国文物之邦云。予问其名，则曰山本文之助，曰堀达之助，曰合原操藏，曰名村五八郎，乃是日本之官也，因而各叙寒暄。

次日，其官馈来萝蔔一艇、鸡二十头、蛋五百枚、柑数箱、葱数担。亚船受之，而答以物，因而与之酌议通商之事。

其官返报大君。大君则筑公馆于横滨，内结绫绉屏障毡席而相会，命林大学头为钦差。合众国钦差大臣、驻中华日本天竺① 等海权官、本国师船提督被理，布列威严，上岸相会。卫廉士为通理国师，呈以通好条约。各官于馆内俱有馔盆饼食，款待不过鲜鱼、蠔蚬、鸡蛋、萝蔔、黄酒而已。其处人民不畜牛羊豚豕，亦不宰生而食客，予见人家畜鸡至数

横滨会谈

①天竺：印度。

年而不宰者。以言食物，则万不及于中国矣。钦差接收条约，五日始有回音。自此每日俱有官至船，给来薪水、鸡蛋、鲜鱼等物。

林鹅殿接条约

有平山谦二郎者，其人纯厚博学，趋而问予中国治乱之端。予将平日纪录之事及《治安策》视之。其付来一信曰："仁台文章焕发，议论正大。昨日宾会之事，未遑详读。愿借册子携回一涉，下日完璧于横滨公馆"云。予因与之。阅毕送返，亦答予书曰：

平山谦二郎来书

尔来契阔，未审起居笔砚清良否？顷者，披视《南京纪事》及《治安策》二册子，熟读数四，始审中国治乱之由；且知罗向乔② 之学术淳正，爱君忧国之志流离颠沛未尝忘，亦未尝不捲卷而叹也！

民情下郁，下情不达，人牧失职，贿赂公行，古今季运之通病也。所以然者，何也？曰利而已矣。

呜呼！利者，人之所共欲，而万害所由胎也。子罕言利，常杜其源也。

言闭关锁国之理由

我祖宗绝交于外邦者，以其利以惑愚夫，究理之奇术以骗顽民。顽民相竞，唯利是趣，唯奇是趣，骎骎乎至于忘忠孝廉耻，而无父无君之极也。原夫天道流行，发育万物之妙理，则茫茫堪

①向乔：罗森别字。

舆之间，虽冰海夜国人，亦孰非天地之赤子？孰非相爱相友之人？所以圣人一视同仁，不分彼此也。全地球之中，礼让信义以相交焉，则大和流行，天地惠然之心见矣。若夫贸易竞利以交焉，则争狠狱讼所由起，宁不如无焉。是我祖宗所深虑者也。

万国交际不宜言利

由是观之，则交际一也。唯有无相通，患难相救，则天地自然之道，所谓太平和好之真者；只逐锥头之末，惟利是务，则人欲争狠之由，不能始终其事者也。两者相去一发，无他，义与利之分而已。古往今来，千百万年，治乱兴废，起戎出好，未尝不决乎此也。凡万国交际之道，宜首讲此义也。

次练兵讲武，代天心以行天讨。各国君王，所以不可一日而缺焉者也。升平之久，忽之则所由衰也。我邦有深省于此者，近顷练兵讲武，演炮制舰，日就月将，不数年驯致乎汤武之正兵，夫然而后始可保万年不朽之太平耳。不然，则或奸臣巨盗，暴乱威劫，无以征之。全地球中强并弱，大吞小，殆庶几乎虎狼之交矣。惟上帝鬼神以父母之心，视其赤子之相欺相争，宁不恻然乎？不悯然乎？

请罗宣扬孔孟之道

全世界中各国布棋，贤君英主，必不乏其人矣。先着鞭以奉行天道者，谁也？方今世界形势一变，各国君主当为天地立心、为生民立命之秋也。向乔寓合众国火轮而周游乎四海，有亲观焉者乎？若不然，请足迹到处，必以此道说各国君主，是继孔孟之志于千万年后，以扩于全世界中者也。

今因完附二册子，录所当志，以告诸罗向乔，并候崇安。

〔以上载一千八百五十四年十一月《遐迩贯珍》〕

日人显示孔武有力

三月初旬，提督再会林大学头于公馆。其时公馆之旁，有茶花数簇，灿烂鲜红，天气严寒。林大学头馈以粟米数百包，每包约二百馀斤重。遣肥人九十馀名，俱裸体，一夫获举二三包，不一时而数百包之粟米尽迁于海畔。再后，复使肥人清服赤体，以武力角于公馆之墀，胜者赏酒三卮。予在公馆阅视数刻，亦足见日本之多勇力人也。

合原操藏，是浦贺府之官。予问其国取士之方，称说文、武、艺、身、言皆取，而诗不以举官。所读者亦以孔孟之书，而诸子百家亦复不少。所谓读书而称士者，皆佩双剑，殆尚文而兼尚武欤？

一月写扇五百馀柄

日本人民自从葡萄牙滋事，立法拒之，至今二百馀年，未曾得见外方人面，故多酷爱中国文字诗词。予或到公馆，每每多人请予录扇。一月之间，从其所请，不下五百馀柄。

三月廿五，林大学头相议条约之事已成．则允准箱馆①、下田②二港以为亚国取给薪水、食料、石炭之处。由是两国和好，各释猜疑。过日，提督请林大学头于火船

①箱馆：今称函馆，在北海道。 ②下田：在横滨西南伊豆半岛南端。

34

宴会。船上彩奏乐，日本官员数十于火船上大宴。有诗为证：

两国横滨会，骓虞一类同。解冠称礼义，佩剑美英雄。
乐奏巴人调，肴陈太古风。几番和悦意，立约告成功。

烧试火车
日人称奇

宴罢，于船歌舞，日暮方终。次日，亚国以火轮车、浮浪艇、电理机①、日影像②、耕农具等物赠其大君。即于横滨之郊筑一圆路，烧试火车，旋转极快，人多称奇。电理机是以铜线通于远处，能以此之音信立刻传达于彼，其应如响。日影像以镜向日绘照成像，毋庸笔描，历久不变。浮浪艇内有风箱，或风坏船，即以此能浮生保命。耕农具是亚国奇巧耕具，未劳而获者。大君得收各物，亦以漆器、瓷器、绸绉等物还礼。

官士叨笃以《元旦试笔》录以视予，曰：

斗转年还改，书生世事厌。空怀宗悫志，终乏武侯才。
诗就聊挥笔，忧多复举杯。依依门外柳，青眼为谁开？

玉斧僧居中以《新阴咏》视予，曰：

昨夜惜华窗下咏，今朝爱绿苑中吟。
人间何识天心意，已变红林作碧林。

予亦咏诗以返之：

①电理机：电话机。　②日影像：照像机。

与日人以诗相酬答

遥见春色偶为吟，日本山川雪尽侵。古径茶花红满簇，群冈松树翠为阴。沙鸥冒雨浮波面，海鸟随风逐浪心。岸侧军营烟漠漠，湾中战舰雾沉沉。横滨筑馆应非远，江户楼台望转深。未识人家何处是，泛舟摇漾到前林。

是日，予游横滨，见郊外只有龙神古庙，以木为之，内悬镜像，俨若兴云致雨之意。有店烧瓦，其瓦坚实，灰色而厚，不同中国之式。再行二三里，则有人居屋，亦或灰或草结盖屋，外多以纸符贴于门上。女畏见外方之人，予横滨只见一妇人而已。

至下田

越数日，事毕，火船由横滨一日而至下田。下田之港在地球图纬线赤道之北三十四度三十九分，经线中华北京偏东二十二度二十九分。其处有山水灌溉，泽边膏腴肥润，以此名曰下田。下田港心，有一小石岛居中，以为该处之水口。船只泊入于内，但见山环海绕，垣局稠密，虽有飓风，亦甚坚稳。其时火船寄泊岛边，一望四围之山，俱有大石盘脚，波浪故不撼塌之。山上树木蔚茂，亦有雉鸡、雁、鹰、鸦、水鸭、猓狸之类。

提督上岸

次日，提督上岸，馆于法顺山了仙寺。其寺有僧，名日净，小徒二名。内有佛殿。殿旁坟所，各家信士信女之墓也。墓以石为坟塔，僧人时时扫除，供奉名花。寺陵有石亭、小鱼池、花果等类。是日在此烹茶，男女千百入寺观看，以物赏之。女亦不羞避，衣长委地，腰后有裙，以红绸束其髻，颜色亦多美艳。少年则朱唇皓齿，及至生育子女后，则以五倍粉染黑其牙。

男女不分

再日，往游街市。见铺屋，或编以茅草，或乘以灰瓦。比邻而居，屋内通连。故曾入门见其人，再入别屋，而亦见其人也。女人过家过巷，男女不分，虽于途间招之亦至。妇人多有裸裎佣工者。稠人广众，男不羞见下体，女看淫画为平常。竟有洗身屋，男女同浴于一室之中，而不嫌避者。每见外方人，男女则趋而争看。双刀人至，则走离两旁。

其街则有大工町、伊势町、店之町、池之町、新町、各等町十馀条。循海滨，过桥里许名柿崎，则有玉泉寺。寺外苍松阴翳，门向石岛，遮拦外洋泙湃之势。兹于寺旁准以一地为亚国之坟所。

拜　佛

其处人民俱重拜佛。虽山边海旁，多以石刻置佛像。坟墓石碑，多刻南无妙法莲华经。予至大安寺，见人拜佛，不设香烛，拜后放钱数文于箱，名曰放生钱。寺有僧二名，以纸求予书。予观山景，则书“峰回水绕”四字与之。某亦题诗曰：

一丈方庵玉座同，寸馀砚石白云通。
黄金毕竟尘中物，不省明朝炊米空。

同座之间，适有女人拜寺，但见：

朱唇皓齿逞娇姿，云髻斜钗淡扫眉。
半面新妆却绝妙，恰如明月挂梅枝。

是日，天气太暖，在寺烹茶。其处之茶味略带甘甜，似同于西樵茶味。步出寺门〔原注：一本作寺外〕一箭之地，有山溪，砂石流泉，水光彻底，堪以濯缨。池之町有一庙，内制偶像，身带弓矢。庙墙每悬一镜，画一船，大抵人家行洋，托赖平安酬恩之意。亦有发髻数十枚挂于墙上，亦是酬恩者。此日本之大略风俗然也。

神庙

其处山岭，杜鹃花甚盛，而各花亦复不少。卫廉士曾采名花数百种，压干以备考览，所谓多识鸟兽草木之名欤！

夫一方斯有一方之善政，日本虽国小于中华，然而抢掠暴却〔劫〕之风，亦未尝见。破其屋，门虽以纸糊，亦无有鼠窃狗偷之弊。此见致治之略，各有其能矣。

谈西洋宗教

是日游山，不识路，得遇僧人引步。行逾五里，有人，村名洲崎。适遇菊地森之助，谈，问亚国所遵何教？予曰："其所奉者独一神，神即造化之主宰。所谓昭事上帝，聿怀多福，其明徵欤！"因在途间，言难悉述，遂作别于松阴之下。

步至海旁，多见大鲍鱼，是下田之土产也。回于町店买物，则以漆器、瓷器为佳。所拣物品，则书名于物上，记价，然后店人送到御用所，交价于官。官者，海关之吏也，近藤良次主之。御用所即其处之海关也，设官数名，而司买物之事。每洋银一元，作钱一千六百文。

御用所即海关

其日本则有当百之大钱，亦有纯金一分，亦有纯金大判，亦有一分银，亦有二朱金。二朱则表金而里银也，世间乃通用，可易当百八枚。一分银可易当百十六枚。四分银可易一小判。黄金大判则以分银百馀方，按时价而兑换。

行历下田七里之遥，未曾见一羊一豕，马则多有以负物，牛则间有以耕田。女人织布与中国无异。打铁做木，亦与中国略同。而女工之顾绣未曾睹也。男人女子俱尚扇。予于下田，一月之间，所写其扇不下千馀柄矣。

黑川嘉兵卫是主理下田事务之官，堀达之助、森山荣之助、中台信太郎等是行事之官，共以扇请书。付诗一首：

避乱夷船亦一奇，吴中鼙鼓不闻知。
翻将万里东来色，快睹芙蓉绝世姿。

关研次诗曰：

横滨相遇岂无因，和议皆安仰赖君。
远方鴃舌今朝会，幸观同文对语人。

合原猪三郎，其于临别赠予墨盒一，诗一，曰：

树外雨收莺语流，声声啼送旅人舟。
不知黄帽金衣客，得解转蓬飘泊愁？

〔以上载一千八百五十四年十二月《遐迩贯珍》〕

至箱馆

四月十六，火船启行。五日至箱馆，在地球图纬线赤道之北四十一度四十九分，经线中华北京偏东二十四度十九分。天气寒热，与盛京同。惟此处僻土偏壤，地多沙漠，生物不毛；故民之食货，恒取给于别埠。北港为船只运货往来之区，因号其名曰箱馆。其港垣局宽旷，海阔山朝。时当五月，尚有白雪于山巅。房屋较下田而壮丽，衣冠人物似富盛于下田。妇女羞见外方人，深闺屋内，而不出头露面。风俗尚正，人民鲜说淫辞。

其处有护国山，山有一寺，画栋雕梁。寺中器皿鲜明，墙悬佛家偶像。寺旁亦坟墓之所。提督遣人于此，绘照日影像，以赠各官。

访问松前大夫公馆

松前大夫勘解〔原注：松前〕由之公馆，幽雅洁净，贴近海滨。登楼眺望，用千里镜窥看，微茫之际，见有人村甚多。遥山远水，如看画图。予同辨地、卫廉士等入而晤之，款接甚恭，人品醇善。

远藤又左卫门是参议，石冢官藏町奉行，工藤茂五郎是县令，关央老〔原注：蛯〕子次郎是近书，代岛刚平、藤原主马是司事，相议于港行步之规，共说必俟江户君主之命，乃能议定。

火船初至人民奔逃

往游町上。百姓卑躬，敬畏官长。人民肃穆，膝跪路旁。不见一妇人面。铺户多闭。因亚国船初至此，人民不知何故，是先逃于远乡者过半。盖以温语安抚百姓，乃敢还港贸易。街上驴马数百，多负食物于远方。此处铺店亦用纸糊，多称野屋、龟屋，与下田无异。此处店内绸绉亦多，但不及中土。惟描金漆器极佳，人多爱之。三日间，于店上品漆器沽之竭矣。此处土产鹿皮、鲍鱼、昆布、白糖、茶叶等项，食物丰美于下田。

越数日，平山谦二郎与安间纯之进等由江户前来，约返下田与林大学头以定箱馆行步之规。予将临别，谦二郎以唐诗录扇赠予曰：

谦二郎写王维诗

渭城朝雨浥轻尘，客舍青青柳色新。
劝君更尽一杯酒，西出阳关无故人。

予答其诗曰：

火船飞出粤之东，此日扬帆碧海中。（原注：一作碧镜）
历览螺峰情不尽，遥瞻蛟室兴无穷。
双轮拨浪如奔马，一舵分流若耿虹。
漫道骑鲸冲巨浪，休夸跨鹤振长风。
琉球乍到云方散，日本初临雪正融。
暂寄一身天地外，知音聊与诉离衷。

是日，远藤赠予画二幅，所绘亦与中国无异。大夫赠书数卷，其书字板胜于中土。予各以香珠答之。即于五月初九扬帆。其官用艇送出山外。

火船行五日，回下田。次日，将官一班，布列威仪，上

官兵排队历游各町

岸，与林大学头宴会于了仙寺。午后，亚国官兵排列队伍，历游各町，男女人民观者如堵。

伊泽氏之侍儿桂正敏，年纪虽小，身佩双剑，志气昂昂，善于应答。复能于公堂之上，描绘亚国各官之像，聪明俊秀，人多悦之。

大医文荃问余中国取士之方。予曰："中国读孔孟书，伸明孔孟之理。以文字分为八股，谓之文章。文章之外，别咏一诗。虽小试、会试，亦复如此。"

越日，有官至船，赠予诗曰：

君产广东我沽津，相逢萍水亦天缘。
火船直劈鲸涛至，看破五湖无限边。

中国之士何归鴂舌

复遇明笃，笔谈曰："子乃中国之士，何归鴂舌之门？孟子所谓下乔木而入幽谷者非欤？"予因寓意吟成七律一首以示之，曰：

日本遨游话旧因，不通言语倍伤神。
雕题未识云中凤，凿齿焉知世上麟。
璧号连城须遇主，珠称照乘必依人。
东夷习礼终无侣，南国多才自有真。
从古英雄犹佩剑，当今豪杰亦埋轮。
乘风破浪平生愿，万里遥遥若比邻。

夏五念二日，林大学头、都筑骏河守等、会议附录条约十三款，彼此恪遵永久。并准箱馆步游五里之遥，明年通商贸易。提督是日请各官于火船宴会，别演火船战法与之看，遇雨而回。

予闻下田云松窝善口笔，请其书画十馀本；但其字多大草，仍有龙飞凤舞之势，人罕识之。

季夏朔日，亚国火船返港，各官泛舟送行。

越六日，还琉球。其官馈来食料，亚船受之。望后一日，总理大臣尚宏勋、布政大夫马良才，请提督各官诣那霸公馆宴会，享受甚丰，相议和好章程，务祈遵守罔替。总理大臣书字一幅赠予，是程明道先贤诗也。

琉球总理书字相赠

六月念五日，予到那霸海旁，于冈脊山见有医馆，英国伯德令在此居住。予入其馆，则宽旷幽雅。时当盛暑，海风徐来，胸怀顿觉爽快。是日，提督传琉球官，将器皿什物陈设公馆，以备亚人采买。其物不过烟包、烟草、花布、蕉布、粗漆器、瓦器等类而已。每银一元准钱一千四百文。外国洋船所取薪水，每千斤亦议定价在条约内，以垂久远。

购买土产

越三日，各船返埠。提督在美士摄被先回香港。予同卫廉士在“鲍了丹”火船，往浙江宁波。船泊于虎靖山外。予上镇海，入县城，用四工钱贸丝，价略低于粤省。其时宁波土人与西洋争闹，亚国排难解纷，而免滋事。七月初二，火船驶至福州。其处水浅，船泊于洋外。是晚风飓。隔日，以小舟棹入一百八十里，是乃府城。七夕，火船驶至厦门。是时，厦

宁波人与洋人争闹

门土匪经清兵荡平，该处人民纷纷贸易矣。七月十四，火船还香港，始知粤省各处之乱。内治安册二十一款，后愿表陈诸君子。

〔以上载一千八百五十五年正月《遐迩贯珍》〕

33d Congress, 2d Session.	HOUSE OF REPRESENTATIVES.	Ex. Doc. No. 97.

NARRATIVE

OF

THE EXPEDITION OF AN AMERICAN SQUADRON

TO

THE CHINA SEAS AND JAPAN,

PERFORMED IN THE YEARS 1852, 1853, AND 1854,

UNDER THE COMMAND OF

COMMODORE M. C. PERRY, UNITED STATES NAVY,

BY

ORDER OF THE GOVERNMENT OF THE UNITED STATES.

VOLUME II—WITH ILLUSTRATIONS.

WASHINGTON:
A. O. P. NICHOLSON, PRINTER.
1856.

アメリカ艦隊による

中国海域および日本への

遠征記

合衆国政府の命を受け
合衆国海軍　M・C・ペリー提督によって
1852、1853、および1854年に実施された。

第2巻—図版付

ワシントン
1856年

JOURNAL

OF

THE SECOND VISIT OF COMMODORE PERRY TO JAPAN.

BY A NATIVE OF CHINA.

Among those who embarked in China on board the squadron, when it left for Japan the second time, was a very intelligent and educated Chinaman, who acted as clerk to our interpreter, Mr. Williams. This observant individual, on his return to China, furnished to the "Overland Register," published at Hong Kong, a copy of the journal he had kept on his visit to Japan, in which paper it appeared in an English translation.

As it is a specimen of the intelligence of an educated Chinaman, and as, besides, it presents briefly the views of an Oriental, uninfluenced by the prevalent opinions of our countrymen around him, (for difference of language prevented much interchange of thought,) it has been supposed that it would not be without interest to the American reader, and a place has, therefore, been reserved for it in the appendix to this volume.

From the "Overland Register and Price Current" of Hong Kong, September 11, 1854.

"*Journal of a visit to Japan.*—Under this heading, in the body of the paper, will be found a very interesting paper. It is a literal translation of a journal kept by a Chinese gentleman who was attached to the United States squadron on its second visit to Japan. The letter addressed to the journalist by *Ping-saw-heem-arh-lang* is especially worthy of attention."

"JOURNAL OF A VISIT TO JAPAN.

"Of late years, the intercourse between China and the State of California, in America, has greatly increased in extent and frequency. In consequence, the government of the United States was anxious that steam vessels should run between the two countries, and it became necessary to have an arrangement by which they could purchase coal at the Japanese islands, which lie between America and Asia. To obtain this, several steamers belonging to the United States visited Japan, in the third month of last year, (April or May,) and it was attempted to negotiate a treaty of peace and commerce, but the Japanese could not at once conclude the matter. An agreement was deferred for some time; and on the 10th of January, 1854, according to foreign computation of time, Mr. ——— asked me if I would go to Japan to assist in the preparation of the contemplated treaty. After some deliberation I consented, and on the 13th we spread our sails—got up our steam rather—and began our voyage. Next day, having prayed and sought for help and teaching, as I stood upon the steamer's deck, I looked up, and was struck by the appearance of clouds in the south and northern quarters of the heavens. In

ペリー提督の第2回日本訪問

ある中国人が記した日誌

2度目の日本訪問に向けて中国から出航する際、通訳のウィリアムズ氏の助手として働いていた、非常に教養があり優秀な中国人［羅森（ルオセン）］がほかの者と一緒に艦隊に加わった。観察眼の鋭い彼は、中国に帰国する際に、日本訪問時に記した日誌を香港の『オーバーランド・レジスター』紙に提供し、それが英訳されて発表された。

この日誌は、教養ある中国人の知性をよく表わしており、また、周囲のアメリカ人の考えに影響されない東洋人（言葉の壁のためあまり意思の疎通がうまくいかなかった）としての見解が記されているため、合衆国の読者にとっても興味深いものと考え、この巻の付録に付け加えた。

1854年9月11日の香港の『オーバーランド・レジスター』と『プライス・カレント』の記事より

「*日本訪問日誌*—本紙のこの題名の記事は非常に興味深いものである。これは、合衆国艦隊の第2回日本訪問に同行したある中国人紳士が記した日誌をそのまま英訳したものである。彼に宛てた平山謙二郎の手紙もとくに注目に値する。」

「日本訪問日誌」

近年、中国とアメリカのカリフォルニア州との交流は規模も頻度も非常に増大している。その結果、合衆国政府は両国の間に蒸気船を就航させたいと考え、そのためには、アメリカとアジアの間に位置する日本の島々で石炭の補給を受けられるよう取り決めることが必要になってきた。この目的を達成するため、去年の旧暦の3月（欧暦の4月か5月）に数隻の蒸気船が合衆国から日本を訪れ、友好通商条約を結ぼうとしたが、日本人はすぐには結論を出せなかった。条約についての話し合いはしばらく延期された。外国の暦でいう1854年1月10日、私は——氏［原文通り］から、日本に行ってこの条約の準備を手伝うよう依頼された。しばらく考えたのち、私は同意し、1月13日にわれわれは「帆」を上げた。いや、蒸気船なので「蒸気」を上げて出発したと言うべきか。翌日、祈りを捧げ、助力と教示を願ったあと、私は蒸気船のデッキに立って空を見上げたところ、空の南と北にある雲の形に驚いた。南には、天頂に向かって飛び上がる翼を持った獅子のような雲があった。一方、北の雲は低くて途切れており、打ち負かされた軍隊のようであった。ちょうど、南の獅子の息によって北から南に向かって小さな雲が流れ、それにより獅子がますます大きくなって、北の雲がだんだん消滅していくような形になっていた。私はこれを見て、友人に、「われわれの遠征は、最初は困難にぶつかるが、結局は成功するということをあの雲が予言している」と言った。友人は、「それは変な話だ。まあ、どうなるか見ていようじゃないか」と言った。

the south they assumed the form of a winged lion, springing up to the zenith, while those in the north were low and broken, like a slaughtered army. A few cloudlets seemed to have floated away from them towards the south, till they were arrested by the lion's breath, whose figure, moreover, continued to dilate, while the clouds in the north gradually disappeared altogether. After looking at these appearances, I said to my friend, 'The heavens prognosticate that our expedition will finally be successful, but difficulties will have to be overcome in the first place.' 'Your words,' said he, 'are strange; let us wait for the event.'

"After three days our vessel steamed right towards the northeast; we passed Formosa, and for some days saw no land. At the same time the wind blew very strong from the north. The steamer was tossed about as if it had been a fan, while all around it there were gulls darting and flying about. In this way we went along for seven days, when we came in sight of land, which was declared to be Lew-k'ew.

"Lew-k'ew, or, as Europeans and Americans call it, Loo Choo, is a small island, about 100 leagues long, and 30 or 40 leagues broad. Its chief town lies in latitude 26° 14′ N., longitude 127° 52′ E.

"From the time of the Ming dynasty, its chief has received investiture from our emperor, having the title of a king. It is a poor territory, yielding only sweet potatoes, some vegetables, a black kind of sugar, vegetable oil, and a few other things. The people bind up their hair in a knot, and wear very large sleeves to their coats. Their shoes are made of grass. The men wear two long pins through their top-knots, and the women one. This is the only distinction between them in their dress, so that when they are young it is not easy to know them from one another, but as they grow up the beard, which is not shaven, sufficiently characterizes the males. One is surprised to see the middle-aged men walking about the streets all with long beards.

"On the first day of our new year, (January 29,) I went on shore for a ramble, and finding a lot of boys on the street, gave them a few cash, which greatly delighted them. The people were very humble. Outside the doors of some of the houses congratulatory sentences were posted up, as in China at the new year, but there was no excitement and no other sign of rejoicing. At Napa I found a temple, and in the garden attached to it the burying place of the families of distinction. The surnames and names of the dead, and the time when they lived, were engraven on tombstones. Every day the priests, I was told, swept them clean, and placed before them flowers and leaves of trees. The tombs of the common people are like those which obtained in China during the time of the Ming dynasty.

"The heights all around were covered with trees. The people I found living in grass huts, put up with enclosures formed of rough stones. Their dwellings had no furniture. For stools and chairs, they use grass mats, on which they *hunker* on their knees and toes, having a pan of fire before them, at which they light their pipes. A few of them can speak and read Chinese. They have no shops, but a market ground, where the business of exchanging commodities is conducted by the women. Thus they do not use money, and care little for the coins of other countries. The common people stand in great awe of their rulers. They are very plain in their diet, and seldom impose on one another. The doors of their houses are merely thin boards, and for windows they use paper, but they pass the nights without fear of thieves; and I have seen, when a man dropped anything on the way, another pick it up and restore it to him. In their public courts there is almost nothing to do—no quarrels to decide, no litigations to settle. Their manners resemble those of the golden age in high antiquity. Whenever we strangers

396

3日後、われわれの蒸気船は北東に向かった。台湾を通過したあと、数日間は陸地が見えなかった。同時に、北から非常に強い風が吹いてきた。蒸気船は扇のように揺れ、周囲にはカモメが飛び交っていた。このような状態で7日間進んだところで陸地が見え、それが琉球だと知らされた。

琉球（欧米人はルーチュウと呼ぶ）は小さな島で、長さは100リーグ［約500キロメートル］、幅は3、40リーグである。代表的な町は北緯26度14分、東経127度52分のところにある。

明の時代から、琉球の首長はわれわれの皇帝から王という称号を与えられている。琉球は貧しい国で、サツマイモ、いくらかの野菜、黒っぽい砂糖、植物油、そのほかわずかなものしかできない。住民は髪を髷に結い上げており、非常に大きな袖のついた上着を着て、草から作った靴をはいている。男は頭上の髷に2本の長いかんざしを刺しており、女は1本だけである。服装の違いはこれだけなので、子供のうちは男女の区別がつきにくい。しかし、鬚を剃らないため、男はすぐ分かる。通りを歩いている中年の男たちが全員長い鬚をたくわえているのを見ると誰でも驚くだろう。

われわれの新年最初の日（1月29日）、散歩しようと上陸したところ、通りに多くの少年がいた。小銭をやると非常に喜んだ。人々はとても質素である。中国の新年と同様、家の外に祝賀文を書いた札が張ってある家もあったが、興奮の声も喜びの声も聞こえてこなかった。那覇で見かけた寺には、付属の庭園に高貴な家族の埋葬場所があった。墓石には死者の姓名と生没年が彫られていた。聞くところによると、僧侶が毎日墓を清め、花や葉を供えるということである。一般の人々の墓は、明の時代の中国の墓と似ている。

周囲の丘はすべて木におおわれている。私が会った人々は草葺きの家に住んでおり、家の周囲にはごつごつした石を積み上げて囲いが作られていた。家に家具はない。腰掛けや椅子ではなく蓙の上にしゃがむ。十能［炭を入れて運ぶ道具］の前にしゃがんで、煙管に火をつける。なかには中国語の読み書きができる者もいる。店はなく、市場で女たちが日用品を物々交換している。このようにお金を使わないため、外国の貨幣に対しても無関心である。一般の人々は、お上を非常に恐れている。食事は非常に質素で、互いに騙しあうことはない。家の戸は薄い板があるだけで、窓には紙が使われているが、夜、泥棒に入られる心配はしていない。また、道でなにかを落としても、誰かが拾って追いかけて渡してやるのを見た。裁判所ではほとんどなにもすることがない。争いも訴訟もないのである。彼らの性質ははるか昔の黄金時代の人々のものに似ている。われわれ外国人がなにかを買いたい場合は、まず行政官に報告して彼にその売買を任せなければならない。

2月3日、ペリー提督および艦隊の大勢の将校は、美々しく着飾って轎［おおいのない輿のこと］に乗り王宮に進んだ。私もこれに同行した。われわれをもてなす席では、総理大臣の尚宏勲が主人役をつとめ、財務官の馬良才に迎えられた。大宴会が開かれたが、素材はわれわれが中国で使うものと同じであった。宴会が終わると、さまざまな役人が客に扇、煙草入れ、絹などの贈り物をした。高価なものではなかったが、王が外国に対して尊敬を表わすための品々であった。アメリカ人の将校もお返しの贈り物をした。王の姿を見ることはできなかったが、話によると、王はまだ子供であるので、外国人を恐れているということであった。王宮は、海岸から3リーグ［約15キロメートル］離れた首里という丘の上にある。王宮への道は両側に大木が植えられており、また、道には祝賀のアーチがいくつもかかっていた。王宮の建物は大きくて美しく、大量の鳳尾草［イノモトソウ］が繁っており、また、多くのタイワンセンダンやそのほかの木が涼しい木陰を作っていた。丘の

wanted to buy anything, it was necessary for us to inform the magistrates, who thereupon managed the business.

"On the 3d of February, Commodore Perry and many officers of the Expedition appeared in full dress and display, and proceeded in chairs to the palace of the king, I also accompanying them. The prime-minister, Shang-hwang-heun, presided at an entertainment which was given to us, and we were received by the treasurer, Ma-leang-tsae. A grand feast was set out, the articles being the same as we use in China, and at the conclusion, the various officers made presents to their guests of fans, tobacco-pouches, silk, and other things. They were not of much value, but this being the way in which their king expresses his respect for foreign nations, the American officers gave them presents in return. The king himself we did not see, but were told that he was young, and would be frightened at us. The palace is on the top of a hill named *Sew-le*, about three leagues from the shore. On both sides of the way to it were large trees, and it was adorned with many commemorative arches. The building itself is large and beautiful, with great quantities of the phœnix-tail grass, and many of the *melia asedarach* and other trees growing about it, and affording a pleasant shade. On the hill-sides and in the fields we saw grain growing, and on the shore there were several salt pans. At this time the moon was advancing to the full, and beneath her light I enjoyed the pleasant scenery.

"Two days after we resumed our voyage, and proceeded towards Japan. For four days we were out of sight of land, and on one occasion I saw a whale more than forty feet long spouting out a jet of water from its head and then disappearing. By-and-by we passed some uninhabited islands, and in two days more the steamers and sailing vessels, amounting in all to nine, cast anchor near to Hwang-pin, called by the Japanese themselves Yoku-hama. The season being spring and the air clear, I saw at a distance, as I judged, of a hundred *le.* inland from Yokuhama a lofty mountain, rising up seven or eight *le.*, its summits covered with snow. From the highest peak lesser though still lofty elevations succeeded to one another, as if in a chain, and reach as far as Keanghoo or Yedo, the capital of the country. When the emperor heard of the arrival of the Expedition, he sent commissioners to negotiate with the visitors, the chief commissioner being of the surname of Lin. I do not give the names of the others, because I really never could distinguish on their cards what was surname and name, what was office and what was place.

"On both sides, this being the commencement of intercourse between their respective countries, there seemed at first to be some suspicions. I observed a fleet of more than a hundred Japanese vessels, all with cloth sails, drawn up some distance off, near the shore, and on the land was a camp full of soldiers and their accoutrements, all in preparation for any hostilities which might arise. Next day two or three government boats came off to see the steamers, carrying at their stern a blue and white flag, with the words 'Imperial Service' on it. The American officers received the parties very courteously, and showed them the guns, trains, and everything on board their vessel. The visitors were greatly delighted. Their dress was wide and loose, with large sleeves. Each man had a couple of swords at his girdle. Their hair was tied up in a knot, a small space over the *pia mater* in front being shaven. They wore shoes made of straw, and their trowsers were of gay and very various colors. Notwithstanding the difference of their language, I could introduce myself to them by means of the pencil, as they understood the Chinese character, and they responded to me in the same way, expressing their admiration of my country, and their pleasure at making my acquaintance. Many of them wrote down for me their names and titles, and a friendship was thus established between us.

397

斜面や畑には穀物が栽培されており、海岸にはいくつかの塩田があった。ちょうど満月に近い頃で、私は美しい風景を楽しむことができた。

2日後、われわれは日本に向けて出航した。4日間は陸地が見えなかった。長さ40フィート［約12メートル］以上もあるクジラが潮を吹いてまた波間に消えるのを1度だけ見た。やがて無人島を通過し、2日後には、蒸気船や帆船合わせて9隻の船が、日本人がヨコハマと呼ぶ横浜の近くに錨を下ろした。季節は春で空気は澄んでいた。横浜から内陸へ私の目測でおよそ100里［約67キロメートル］のところに大きな山があった。高さは7、8里で頂上は雪でおおわれていた。その周囲には、これよりはやや低いものの、高山が連なっており、これは首都である江戸（ジャンフー）あるいはエドまで続いている。艦隊の到着を聞いた大君［将軍］は、訪問者と協議するために委員らを派遣してきた。首席委員の名字は林（リン）といった。そのほかの委員の名前は、名刺を見ても名字や名前、役所名や地名の区別がよく分からないのでここにはあげない。

日米双方とも、これが初めての取り引きであるため、最初はいくらか疑心暗鬼であった。日本側は、海岸近くに帆を張った100隻以上の船を遠巻きに待機させ、また、陸上には多数の兵士と装具をそろえて交戦という事態に供えていた。翌日には、船尾に『御用』と書かれた青と白の旗をつけた政府の用船が2、3隻、蒸気船にやってきた。アメリカの士官はこの一行を丁重に迎え、蒸気船にある銃砲、輪機［機関車］などすべてを見せた。訪問者は非常に喜んでいた。彼らの衣服は幅広くてゆるやかなもので、袖が大きかった。それぞれが腰に2本の刀を差していた。彼らは、前頭の軟膜の上にあたる部分を剃り、髪を髷に結っていた。藁（わら）で作った靴をはき、華やかでさまざまな色のズボンをはいていた。言葉の違いはあったものの、彼らは漢字が読めるので、私は筆を使って筆談で自己紹介をすることができた。彼らも筆談で、私の国に敬意を表すること、また、近づきになれて光栄だということを表わした。このようにして訪問者の多くがそれぞれの名前と役職名を書いてくれ、双方に友好関係が生まれた。

翌日、蒸気船に贈り物が届いた。小舟一杯のカブ、鶏20羽、卵500個、ミカン数箱、タマネギ数担［1担は約60.5キログラム］を受け取り、お返しに相応の贈り物をした。そのあと、交渉開始が提案された。これに対して、日本の委員らが首都に指示を仰いだところ、訪問者を受け入れるための建物を海岸付近に建設する命令が出された。これはすぐ実行に移され、立派な建物が建てられた。公衆の目をさえぎるために周囲には絹の布が張りめぐらされ、床には畳や毛氈（もうせん）が敷かれた。日本側の首席委員は林——［原文通り］、アメリカ側の首席は東インド、中国、日本海域合衆国海軍司令長官マシュー・C・ペリーであった。合衆国側の通訳としてウィリアムズ博士がついた。この会見に出席した士官に出された膳の上には、新鮮な魚、牡蠣などの貝、鶏の卵、カブを使った料理と黄色っぽいワインがのっていた。日本人は羊、牛、豚を飼うことはせず、また、動物を殺して訪問者に料理を出すこともしない。鶏も多数飼われているが、多くはかなり歳をとるまで生きのびている。日本人の食事だけを見ると、中国の食事よりかなり貧しい。

日本側の委員は、合衆国側が提案する条約の項目を受け取り、その5日後に返事を持ってきた。それ以来、毎日のように役人が船にやってきて、燃料、水、卵、魚の供給が行なわれた。われわれの船にやってくる役人のなかに、平山謙二郎という、学問にすぐれた立派な人物がいた。彼は私の国で現在起こっている騒乱についてたずねた。私は彼に、この暴動について私が書いた報告書と、良い政府の原理についての論文集を1冊見せ

Next day a present came off to the steamer, consisting of one boat of turnips, twenty fowls, five hundred eggs, several boxes of oranges, and several piculs of onions. These things were received, and corresponding presents were returned, after which it was proposed to commence the negotiations. On this the commissioners sent for instructions to the capital, and received orders to erect a building on shore, where they should received the visitors. This was soon done, and a fine building it was, hung round with silk, screened off from the public gaze by elegant curtains, the floor being laid with mats and carpets. Lin ——— was the chief commissioner on the Japanese side, and on the American side was Matthew C. Perry, commander-in-chief of the United States naval forces in the East India, China, and Japan seas—with him was Dr. Williams, interpreter for the United States. For every officer present at the interview there was placed an entertainment on a small table, but it consisted merely of fresh fish, oysters, and other shell-fish, fowls' eggs, turnips, and a yellow looking wine. The Japanese, indeed, do not keep sheep, nor oxen, nor pigs, nor do they kill animals to entertain visitors with. I saw that many even of the fowls, which they do breed, obtained a most venerable age. If we look only at the diet of the people, it is immeasurably inferior to that of the Chinese.

The commissioner having received the articles of the treaty as proposed by the Americans, returned a communication after five days, and from that time, every day, there were officers coming to the ships, and supplies were sent of fuel, water, eggs, and fish. Among those who came to our vessel was a gentleman, named Ping-san-heen-urh-lang, of an ingenious nature and great learning, who asked me about the troubles which are at present distracting my native country. I showed him an account of the insurrection which I had drawn up, and a volume of essays on the principles of good government. These he borrowed of me the next day, in a polite manner, and returned them before long with the following letter:

"I trust that since I saw you, you have been well, and pursuing with pleasure your literary avocations. I have read carefully the record concerning the affairs at Nanking, and the volume of essays, with the perusal of which you favored me. I have learned two things from them, for, in the first, place they have made me acquainted with the causes of the present confusion in China, and, in the next, they display your own learning and worth. In times of disorder and difficulty, you have not forgotten the regard for your sovereign and interest in your country, which every good man ought to cherish. As I have shut up your volumes, my feelings have found vent in sighs.

"The common people are oppressed and miserable, and the rulers pay no attention to their feelings. They who should be the pastors of the nation fail to dischage their duties; bribery and venality widely prevail; such it seems is the condition of China, from antiquity to the present time—the common diseases of a decaying empire. The essential evil of such a state may be described in a single phrase—it is the desire of gain. Now, the desire of gain is common to all men, and is the pregnant womb of all evil. Confucius seldom spoke of gain, wishing to check the lust of it in its source. This, also, was the reason why my ancestors cut off all intercourse of foreign nations with Japan, because the desire of gain led astray the ignorant people, and wonderful arts in the investigation of principles deceived the perverse,* so that they got striving together, seeking gain and hurrying after what was wonderful, till filial duty, modesty, and the sense of shame were all forgotten. To a man who has reached this stage of evil, neither his father nor his sovereign is anything.

* The Japanese gentleman writes Chinese with great freedom. Few, if any, Sinologues from the west could compete with him. Yet his composition might be plainer in some parts than it is. It is not easy to make out his meaning here, where he is touching on an interesting topic—the reason which induced the exclusion of foreigners from Japan.

398

た。翌日、彼はこれらの本を礼儀正しく私から借りだし、まもなく次の手紙と一緒に返してくれた。

「先日お会いして以来お元気で、著述に励まれていることと存じます。おかげさまで、南京で起こっている事件の記録と論文集を熟読することができました。これらの本から2つのことを学びました。1つは、現在の中国で起こっている混乱の原因です。もう1つは、本に現われているあなたの教養と徳です。混乱と困難の時代にありながら、あなたは故国の独立性と利益を忘れてはおられません。これは正義ある人間が守るべきものであります。あなたのご本を読み終えて閉じたとき、溜息が出ました。

一般の人々は抑圧されて惨めな状態にあるのに、統治者はこれらの人々の感情に無関心です。国を守るべき立場にある人々はその義務を果たしていません。賄賂と不正が蔓延しています。これが中国の現状であるようです。古代から現在まで、これは傾きつつある帝国に共通する病です。このような国の悪の根源は、欲の一語で表わせると思います。この欲はすべての人間にあり、これこそがすべての悪を育むのです。孔子は、欲を生じる心を戒めようと望み、利についてはほとんど語っていません。これも、われわれの先人たちが外国との交流を絶った理由の1つです。といいますのも、欲がありますと無知な人間は道を失い、道を踏み誤った人々には道を追求したせっかくのすばらしい学問も意味をなさず、* 彼らは集まって利益を得ようと争い、焦ってなにかすばらしいものを得ようとしたため、ついには子としての義務、謙遜、羞恥心を忘れてしまったのです。このような悪徳を身につけた者は、父親や国の独立性など歯牙にもかけないのです。

天の道は偉大です。宇宙全体のすべての物を育みます。氷の海の暗黒の国にさえ、天と地の子でない人間はいないのです。隣人を愛し、みなと仲良く暮らさねばならないのです。このため、賢人たちは、誰彼の区別なくすべての人々を同じ慈悲深さで抱擁したのです。相互交流という原則は、世界のどこでも共通です。大切なのは礼儀、親切、誠意、正義です。これを守るならば尊い調和が広がり、天地の心があますところなく現われるのです。

これとは逆に、利益だけを求めて商売を行なえば、争いや訴訟が起こり、喜びではなく呪いとなります。われわれの先人たちはこのような事態を心配したのです。問題をこのように見ると、交流における主題は、人々が豊富に持つ品々を、豊富に持たない品々と交換する方法、つまり、ある国がほかの国をいかにして助けるかに尽きます。その繁栄は天理によってのみ定められ、真に重要な成果は平和、調和、厚情を得ることです。しかし、もし、交流で利益だけを求めるならば、人間の欲望とあさましい情熱を増長させるだけです。このような交流ならば、最初は吉兆のもとではじまったとしてもかならずや悲しむべき結末となるでしょう。結果がこのどちらになるかは本当にわずかな差なのです。利己主義が手綱を握れば、正義はたちまちのうちに欲に飲み込まれてしまうのです。

古代から現代まで、何百年、何千年と繰り返されてきた混乱と無秩序、国の興亡、武力衝突と平和は、すべてこれにより左右されてきました。国が互いに交流を望むなら、正義を重んじるという点を明確にせねばなりません。そして、天による制裁が求められる場合には、兵を動員して戦争の動機について論議を行なえばよい

*この日本の紳士の漢文は非常に流暢である。西洋の中国学の学者にも彼ほどの者は少ないだろう。しかし、ときによっては不備な部分も見られる。日本の鎖国の理由について述べたこの興味深い部分で、彼がなにを言おうとしているのかを理解するのはむずかしい。

"The ways of Heaven are great. It nourishes all things in the universe. Even among the dark countries who dwell by the icy sea, there is not an individual who is not a child of Heaven and Earth—not one who is not made to love his fellows, and be friendly with them. On this account the sages embraced all men with a common benevolence, without distinction of one from another. The principles for mutual intercourse, all over the globe, are the same—propriety, complaisance, good faith, and righteousness. By the observance of these a noble harmony is diffused, and the heart of Heaven and Earth is abundantly displayed.

"If, on the contrary, commerce is conducted merely with a view to gain, quarrels and litigations will spring from it, and it will prove a curse instead of a blessing. Against such a result my ancestors were profoundly anxious. Looking thus at the subject, the one topic of intercourse, it is the means by which people exchange the commodities which they have abundantly, for those which they have not, and one nation succours the distresses of another; its prosperity is plainly indicated by Providence, and peace, harmony, and good feeling are its true results. Yet if gain—gain—be what is sought for by it, it will only develope the lusts and angry passions of men, and there will be a melancholy termination to what may be begun under good auspices. It is but a hair's breadth which separates those different results; for, give selfishness the reins, and righteousness is instantly merged in the desire of gain.

"From ancient times till now, for hundreds and thousands of years, confusion and disorder the rise and fall of states, recourse to arms and words of peace, all have been determined by this. Whenever nations agree to carry on intercourse together, they should speak clearly on this point of righteousness, and then let them exercise their soldiers and discuss the subject of war, that they may be prepared to inflict any punishment which Heaven demands. No sovereign of any kingdom should be unprovided for this.

"It happens, however, that when peace has long prevailed, these important matters are slighted, and thence comes the decay of States. But, in our country, the due precautions for safety have been well attended to. Our soldiers have been trained; the art of war has been discussed; guns have been cast; ships have been built, day after day, and month after month, for many years, and now our troops are like those of the ancient heroes T'ang and Woo. It is in this way that we have secured the continuance of our peace. If we had not done so, some nefarious ministers or powerful thieves might have arisen to excite confusion, and to begin to plunder, and we should be unable to punish them. All over the globe the strong destroy the weak, and the great swallow the small, as if societies of men were like collections of tigers and wolves. God, by his spiritual pervasion, however, sees, with a parent's heart, how His children impose on and strive with one another. Must he not be grieved? must he not be moved to pity?

"But the world may be compared to a chessboard, and every nation, also. There cannot be wanting worthy princes and heroic lords. Who is he that shall go before his fellows, whip in hand, to execute the laws of Heaven? Now great changes are occurring. It is a time of revolutions, when every prince should set his heart to act in obedience to providence, and labor for the good of his people. You ——— now live in a steamship of the United States, and you wander over the seas. Have you seen such a man as I indicate? If you have not, I pray you, wherever you go, to inculcate the principles I have stated on every sovereign and ruler; so shall the wishes of Confucius and Mencius, so many centuries after their time, be made to shine conspicuously in the whole world.

399

のです。独立国家はこのような準備を怠ってはなりません。

しかし、平和が長く続くとこれらの重要なことがおろそかにされて、国家の崩壊がはじまります。しかしわが国は、安全のための準備を怠っていません。何年にもわたって、毎月毎月、日々怠りなく、兵士の訓練、兵法の研究、銃の製造、船の建造が行なわれています。いまやわれわれの軍隊は古代の英雄湯（タン）［湯王。殷王朝の初代の王］と武（ウー）［武王。周王朝初代の王］のようです。われわれはこのようにして平和を守ってきたのです。そうでなければ、不埒な大臣や強大な泥棒が混乱を引き起こし、略奪を始め、しかもこのような輩が処罰されない状態に陥っていたでしょう。人間の社会はあたかも虎や狼の群れのようになり、世界中のいたるところで強者が弱者を破滅させ、大が小を飲み込むことになるでしょう。しかし、天はその広い心で、親のように、子供たちが互いに傷つけあい、争う姿を見ています。天は悲しんで哀れをもよおされるでしょう。

しかし、世界もそれぞれの国も碁盤にたとえられます。有徳の諸侯や英雄は必ずいるでしょう。笞（むち）を片手にみなの前に立って天の法律を実行するのは誰でしょうか。いまや大きな変化が起こりつつあります。諸侯はいまや天理に沿って行動し、その臣民の幸福のために心を砕くという革命の時代なのです。あなたはいま、合衆国の船に乗って海を旅していらっしゃいます。私が述べたような人物にお会いになったことがおありでしょうか。もしいまだお会いになっていないならば、あなたの行く先々で、その国と統治者にこの原則を説いてくださるようお願いいたします。そうすれば、孔子と孟子の願いが、何世紀も経過してやっと世界全体を明るく照らすようになるでしょう。

ここに私の意見を述べさせていただきました。ご本をお返し致します。ご多幸をお祈りしております。」

この手紙に対して、私は次のような返事を出した。

「時は春の第3月に近づき、風景はだんだん美しくなりつつあります。すばらしいお手紙をいただき、大変感動いたしました。私たちは水面を流れる葉のように出会い、あなたのご教示は私に光をなげかけてくれました。世界中のすべての人間は天地の子供であり、天理、礼儀、誠意、正義の原理にしたがって互いを遇するべきだというあなたの言葉はすばらしく、その通りだと思います。また、宇宙の寛大な心とわれわれの賢人の教えにある平等の慈悲心を十分に表わしていると思います。お手紙の一語一語に感謝しております。お言葉を常に心に刻みつけて忘れぬようにいたします。

現代は古代とは非常に異なった時代です。それを知りながら心ある者が見て見ぬふりをすることができるでしょうか。凡才の私ではありますが、何年も世界の出来事に関わってまいりました。イギリスとの戦いにおいても、勇敢な者たちを率いて、全力を尽くして故国のために戦ってまいりました。しかし、私腹を肥やすことだけに熱心な政府の役人は、私の貢献や努力を一顧だにしませんでした。このため私の心は外国に旅することに向けられ、この蒸気船に乗ってここまでやってきたのです。革命が起ころうとしています。権力と利益だけを求める取るに足らないような者が権力の座につき、志と大きな目的を持った者が彼らにより災難に追いやられ、破滅させられているのです。かの賢人の言葉を思い出さねばなりません。『国の政治が良いときには自分の考えを表わしてもよいが、国の政治が悪いときには隠れていよ。』しかし、私はこのような状態から目をそらすことはできませんでしたので、誰かが、その行動と考えで、民衆の良い部分を育て、祖国を永遠に繁栄へ導いてくれることを願って本を2冊書きました。あなたがお読みになったのはその本です。私の望みは、この目

"Herewith, with these observations, I beg to return to you your documents, and wait upon you with my desires for your happiness."

To this letter I returned the following reply:

"Now it is drawing towards the third month of spring, and the landscape is assuming aspects of beauty. I have received your admirable letter, and my poor mind has been not a little enlarged by it. We have come together like the leaves of plants floating on the water, and on me has fallen the light of your instructions. When you say that all in the world are the children of heaven and earth, and that they should treat each other according to the principles of propriety, complaisance, good faith, and righteousness, your words are great and correct, and are sufficient to show the generous spirit of universal and equal benevolence which belongs to the school of our sages. For every word in your letter I shall ever be grateful. I shall wear it at my girdle, and always keep it in remembrance.

"The present age is very different from the times of antiquity; but who, with a conscience, can altogether disregard it? Notwithstanding my want of talent, for years I gave myself to the business of the world. During the war with the English, I led a body of braves, and put forth all my strength in the service of my country. Yet, afterwards, the officers of the government, bent on nothing but gain, made no account of my devotion and efforts. It was this neglect which set my mind on travelling abroad, and led me to my present position on board this steamer. Revolution is impending. Mere ordinary men, whose objects are power and profit, get into the possession of authority, and men of spirit and generous aim are likely to be pushed by them into calamity and driven to ruin. The maxim of the sage must be observed: 'When the empire is well governed, you may show yourself; when it is ill-governed, live in obscurity.' Yet, I have been unable to banish from my mind all interest in the condition of affairs, and, therefore, drew up the two works which you have read, hoping that some man will arise who, by his deeds and principles, shall promote the good of the people, and establish the prosperity of the country on a permanent basis. This is what I deeply desire; would, for the good of my country, that this end were gained!

"As to making compositions, jingling sentences, and seeking poetic inspiration from the moon and from flowers, this sort of thing I have long given up; yet, to dissipate my melancholy and moodiness, I have made a couple of odes, to which I beg you to apply the axe of your correction, and herewith I wait upon you with my desires for your happiness."

In the first decade of the third month (March or April) the commodore had a conference on shore with the Japanese commissioners, on which occasion rows of *japonicas*, in full flower, were arranged outside the building. Lin, the chief commissioner, had several hundred bags of grain, each weighing more than two hundred catties, set down close by, and, soon after, there appeared eighty or ninety burly fellows, naked, excepting a cummerbund, though the weather was extremely cold, and taking up the bags, one man two or three sacks at a time, they removed them, in a twinkling, to the shore. These men were not of uncommon height, but very stout, and immensely muscular. After they had removed the sacks of grain, they were made to exhibit their strength in wrestling and fighting, in an open space in front of the reception hall—the victor being rewarded with three cups of wine.

At that time I talked with an officer of the district of Poo-ho, by the name of Hop-yuen-tsaon-chwang, and asked how they proceeded in Japan in the appointment of men to official situations. He told me that both in the civil and military departments, officers were appointed after examination, only importance was not attached, as in China, to the making of verses;

400

的が達成されて故国が良くなることです。

文章について言えば、私はかなり前から韻文や、月や花を題材にした詩的な表現を使うのをやめています。しかし、私の沈む気持ちとやるせない思いを詠んだ賦［詩経の六義の1つ。感ずることをそのまま述べ表わす詩］を2編お目にかけます。どうか添削をお願い申し上げます。ご多幸をお祈りし、ここに筆を置きます。」

旧暦3月（3月または4月）の初旬、提督は日本側の委員と陸上で協議した。建物の外側は満開の椿の垣で囲われていた。首席委員の林は、一袋200斤［120キログラム］以上の米俵を数百も近くに並べさせた。そのあとすぐに80から90人の大男たちが入ってきた。非常に寒いにもかかわらず、まわしを巻いただけの裸であった。それらの男たちは同時に2、3個の俵を持ち上げすばやく海岸に運んでいった。彼らは非常に背が高くてがっしりしており、筋肉も非常に発達していた。米俵を取り除いてから、レセプション・ホール前の野外で相撲が披露された。勝者には3杯の酒が与えられた。

このとき、私は浦賀の役人合原操蔵と話をし、日本ではどのようにして公式の場に出る人員を選ぶのかをたずねた。彼が言うには、役所でも軍隊でも、試験を行なうということである。しかし、中国とは異なり、詩を作る能力は重要視されていないという。また、勉強する本は孔子や孟子、およびその学派の学者が書いた本で、試験に合格して役所の仕事につけるようになると、それらの人々は刀を2本差すことが許されるという。

日本人はこれまでの200年間、外国人との交流を断ち切ってきた。そのため、長崎での交易が許されている少数の中国人やオランダ人を除いては外国人を見たことがなかったのである。私も珍しそうに見られているのを感じた。日本人は漢字や漢文を非常に尊重しているため、私は行く先々で、自分の扇子になにか書いてくれと頼まれた。横浜滞在中の1ヵ月の間に、私は少なくとも500本の扇子に漢文を書いた。実際のところ、このような依頼には困惑したし、書くにも時間がかかったが、彼らの熱心な頼みを断るのはむずかしかった。

力士の相撲が披露されたのと同じ日に、条約の条項が取り決められ、箱館と下田、日本語ではハコダテとシモダの2港が合衆国船に対して開放され、そこで薪、水、食料、石炭の補給を受けられるようになった。日本側も合衆国側も非常に友好的で、双方の疑念も解消されたかのようであった。数日後、ペリー提督は、旗艦ポーハタン号に日本側委員の林を招待した。ポーハタン号はこのために美しく飾りつけられていた。この宴会について私は次の詩を作った。

両国の代表は横浜で会合した。	両国横浜会
人間としての兄弟愛を表わすために、喜びの宴が催された。	驩虞一類同
代表らは帽子をとって親しく挨拶をかわし、	解冠称礼義
大小を差した英雄らは、誇りに満ちて立ち並ぶ。	佩剣羨英雄
泡立つ杯を差し上げて心からの平和を願うことを約束した、	楽奏巴人調
ドラムの響きと鐘の音が耳を聾するなか。	殺陳大古風
すべての人々の口からは愛という言葉が聞かれ、人々の目は喜びに輝いている、	幾番和悦意
この条約が永遠に続き、安全が保たれんことを！	立約告成功

that the books which they studied were those of Confucius and Mencius, and the writers of their school, and that after passing the examinations, and being approved as competent for office, parties were privileged to wear two swords.

As the Japanese for two hundred years have had no intercourse with foreigners, and have seen none, excepting the few Chinese and Dutch who carry on the trade at Nanga-saki, I found myself quite an object of interest; and as they set a great value on Chinese characters and compositions, whenever I went to the hall of reception many of them were sure to ask me to write on fans for them. The fans which I inscribed during a month while we were at Yokuhama could not be fewer than five hundred. The applications were, indeed, troublesome, and the writing took up much of my time, but it was difficult to decline acceding to their pressing requests.

On the same day on which the exhibition of athletes took place, the articles of treaty were settled, and it was arranged that the two ports of Seang-Kwan and Hea-teen, called by the Japanese, Hakodadi and Simoda, should be open to vessels from the United States, which should there be supplied with firewood, water, provisions, and coal. The most friendly feeling was displayed by both the contracting parties, and there seemed to be an end of their suspicions. A few days after, Commodore Perry gave an entertainment to Commissioner Lin on board his flag-ship, the *Powhatan*, which was decked out for the occasion. I made the following lines upon it:

Two nations' representatives at Yokuhama met;
To show their human brotherhood, the feast of joy was set.
Here were the chiefs who doff the hat and friendly greetings pay,
And there the heroes with two swords, in proud and bold array.
They raised the sparkling cup to prove their words of peace sincere,
While roll of drums and clash of bells came thundering on the ear.
Love spake from every lip, strained every eye with pleasure,
Ever may the treaty last, a good securing measure!

After the feast there were some theatrical performances; and when it was evening the Japanese returned to the shore. Next day the presents brought from the government of the United States to the Emperor of Japan were exhibited. There was a model of a railway engine and carriage, a life-boat, an electric telegraph apparatus, the instruments for taking daguerreotype pictures, various implements of agriculture, and other things. A circular railroad had been laid down outside the town, on which the engine and carriage swept round and round with great rapidity, to the astonishment of the beholders. The use of the electric telegraph was by means of copper wires to convey intelligence instantaneously from one place to another. By the daguerreotype apparatus pictures were taken by the reflection of the sun's light from the object on plates of metal. There is no need for pencils or drawing, and the pictures last long without fading. The life-boat was fitted with air-boxes, by means of which it was kept from sinking. On occasions of shipwreck, parties may be saved by means of this invention. The implements of agriculture were the most ingenious contrivances for purposes of husbandry used in the United States. The Emperor of Japan received all these things, and gave in return presents of lacquered ware, what might be called fine China ware, if it were not made in Japan, silks, &c. There was one gentleman, a Mr. Hop-yuen-choo, who conversed with me on this occasion, and gave me a case for pencils, along with these lines:

"The rain is gone; the nightingale
Sings loud among the trees;
Its notes to the foreign vessels
Are borne upon the breeze.

401

宴会のあとには、ちょっとした寸劇があった。夜になると日本人は陸に戻った。翌日、合衆国政府から日本の皇帝への贈り物が披露された。模型の機関車と客車、救命ボート、電信機、銀板写真機、さまざまな農機具などである。町はずれに模型機関車用のレールを円形に敷き、そこで機関車と客車をかなりの速度で走らせたところ、見物人は非常に驚いた。電信機は、銅線を使ってある場所からほかの場所に瞬時に情報を伝える装置である。銀板写真機は、太陽光線の反射を金属板に投影して写真を撮るものである。筆や写生は必要なく、写真は薄れることなく長持ちする。救命ボートは、空気ボックスがついており、沈まないようになっている。この発明品により、船の難破の際に乗組員の命を救うことができる。農機具は、合衆国の農業のために考案された便利な機具ばかりであった。日本の皇帝はこれらの品々を受け取り、返礼として漆器、陶磁器、絹などを贈った。このとき合原猪三郎という紳士と話したが、彼は筆入れと一緒に次の詩を贈ってくれた。

雨はあがった。ウグイスが木立の中でさえずっている。	樹外雨収鴬語流
そよ風に乗せて外国船に向かって歌っている。	声々啼送旅人舟
愚かな鳥よ、お前はあの船の帆がすぐに向きをかえてしまうのを知らないのだ。	不知黄帽金衣客
黄色い帽子と金モールをつけた人々は去っていき、私たちは悲しみに取り残されるのだ。	得解転蓬漂泊愁

同じときに、明篤(ミンドゥ)という役人が、元旦に作ったという賦を見せてくれた。

北斗七星がふたたびめぐりはじめた。	斗転年還改
世界は冷たく無情に見える。	書生世事灰
宗愨の志により私の魂は呼び起こされる。	空懐宗愨志
しかし私の中には武侯の炎がない。	終乏武侯才
詩人の筆を手に持ち、	詩就聊揮筆
杯を傍らに置いた私は、	憂多復挙杯
家の軒の柳の葉ずれの音を聞き、	依々門外柳
目のように細い葉を透かして見る。	青眼為誰開

また、僧居中の玉斧という役人も、春について歌った次の詩を見せてくれた。

昨晩、花の中を私は歌いながら歩き、	昨夜惜華窓下詠
今朝、私の声は森の中で響いている。	今朝愛緑苑中吟
人知の及ばぬところに天の高い道がある！	人間何識天公意
この春の緑が天の慈愛を示してくれる。	己変紅林作碧林

Ah! silly bird, thou knowest not
Their sails they soon will turn,
The yellow hats and lace of gold
Go and leave us to mourn."

At the same time, an officer named Ming-tuh showed me an ode which he had made on the first morning of the year. It ran:

"The bear begins his course again;
To me the world seems cold and vain.
Tsing Hok's high aim my soul inspires;
But not in me are Woo-how's fires.
With poet's pencil in my hand,
And wine cup near me on the stand,
I hear the willow rustling at my eaves,
And watch the opening of its eye-like leaves."

Another officer, named Yuk-foo Sank-kew-chung, also brought me some lines on the spring. They were:

"Last night among the flowers I walked and sang,
This morn again my voice in green woods rang.
Beyond men's ken the way of God above!
This greenery of spring well proves his love."

This piece was composed in the hall of reception, and it seemed incumbent on me to produce something of the same kind, so I took my pencil and wrote:

O face of spring, that now revisitest
The earth, my soul is stirred by thee to song.
Though still the winter snow clothes all the hills,
The rural paths are bright with blushing flowers,
And on the mountain sides the firs shine green.
Amid the waves see how the sea gulls play,
And find their home upon the ocean's breast.
Along the shore the smoke curls from the camps;
The hovering mists close shroud the ships of war.
Here in this hall the east and west are met;
There rise the towers of Japan's capitol.
Where shall I go to taste the inspiring cup?
I'll row my boat to yonder clump of trees.

On the same day, Wau-che-choo, of Shan-pun, asked me to inscribe a fan for him, and presented to me the four following lines:

"Say not our meeting here was all of chance;
To you we owe the treaty and our peace.
From far the strangers came, their language strange,
'Twas well we had your pencil and your tongue."

I took the opportunity that day to take a long walk, and not far from the town came upon an old temple dedicated to the dragon spirit. It was built of wood, and in the inside were hung, in frames, a great many pictures. Near by was a brick manufactory. The bricks were different from those we use in China—hard and large, and of an ashy color. Strolling on two or three *le*, there were a good many dwellings of the common people, some covered with tiles, and some thatched with straw. Most of them had pasted on the door Buddhistic charms, written on strips of paper. The women, afraid of a foreigner, kept all out of sight. During all the time we were at Yoku-hama, indeed, I saw only one woman.

After some days, the business of the expedition at this port being concluded, the steamer left Yoku-hama, and in one day reached Simoda, called in Chinese "Hea-teen," which would be in

402

この詩はレセプション・ホールで作られた。私も同じような詩を返すべきだと感じたため、筆をとって次のように書いた。

春よ、またぬぐってきた春よ、私の魂は揺さぶられ、歌わずにはいられない。　遥見春色偶為吟
丘にはまだ雪が残っているが、　日本山川雪尽侵
田舎の道は咲く花で明るく、　古径茶花紅満族
山腹のモミの木は緑に輝いている。　肇岡松樹翠為陰
波間にはカモメが遊び、　沙鴎冒雨浮波面
海の胸を家にしている。　海鳥随風逐浪心
海岸の野営地からは煙が立ちのぼり、　岸側軍営烟漠々
ただよう霧は戦艦を包む。　湾中戦艦霧沈々
この館で東と西が出会い、　横浜築館応非遠
彼方には日本の首府の塔がそびえている。　江戸楼台望転深
この喜びの酒をどこで飲もう？　未識人家何処是
船を漕いで木立の向こうへ行こう。　泛舟揺漾到前林

同じ日、扇子になにかを書いて欲しいと頼みにきたShan-punの関研次という人は、次の詩を見せてくれた。

私たちがここで出会ったことはまったくの偶然でしょうか、　横浜相遇豈無因
条約と平和が得られたのはあなたのおかげです。　和議皆安仰頼君
遠くから見知らぬ人々がやってきて、言葉も分からない私たちは、　遠方鴃舌今朝会
あなたの筆と舌がなければどうなっていたことでしょう。　幸観同文対語人

その日私は長い散歩をしたところ、町からそう遠くないところで竜神を祭った古い寺に行きあたった。木造の寺で、内部には額に入った実に多数の絵がかかっていた。近くには瓦工場があったが、われわれが中国で使う瓦とは異なり、固くて大きく、色は灰色だった。さらに2、3里行くと、庶民の家々が多数あった。瓦葺きの家もあれば、藁葺きの家もあった。大多数の家の戸には仏教の御札が張られていた。外国人を恐れて、女たちはまったく姿を見せなかった。横浜に滞在中、私が見かけた女はたった1人だけだった。

数日後、横浜の港での仕事が完了したため、艦隊の蒸気船は横浜を出発し、1日で下田に到着した。中国語で「Hea-teen」と呼ばれる下田は英語では「Low fields」という意味である。位置は北緯34度39分、東経138度57分である。富をもたらし土地を肥沃にしてくれる川の流れる山の麓にあることが、この名の由来である。湾内には岩でできた小島［犬走島］があり、波よけになっている。湾内では船はまったく安全である。前には高い山々が連なり、外側には海が広がっていてまるで円形劇場にいるようである。しかし、ここで嵐が荒れ狂っても、船は静かに落ち着いて進めるであろう。蒸気船は先の岩でできた小島の付近に錨を下ろした。陸地の方は急峻で断崖になっていたからである。実際、岩だらけの崖は、波にどれほど洗われようとも削られそうになかった。山や丘は木が豊かで、キジ、タカ、カラス、キツネがたくさんいた。低地にはカモが多かった。

English "Low-fields." It lies in latitude 34° 39′ north, longitude 138° 57′ east, and takes its name of Low-fields from its lying at the foot of high hills, from which streams come down, making the country around rich and fertile. There is a small, rocky island in the middle of the harbor, which serves the purposes of a break-water. Within it vessels may lie in perfect safety as in an amphitheatre, with lofty hills rising one above another in front and outside the great ocean; but whatever storms rage there, they may ride quietly and undisturbed. The steamers anchored close by the rocky island, the shore of the mainland being steep and precipitous, rocky cliffs, indeed, against which the waves might beat and chafe for ever without making any impression. The heights and hills are well wooded, and abound with pheasants, hawks, crows, and foxes. In the low grounds teal are abundant.

On the day after our arrival, the commodore went on shore, and took up his quarters in the Leaou-seen temple, on Fae-shun hill. There was a priest in charge of the temple called Yis-tsang, and two neophytes with him. Inside was a large hall for the worship of Buddha, and along the sides of it were many tombs—small structures made of stones—which it was the duty of the priests to sweep and keep clean, and where they presented daily offerings of flowers. The parties buried in them had, during their lifetime, made contributions to the temple. Behind the temple was a small pillared dome, built of stone, a small fish-pond, and many flowers and fruits. While we were taking some refreshments, hundreds of the people, men and women, came in to look at the strangers and receive presents. The women came and went without any appearance of bashfulness. They wore their dress long, had an apron behind instead of in front, and their hair was bound up with a strip of red silk. Most of them were good looking, and before marriage their teeth are beautifully white. After they have children, however, they stain the teeth black with gall-nut powder.

On another day I walked through the streets, and looked at the shops and houses. Some of them were built of bricks and covered with tiles, while others were merely huts of straw. They were mostly connected together, so that one could walk a long way, just passing from one house to another. The women moved about in the houses and streets as freely as the men. They came readily on the streets to me when I called them; many of them I saw working with the upper part of their bodies uncovered. Many of the men go about without any covering but the cummer bund, and the women think nothing of looking at obscene pictures. There are bathing houses, to which both the sexes resort without distinction. The women came always in crowds to see a foreigner, but ran off when any of the two-sworded gentry made their appearance.

The streets are all named. There are "Great Work street," "New street," "Shop street," and half a score besides. Passing along the shore and crossing a bridge, after walking a little more than a *le*, you are in the district of Tsze-Ké, and come to the temple of the "Gemmeous spring," shaded by old fir trees, and fronting the rocky island in the harbor, of which I have spoken. Here a piece of ground has been assigned as a burial place for strangers from the United States.

The people are all Buddhists. All about, on the hill sides and by the seashore, are images of Buddha, and on most of their tombstones are engraven some words from the "water lily," classic. At the temple of "Great Repose," I saw people worshipping Buddha, without either incense or lighted candles. When they had finished, they put some money in a box, calling it "Let-go-life money," with reference to the Buddhist doctrine which forbids the killing of animals. There were two priests in the place, who asked me to write some characters for them,

403

われわれが到着した翌日、提督は上陸して、法順山了仙寺を宿営場所とした。寺を守るのは日浄という僧と2人の小僧であった。寺の中には仏を祀った大きなお堂があり、両側には多くの墓があった。墓は石で作られた小さなもので、僧が毎日掃き清めて、花を供えていた。ここに葬られている人々は、生前に寺に喜捨をしていたのである。寺の裏には石でできた柱のある小さなドームと、小さな池があり、花と果実が豊富に実っていた。われわれが軽く食事をしていると、何百人もの男女がやってきてわれわれ外国人を眺め、贈り物をもらおうとした。女たちも恥ずかしがるふうでもなくやってきては帰っていった。女たちは長い着物を着て、エプロンを前ではなく後ろにして、髪は赤い絹の紐で結い上げてあった。美しい女も多く、結婚前には歯も白い。しかし、子供を生んだ女はフシの粉でお歯黒をする習慣がある。

後日、私は道を歩いて店や家を見てまわった。煉瓦作りで瓦葺きの家もあれば、藁葺きの粗末な家もあった。大部分の家はつながっているので、歩き続けると何軒もの家の前を通ることになる。女も男と同じように、家や通りを行ったり来たりしていた。私が呼びかけると嫌がりもせず、道のところまで出てきてくれた。私が見かけた人々の多くは上半身が裸だった。男たちも多くはふんどし1枚で歩き回り、女たちもそれを見苦しいとは思っていないようだった。男女混浴の浴場もあった。女たちは外国人を見に集まってきたが、大小を差した武士の姿が見えると逃げていった。

道にはそれぞれ名前がついており、「大労道」や、「新道」、「店道」やそのほかいくつもの名前があった。海岸沿いに1里強歩いて橋を渡ると柿崎区に入る。そこには、古いモミの木の陰に、玉泉寺という寺がある。先に述べた湾内の岩だらけの小島はちょうどその前に見える。ここに、アメリカ人が亡くなった場合の埋葬地としていくらかの土地が割り当てられている。

日本人はみな仏教徒である。山でも海でも仏像がいたるところに見られる。また、墓石には、多くの場合、古典の「蓮華（れんげ）」からの言葉［南無妙法蓮華経］が彫りつけられている。大安寺では、線香も灯明もあげずに仏に祈っている人々を見た。祈りが終わると、箱にお金を入れていたが、そのお金を、動物の殺生を禁じる仏教の教えにちなんで「放生銭」と呼んでいた。ここには2人の僧がいて、私はなにか一筆書くよう求められた。私は、まわりの景色に感動して「峰廻水邊」［取り巻く山々、囲む海］という意味のことを書いた。これに対し、僧は、次のような詩で心境を表わした。

この小さな部屋に私たちは座り、　　一丈方庵玉座同
硯のまわりで白い雲が出会う。　　寸余硯石白雲通
珍しい金でさえ私たちには塵にすぎない、　　黄金畢竟塵中物
この先に憂うることもなし。　　不省明朝炊米空

彼らと一緒に座っていると、祈りに訪れた女がいた。その美しさにうたれて私は次の詩を詠んだ。

彼女の唇は赤く、歯は白い　　朱唇皓齒遈嬌姿
明るい眉の上に結われた雲のような髷。　　雲髻斜釵淡掃眉
きらめく髪飾りの下でその美しさは星のようだ　　半面新粧却絶妙
梅の木の枝を通して見る月のようだ。　　恰如明月掛梅枝

on which, struck by the scenery around, I wrote "encircling peaks, girdling waters." They in return described their position in the following lines:

> "Here in our little cells we sit,
> Round our inkstones the white clouds meet.
> Mere dust to us is gold so rare,
> The future gives us not a care.

While I was sitting with them, there came a woman to the temple to worship; the sight of beauty greatly stirred me ;—

> "Her lips vermillion red, her teeth were white,
> Her hair in clouds rose o'er her eyebrows bright.
> In glittering head-dress starlike was her sheen,
> Or like the moon through plum tree branches seen."

The day being very warm, the priests had tea brought in, and I found it sweetish, like that produced at the hill of Se-tseaou, not far from Canton. About a bow-shot from this temple is a mountain gully, where a stream flows clear over a bed of sand and pebbles—a beautiful place for bathing.

In "Pond" street is a temple, where I found an idol grasping in his hands a bow and arrows. On the walls were hung many paintings of ships, which I supposed to be votive offerings from parties on their safe return from sea. Many people had hung up in the same temple the hair of their head, having vowed in a time of danger to cut it off, and present it, should they be delivered. Such are some of the customs of the Japanese.

The *azalea* is very abundant on the hills about, nor are other flowers rare. My friend made large collections of them, which he afterwards dried and preserved for future study, showing himself worthy to be a disciple of Confucius, who advised his followers to read the book of Odes, that they might become acquainted with the names of birds and animals, plants and trees.

Now every village has that which is good in its order and government. Though Japan is a smaller country than China, yet robbing and oppression are unknown in it. The doors of the houses are for the most part but thin boards, or frames with paper pasted over them, yet a case of theft is hardly ever heard of. Surely these things are sufficient to prove the excellence and ability of its rulers.

One day, wishing to ramble over the hills, I got a priest to guide me, and after walking five or six *le*, came to a village called Seu-Ke, by the sea-shore. There I saw large quantities of the shells of the pickle fish, which is found largely in the neighboring waters. Returning to the town I went into several shops. Among articles for sale in these, laquered-ware occupies the first place. When I made any purchase, I wrote my name on the article and also the price. The shop keeper then carried it to the officer of customs for the port, who, with his assistants, superintended all matters of buying and selling. A dollar was taken as 1,600 cash. The Japanese themselves have a large copper coin, equal to 100 cash. They have also several coins of gold and silver, and one piece of silver gilt. Within a circuit of seven *le* around Simoda, I did not see a single sheep, goat, or pig. Herds, however, were not uncommon, and were used for carrying burdens. Cows and oxen are used by the people for ploughing. The women weave cloth just as they do in China. Blacksmiths and carpenters seemed to go about their work as among ourselves; but I did not see any pieces of women's work in embroidery. Both men and women are fond of carrying fans. While I was at this place I am sure I inscribed more than a thousand fans. The governor and the various officers conducting the intercourse

404

その日はとても暖かく、僧はお茶を出してくれた。そのお茶は、広東に近い西樵で生産されるお茶と同じくらいおいしかった。この寺からごく近いところに山の小谷があり、澄んだ水を通して底の砂と小石が見える。水浴びには美しい場所である。

「池」通りにも寺があり、そこには弓と矢を手に持った像があった。壁には船の絵がたくさんかかっており、海の安全を願って奉納されたものだと思われる。この寺にはまた髪の毛も奉納されていた。危険が迫ったときに、これから逃れられたら髪を切ることを宣誓し、祈りが叶えられたらこれを納めるのである。これも日本の習慣の1つである。

周囲の山にはツツジやそのほかの珍しい花がたくさん見られた。私の友人はこれを集めて乾燥させた。保存してのちに研究するのである。孔子の弟子というにふさわしい行ないだ。孔子は鳥、動物、植物、木の名前を知るために、頌［詩経の六義の1つ。人君の盛徳をほめて成功を神に告げる詩］を集めた本を読むように弟子に教えたのである。

日本ではどの村も秩序が保たれよく治められている。日本は中国より小さな国だが、泥棒や圧政は見かけられない。家々の戸はほとんどが薄い板や障子であるが、泥棒が入ったという話はほとんど聞かない。これは統治者の有能さを十分示すものであろう。

ある日、丘を越えて散歩しようと、僧に案内してもらった。5、6里歩くと、海岸近くの洲崎という村に着いた。ここで私は、塩漬けにする貝の貝殻が大量にあるのを見た。近くの海で大量にとれるのである。町に戻っていくつかの店を覗いてみた。さまざまなものが売られているが、まず目につくのは漆器である。なにか買い物をしたいと思ったら、私は名前と値段をその品物に書かねばならなかった。店主はそれを持って港の税関に行き、税関の役人とその助手が売買の最初から最後までを監視するのである。1ドルは銅銭1,600文で交換できた。日本人は大きな銅貨を使っており、それ1枚は100文であった。ほかにも金貨や銀貨があり、また銀メッキのものもあった。下田の周辺7里四方には、羊、山羊、豚は1匹も見当たらなかった。しかし牛はよく見られ、荷物の運搬に使われていた。牛はまた田畑を耕すのにも使われていた。女たちは中国と同様に機を織っていた。鍛冶屋や大工もわれわれの国と同じように働いていた。しかし、女たちが刺繍をしている姿は見られなかった。また男も女も好んで扇子を持ち歩くようである。ここに滞在している間、私は頼まれて少なくとも1,000本の扇子に漢文を書いた。奉行やアメリカ人との交渉を担当するいろいろな役人、誰もが私に同じことを頼むのである。彼らは次のような感謝の言葉を贈ってくれた。

外国の船に乗ってあなたは旅する、	避乱爽船亦一奇
故国災いを離れて。	兵中鼙鼓不聞知
大海を渡って東の国に、	翻将万里東来色
あなたはやってきて、私たちに平和をもたらしてくれた。	快観芙蓉絶世姿

これに対し、私は次のような返事をした。

東に向かい、私は火の船に乗った、	火船飛出粤之東

with the Americans, all requested my services in this matter. They sent me the following complimentary lines:

"In foreign ships abroad you roam,
Escaping from the ills of home.
O'er the wide ocean to the East,
You've come, and us with peace have blessed."

I returned to them this reply:

"Eastward my course, the ship of fire I joined,
On travel bent, new scenes absorb my mind.
What mountains rise to bless my wandering sight!
O'er ocean's fields I gaze with vast delight;
Our wheels! like wings whose power the eagle wields;
Our helm! t' its lightest touch the vessel yields;
We dash along, a car whose steeds are whales;
Like osprey strong, we sport with furious gales;
By moonlight calm I saw Lew Chew's fair isle;
I've marked of Japan's hills the snowy pile.
Deeply my insignificance I feel,
Not vain to friendship, these things I reveal."

On the 16th day of the 4th month (12th May,) the commodore sailed from Simoda, and in five days reached Hakodadi, the second of the ports appointed in the treaty. It lies in latitude 41° 49′ N., longitude 140° 47′ E., and its climate is very much the same as Moukden. It is a retired and small place, surrounded by a barren country, where the trees are few and the grass is scanty. The people consequently are dependent for their food on supplies from other places, and vessels are constantly coming and going to it. From this circumstance it has received the name in Chinese of Seang-kwang, *i. e.*, "Hall of boxes." The harbor is wide, an open bay indeed, the hills on shore standing round it, as if in audience of the sea. When we were there the snow was still to be seen on the tops of the mountains. The houses are superior to those of Simoda, and the dress, ornaments, and vessels of the people are all indicative of more wealth. The women kept in their houses, and did not allow themselves to be seen by foreigners. The morals of the inhabitants appeared to be good. Obscene language was rarely heard.

Near Hakodadi is "Kingdom-protecting" hill, on which there is a temple where the pillars and beams are covered with carvings. All the articles in it are new and beautiful, and many pictures are hung round the walls. On each side of the principal hall are many graves. The commodore had several pictures taken in this building with a daguerreotype apparatus, and distributed among the Japanese officers.

Some difficulty arose in arranging about the distance to which the American citizens might travel round the port of Hakodadi, and a reference upon the subject was made by the Japanese to Yedo. During the time which thus elapsed, there was free intercourse with the people, and one could not but be struck with their quiet and submissive habits. They would kneel down by the way-side when they saw an officer. I did not see a single woman. On our first arrival, indeed, most of the shops and houses were shut, for the people, alarmed by the appearance of the foreign vessels, had fled to distant villages. Gradually, however, they regained their confidence, and came back and resumed their occupations. Hundreds of horses and some asses were to be seen upon the streets, bringing and carrying burdens of food. The windows were mostly of paper, as in other places where we had been, and upon many of the doors were pasted Chinese characters, signifying "Wilderness House," "Tortoise House." In the shops there was abundance of silks, but of a quality inferior to those of China. Their lacquered ware, how-

旅をして、新しい風景に私の胸は踊る。	此日揚帆碧海中
私の目に、山々がなんと美しく映ることか！	歴覧螺峰情不尽
はるかな海原を眺める喜び、	遥瞻蚊室興無窮
蒸気船の外輪は鷲の翼のように力強く、	双輪抜浪如奔馬
舵は軽々と船を操る、	一舵分流若耿虹
私たちは進む、馬のかわりに鯨をつけて、	漫道騎鯨冲巨浪
ミサゴのように力強く、激しい風と戯れながら、	休誇跨鶴振長風
静かな月夜に浮かぶ美しい琉球の島、	琉球乍到雲方散
雪を頂く日本の山々。	日本初臨雪正融
私はなんとちっぽけな存在であろう、	暫寄一身天地外
私は言おう、友好に虚栄はいらない。	知音聊与訴離衷

旧暦の4月16日（5月12日）、提督は下田を出航し、5日後に箱館に到着した。箱館は条約で開港が取り決められた第2の港である。北緯41度49分、東経140度47分に位置し、気候は盛京（ションジャン）と似ている。箱館はへんぴな小さな町で、周囲の土地も不毛である。木も草も少ない。住民はほかの土地に食料を頼っており、船がたえず出たり入ったりしている。箱館、つまり「箱の館」という名前はこのような状態に由来しているのだという。港は大きくて湾は開けている。海に向かって観客席のように周囲を山が囲っている。ここに到着したときには、まだ山頂に雪が残っていた。下田の町より家々は立派で、人々の着物や装飾品、船を見ても下田より富んでいることが分かる。女たちは家に閉じこもり、外国人に姿を見せようとはしなかった。住民のモラルは高いようであった。汚い言葉を聞くことも稀であった。

箱館の近くにある「護国山」には寺がある。その柱や梁には彫刻がほどこされており、中の品々はすべて新しくて美しく、壁には多数の絵がかけてあった。大きなお堂の両側には墓がたくさんあった。提督はこの建物の中で銀板写真を何枚か撮影し、それを日本の役人に配った。

箱館港周辺でアメリカ人が移動できる範囲についてちょっとした問題が発生し、この件について日本側は江戸に照会する必要があった。この返事が来るまでは、住民と自由に交流することができたが、その静かで純朴な様子には驚かざるをえなかった。彼らは役人を見かけると道の端に寄って跪く。また、女は1人も見かけなかった。初めて到着したときは、店や家の戸は閉ざされていた。住民は外国の船の出現に驚いて遠くの村に逃げていってしまったのである。しかし、段々に落ち着きを取り戻し、家に戻って仕事を再開した。道には、食料の荷を運ぶ何百頭もの馬や数頭のロバが見られた。われわれが訪問したほかの町と同様、窓は主に紙でできており、戸には「原屋」や「亀屋」などの漢字の札が張ってある家が多かった。店には絹が多数あったが、品質は中国のものより劣っていた。しかし、漆器はすばらしく、すぐに売り切れになってしまった。鹿革、鯉、薬用になる海草が大量にあった。住民は下田より良いものを食べていた。

数日後、江戸から返事が到着し、艦隊が下田に戻ること、また、箱館周辺の外国人の遊歩範囲については委員の林との話し合いで決定されることが伝えられた。型通りの挨拶が済んだあと、港を去るときに遠藤という

ever, was admirable, and the shops were soon emptied of it by their visitors. Deer skins, the roach fish, and medicinal sea-weed were to be seen in large quantities. The food of the people was of a better quality than at Simoda.

After some days, a request arrived from Yedo that the expedition would return to Simoda, that the question how far the country around Hakodadi should be considered open territory might be determined in conference with the Commissioner Lin. Besides the usual verses of compliments, an officer, called Yuen-tang, presented me, on our leaving the port, with two pictures in rolls, not to be distinguished from those common in China. Another gave me a good many volumes, I always acknowledging the gifts by the return of strings of fragrant beads. On the 4th of June, the commodore commenced his return to Simoda, the passage back occupying the same time as the passage from it had done. The day after his arrival, he and his officers, all in full dress, were entertained by Lin in the Leaon-seen temple, and in the afternoon the American soldiers marched in order through the streets, there being a general turn out of the population to look at them. Among the attendants of one of the commissioners was a young gentleman named Kwei-ching-min, of much intelligence and liveliness. All the visitors were very fond of him, and he had a great knack of drawing their likenesses. One of the imperial physicians, Wan-tsuen, asked me on this occasion about the manner in which officers were advanced to government employment in China. I endeavored to explain the subject to him, and we afterwards exchanged stanzas.

On the 17th of June, Lin and the other commissioners completed the negotiations connected with the treaty, which was arranged in thirteen articles. It was agreed, also, that American citizens should be free to ramble to the distance of five *le* all round Hakodadi. These are Japanese *le*, and the five may be equal to ten English miles. On the same day the commodore gave a grand entertainment on board the steamer, and exhibited a mimic specimen of a naval fight, for the entertainment of his Japanese guests, but the festivities were sadly interrupted by heavy rains.

Having heard that in Simoda there was one Yun-ts'ung-wo, famous for his skill in writing with his mouth, I went to him and got him to draw and inscribe for me about a dozen pictures.

On the 25th of June, all the business being concluded, the squadron left Japan, many officers escorting it in their own boats. Six days brought us to Lew-Chew, where the native authorities received us courteously, and supplied the ships with provisions. When we sailed from Lew-Chew in February, the commodore had left some sailors who were sick, and circumstances came to light concerning the death of one of them, which required investigation. He and two others had been drinking, and he in particular had provoked the people till they began to stone him. They probably killed him and threw him into the sea; but the authorities concealed the fact of his having been stoned, and merely said that he had disappeared, leaving his companions drunk, and they knew nothing of him till he was reported as found drowned at a certain spot. The fact of his having been stoned coming out, one of the men concerned in the case was brought before the Commodore, who, after inquiry, delivered him to the Lew-Chewan authorities, to be dealt with according to justice. He was banished, I understood, to Kew-chung hill, and the local magistrate was deprived of his pay, but retained in office.

On the 11th July, the prime minister and the treasurer, at an interview with the commodore at Napha, concluded articles of a treaty between the United States and Lew-Chew. This being settled, the steamers separated, and we sailed for different ports of China.*

* Although there are some errors in the descriptions of the Chinese writer, his paper has been faithfully copied.—M. C. P.

406

役人が2巻の絵巻物を私に贈ってくれた。中国のものとよく似ていた。もう1人からは何冊もの本をもらった。私はいつも贈り物へのお礼として、紐に連ねた良い匂いのする玉を贈ることにしていた。6月4日、提督は下田に向けて出航した。来るときと同じ日数をかけて下田に戻った。到着の翌日、提督と士官は盛装して了仙寺に赴き、林の歓迎を受けた。その日の午後には、アメリカ人たちは整然と町を行進した。彼らを見ようと住民のほとんどが見物にやってきた。日本側の委員の中に、桂正敏という若くて聡明で元気のよい紳士がいた。アメリカ人にも非常に人気があり、似顔絵を書くのが上手であった。このとき、皇帝の医師の1人である文荃が、私に中国政府内における役人の昇進についてたずねた。私はこれについて彼に説明し、そのあと私たちは詩を交換した。

6月17日、林とそのほかの委員たちは13項からなる条約に関する交渉をすべて終えた。また、アメリカ人は箱館周辺5里四方を自由に歩行してよいことになった。これは日本の単位の里で、5里［約20キロメートル］はおよそ10英国マイルにあたる。同日、提督は蒸気船で大宴会を開き、日本の客をもてなすために模擬海戦を披露したが、大雨のために残念ながら中断された。

下田に口に筆をくわえて字を書くことで有名な雲松窩膳という人がいることを聞いたので、出かけていって10枚ほどの絵と署名を頼んだ。

6月25日、すべての作業が終了したため、艦隊は日本を離れた。多くの役人が自分の船で見送ってくれた。琉球までは6日かかったが、現地当局はわれわれを丁重に迎え、食料を補給してくれた。2月に琉球を出発した際、病気の船員を数名残していったが、そのうちの1人の死に疑問があったため、調査が行なわれた。その船員ともう2人は酒を飲み、とくにその船員は住民の怒りをかって石を投げつけられたという。おそらく住民は彼を殺して海に投げ込んだのだろう。しかし、当局は彼が石を投げつけられたことを隠し、ただ、酔っぱらった仲間を残して消えてしまった、ある場所で溺死しているのが報告されるまではなにも知らなかったと述べた。しかし、彼が石を投げつけられたことが明らかになり、それに関わった男が1人提督の前に連れてこられ、取り調べののち、琉球当局に引き渡され、法に従って処罰されることになった。おそらく、彼はKew-chungの丘に追い払われ、行政官は給料停止になっただろうが、職は追われなかったと聞いている。

7月11日、提督は那覇において総理大臣、財務官と会談し、合衆国と琉球の間の条約の項目について取り決めた。これが終了したあと、蒸気船は出発し、われわれは中国の港に向けて出航した。*

［本章の人名・地名および漢詩は、『大日本古文書　幕末外国関係文書』1～3（明治43、44年東京帝国大学資料編）より引用］

*この中国人の記述にはいくつか誤りはあるが、すべてそのまま掲載した。——M・C・P

滿清紀事
全
LM2

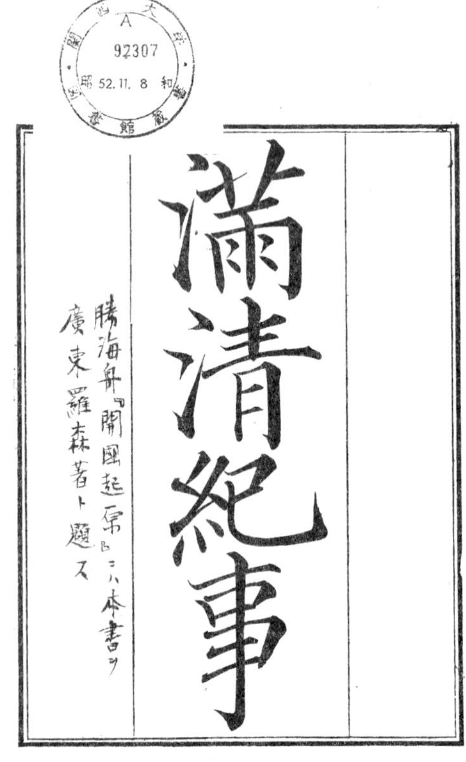
A
92307
52.11.8
滿清紀事
勝海舟『開國起原』ニハ本書ヲ
廣東羅森著ト題ス

滿清紀事（此編本無標題世或呼爲滿清紀事今姑從之）

山谷清涼樹木陰蔚羣巒疊翠石澗飛泉于此閒遊打坐正可敲棋琢句亦乏（足）論古談今非謂已之多聞亦本衆人所共知者耳古人有言曰不知天文不知地理不知敵國之言不可以爲將故曰知彼知己百戰百勝而不禁慨然於中華也中華地廣人衆財物豐饒聖天子在上俱以德教爲政治禮義以交孚積明壽考勤政愛民幅幀廣大四海安寧盤古至今未有如茲之盛潮自清朝開國以來順治在位十八年康熙在位大免天下民税一次當時章程尚未定而

聖祖力以成之在位六十一年及至雍正明而畧刻貶削親王數年羮堯在位十三年乾隆登位時際上元民豐物阜開闢新疆數千里大免天下民税一次遊江南二次時臺灣叛逆命福康安帶兵不數月而平之在位六十年而與子另爲太上皇三年嘉慶即位各國夷人旺于廣州貿易海關年中入息甚多夷人每受官民挾制番人勢弱未可如何道光登極越年省城大火燭癸巳（我天保四年清道光十三年）兩大水時鴉片大盛蔫遍民寰皇上命林文忠來粵禁烟唐番互結鴉片毀消人民遵從義律被困功效將成忽然罷任

再命琦善奕山到來夷人揚眉吐氣義律伯貊提兵攻擊廣城稱言要償還鴉片烟項舉人秀才多獻善策統率州民殺却伯貊各處百姓奮力三元里義勇齊出大將軍恐懼而開城以六百萬金而退敵於是英人復乘火船上天津攻鎮江所到之處勢如破竹連河阨要之區泪塞京城人心爲之震動皇上乃以二千一百萬分三年而與之准其於寧波上海福州廈門香港五所開港貿易與耆英議設三十六款章程以爲永遠和好之計初時民心尚多疑惑及見番人設立學校教育士女英材委命有司批斷民訟曲

直無月糧以催士民凶趨進番人之路派經書於舖戶人多知有上帝之書自是開港至今唐番互處則無分于爾我矣然而世情自此縱橫贈大刼掠當舖渡船之事漸多又不得淸明才德之官來茲東粵故世情愈趨而愈下盜匪愈殺而愈多竊自夷人滋擾之後黃恩相爲台余溥淳爲廣府俱不理民情亂爲番人使役士人惡之故罷塲而不考府試再有劉濤爲廣府年輕驕傲菲薄士民出街鳴鑼作威看見舖民有不避起立者每每事在街心連笞數十時雙門底内醬園挑醎趨避未及被笞數十另繫於獄街坊

聯呈保之不允衆民忿激是晚公熱文上發起大堆
有穿好白衣裳者多人超入取其珍寶玩器不計括
搶出外盡放于火中焚燒劉得從後門走去事後有
愚民在此觀望被南海縣史樸獲捉數十名殺之原
史樸于初上任新舊交代爭取漏規與吳舊令相歐
于学上註子聞而鄙之是年縣試士子皆嫌卷金太
多罷考要其覩筆爲例此後每場卷金定收六分而
已此粵東一禾兩穗筋竹園處開花徐廣縉爲總督
數年不發一示番人回前看英之書三年之後入城
遊玩法時故以文書復往問徐徐辭不允親詣虎門

三

拥入勒贖梁懷本差委捉拿彼亦畏懼拆爛懷本之
屋後率其結拜之兄弟數千往廣西會同大頭羊大
鯉魚等聚黨爲盜劫掠此方日甚猖狂官兵難獲斯
時路上汛塞經營到處打單貨價不定該鄉市鎮亦
恭迎富饋禮物此鄉妥靜如不從順掠不留情世界
日擊於禍亂貧富日夜而心驚是以某某鄉因議設
立保良攻匪會馮雲山洪秀泉二人在列自立會后
如或盜匪一至該鄉民須要齊出守望相助同心聯
絡盜匪因此不敢藐覷其鄉該鄉亦賴打單于匪得
其不相侵犯而已時皇上洞悉林文忠才知兼優故

四

再召其出身往廣西辦匪事先聲奪人盜匪聞風散
了一半詭臣中途陷害之皇上精明故斥穆彰阿而
不任也時兩廣總督徐廣縉庸碌無才專以夷務推
辭不辨匪事性傲乖張殘殺沉米義士監斃梁友竹
擎捉潘鏡泉刻薄百姓士子亂作威福神人共憤故
廣西之賊聞知而復聚爲茲說會內之洪秀泉自小
家有膽畧結納英豪中年讀貧客鬱鬱而不得志聞
知番人教讀每月工銀可有數元故于廿八年到港
詣進郭士笠門講論上帝書理心內明智番人因予
工食往廣西而傳道寓住某某鄉故得入名於保良

五

會內馮雲山亦因貧乏須問太教頓番人工食往西
教書初年寓居黃宅次年寓曾宅有秀才張姓者言
他邪教指其毀爛社壇廟宇向臬官官即飭差拿黃
會二人及馮雲山於獄將黃會二人抑斃馮雲山用
些小錢賄囑差房照徵是以知縣見他雖是邪教並
未悔出事端故寬之而逸解回花縣回家既久難覓
生涯復往廣西官差查覺再來戈獲遍友兄弟好報
不半將差敵打或至被傷差走稟官稱爲叛逆官即
提兵以勦其鄉此時危急騎虎難下洪秀泉馮雲山
故糾合鄉民而與官兵相拒同小致大已酉皇命周

天爵向榮提兵剿之相持久不克洪秀泉等乃率其鄉民蓄髮易服不准搶掠百姓法律甚嚴行軍肅虔創志恢復明朝年與滿州爲敵奮勇直前比楚項羽之破釜沉舟採用機謀效漢光武之中興起義初時鄉民婦女共計不過數萬官兵四伏環而攻之洪秀泉倡與鄉民冬踞山谷合理山內之家及婦女操戈禦敵男則當兵女則供食分行暫伍視死如歸官員數次引兵入洞剿其巢彼每誘敵而取勝斯時盜首大鯉魚等已降官兵隨營用命官遣其爲先隊令攻洪黨洪黨深溝高壘待未銳氣一墮而沖之士卒死

傷丘積矣行都統烏蘭泰者自請奮勇當先帶兵相拒年餘被炮傷足而斃張敬修招集壯勇耗費多資屢次交鋒未能殺勝所招義勇反擾鄉民兵勇所至財物一空盜匪掠民猶留餘地故百姓之懼兵勇亦甚于盜賊也是年八月日食殆甚皇詔頒行輕徵民稅秋闈闔省武秀欲聯罷試爲顧登宪不英清曾昌擾置數月撫台葉廷琛帶兵滅之另黨凌十八擾亂翁源也於羅境墟內葉廷琛帶兵圍之意欲絕其糧食連該處之良民老幼俱皆餓死入境內而臭穢不堪此葉廷琛之亦損於陰隲已且夫蒼生國賓也兵

戈係事也戰勝攻取之機不患無策然而行軍紀律須本於愛民果能得法以視民如子曾見簞食壺漿恭迎母寧而之師矣果能不愧於爲民父母亦見從征犯難斷無委而去之民矣善用兵者不惜其地而惜其民善將兵者不攻其民而攻其心故曰得道者多助失道者寡助而不奈令人道憶才今日也夫令日於太平無事之時官門上下無非以利交征即此有事之秋大小官員而亦專門粉飾佐愈尊而愈驕總無肯於下問雖有功能非錢不錄苟莬美行枉鬱難伸官隸差房倚權恃勢官門訟獄財富惟親所貴

皇上英明鼎新革故若不洗除舊染之污則民心也離而在彼無怪兵民之棄甲曳兵矣此時洪秀泉會內人漸充多辛亥八月初一向榮提兵伏道剿之洪黨亦以兵相拒自辰至酉勝敗未分洪黨還韋正暗渡斜谷遠出兵後官兵相拒之際而不知永安已陷矣於是官兵退後數里無營洪秀泉亦以永安添守壬子正月（我嘉永五年清咸豐二年）廣西梧州府忽有波山艇數十號突到關前關吏不阻暫查船內冲出多人提刀舞牌直扨關廠梧州府閉城數日賊乃獲利而去二月洪黨大隊人攻却永安州俄圍桂府至四月初一

日忽解圍入湖南四月十四攻郴州傍東統道連陷
道州桂陽嘉禾永興安仁醴陵攸縣竟于七月二十
八日徑至長沙圍其城于夜又解圍北向途中出示
奉承□天運太平國總理機都督大元帥萬大洪
爲剴切曉諭伐暴救民事照得天下貪官甚于強
盜衙門活吏無異虎狼皆由君上之柔懦遠君子
而近小人賣官鬻爵壓抑賢才以致利風日熾上
下交征富貴者縱惡不究貧窮者宛莫伸言之痛
心殊堪髮指即錢漕一事近益數倍三十年之粮
銀免而後再徵民之財盡矣民之苦極矣我等仁

人善士觸目傷心故將各府州縣之賊官狠吏盡
行除滅救民于水火之中也刻下大兵雲集廣西
已定長州太平將近江西等處不得不先行曉諭
恐我百姓不必驚慌農工商賈各安生業富貴須
備辦糧食助吾之兵餉多寡數目親自報明各給
回借卷以憑日后清償餉等如有勇力者智謀者
同心竭力共成美舉侯承平之日幸資榮封現在
各府州縣官員逆吾者斬順吾者昌著即付印回
繳其餘豺狼差役概行勦除縣首示衆恐有流賊
藉端滋事准爾等指明具投隨即判除倘有鄉民

敢助賊官爲官以敵吾之士卒者無論各府州縣
鄉村盡行洗滅凜之慎之毋違特示
示賠各處此將皇上知賊勢猖狂憫憐生民紊事故
屢次上諭催徐廣縉往西辦理然其則遲遲行也因
此洪黨于十一月初三克洞庭湖之岳州府各路防
堵皆空洪黨先使八十餘人坐大船二隻小船四隻
遂于十一月初九到湖北之漢陽府鸚鵡洲灣船等
候大隊入民打攻漢陽十三日洪黨見漢陽城外官
兵駐劄營內有一班膽者云我們先去攻打官兵試
可能否于是八十餘人攜了鳥鎗軍器藥獎一人手

執大旗先行上岸大聲喝殺官兵其賊上官兵見賊
上岸以爲大隊人馬不知多少前來攻賊各人心甚
驚慌遂放鳥鎗數日即刻逃走彼見官兵趕到城邊
擲藥□數十個燒著民房數間官兵盡行走淌遂來
勢攻破城地另焚棄撫台之村塌其舡墳入到漢陽
府衙門劫了倉庫出示安民示曰
大漢軍師兼理內外政教統理官吏軍民開國承
相靖國王爲上諭宣布外事照得安邦定國弔民
非所以害民發政施仁戡亂非所以擾亂村鄉而
鎮不用驚惶士農工商各安本業夷滿當滅漢祚

當與久合必分亂極復治天地循環自然之理也茲因君弱臣暗臣強盡奪而暴斂日甚況且朝中文武權重者盡屬旗滿之人外省職員無非捐納之子則士子窗前勤學就是巷儒難以抱負雖奇才經綸終難展用朝無善政野有遺才大員盡屬貪贓小吏能無索賄上有好者下有甚焉故張嘉祥等因攔截江河擾亂鄉里逞其虎狠之性魚肉生民肆其狐狗之心室家受害求渠等又攬感而與扁擔集匪徒傷殘黎庶沿江望氣而赴兩散官司爲不究貓鼠誰非同眠嗟嗟生民際此塲生何

賴是以我聖神皇帝心存惻隱日夜焦勞故聚天下之義士弔民罰罪爰舉義旗以靜魔妖自于八月初一兵入永州安城陛下待庶民如保赤子本王深體陛下之意自從出兵以來不許部下妄搶一物與傷一人倘有抗拒不遵本王定必重究免其以暴所以各省州縣地方所在必宜更變被髮左衽之非而奮厥乃心成其偉績則效力有功定給獎賞且候平定各省勦滅本燕擒獲鑾居問其猾夏之罪贊成四海之休賞德論功各設刑罰爵祿自有常典爲此特示勿違凜遵

越日出城往海搶了糧船約一千號其有不從者用火燒去四五十號十六日有數百人到了又攻打漢口兩路來往十九大隊人馬到齊就在漢口居住其頭人住廣東安徽各會館內連日齊備攻打武昌先圍城後洪秀泉馮雲山二人乃到十二月初四被地雷火藥轟陷城地遂破武昌城中大小官員常大淳等俱死盡節計壞官兵百姓數千血流成渠聞係廣東人則不殺閉門不出者亦不殺洪秀泉在武昌分派人馬攻打各處十二月十四攻破黃州十九攻破波縣得兩處以爲門戶獲銀七十餘萬就在武昌過

年有姓錢名江者浙江人也素有膽略博學多聞林則徐辦烟時同他來粵辦理書文事務因林則徐敗流落粵東當時番人見伏後其再欲鼓衆以拒夷聯同紳士上明倫堂官又主和其猶辦論梁星源謂其刁蠻獲而審之彼立不跪官怒責之監其數月遞解回籍自此在家悶悶而不舒適聞洪秀泉破了武昌其挾宿恨欲報前仇故不遠千里而相見勸洪黨舍西而東因獻一策于洪秀泉其策內所言西川不可守如劉先主當日先有諸葛之賢後有姜維之勇六出九伐不得中原寸土今欲以區區之地而敵天下

决然不可不若取了南京心腹之地建都以圖進取內有與王策數欸秀泉覽而悅之即遵其計行事明年（我嘉永六年 咸豐三年癸丑）正月初四洪秀泉盡行上船居住共有船二千餘只順流東下十一日攻破九江府官兵退守小姑山洪黨由北口而出由大江直落官兵不敢動他獨有上海道台吳爽招得廣東頭猛船華船十餘隻裝有紅毛大砲六百餘位在小狼山奮力到劉他屯海邊築堤相拒是夜二鼓即於堤內登起燈籠而轟之連放傷殘六十餘人及至天明廣船人少吳爽之大砲船隻盡爲所得正月十八攻破安慶廿二攻破蕪湖殘殺官兵數百得銀三十餘萬另獲糧米婦女不可勝計官兵退守南京及鎮江府總督陸建瀛盡引其兵屯于城內不與屬員商議將軍三司會銜奏之吳爽得冦信付于番人請其火船往攻洪黨于此夜用酒埋以兩桶相盞每埋掛明燈一枝浮於水面順流而至黑夜之際清風蕩漾其埋似有人遊於水面番人懼其將近速即放砲轟之火藥將竭洪黨乃以伏兵齊出拿住火船之大使一名番人仍以兵糧爲禮說安二月初十日寅時洪黨用雲梯登城越入天明已將南京四門盡閉截殺官兵旗滿兩者不計其數百姓跟從官兵逃出亦殺害十三日開城捉百姓去搬尸首十五日閉城拘百姓入隊不入者斬之計洪黨自廣西猖獗以來算南京殺人至多淮河之水俱紅臭不堪總督陸建瀛將軍祥厚各大員等或有盡節或有砲死眞是聞者傷心見者流淚據梁星源則被錢江殺分爲數段以報前仇于是洪秀泉在南京修整明舊宮殿居住內外掛聯二對其聯曰

獨手擎天重整大明新氣象
單心報國除清外域異衣冠

虎賁三千直掃幽燕之地
龍飛九五重開堯舜之天

連日飲太平宴三日大封會友以錢江爲大司馬總理軍民事務又命良工加築砲台于城外固守撥其新入隊者守之湖南湖北入隊者守二重城其長髮者守裏重城洪秀泉上戴天冠身穿黃龍袍用黃綢紗脇其衣用紅紬又衣用紅布洪黨人馬合理多少未知其詳時濮倘阿爲欽差剿辦匪事八品人純柔懦太過心存惻隱不事殺人故以之爲太平宰相則有餘以之爲征討大員則不足徐廣縉專巧欺瞞混

詳報勝賜遇必隆亦不明於賞罰擁兵自護怯懦不前上諭屢責其當頭剿截而不進賊已陷城數日尚不覺故皇上震怒將他拿解還京二月廿五日洪黨分發人馬兩隊一打破揚州一打破鎮江正欲進兵適遇京兵萬餘蒙倫七千山東河南山西陝西四川甘肅各省共兵二萬餘又欽差向榮帶兵三萬五千廣東壯勇一萬餘俱已到齊離南京十餘里或數十里下營商議合兵攻剿此次洪黨之心亦慌故將揚州鎮江人馬暫回南京拒守所以人馬亦不暇進兵而前也上海蘇州松江三四府地方于三月初七夜

大震丑時微震寅時小震連日俱有奉賢縣離海上約七十里地近海邊崩陷數里初時民心甚驚令惟累定將來南京料有數場大戰若欽差向榮果有勇謀又有官兵如此之多行軍奮力向前賞罰義以爲倘何憂地方之不平服也哉時届三月連日風雨向榮探察軍營地利議于初六無月朦朧人馬啣枚潛于隘險突然鳴鼓而相攻鎗砲噴筒而截殺鍾山地面有隊新入洪黨者投出倉惶之間向榮以糧米給其散去四面疊攻取勝獲回器械甚多十三洪黨擁兵北門直撲琦善營[illegible][illegible]兩下攻打之際陳金綬以

青州駐守之兵繞過山前會合截殺勝保又著火器營兵以銅砲在高轟下以火箭射入土城焚燬營盤三處洪黨敗走回城次日洪黨再欲決戰錢江止之曰彼既得勝銳氣方剛不若調回人馬以守瓜州往撤同心以據泉厦則我軍糧食可裕敵軍糧用難通以時養精蓄銳以逸待勞俟至秋凉然後決戰洪黨從之是月厦門偶失守一夜賊用火燒燬衙門殺却地方官府並未搶掠番人物件另以緘書送與番人番人閱其書內道理心相契洽於是擬番親乘火船上長江以探其實即于三月十五日解纜十九到焦

山越日抵江寧洪黨偶望火船駛至以爲火船助官攻已即以大砲桃岸轟之壞其船尾番人見其砲火猛鍊因不還砲乃升白旂洪黨內有識升旂事例者故以小艇綁船問之曰君處南海寡人處北海風馬牛不相及也不知君之到此何居曰我國商人雲集上海南京失守恐君逼近此日之來秖爲調護況有給言洪黨與英爲仇故火船來探問茲知釁端于我兩不相助于爾勿害通商書曰四海之內皆兄弟也畀其諭之洪黨見其言婉意皆欣洽遂與歷覽各營以軍容之盛示之因復曰通商大局理所底然如果

得志彼此相安至若洋煙一切永中國議論爾後火船遂于三月二十四日離江寧溯流而兩回上海二十九日總兵鄧肇良進攻鎮江城外之觀音山洪黨蜂擁而出兵勇各以鎗炮迎敵洪黨漸退分股抄出官兵之後官兵駐于京江分頭回戰互有損傷四月初二和淳督帶師船乘風直至焦山洪黨即以其船開砲迎拒師船復駛向瓜州此處洪黨船隻甚多岸上施放連環大炮不絕該師船因有帆風亦放砲衝擊南北兩岸初七日向榮預派兵勇分作五路以路致江寧通濟朝陽二門洪黨又出兵二三千分頭迎

擊是日戰且走官遍近誘敵洪黨悟終不前十一日向榮札營于紫金山恐其占據形勝突出數千劫掠營寨向榮分頭接仗是日長江上游盧應翔會同楊煥章各帶砲船砲勇遶出夾江沿江北潛于南岸楊煥章分兩隊遶至夾口蘆葦中張疑設伏以爲援應于總黄秉忠督大小砲船遶進夾山直打橫塞溢口之鹽船三隻其餘鹽船順流退下放砲拒迎楊煥章伏葦岸接應先向望樓燒壞殲斃數名乘機催船齊進洪黨泊船相拒岸上砲台七座均向官船開砲轟盧應翔率勇抄截楊煥章麾兵應之黄秉忠復迴環衝

擊互開鎗砲數時陳嘉率勇登岸赴援斃却執黄旗首目洪黨逃潰兵勇乃折斷夾口木排奪得大砲黄旗器械等物越日洪黨計議云虛虛實實用兵之方前有大兵之扼又無用武之地勝負難决不若舍而支[illegible]從左潛入守候機宜而進也是以分股支援滁州復占據臨淮關直趨鳳陽府知府裕泰等于四月二十一日酉時在北門外與之接仗洪黨另分一股從小路潛入東門城内烟火突起九華山與興龍寺前有會黨兩股望見火光即向北門左右衝散鄉男遂陷府城二十五日洪黨另一股自汴梁西竄于汜

水縣據城中安設鎗砲守禦將軍托明阿提兵進剿洪黨官兵以連環鎗砲四面圍攻傷殘無數黨見孤城難守自東門竄出屯于東西兩土山上糾合三路以爲犄角分援于河南蔓延于山陝皇上命江南安徽各路大員添調精兵分路防剿令總兵董占元陞任山東兗州花里遜布督帶大名宣化正定官兵馳赴河北會同河北總鎮亦埋防勦事務直隸總爾經額即日出省統兵接應蒙古三盟王哲里木等各派兵古斤由熱河圍場前來調集察哈爾官兵近畿一帶大兵雲集欽命訥爾經額總督各路帶兵大員備

勇前進以為山東河南後路應援京師十萬禁兵均已調齊以俟攻剿都統西凌阿督帶黑龍江官兵在浦散任民房來安盤洪黨乘其無備暗兵襲之由洛湖河擾及溫縣亳州失守知州孫椿等陣亡復潛往于劉家山住南岸施放鎗砲總兵邵辰等巡防渡口同時星散北岸師船概自燒燬兩日不見回踪斯來得救兵互護五月初七搶入府城帰德守河南巡撫陸應穀奏稱賊匪竄互汴梁是夜大雷大雨賊管火藥皆濕賊外濠水驟深數丈十三連日賊匪攻城屢敗據衆傳說夜深攻城緊急之時一長身赤面人手

執大刀往來指揮左右前後隨護之人亦復不少且見兵勇下城每有持燈指引者行走如飛賊由敬畏不前以致敗遁請加封號時湖北廣濟縣葵涌琛徵□民佃既經兵火者未曾分開應徵應免之處希圖一律蠲緩鄉民不服持戈聚抗官此後有鄉民欲赴隸縣收著為別處鄉民設詞攔阻鮑署令不善調停反帶兵勇殲拴數十因此鄉民愈聚愈多該縣復請上憲發兵勦捕琦善咨調叛殘九百予之兵不堪用是晚衆鄉民一齊闖至縣署聲稱要尋鮑令報仇鮑令率同縣守挺身出外彈壓均被殘害衙署亦被焚

燒臬司江忠源統帶楚勇千餘東下一面會同提督阿勒經阿挑選兵丁配齊器械刻日帶赴廣濟接辦以期迅速蔵事但須善力乃不致遏手附會也月中廣西興安縣爲坪村土匪聚衆拜會知縣蔡映符前往查拿會斜移黨闖入縣城戕官奪犯竄入靈川盤踞城內安砲抗拒許祥先張敬修分路進攻賊始棄城潰逃暹羅貢使行抵商邱所有賞賚各物御書均被搶去著補償還改道護送回國湖南桂東縣有江廣會黨二千餘盤踞三都橋肆行劫掠焚燬汛署二十九日未刻撲城該縣會同武營分兵出城堵禦衆

寡不敵會黨分股擁進城門斷絕歸路諸兵放護會黨闖分股于上猶龍泉等縣城內衙署門格均打毀錢糧倉庫搶去無幾禁犯乘間脫逃居民或被搶掠獲又散擾于永興縣由山路竄入三河州地方山頂駐札伐木結寨該處係高仙峻嶺有徑三條官兵兩路堵衆俾留一路出入架砲防堵衡州府屬安仁縣復有一股竄集請兵防堵駱秉章遂飛咨于江西巡撫不分畛域一體勦辦六月初八訥爾經額奏稱永定河南水漫堤頂自未至中長水一丈九尺連原底共深二丈餘啣當畢夜水勢猛驟入力難施埸抑三

十七丈掣動大溜氏間房舍田禾間有冲壞淹浸相應請旨飭監督修毋致塌刷捻寬一面行查被淹各村庄輕重情形應否撫卹具奏十九合兵進攻商定此股多係粵西湖廣會黨形踪譎巧或分五六股突出一見官兵又復嘯聚藏匿並於懷慶城之東南一帶接連豎立木壘暗施鎗砲各隘口設有陷坑竹地雷埋伏遍插旗幟遙作聲援虛實無辨參將崇安奮攻木壘砲傷陣亡二十一給事中張祥晉以粵西興軍兩載以來所費不下三千餘萬之多奏亟籌經內費以濟餉需一請開內地罌粟花稅比照茶酒等物一律收稅一請將內府舊有金器收鑄金錢與紋銀一律並行一請將京城現鋪程章程推廣各直省一體辦理硃批該部議奏七月中旬彗星見于西方廣西梧州府陳因大鯉魚雖有歸降之名究無降順之實六月廿七恩華親督文武員弁統帶吉林黑龍江及直隸山東各省兵由二十里鋪直抵丹河會黨分旗從林內轉出官兵以連環鎗砲拒敵洪黨退后官兵將其房舍燒燬百餘間二十九連日復督官兵過河捲殺會黨退入木城不出情形巧詐營壘尚多官兵亦不敢遽進至大名鎮董占元先于二十一日帶

兵前搗懷慶北關督率遊擊薛成龍等官員共一十二名員兵攻察俱被受傷陣亡兵丁亦復不少七月二十二日府遣其子先代勇士誘于廟擒而戮之另將衙內之首目舞弊者斬却地方賴安七月中旬上海吳爽行文到粵東調發南洋船數十號壯勇數千由洋而往上海不料八月初旬劉元預伏黨友數百于是夜登岸而用火擲下衙口將其誘出伏兵統從兵獲勝兵勇一時逃散吳爽被押于會館會黨監與之盟方要佗賞將洋船寫明送是晚吳爽失了印信一顆移知林旂領事帶入行商二十三日分兵各剿捍聯阿若藤等攻其北勝保攻其東南黨仍堅閉暗施鎗砲抵敵官兵列隊前進黨亦分股突出各放鎗砲互有損傷黨于心隄淺水之處分股接應官亦分兵排截而退二十六日復分馬步各軍前進黨于木城內及各隘口施放鎗砲或出或入官兵亦不敢直前二十七辰早勝保攻其南托明阿等分擊其北兩面屢由隄北邊出兵後東北木壘遍插旗幟暗放大砲兵傷百數官兵鎗砲直進亦斃會黨不少天已昏暮正在收隊黨于東南北衣路以出禾內突出因將黑夜馬隊官兵未能擊毀傷殘官兵甚多亦是退下

列營善祿即著兵丁拈鎗拈砲並放一時之久黨乃

擊退

有所不爲齋雜錄 第二十

治安策 滿清記事 咸豐帝上諭
清國擾亂數種

治安策

南海 羅森

粵自番人見伏之後、游民自此縱横胆大、拜會掠劫之事漸多矣、廣西之纍、由此伏矣、朝廷洞悉林文忠（則徐）才智兼優、故再召出身、往西勦辦、先聲奪人、盜匪聞風、一時幾于盡散、厥後中途病故、承辦之官、多招壯勇、反擾鄉民、兵勇所至、財物一空、盜寇掠民、猶留餘地、由是百姓之惡兵勇、更甚於盜賊、夫蒼生國寶也、兵戈危事也、戰勝攻取之機、不患無策、患無愛民之心。故善用兵者、不惜地而惜其民、善將兵者、不攻民而攻其心、予於今日竊慨然矣、當今之時、官門上下、惟利交征、衙吏官員、專門粉飾、皀隷房差、倚權恃勢、官司訟獄非不行、而爲上者、又復驁傲自居、不體下情、無怪民離散在彼而不在此也、竊自粵西興軍、兩載以來、所費不下三千餘萬、曠日持久、迄無寸效、何者彼實未覩於先後虛實之說耳、方今四方鋒□、出沒靡常、我若以實兵攻之、則彼必乘虛而入、惟我以虛兵誘其實、另以實兵勦其支、斯枝削則本搖、而盜氣可屈、獨是最難强者、百姓之從違、最易覘者、羣情之向背、故欲操必勝之權、莫先於民、而民心之得、尤在於推好惡同憂樂明賞罰嚴號令肅隊伍密巡邏、上下聯以一心、庶收臂指之效、古人有言曰、剋敵之要、在乎將得其人、固守之方、在乎民得其心、此之謂也、爰陳管見、謹列於左、

一申軍令以彰國條、清朝開基以來、英明遞禮、威震中華、雖金川臺灣之叛、不數月而平矣、由此太平日久、民不知兵、兼之粮餉羈微、兵暇分心而貿易、一□時當服役、砲響畏怯於軍前、鋒鏑既接、誰欲當先、前途倒戈、後卽逃潰、夫人情莫不怯死而貪生、法度不嚴、何以整軍容肅士氣、王者之師、愛民爲先、所過秋毫無犯、師律貞而武功立、此爲將任之一端也、

一明賞罰以服衆庶、一輕一重、理亂攸關、宥之以恩、自新者思歸命、斷之以法、懷懼者姑免偷生、勿徇私情、以杜姑息之漸、勿爲吝嗇而啓怨忿之端、自昔能建奇功、或拯危厄、未必皆是絜矩純良之士、珠玉不以瑕纇而不珍、髦彥不以過失而不用、古有始爲□讎、

終爲鄉相者、驅駕擾馴、唯在所馭、明黜陟而鼓士氣、此爲奬勵之一端也、

一備兵器以壯攻守、兩陣對壘、巨砲爲先、所貴鐵模鑄就、界尺居中、轟擊可能達遠而有準。兩接仗、鎗矢開排、更宜花筒爲備、矢革衞前、駐扎自有所靠而不驚、若夫火藥、須按泰西銅鍁之法、傾滓製造、勢力倍增、各器必使兵丁輪日磨刷、廼器物光瑩奪目、爲用自有威嚴、鼓之則進、金之則止、一吹而行、再吹而聚、所謂工欲善其事、必先利其器、此爲武備之一端也、

一嚴防守以決軍機、虛〻實〻、敵人莫得窺伺其微、行迎駐守、敵人莫俾屯於地利、故善防守者、防於所不守也、守而固者、守於所不攻也、故所欲戰、敵雖高壘深溝、不得不與我戰者、攻其所必救也、所不欲戰、雖畫地而守、敵不得與我戰者、乖其所之也、玆之城垣市鎭、守禦俱疎、巡緝廢弛、敵人或潛跡而莫知、內患或將萌而莫覺、詩云戰〻兢〻、亦爲防虞之一端也、

一教隊伍以從法度、聖天子偃武而不忘武備、養兵而不弛兵威、今之食粮當兵、〻荒韜演、進退而依隊伍者少、孫子曰、將弱不嚴、教道不明、吏卒無常、陣兵縱横、敗之道也、按泰西之兵、取無室家、與足粮食、次之進退步履、無有參差、以之防守巡邏、無得懈坐、統以六卿、帥以夫長、頭陣勝、四倍奬、再陣勝、八倍奬、連勝三陣、乃全給之、若於第三次敗、而頭二次之功、半歸烏有、此故初奮力、而終吏如財命相連矣、奬勵若是、總之教練宜多、此爲壯軍之一端也、

一聯鄉曲以靖閭閻、各處鄉民、俱有表率、一方公所、亦有主持、但今世道澆漓、後生強悍、識理者轉多緘口退避、此誠父兄之教不行、衿耆之權不振耳、爲民上者、若肯平心下氣、詢于蒭蕘、聯絡衿耆、不耻下問、無事則遣族老以導愚頑、有事則聯族老而商辦理、各鄉老戴慕於已、即各鄉老爲已用矣、子弟豈有不相率而從事哉、間有不遵約束者、在上之耳目亦近、由近及遠、擇善奬之、亦爲致治之一端也、

一設義學以化童蒙、古者亦有義學之舉、故士習端方、人材蔚起、近今文風日薄、師道不隆、民間年中、簽題雖多、反喜於建醮會景之用、甚嘆世人以有用之錢財、耗費於無益之地也、爲民上者、果能着油鹽茶當、綢緞各行、按年簽助規餉、以于官荒地段、多建義學、訪薦明師、教育貧富子弟、無庸束脩、月中講論善書聖訓、教人以悔過行功、有德者薦而升之、有才者拔而用之、師道立、則善人多、此爲文教之一端也、

一親賢才以輔國政、文藝爲後、德行爲先、故聖王不以辭盡人、不以意選士、凡制爵祿、衆公之、先論其才、乃授以職、所學必試以事、而考于成、然後苟妄不行、眞實在位、若知賢而用之、則勿以資格而拘之、古之賢侯將相、多出微賤、一旦感遇知音、振奮之情彌切、當今財勢是重、正比英雄蠖屈之時、即大臣保奏者、無非公侯世官之子、豈知貧賤憂戚、正彼蒼磨勵英豪之資、險阻艱難、悉上帝鼓舞賢才之具、古者闢門籲俊、此爲輔理之一端也、

一崇朴儉以重淳風、今人專言勢利、俗尚奓華、而冠婚喪祭之繁華無論已、誠有取數十年之蓄積、不足以供一朝之用、以天地造物之生成、而給一人嗜慾之私、由是門風日大、敷演日繁、一不知稼穡之

艱難、迨後不賸而困苦、因此倖幸之心腸日作、貧窮遂不甘於守分、故聖人制禮、惟於相稱、禮以多爲貴、不得簡略以爲安、禮以少爲貴、不得奢靡以相尙、崇朴儉而得中、亦維世道之一端也、

一清訟獄以免民累、清之法主於明、ゝ則能判曲直、不致糊塗而尸位、夫訟乃輿情所屈、愼勿遷擱游□、延阻蒼生之望、獄乃性命所關、愼勿偏情率性、致乖好生之心、逼勒口供、混拿了案、窃睹房差之大無良者矣、案懸不結、尋節生枝、歷見爲官多等如是者矣、方今朝廷愛民誠切、在下総非認眞、因想古人折獄、而民畏之如雷霆、理訟、而民仰之如日月者、誠爲愛民之一端也、

一省威猛以撫羣黎、大平盛世、愚民安分、官威尙可懾服之、今時特威則無益矣、甞見位尊而高堂ゝ、傲氣作威、迤ゝ聲音顏色、拒人于千里之外、無怪善言之難近、志士之裹足不前也、今天下言州縣爲親民之官、亦曰父母官、無如居移氣、養移體、是有父母之名、遂失父母之實、古聖人天下爲一家、如慈父之愛子、好問察言、敬敷五敎在寬、夫恭不侮而寬得衆、此爲親民之一端也、

一察房差以免積弊、世間皀役、多是倚權恃勢而凌民者、語云富不與官爭、小民懦弱、何敢與之而抗氣、一法立、一弊生、若不嚴防皀役、官規所以日壞、民情所以受屈也、體邺民者、盍其勗諸、夫差役下流人耳、居上而使下、理應按月給以工銀、則何今之承充差房者、反需饋禮數千而後得哉、此一旦當差、其中□弄可不問而知矣、毋得執票勒索、毋得倚勢欺民、毋得窩娼開賭、毋得苛刻案件之人、時稽訪察、誠爲除暴之一端也、

一輕狀金以伸民望、稟費難免、多亦非宜、議限微些、以截滋擾、外國規條猶是、誠以百姓之案件紛繁、群黎之貧富不一、若照今時事例、則每入一稟、須銀數元、到訊另要派堂規矩、行牌亦要票金、差房亦要使用、種ゝ苛求、不一而足、是朝廷設官以理民、悉足以病民耳、彼小民之欲行赴愬者、無如費用難支、是以被屈、寧甘忍受、寃枉終以難伸、通世務以快輿情、亦爲行政之一端也、

一免加征以遂民業、如欲革其積弊、須窮致弊之由、小民賴此產業以養家、生齒日繁、支用尙且不足、仍復子租稅而加之、民情既苦而益苦矣、或以大斗而收、或以大秤而入、或以公務而添征、或以官佃而增稅、此加征故多釀成禍患也、先王之制賦入、故必以丁夫爲本、無求于三則之外、不以務穡增其稅、不以輟稼減其租、民安居而樂業、此爲撫邺之一端也、

一遏淫風以正人心、近來風俗不古、差役多是窩娼漁利、凡女子之有顏色者、自小買育寮中、以求出息、而貪利之徒、又不計及陰隲之事、故娼寮日盛、而私寨亦多、更有三姑六婆、每煽良婦、而爲不法之事、故于街前粘貼下胎之藥甚多、此見人心風俗之變矣、聖人治世、必宣正道以遏淫風、遏之則莫如禁賣爲娼、重稅娼寮、輕限妓價、其難綱利害自消除、則爲新民之一端也、

一禁賭博以塞盜源、民間子弟、好賭必難守業、僥倖之心遂生、故嬴錢則風花雪月、輸錢則鼠窃狗偸、以覔生涯則怠惰、而習與性成、以使傭工、則畏勞而貪婪不足、近今盜匪日多、好賭者居于大半、試思市城賭館大、則每月衙規九百、中亦數百、此豈眞能公道交易哉、入門則望以幇其費用、此不問而知矣、不賭是嬴錢、亦爲興利之一端也、

一屛異端以維正道、聖王治天下、無外脩齊之理、而異端不貴焉、世間無父無君、眞欲出家者、世無幾人、果有此人、此人猶不害于世界、然世無幾人、而異端之害人深矣、嘗見近今、僧尼雖有食齊之名、究無食齊之實、或於市井言世利、或於民間煽惑人、更有代夫不善者、而拜神求禱、多方賺錢、言難悉數、所宜置寺門于海外、俾其不得而入市廛、亦爲風化之一端也、

一超女苦以布王猷、聖王治天下、必先於鰥寡孤獨、而況女子之無辜受屈者哉、蓋一陰一陽、上帝造端乎夫婦、于今生齒日繁、貧富不一、故有買奴買婢之條、亦有三妻五妾之例、此毋論已、然而被賣爲娼者、非其所欲、即宜矜之、矜之則莫若出示任其從良、一到官前問明、立即任其所往、買主毋得以身價留難、差房毋得倚勢而勒索、此外國亦有是例、嘗見今之買女爲娼者、多寫身價、故自少至老、終不脫離其苦、此中國從良之例不行矣、至若以女子束脚而悅心目、奔走艱難、心誠何樂、貧寒之家、自行作事、受苦益深、故超女苦、亦爲施德之一端也、

（朱）嘉永甲寅五月廿二日一校了

（朱）滿清紀事

山谷清涼樹木陰蔚群巒疊翠石澗飛泉于此間遊打坐正可敲棋琢句亦足論古談今非謂己之多聞亦本衆人所共知者耳古人有言曰不知天文不知地理不知敵國之言不可以爲將故曰知彼知己百戰百勝而不禁恍然於中華事也」中華地廣人衆財物豐饒聖天子在上俱以德敎爲政治禮義以交孚精明壽考勤政愛民幅隕廣大四海安寧盤古至今未有于玆之盛」溯自清國開國以來順治在位十八年康熙在位大免天下民税一次當時章程尙未定而聖祖力以成之在位六十一年及至雍正明而畧刻貶削親王戮年羹堯在位十三年」乾隆登位時際上元民豐物阜開闢新疆數千里大免天下民税一次下遊江南二次臺灣叛逆命福康安帶兵不數月而平之在位六十年而與子另爲太上皇三年嘉慶即位各國夷人旺于廣州貿易海關年中入息甚多夷人每受官民挾制番人勢弱未可如何」道光登極越年省城大火燭癸巳而大水時鴉片太盛毒遍民衆皇上命林文忠來粵禁烟唐番互結鴉片毀消人民遵從義啡被困功效將成忽然罷任再命琦善奕山到來夷人揚眉吐氣義啡伯貊提兵攻擊廣城稱言要償還鴉片烟項擧人秀才多獻善策統率壯民殺却伯貊各處百姓奮力三元里義勇齊出大將軍恐懼而開城以六百萬金而退敵於是英人復乘火船上天津攻鎭江所到之處勢如破竹運河扼要之區阻塞京城人心爲之震動皇上乃以二千一百萬分三年而與之准其於寧波上海福州厦門香港五所開港貿易與耆英議設三十六欵章程以爲永遠和好之計」初時民心尙多疑惑及見番人設立學校教育士女英材委命有司折斷良頑曲直重月粮以僱工民因趨進番人之路派經書於舖戶人多知有上帝之書自是開港至今唐番互處則無分于爾我矣」然而世情自此縱橫胆大劫掠當舖渡船之事漸多又不得清明才德之官來玆東粵故世情愈趨而愈下盜匪愈殺而愈多」竊自夷人滋擾之後黃思桐爲撫台余溥淳爲廣府俱不理民情祇爲番人使役士人惡之故罷場而不考府試」再有劉潯爲廣府年輕驕傲非薄士民出街鳴鑼作威看見舖民有不暇起居者每每牽在街心連笞數十時双門廷內醬園挑醢超避未及被笞數十另繫

於獄街坊聯呈保之不允衆民忿激是晚公堂之上發起大堆有穿好白衣裳者多人超入取其珍寶玩器不許拈搶出外盡放于火中焚燒劉潯從後門走去事後有愚民在此觀望被南海縣史樸獲捉數十名殺之」原史樸于初上任新舊交代爭取漏規與吳舊令相毆于堂上士子聞而鄙之是年縣試士子皆嫌卷金太多罷考要其親筆爲例此後每場卷金定收六分而已」時粵東一禾兩穗筋竹闔處開花徐廣縉爲總督經年不發一示番人因前耆英書納三年之後入城遊玩至時故以文書復徃問徐徐辭不允親詣虎門求返前者之書番人對曰此乃小事允不允亦無關於緊要也遂以前書還之」既回彼於愚民耳目之前舖張揚大其事連夜換轉城門又着舖戶每出一壯丁持戈遊歷城廟內外比如廟宇出遊一般及晚着令該縣每街各以燒楮奬民愚民益增興趣矣一連出遊數日枉費多資豈知番人並無必要入城之事」其乃稱言督率各處鄉民以使夷人畏服不敢進等語欺瞞皇上皇上謂其不發一卒不費一矢功成勝如爭戰所以賜之以世襲子爵實是平地風波瞞戲皇上者且又托賴於百姓者耳而孰意其後來之刻薄百姓若此哉英清地方欠粮不納上召委差捉獲茲事時史樸任滿例陞、（句讀ハ原ノマヽ）意欲邀功、自帶壯勇、往緝捕、乘轎鳴鑼而入、恃官威欲以壓民、不料匪人持戈逐之、棄轎而奔、觸石跌步遺靴、被匪擄獲羈留半月、其子探之連夜到匪巢說明、價銀一萬取贖、乃以平昔所得之贜物、加收民佃之資財、運在途中、彼此易換、史樸方回、百姓鄙之、民情之變自此始矣、道光在位三十年之事也」咸豐卽位、黃河偶缺、盜寇頻興、粱十五擄得民船數百、沿海肆掠、英人率火船二隻敗之、後來歸降官府、隨營效力、當時有羅單德霸氣擄人勒贖、梁懷本義委捉之、彼亦不懼、拆爛懷本之屋、後率其結拜之兄弟數千、往廣西會同大頭羊大鯉魚等、聚黨爲盜、刼掠地方、日甚猖狂、官兵難獲」斯時路上阻塞、經營到處打單、貨價不定、該鄉市鎭、亦要恭迎、當饋禮物、此鄉安靜、如不從順、掠不留情、世界日擧於禍亂、貧富日夜而心驚、是以某某鄉、因議設立保良攻匪會、「馮雲山洪秀泉二人在列」自立會後、如或盜匪一至、該鄉民須要齊出守望相助、同心聯絡、盜匪因此不敢藐視其鄉、該鄉亦願打單于匪、俾其不相侵犯而已、時皇上洞悉林文忠才知兼優、故再召其出身、往廣西而辨匪事、先聲奪人、盜匪聞風散了一半、讒臣中途陷害之、皇上精明故斥穆彰阿而不任也、時兩廣總督徐廣縉庸碌無才、專以夷務推辭、「不亦匪事、性傲乖張殘殺、沈米綫士監甕梁友竹、怒捉潘鏡泉刻薄百姓士子亂作福威神人共憤故廣西之賊聞知而後聚焉茲說會內之洪秀泉自小素有胆略結納英豪中年讀書貧寒鬱々而不得志聞知番人敎讀每月工銀可有數元故于廿八年到港詣進郭士笠門講論上帝書理心內明晰番人因予工食往廣西而傳道寓在某々鄉故得入名於保良會內憑雲山亦因貧于澚門入敎領番工食往西敎書初年寓居黃宅次年寓曾宅有秀才張姓者他邪敎指其毀爛社壇廟宇而禀官官卽飭差拿黃曾二人及憑雲山於獄將黃曾二人押甕憑雲山用些小錢賄囑差房照顧是以知縣見他雖是邪敎並未滋出事端故寬之而遞解回花縣」回家既久難覔生涯復往廣西官差査覺再來戈獲適友兄第好報不平將差毆打或至被傷差是禀官稱爲叛逆官卽提兵以剿其鄉此時危急騎虎難下洪秀泉憑雲山故糾合鄉民而與官兵相拒因小致大已酉皇命周天爵向榮提兵剿之相持久不克洪秀泉等乃率其鄉民畜髮易服不准搶掠百姓法律整嚴行軍肅虔創志恢復明朝專與滿州爲敵奮勇直前比楚項羽之破釜沉舟採用機謀效漢武之中興起義初時鄉民婦女共計不過數百官兵四伏環而攻之洪秀泉倡其鄉民入踞山谷

一三九

合理山內之家及婦女操戈禦敵男則當兵女則挑食分行束伍視死如歸官員數次引兵入洞剿其巢彼每誘敵而取勝斯時盜首大鯉魚等已降官兵隨營用命官遣其爲先隊合攻洪黨深溝高壘待夫銳氣一墮而冲之士卒死傷如積矣有都統烏蘭恭者自請奮勇當先帶兵相拒年餘被炮傷足而斃張敬修招集壯勇耗費多資屢次交鋒未能殺勝所招義勇反擾鄉民兵勇所至財物一空盜匪掠民猶留餘地故百姓之惡兵勇而更甚于盜賊也是年八月日食殆甚皇詔頒行輕徵民稅秋圍闈省武秀欲聯罷試爲顧登寃不果英淸會昌擾亂數月撫台葉廷琛帶兵滅之另黨凌十八擾亂翁源屯於羅境墟內葉廷琛帶兵困之意欲絕其粮食連該處之良民老幼俱皆餓死入境內而臭穢不堪此葉廷琛之亦有損於陰隲已且夫蒼生國寶也兵戈危事也戰勝攻取之機不患無策然而行軍紀律須本於愛民果能得法以視民如子曾見簞食壺漿恭迎毋畏寧爾之師矣果能不愧於爲民父母亦見從征犯難斷無委而相去之民矣故善用兵者不惜其地而惜其民善將兵者不攻其民而攻其心故曰得道者多助失道者寡助而不禁令人追憶于今日也夫今日於大平無事之時官門上下無非以利交征即此有事之秋大小官員而亦專門粉飾位愈尊而愈驕總無肯於下問雖有功能非錢不錄窮薨美行枉屈難伸皂隸差房倚權特勢官門訟獄財富惟親所貴皇上英明昇新革故若不洗除舊染之汚則民心已離而在彼無怪兵民之棄甲曳兵矣此時洪秀泉會內人漸充多辛亥八月初一向榮提兵伏道勦之洪黨亦以兵相拒自辰至酉勝敗未分洪黨遣韋正暗渡斜谷遶出兵後官兵相拒之際而不知永安已陷矣於是官兵退後數里爲營洪秀泉亦以永安添守壬子正月廣西梧州府忽有波山艇數十號突到關前關吏不及稽查船內冲出多人提刀舞牌直劫關廠梧州府閉城數日賊乃獲利而去二日洪黨大隊人雖劫永安州俄圍桂林府至四月初一日忽解圍入湖南四月十四攻柳州傍東繞道連陷道州桂陽嘉禾永興安仁醴陵攸縣竟于七月二十八日逕至長沙圍其城于夜又解圍北向途中出示

奉承　天運太平國總理軍機都督大元帥萬大洪爲剴切曉諭伐暴救民事照得天下貪官甚于强盜衙門活吏無異虎狼皆由君之柔懦遠君子而近小人賣官鬻爵壓抑賢才以致利風日熾上下交征富貴縱惡不究貧窮者有寃莫伸言之痛心殊堪髮指即錢漕一事近益數倍三十年之粮銀免而後再徵民之財盡矣民之苦極矣我等仁人善士觸目傷心故將各府州縣之賊官狼吏盡行除滅救民于水火之中也刻下大兵雲集廣西已定長洲太平將近江西等處不得不先行曉諭凡我百姓不必驚慌農工商買各安生業富貴須備辦粮米助吾之兵餉多寡數目親自報明各給回借卷以憑日後淸償爾等如有勇力者智謀者同心竭力共成美舉俟承平之日聿資榮封現在各府州縣官員逆吾者斬順吾者昌着即付即回籍其餘豹狼差役慨行勦除縣首示衆恐有流賊藉端滋事准爾等指明具投隨即剿除倘有鄉民敢助賊官爲害以敵吾之士卒者無論各府州縣鄉村盡行洗滅稟之愼之毋違特示

示貼各處此時皇上知賊勢猖狂憫憐生民荼毒故屢次上諭催徐廣縉往西辨理然其則遲〻行也因此洪黨于十一月初三克洞庭湖之岳州府各路防堵皆空洪黨先使八十餘人坐大船二隻小船四隻遂於十一月初九到湖北之漢陽府鸚鵡洲灣船等候大隊人馬打攻漢陽」十三日洪黨見漢陽城外官兵徃劄營內有一壯膽者云我們先去攻打官兵試之可能否于是八十餘人携了鳥鎗軍器藥煲一人手執大旗先行上岸大聲喊殺官兵其城上官兵見賊上岸以爲大隊人馬不知多少前來攻城各人心甚驚慌遠放鳥鎗數口即刻逃走彼見官兵趕到城邊擲藥煲數十個燒着民房數間官兵盡行走淸

遂承勢攻破城池另焚棄撫台之材掘其祖墳入到漢陽府衙門刼了倉庫出示安民示曰大漢軍師兼理內外政教統理官吏軍民開國承相靖國王左爲
上諭宣布中外事照得安邦定國弔民非所以害民發政施仁戡亂非所以擾亂村鄉市鎮不用驚惶士農工商各安本業夷滿當滅漢祚當興久合必分亂極復活天地循環自然之理也茲因君弱盡暗臣强盡貪而暴弱日甚況且朝中文武權重者盡屬旗滿之人外省職員無非損納之子則士子牕前勤學統是巷儒難以抱負雖奇才經綸終難展用朝無善政野有遺才大員盡屬貪賍小吏能無索賄上有好者下有甚焉故張嘉祥等因攔截江河擾亂鄉里逞其虎狼之性魚肉生民肆其狐淫之心室家受害求渠等又觀感而興焉招集匪徒傷殘黎庶沿江取稅到處打擾搶掠商民當之者迎刄而倒風行士庶聞之者望氣而趁雨散官司爲不宄猫鼠誰非同眠嗟々生民際此聊生何賴是以
我聖神皇帝心存惻隱日夜焦憂故聚天下之義士弔民罰罪爰擧義旌以靜麼妖自于八月初一兵入永安州城陛下待庶民如保赤子本王深體陛下之意自從出兵以來不許部下妄傷一人倘有抗拒不遵本王定必重究免其以暴所以各省州縣地方所在必宜更變披髮左衽之非而奮厥乃心成其緯績則效力有功定給奬賞且候平定各省勦滅北燕擒獲蠻君問其割夏之罪贊成四海之休賞德論功各設刑罰爵祿自有常典爲此特示毋違凜遵」越日出城往海搶了粮船約一千號其有不從者用火燒去四五十號十六日有數百人到了又攻打漢口兩路來往十九大隊人馬到齊就在漢口居住其頭人住廣東會舘廣西安徽各會舘內連日齊備攻打武昌先困城後洪秀泉憑雲山二人乃到十二月初四被地雷火藥轟陷城池遂破武昌」城中大小官員常大淳等俱死盡節計壞官兵百姓數千血流成渠聞係廣東人則不殺閉門不出者亦不殺洪秀泉在武昌分派人馬攻打各處十二月十四攻破黃州十九攻破波縣得兩處以爲門戶獲銀七十餘萬就在武昌過年有姓錢名江者浙江人也素有膽略博學多聞林則徐辨烟時同他來粵亦理書文事務因林則徐被貶流落粵東當時番人見伏後其再欲鼓衆以拒夷聯同紳士上明倫堂官已主和其猶辨論梁星源謂其刀蠻獲而審之彼立不跪官怒責之監其數月遞解回籍自此在家悶々而不舒適聞洪秀泉破了武昌其挾宿恨欲報前仇故不遠千里而相見勸洪黨舍西而東因獻一策于洪秀泉其策內所言西川不可守如劉先生當日先有諸葛之賢後有姜維之勇六出九伐不得中原寸土今欲以區々之地而敵天下決然不可不若取了南京心服之地建都以圖進取云云內有興王策數欵秀泉覽而悅之即遵其計行事」明年正月初四洪秀泉率衆盡行上船居住其有船二千餘只順流東下十一日攻破九江府官兵退守小姑山洪黨自北口而出由大江直落官兵不敢動他獨有上海道臺吳爽招得廣東頭猛船華船十餘隻裝有紅毛大砲六百餘位在小狼山奮力攻剿他屯海邊築堤相拒是夜二鼓即於堤內豎起燈籠而轟之連夜傷殘六十餘人及至天明廣船人少吳爽之大砲船隻盡爲所得正月十八攻破安慶廿二日攻破蕪湖殘殺官兵數百得銀三十餘萬另獲粮米婦女不可勝計官兵退守南京及鎮江府總督陸建瀛盡引其兵屯于城內不與屬員面議將軍三司會衔參之吳爽復寫信付于番人請其火船往攻洪黨于此夜用埕以雨帽相蓋每埕掛明燈一枝浮於水面順流而至黑夜之際清風蕩漾其埕似有人遊於水面番人懼其將近連即於炮轟之火藥將竭洪黨乃以伏兵齊出拿住火船之大伙一名番人乃兵粮爲禮說妥二月初十日子時洪黨用雲梯登城越入天明已將南京四門盡開截殺官兵旗滿死者不計其數百姓跟住官兵逃出亦被殺害十三日開城捉百姓去搬尸首十五日閉城拘百姓入隊允不者隨之計洪黨自廣西猖厥以來算南京殺人至多淮河之水俱紅

一四〇

臭不堪總督陸建瀛將軍祥厚各大員等或有盡節或有炮死眞是聞者傷心見者流淚惟梁星源則被錢江數分爲數段以報前仇于時洪秀泉在南京修整明朝舊宮殿居住內外掛聯二對其聯曰獨手擎天重整大明新氣象單心報國除淸外域異衣冠」虎賁三千直掃幽燕之地龍飛九五重開堯舜之天」連日飲太平宴三日大封會友以錢江爲大司馬總理軍民事務又命良工加築垊炮臺于城外固守撥其新入隊者守之湖南湖北入隊者守二重城其長髮者守裎重城洪秀泉上藏天官身穿黃龍袍用黃縐紗腰帶其次用紅綢又次用紅布洪黨人馬合埋多少未知其詳時賽尙阿爲欽差勦辦匪事人品太純柔懦大過心存惻隱不事殺人故以之爲太平宰相則有餘以之爲征討大員則不足徐廣縉專巧瞞混詳報勝賜遏心隆力亦不明於賞罰擁兵自護怯懼不前上諭屢着其常頭勦截而不邀賊已陷城數日尙不覺故皇上震怒將他拿解還京二月廿五洪黨分發人馬兩隊一打破楊州一打破鎭江正欲進兵適遇京兵萬餘索倫七千山東河南山西陝西四川甘肅各省共兵二萬餘又欽差向榮帶兵三萬五千廣東壯勇一萬餘俱已到齊離南京十餘里或數十里營商議合兵攻勦此次洪黨之心亦慌故將楊州鎭江人馬暫回南京拒守所以人馬亦不暇進兵而前也上海蘇州松江三四府地方于三月初七夜大震巳時微震寅時小震連日俱震有奉賢縣離上海約七十里地近海邊崩陷數里初時民心甚驚今惟略定將來南京料有數場大戰若欽差向榮果有勇謀又有官兵如此之多行軍奮力向前賞罰義以爲尙何憂地方之不平服也哉時屆三月連日風雨向榮探察軍營地利議于初六無月朦朧人馬銜枚潛于隘險突然鳴鼓而相攻鎗炮噴筒而截殺鍾山地面有隊新入洪黨者投出愴惶之間向榮以粮米給其散去四面疊攻取勝獲回器械甚多十三洪黨擁兵北門直撲琦善營寨兩下攻擊之際陳金綬以青州駐守之兵繞過山前會合截殺勝保又着火器營兵以銅炮在高轟下以火箭射入土城焚燬營盤三處洪黨敗走回城次日洪黨再欲決戰錢江止之曰彼旣得勝銳氣方剛不若調回人馬以守瓜州徃檄同心以據泉厦則我軍粮食可裕敵軍粮用難通以時養精蓄銳以逸待勞俟至秋涼然後決戰洪黨從之是月厦門偶失一夜用火燒燬衙門殺却地方官府並未搶掠番人物件另以經書送與番人番人閱其書內道理心相契洽是擬番親乘火船上長江以探其實卽于三月十五日解纜十九到焦山越日抵江寧洪黨偶望火船駛至以爲大船助官攻已卽以大砲枕岸轟之壞其船尾番人見其炮火得鍊因不還炮乃升白旂洪黨內有識升旂事例者故以小艇開船問之曰君處南海寡人處北海風馬牛不相及也不知君之到此何居曰我國商人雲集上海南京失守恐君逼近此日之來祇爲調護況有給言洪黨與英爲仇故大船來探問玆知釁端于我兩不相助于爾勿害通商書曰四海之內皆兄弟也君其諒之洪黨見其言婉意皆欣洽遂與歷覽各營以軍容之威示之因復曰通商大局理所應然如果得志彼此相安至若洋烟勿來中國議論之後火船遂于三月廿四日離江寧溯流而西卽回上海廿九日總兵鄧肇良進攻鎭江城外之觀音山洪黨蜂擁而出兵勇各以鎗炮迎敵洪黨漸退分股抄出官兵之後官兵駐守于京口分頭回戰互有損傷四月初二和淳督帶師船乘風直至焦山洪黨卽以其船開砲迎拒師船復駛向瓜州此處洪黨船隻甚多岸上施放連環大砲不絕該師船因有帆風亦放炮冲擊南北兩岸初七日向榮預派兵勇分作五路攻江寧通濟朝陽二門洪黨亦出兵二三千分頭直撲且戰且守官兵逼近誘敵洪黨始終不前十一日向榮扎營于紫金山洪黨恐兵占據形勝突出數千刼掠營塞向榮揮兵分頭接仗是日長江上游盧應祥會同楊煥章各帶炮船炮勇遶出夾江沿江北潛于南岸楊煥章分兩隊遶至夾江蘆葦中張疑設伏以爲援應

千總黃秉忠督大小炮船遶進夾江直擊橫寨隘口之鹽船三隻其餘鹽船順流退下放炮拒迎楊煥章從葦岸接應先向望樓踢壞殲却數名乘機催船齊進洪黨泊船相拒岸上炮臺七坐均向官船開炮轟擊盧應祥率勇抄截楊煥章麾兵應之黃秉忠復廻環沖擊互開鎗炮數時陳喜率勇登岸赴援斃却執黃旗首目洪黨逃潰兵勇乃拆斷夾口木排奪得大炮黃旗器械等物越日洪黨計議夫虛々實々用兵之力前有大兵之拒又無用武之地勝負難決不若舍前支西從虛潛入宜候機宜而進也是以分股支擾滁州復占據臨准關直超鳳陽府知府裕泰等于四月廿一日酉時在北門外與之接仗洪黨另分一股從小路潛入東門城內煙火突起九華山與興龍寺前有會黨兩股望見火光即向北門奔去沖散鄉勇遂陷府城廿五日洪黨另分一股自汴梁西竄于汜縣盤踞城中安設鎗炮守禦將軍托明阿提兵進勦滿漢官兵以連環鎗炮四面圍攻傷殘無數洪黨見孤城難守自東門竄出屯于東西兩土山上糾合三路以爲犄角分擾于河南蔓延于山陝皇上命江南安徽各路大員添調精兵分路防勦令總兵董占元陞任山東袞州花里遜布督帶大名宣化正定官兵馳赴河北會同河北總鎭亦理防勦事務直隸總督訥爾經額即日出省統兵接應蒙古三盟王哲里木等各派蒙古兵由熱河圍場前來調集察哈爾官兵近畿一帶大兵雲集欽命訥爾經額總督各路帶兵大員奮勇前進以爲山東河南後路應援京師十萬禁兵均已調齊以俟攻勦都統西凌阿管帶黑龍江官兵在浦散住民房未安營盤洪黨乘其無備暗兵襲之由洛渡河擾及溫縣亳州失守知州孫椿等陣亡復潛徑于劉家口在南岸施放鐵砲總兵邵懿辰等巡防渡口同時星散北岸師船概自燒燬兩日不見回踪斯未得救兵至護五月初七搶入府城歸德失守河南巡撫陸應穀奏稱賊匪竄至汴梁是夜大雷大雨賊營火藥皆濕城外濠水驟深數丈十三連日賊匪攻城屢敗據衆

傳說夜深攻城緊急之時一長身赤面手執大刀往來指揮左右前後隨護之人亦復不少且見兵勇下城每有持燈指引者行走如飛賊因儆畏不前以致敗遁請加封號時湖北廣濟縣蔡潤琛徵收民佃既經兵火者未曾分開應征應免之處希圖一律錙緩鄉民不服持戈聚抗官此後有鄉民欲赴該縣收首爲別處鄉民設詞攔阻飽署令不善調停反帶兵勇殲捡數十因此鄉民愈聚愈多該縣復請上憲發兵勦捕琦善咨調疲殘九百予之兵不堪用是晚衆鄉民一齊闖至臬署聲稱要尋飽令報仇飽令率同縣守挺身出外彈壓均被戕害衙署亦被焚燒縣司江忠源統帶楚勇千餘東下一面會同提督阿勒經阿挑選兵丁配齊器械刻日帶赴廣濟接應亦以期迅速藏事但須善辦乃不致逼于附會也月中廣西興安縣馬坪村土匪聚衆拜會知縣蔡映符前往查拿會糾夥黨闖入縣城戕官奪犯竄入靈川盤踞城內安炮抗拒許祥光張敬修分路進攻賊始棄城潰逃暹羅貢使行抵商邱所有賞賚各物御物均被搶去着補須還改道護送回國湖南桂東縣有江廣會黨二千餘盤踞三都橋肆行刼掠焚燬汛署二十九日未刻撲滅該縣會同武營分兵出城堵禦衆寡不敵會黨分股擁進城門斷絕歸路請兵救護會黨聞風分股于上猶龍泉等縣城內衙署門捛均打毀錢糧倉庫搶去無幾禁犯乘間脫逃居民或被搶掠復又散擾于永興縣由山路竄入三河洲地方山頂住扎伐木結寨該處係高山峻嶺有徑三條官兵兩路堵塞僅留一路出入架炮防堵衡州府屬安仁縣復有一股竄集請兵防堵駱秉章遂飛咨于江西巡撫不分畛域一體勦辦六月初八訥爾經額奏稱永定河南水漫隄頂自未至申長水一丈五尺連原底共深二丈餘時當黑夜水勢猛驟人力難施塌却三十七丈掣動大溜民間房舍田禾間有沖壞淹漫相應請旨赴緊監修毋致塌刷愈寬一面行查被淹各村庄輕重情形應否撫邺其奏十九合兵進攻商定此股多係粵西湖廣會黨形踪

諭巧或分五六股突出一見官兵又復嘯聚藏匿並于懷慶城之東南一帶接連竪立木壘暗施鎗炮各隘口設有陷坑竹簽地雷埋伏遍插旗幟遙作聲援虛實莫辨參將崇安奮攻木壘炮傷陣亡二十一費以濟時需一請開內地罌粟花稅比照茶酒等物一律收稅一請將內府舊存金器改鑄金錢與紋銀一律並行一請將京城現收舖租章程推廣各直省一體辦理硃批該部議奏七月中旬彗星見于西方廣西梧州府陳因大鯉魚雖有歸降之名究無降順之實六月廿七恩華親督文武員弁統帶吉林黑龍江及直隸山東各省官兵由二千里舖直抵丹河會黨旗從林內轉出官兵以連環鎗炮拒敵洪黨退後官兵將其房舍燒燬百餘間二十九連日復督官兵過河掩殺會黨退入木城不出情形巧詐營壘尚多官兵亦不敢遽進至大名鎮董占元先于二十一日帶兵直搗懷慶北關督率遊擊薛成龍等官員共一十二名直兵攻寨俱破受傷陣亡兵丁亦復七月廿二日府遣其子先伏勇士誘于席棬而戮之別將衞內之差目舞斃者斬却地方賴安七月中旬上海吳爽行文到粵東調撥南洋船數十號壯勇數千由洋面往海上不料八月初旬劉元預伏黨友數百于是夜登于瓦面用火擲下衙日將其誘出伏兵統後兵獲勝廿三日分兵各勦托明阿善祿等攻其北勝保攻其東南黨仍堅閉暗施鎗炮抵敵官兵列隊前進黨亦分股突出各放鎗炮互有損傷會黨于沁隄淺水之處分股接應官亦分兵拒截而退廿六日復分馬步各軍前進黨于木城內及各隘口施放鎗炮或出或入官兵亦不敢直前廿七日辰早勝保攻其南托明阿等分擊東北兩面屢由隄北遶出兵後東北木壘遍插旗幟暗放大炮兵復百數官兵鎗炮直進亦斃會黨不少天已昏暮正在收隊黨于東南北各路以田禾內突出因時黑夜馬隊官兵未能擊壓傷殘官衆甚多于是退下列營善祿即著兵丁招招鎗炮並放一時之久黨乃擊退給事中張祥晉以粵西興軍兩載以來 所費不下三千餘萬之多奏爲亟籌經內兵勇一時 逃散 吳爽 被押會館于會黨監與之盟方要他實將洋船寫明送是晚吳爽失了印信一顆後賴花旂領事帶入行高

紀事道光癸巳至咸豐三年癸丑八月按廣東羅森避亂亞黑利加癸丑八月駕鮑厦丹師船甲寅正月抵浦賀港故所見聞記事止于此

香港開埠初期文教工作者羅向喬事蹟述釋

羅香林

一

羅向喬名森、一名祥、廣東南海西樵人。父羅介人、爲淸學人，嘗著書言天文地理之學。向喬自少往來廣州澳門等地。嘗爲馬禮遜之子約翰馬禮遜講解中文。（註一）自英軍接管香港，開爲商埠，向喬未幾亦來居香港，與何福堂及理雅各相友善。（註二）其姪女卽出字何福堂長子。理雅各翻譯中國經典，曾得王韜助力最大。然據其所譯詩經首冠序文，及理海倫所撰「理雅各傳」，謂有相助之史超活（Dr. Pradench Stewart）及羅君等。（註三）。史超域曾膺官立中央書院之首任校長，（註四）。羅君卽羅向喬，其畫像照片、（照片附後），正見於理海倫所撰之「理雅各傳」也。（註五）。

向喬子觀漢、字彬湖、嘗任兩廣督標。孫羅延年，至今仍居香港，已年八十二歲。本年（一九七〇年）八月十二日余曾於香港怡和酒家，與彼會晤。據云：向喬公於七十八歲去世，時彼已十一歲。依此推算，向喬於七十一年前去世，時爲一八九九年，卽淸光緒二十五年，由此上推七十八年，爲一八二一年，卽道光元年，是爲向喬生年，向喬乃生於淸道光元年，卒於淸光緒二十五年。延年先生又謂：向喬公往來香港與日本，及香港與北京之間。在港時曾反對開賭最力，獨自致電倫敦，力爭禁賭，終於得直，關係於香港社會者甚鉅。又謂日本明治天皇嘗聘向喬公爲顧問，曾贈名畫與彼（註六）。是向喬亦香港開埠初期一重要人物也。

二

日本增田涉先生，謂向喬曾撰「滿淸紀事」卽最先記載太平天國在南京事蹟之「南京紀事」，及「日本日記」等二書。（註七）據云：

『「開國起原」的「滿淸紀事」，標「廣東羅森著」，與「近世中國秘史」，稱「日本某著」有異。而詢井經夫氏的「太平天國」（日本昭和二十六年岩波新書）寫道：「滿淸紀事」爲再度來航至浦賀之彼理（Perry）艦隊乘員廣東人羅森所帶來。彼抄寫流布之後，以木活字印成一册出版，上題「羅森著」。筆者所藏木活字本，並無標名羅森，文中亦不見此名。是否有標名與不標名的二種木活字版本？抑是增井氏的記錯？』

『再說增井氏認爲「滿淸紀事」的來歷，是由「再度來航至浦賀的彼理（Perry）艦隊乘員廣東人羅森所帶來」，是誰說的？還是哪本書上寫的？沒有表示一點足爲證據的文獻。然而「開國起原」也稱「羅森著」、則必有什麼根據。於是，筆者雖不敢斷定絕對的確實，姑舉一二似乎牽涉此人的文獻，以爲參考。』『筆者藏有標題「日本日記」的寫本一册，係一八五四年連載於「遐邇貫珍」（Chinese Seria）十一號至十三號的「日本日記」。一八五四年卽嘉永七年，爲彼理再度航抵日本的一年。據戈公振的「中國報學史」稱：「遐邇貫珍」爲一八五二年八月發行於香港的月刊雜誌（十二頁至二十四頁），開始由麥都思（W.H. Meadhurst）主筆，翌年由奚理爾（C.B. Hillier）主筆，一八五六年由理雅各（J. Legge）主筆，不久卽告停刊。「遐邇貫珍」於我國幕末，被視爲一種海外情報資料。』

『現在看這本「日本日記」，冒頭爲編者的前言，「遐邇貫珍」數號，每記花旗國與日本立約之事，至第十號則載兩國所議定約條之大意。「今有一唐人（主筆的奚禮爾？）平素知己之友，去年搭花旗火船，遊至日本與叻立約事。故將所見所聞逐日詳記，編成一帙，歸以授余。玆特著于貫珍之中，以廣讀者之見聞，庶幾耳目爲之一新。以下便是此「一唐人」的日本見聞記。』

『內容是說：癸丑（一八五三年、日本嘉永六年）三月，商議合衆國之汽船通商日本，未遽而得許。是年十月廿三日，某友請余同行，共議條約，遂於十二月十五日出航云云。日期皆記舊曆，然未記此「一唐人」由何處啓航。由彼理的航海誌推測，大概在香港登船。又此「日本日記」最後處，記載七月十四日，汽船回到香港。首先寫琉球的見聞，接着正月抵橫濱（浦賀？）。以後便將日本預備會議的官員登艦來訪、及交涉經過，或船員下船遊覽橫濱與下田，或日本官員的風貌，或雙方應對的筆談，詩之應酬等。停留中的見聞，皆一一詳錄之。文中叙述於正式與林大學頭，鵜殿民部少輔，伊澤美作守，井戶對馬守等交涉之前，先會見被派遣來作預備會的小吏。他與那些人交換筆談，問其名，有山本文之

助、合原操藏，名村八郎。其後數日，平山謙二郞（此人爲幕府之「徒目付」卽「目付」岩瀨肥後守之部下，後與橋本左內往來甚密，見「橋本景岳全集）、因「問余中國治亂之端」，故「余將平日記錄之事及治安策視之」，遂將此書借與他。又說借書回去（想於這期間抄寫）的平山，於還書時，寫了一封長信給他，信中有云：「頃者，視南京紀事及治安策二册子，熟讀數回，始審中國治亂之由，且知羅向喬之學術淳正，愛君憂國之志，流離顚沛未嘗忘，亦掩卷而歎也。」（原文）這封信的受信人署名羅向喬。』

『此處所謂「南京紀事」（太平天國建都南京），係指最初沒有標題而後來在日本被命名爲「滿淸紀事」一書；所說「羅向喬」卽羅森、向喬是字號。』

『羅向喬說：於下田一月間，被請揮毫於扇面者千餘，（某處則寫五百以上）。其中有主理下田事務的官員黑川嘉兵衞行事官堀達之助，森山榮之助，中臺信太郎等，要求贈詩於扇面，下文遂錄其詩，中有一句：「避亂乘船亦一奇，吳中鼙鼓不聞知。」聽這口吻，叫人覺得他好像最初身處亂中，對於太平軍之亂，相當淸楚。以下錄日本人贈給他的詩，中有一句：「君產廣東我沾洲，相逢萍水交天緣。」生於廣東，想是他自己告訴日本人的吧。』

『以上看來，所謂「滿淸紀事」，便是羅向喬所寫的，而羅向喬卽羅森，如是斷言，當無差池。』

『羅向喬與日本人贈答之事及詩，皆記載於「日本日記」，而根岸橋三郎於其「幕末開國新觀」（日本昭和二年博文館），介紹了「丑寅俳句」，（原題「丑寅キのはづけ」））一

篇。該篇似爲當時的瓦版，未明記出處，內容係諷刺癸丑（一八五三年），甲寅（一八五四年）間，卽彼理來航時社會的物情騷然，其中稱「可怕者」爲「與羅森贈答的腐儒。」此亦可證羅森與彼理同時來日本，且與日本人贈答了詩的「日本日記」之羅向喬，卽是羅森。』

據此，可知羅向喬卽爲於一八五三年與彼理艦隊同至日本參與商訂日美汽船通商條約者。其人其學，又爲當時日人所甚敬重，則其後受日本明治天皇聘爲顧問，非無前因也。

三

向喬嘗在港敎學，政府中人，多從之遊。昔年於中環，亦頗置地產。延年先生嘗任警察署文案，清末頗與孫中山所組織之興中會及同盟會諸志士相往還，孫太夫人在九龍去世，卽由彼設法購得百花林墳場安葬者，詳余另著「國父在香港之歷史遺蹟。」(註八)延年先生有子八人：長廣威、碩士，次廣耀、學士，三廣德、航空指揮官，四廣洪、亞細亞公司任職，五廣福、市政局邦辦，六廣儒、工程師，七廣霖、渣打銀行電報員，八廣熙、咸豪置業公司經理，一門英秀。惜自第二次大戰後，其家中所藏向喬公有關文籍，皆已無存云。(註九)

惟幸日本所藏「開國起原」所載之「滿清紀事」卽「南京紀事」尚有木刻活字本一種，明載「廣東羅森著」，蓋爲羅向喬於一八五三年由香港乘再度赴日本之彼理（Perry）艦，而帶往日本，卽由彼邦書坊所傳印者。此書如非卽爲羅向喬所自撰，亦必與其有密切之關係，且必最先曾出現於香港。

考洪秀全由拜上帝會所組織之太平軍，於道光三十年卽一八五〇年六月，始起義於廣西桂平之金田村，至咸豐元年卽一八五一年閏八月，進據永安，卽今廣西蒙山縣，始建號曰太平天國。咸豐二年四月，攻陷全州、東出湖南，至七月抵長沙，十一月東下長江。咸豐三年卽一八五三年二月遂攻克南京，建爲首都。西人之撰文報告太平天國起義經過者，首爲一八五二年羅孝全牧師（Rev. I.J. Roberts）所作「洪秀全革命之眞相」一長函。(註十)繼有一八五三年八月「遐邇貫珍」第一號所載之「西興括論」及一八五四年同誌第二、三、四號所載之「太平天國新聞雜輯」(註十一)與一八五四年韓山明牧師（Rev Theodore Hamburg）所撰之「太平天國起義記」（The Vissions of Hung Siu-tsuen and Origin of the Kwang-si Insurection）。(註十二) 國內文人之撰文紀載太平軍攻克南京及其各種措施者，則首有咸豐三年上元鋒鏑餘生所撰「金陵述略」一短文，(註十三)，及咸豐五年張德堅所撰之「賊情彙纂」一專書，(註十四)，與咸豐六年滌浮道人所撰之「金陵雜記」一小書。(註十五)。而此「滿清紀事」卽「南京紀事」，乃於一八五三年十二月，傳入日本，則其撰書，亦必卽在是年二月以後十二月以前，與「遐邇貫珍」所載「西興括論」之撰作時期及「金陵述略」之作期，爲大略相同。較之韓山明所撰「太平天國起義記」爲早出一年，視張德堅所撰「賊情彙纂」爲更早出二年。是此日本一種木刻活字本所載「廣東羅森著」之「南京紀事」，乃爲關於太平軍攻入南京之較早記錄，就史料之性質言之，亦爲極可貴者，以此更知羅向喬在咸豐初期之重要性矣。

四

羅向喬所撰『日本日記』所述事蹟，始自一八五三年十二月十五日、自香港出發、途經琉球，至一八五四年正月，抵達橫濱(浦賀?)見及日本德川幕府末期各官員，及文化教育界各鉅子

理雅各與助其翻譯中國經典之羅向喬左起第一人為理雅各第二人為羅向喬

，相與協助商訂日美通商條約，並與日本愛好中國詩文之人士相互酬唱，而止於一八五四年七月十四日之間抵香港。首尾僅滿七月，時間短促，篇幅非富。然就清代中國文人所記日本史地與國情之載籍言之，亦似有其應得地位。蓋前乎此書之載，多為見於正史外國傳之日本國傳，即有獨自成書者，所記亦每止於豐臣秀吉時代或德川幕府之初期，如明季李言恭郝杰同撰之『日本考』五卷，(註十六)薛俊撰之『日本考略』三卷，鄭若曾撰之『日本圖考』二卷，(註十七)及清初戴名世撰之『日本風土記』一卷，(註十八)，是其例也。其通記日本全史，或詳述日本政教者，其撰作又多已在德川幕府歸政天皇、即明治維新以後，而尤以記述日本已達強盛時期之情況者，為較顯著，如傅雲龍撰之『日本圖經』三十卷，(註十九)黃遵憲撰之『日本國志』四十卷(註二十)，及何如璋撰之『使東略述』，(註二十一)，與吳汝綸撰之『東遊叢錄』，陳家麟撰之『東槎聞見錄』等，(註二十二)，是其例也。羅向喬之『日本日記』，則為屬於德川幕府末期之見聞，雖篇幅與聲名不足與上述各書相比擬，然亦有其所代表之時期。吾人不言德川幕府末期之見聞則已，不然則不能以羅向喬『日本日記』之篇幅較短而輕視之也。

附註

註一、見拙作「乙堂隨筆」「約翰馬禮遜與羅向喬」條。(一九五四年四月五日於九龍好彩發室據羅延年先生口述所記錄)。

註二、見拙著「香港與中西文化之交流」(一九六一年香港中國學社出版)第二章「香港早期之教會與理雅各歐德等之翻譯中國要籍」註五三。

註三、見理海倫(Helen Edith Legge)撰「理雅各傳」James Legge Mis—

sionary and Scholas, 1905 第四章「香港及中國經典」 Hong Kong and Chinese Classics)。

註四、香港官立中央書院（Government Central School）創立於一八六二年，即今皇仁書院（Queen's College）之前身。史超活事蹟見史鐸士（Gwenneth Stokes撰「皇仁書院百年史」Queen's College, 1862—1962）第二章「史超活博士」（Dr Frederick Stewart, 1862—81）。

註五、理海倫所撰「理雅各傳」，附有「理雅各及其助手」油畫照片一幀，照片內坐者二人，立者二人，自左而右，第一坐者爲理雅各，第二坐者，據羅延年先生就其形貌研究，謂即爲其祖羅向喬公也。

註六、羅向喬之赴日本，始於一八五三年，時尚爲德川幕府當政之末期。後至一八六七年（清同治六年）明治天皇即位，積極變法維新。向喬以早嘗來往日本，助訂日美商約，熟悉國際情況，其受聘爲顧問，殆可信也。羅延年先生謂明治天皇贈向喬公之名畫，共爲四幅，至第二次大戰時，始不幸失去。

註七、見大陸雜誌（臺北市大陸雜誌社編印）第四十卷第六期增田涉著張良澤譯「雜書雜談」第五節（原著載日本平凡社所刊「中國古典文學大系月報」第二十二號。

註八、見「國父百年誕辰紀念論文集」（中華民國各界紀念 國父百年誕辰籌備委員會學術論著編纂委員會編印）第一册一八九頁至二一六頁。（民國五十四年十二月出版）

註九、據本年（一九七〇年）八月三十一日羅延年先生至余寓（香港麥當奴道二十二號二樓）所口述。

註十、羅存全牧師所撰「洪秀全革命之眞相」長函，原刊於 TheChinese and General Missionary Gleaner.（London, Oct, 1852）此據簡又文先生譯文（見中國史學會主編「太平天國資料」第六册）。

註十一、見金毓黻編「太平天國史料」（一九五九年中華書局重版）第四部分「中外記載」。

註十二、韓山明所撰「太平天國起義記」原以英文書寫於一八五四年出版於香港。此據簡又文先生譯本（亦載同上「太平天國資料」第六册。

註十三、上元鋒鏑餘生所撰「金陵述略」，原件今藏倫敦大英博物館。此據同上「天平天國史料」第四部分。

註十四、張德堅所撰「賊情彙纂」十二卷，原僅有鈔本，其後南京國學圖書館乃據鈔本影印，乃始流通。今所據排印本則見同上「太平天國資料」第三册。

註十五、滌浮道人所撰「金陵雜誌」，今亦見同上「太平天國資料」第四册。

註十六、李言恭郝杰同撰之「日本考」五卷，今所見爲北平圖書館影印之「善本叢書十二種」本，蓋爲影印明萬曆刊本者。

註十七、薛俊撰「日本考略」三卷，及鄭若曾撰「日本圖考」二卷，均見黃虞稷「千頃堂書目」及紀昀等撰「四庫全書存目」。

註十八、臧名世撰「日本風土記」一卷，見友人彭國棟先生纂修「重修清史藝文志」二史部地理類「外志之屬」。

註十九、傅雲龍撰「日本圖經」三十卷，見同上「重修清史藝文志」「外志之屬」。

註二十、黃遵憲撰「日本國志」四十卷，於光緒十六年（一八九〇年）刊於廣州文富齋，自是風行全國，爲國人研究日本全史者之創始。

註二十一、何如璋撰「使東述略」，義年何氏後裔何壽朋先生，曾於廣州排印行世。

註二十二、吳汝綸撰「東遊叢錄」見同上「重修清史藝文志」「外志之屬」。陳家麟撰「東槎聞見錄」見王錫祺輯「小方壺齋輿地叢鈔」第十帙。

民國五十九年九月二十二日爲紀念包龍溪先生而作。

H　羅森関係

「

延年宗長簡介—革命老人羅延年先生—（羅森関係資料）

郷原羅延年先生、粤南海西樵羅村人。早歳追随国父孫中山先生、致力革命、建立民国、勲労卓著、為国父及其胞兄孫眉先生倚重。国父哲嗣哲生先生公子治平、治強二君、且以先生為誼父、足見交好之深。

先生世代書香、曽祖介人公前清孝廉、祖父向喬公字祥、又名森、学貫中西、為我国近代外交先進、父観漢、字彬湖、清室武官、以敉〔救〕平広西南寧八排匪乱有功、獲清室賞賜藍翎、当時引為殊栄。

先生幼已茁生民主思潮、受西方教育後、志益堅決、後且加入同盟会従事国民革命、実受其祖父向喬公自幼薫陶之影響。

向喬公任職英国駐華大使館秘書時、以才気横溢、見重清廷、旋擢外交官、出任我国駐日本領事、為日本朝野及当地僑胞敬重、甚有政声。厠身外交工作多年、深明国際情勢、於民主政制、至為傾慕、復以清廷政治窳敗、国弱民貧、以是任満退出政壇、視富貴如浮雲、寧返香港作寓公、授西人華語以餬口。所著南京紀事（日本標題満清紀事、内容誌太平天国事蹟）及治安策、流伝日本、始則抄伝、継而以活字版一再重印、備受日人重視。

一八五二年春、美使至日議訂通商条約、未得要領、返。同年十月、復銜命率彼理艦隊再度赴日重開談判、知公名重東瀛、為日朝野所重、経港時、邀公協助。於是随同出発、抵日後、公従旁斡旋、力促其成、美日通商条約於焉締結。公十月三日自港啓程以迄翌年七月十四日回航返港、逐日詳誌経過、洋

洋大観、為港報「遐邇貫珍」主筆奚礼爾欣賞、商請在報章発表、遂付与該報以中英対照闢欄連載、題為「日本日記」。遐邇貫珍在我国報業史上、推許為香港出版最早之華文報、所載各国動態翔実、被視為珍貴情報資料、見重於国際政壇。由是向喬公名傾中外、許為傑出外交人材。

嗣香港政府以政費支絀、決開賭以挹注、公憂賭禁一開、貽害港僑、毅然上書港督諫阻、不為採納、且一意孤行、因又逕電英廷、呼籲制止。英廷卒電港府厳行賭禁、並復電嘉勉、公之得英廷尊重、可以想見。香港今日之一直以賭博懸為厲禁、不致貽害社会、実拜賜向喬公当年運用国民外交之功。

延年郷先生於一八八九年誕於香港、母李太夫人分娩前夕、夢白鶴繞室飛翔、及先生出生、親友知其事者、咸謂此子有福寿雙全吉兆。今先生年登寿城、児孫満堂、蘭桂騰芳、逾九十二高齢、紅顔白髪、歩履軽盈、猶経常参加社団活動、膺任不少社団要職、李太夫人夢兆、実信而有徵矣。

先生幼聡穎、得乃祖歓。六歳、挈之至穂、延師授中文、向喬公親課西語、暇輒以世界珍聞相告、先生深受薫陶、民主思潮、油然而生。迨十一歳、祖父棄生、李太夫人卓有遠見、与愛子重履香港受西方教育、入聖士提反小学攻読。先生聡穎過人、試必名列前茅、五年学制僅三年即因一再跳級而畢所学、為師長器重。旋升学皇仁書院、復利用下午課余、至華民政務司従黄宝寿習譒訳。及中学畢業、以学優獲選官学生、入牛津大学深造英文、旋奉任九龍城警署譒訳官、継遷海事署、教育司、警察総部等要職。在海事署時、譒訳工作外、身兼秘書、海員監考、洋船註冊数職、治事廉明、為上司倚畀。

一九二七年以耳疾申請采休、其後転而従商、任旧沙宣洋行買弁、継経営採礦及船務、購置上環香港第六号永遠碼頭、加以修建、定名広徳碼頭、以発展航業。長袖善舞、一帆風順、業務鼎盛。歴任僑社要職及東華三院首席総理、於社会慈善福利工作、力行不替。

方其任職九龍城警署時、公余散歩海浜、獲交国父胞兄孫眉先生、志同道合、

尋成知己。時孫氏奉国父命在港秘密主持革命機関、以先生傾向民主思想、邀請参加同盟会、先生欣然応命、乃由革命元老鍾景南先生之介、孫眉先生監誓、加入同盟会、躋於革命行列。

先生遺身香港警署、消息霊通、対同志掩護照顧、至為週全。既而国父令慈楊太夫人病逝九龍城、親友顧慮英廷、多所引避、先生挺身而出、主持治喪、為楊太夫人卜葬飛鵝嶺濠涌百花林、喪礼隆重。会港府受清廷圧力、捕孫眉先生、将遣返中国、先生遣同志走報駐港美領事、及時営救、以孫氏美籍華僑、提出交渉、得免於難。由是見知於国父、其後国父之哲嗣哲生先生、且以公子治平・治強・拝先生為誼文、成通家之好。

民国肇造後、先生返国 任中国鉄路購料委員会委員長、貴州省政府 経済顧問、広東礦務専員等職、嗣因淡泊仕途、辞官返港、重振所業、発展礦務、航業、地産、股票者歴数十年、為本港知名股商。

先生侍母至孝、李太夫人七十六歳時、雙目失明、先生以古人有子舐母、復明之説、認為孝足感天、試試、果漸復視覚、重覩光明、親及嘆為奇蹟。西樵羅村郷長感太夫人教子有方、侍姑尽孝。又曽割股療太翁病、閭里称賢。臚列事実報県呈層憲、奉国府題頒「筠節瑩和」牌坊表揚。

先生於民国四十一年与旅港宗彦発起組織羅氏宗親会、得衆望膺任首届理事長、嗣後蟬联会長至今。茲者、年登上寿、与退休名法官羅顕勝太平紳士、同為旅港宗人尊称羅氏人瑞、而先生固碩果僅存之同盟会革命老人也。（羅氏源流考刊載・一九八〇年末、羅延年博士より受く）

「

羅森扇面の詩。口絵⑨参照。安政元（一八五四年）、ペリー艦隊通訳官羅森が、箱館にて松前勘解由に進呈した扇面の詩。（松前城資料館蔵、加藤昌市氏より）

三三四

火船駛向粤西東。此日登程霽色融。歴覧層山情不尽。遙看巨海目無穹。雙輪飛出蒼溟外。一舵軽浮浩蕩中。勢若騎鯨衝巨浪。快如奮鶚振高風。月明遠照琉球島。雪白横堆日本峰。身覚渺然於天地唯与知音訴己表。両国横浜会。欣情一類同。解冠称礼義。佩剣羨英雄。共説傳杯盞。和懐奏鼓鐘。咸覩歓楽。徳被永無窮。

大夫勘解由政 甲寅夏五月書為 広東羅森

火船①は駛せて向う粤の西②東。
此の日程③に登りて霽色④融なり。
層山⑤を歴覧して情尽きず。
遙るかに巨海を看れば目に穹るなし。
雙輪⑥の飛び出ずるは蒼溟⑦の外。
一舵の軽く浮ぶは浩蕩⑧の中。
勢は鯨に騎る若くして巨浪を衝く。
快きこと奮鶚⑨の如くして高風を振わす。
月明⑩遠く照らす琉球の島。
雪白⑪横堆す日本の峰。
身に覚ゆ天地に渺然⑫たるを。
唯だ知音⑬の与めにのみ己を訴え表す。
両国、横浜に会う。
欣情⑭、一類にして同じ。
冠を解けば礼義に称い。
劔を佩ぶれば英雄を羨む。
共に説⑮びては杯盞⑯を傳け。
和懐⑰しては鼓鐘を奏す。
咸な歓楽を覩⑱て。
徳被⑲は永に窮り無し。

①蒸汽船。②粤‖越　広東、広西。③門出。④晴天。⑤幾重も連る山々。⑥双輪船。⑦青海。⑧広大な水域。⑨鶚。みさご。とび。奮は猛く勇しい。⑩明るい月。⑪白雪。⑫きわまりない。⑬親友。⑭よろこび。⑮‖悦（えつ）　共説（えつ）‖共悦（えつ）。⑯酒盃。⑰なごみよろこぶ。又は懐（こころ）を和やかにして。⑱咸覩歓楽。の下に一字脱落か。⑲徳被、徳のあまねきこと。

「

サミュエル・ウィリアムズ扇面の文。口絵⑩⑪参照。安政元年、ペリー艦隊通訳官、サミュエル・ウイリアムズがつくり、羅森が中訳して箱館にて松前勘解由に進呈した扇面の文。（松前城資料館蔵、加藤昌市氏より）

素企高風殊深。仰
慕依恋
之誠恒切肺腑間
也。兹将
揚帆。未卜何時而
再会、以
得追随几席領承
教益哉。
聴高山流水以快
積懐。覩
各邦風景而増識
見。但恐
煩言鄙瑣不報為
台駕談
耳而姑勿論再者。
本艦即
将揚帆別往。今有
煩言陳
子。如後亜国戒有
船至此、
祈願台駕以民胞
物与之。
懐尽心力以照保
約行事。
此則国家之福而
遠近官
民之戴慕於台駕
徳者深
也。甲寅夏五月書為
大夫勘解由政
三畏衛廉士

平山省齋先生墓表

參國家之機務。而當外交之要衝。維持風教。而誘掖後進。有一於此。足以傳於千載。況幷有之如我省齋先生者乎。先生諱敬忠。字安民。稱謙二郎。省齋其號。後以爲通稱。考曰黑岡活圓齋。以擊劒事三春藩。妣鹽田氏。先生弱冠。讀伊洛淵源錄。有以道學自任之意。旣而自謂爲儒教人。不得志於當世者之所爲。大丈夫應顯君澤民。以報國家爾。於是。游江戶。繼幕臣平山氏後。嘉永四年辛亥。擢徒目付。六年癸丑五月。米利堅國使節彼理入浦賀港。物情騷然。先生受命。巡視房總相武沿海地形。安政元年甲寅春。米使再到金川港。二年又來下田港。先生伻參應接之事。又與目付堀利熙等。巡視蝦夷。窮唐太島。遂巡東北沿海而歸。四年丁已。與勘定奉行水野忠德目付岩瀨忠震赴長崎。會露西亞和蘭二公使。議貿易事。廢歲輸丁銅之約。五年七月。補書物奉行。先是。先生屢進秩加俸。至此又有斯命。盖異數也。當是時。幕府政衰。內憂外患並至。而大將軍溫恭公暴薨、昭德公襲職。井伊直弼爲大老。大興黨獄。先生坐罷職。謫于甲府。居三年。起補函館奉行支配組頭。班布衣。慶應元年乙丑十一月。轉二丸留守、攝外國事務。尋改目付。會幕府奉勅討毛利氏。先生從老中小笠原長行。

赴小倉。監鎮西諸藩兵。二年八月。補外國奉行。叙從五位下。任圖書頭。三年丁卯四月。擢若年寄並外國總奉行。是冬受命。使朝鮮。到京師。見大將軍內府公。稟使事。會公復政權赴大坂。尋有伏見之變。乃從公東歸。補若年寄。移病不參衙。無幾罷職。明治元年戊辰四月。先生被朝譴、屏居于家。頃之移于靜岡。從德川氏也。先生爲人沈毅堅忍。最惡宴安、奉身儉素。而興公益救人急。莫所顧惜。幼好讀書。亦無常師。其在甲府及靜岡也。集徒教授。諄諄不倦、雖在官日。弟子不絕跡。先生起於寒微。陞顯達。當外交始興議論鼎沸之際。常周旋于其間。拮据鞅掌。解紛糾理盤錯者不可勝數。其從長行監軍于小倉也。諸藩兵概懷觀望。逗撓不進。而昭德公之訃適至。長行乘夜航于長崎。先生知事不可爲。晝夜兼行到長崎。則長行既東歸矣。後先生常語人曰。余閱世故當難局多。然苦心焦慮莫過此時。一念及此。爽然自失焉。三年正月。先生遇赦歸東京。卜居于城北白山。號素山道人。自此絕意官途。以振張國教爲已任。周游東西。述敬神愛國之道。遂立一派。稱神道大成教。信徒甚衆。嘗慨大宮氷川社頹敗。請官募資。再造殿宇。又奏請陞東京日枝社爲官幣社。先是。先生補權少教正。兼氷川神社宮司。及日枝神社祠官。後累進大教正。敘從六位。

二十三年五月二十二日病歿。壽七十有六。神宮祭主久邇宮賜謚曰素山彦弘道命。葬于谷中之塋域。配桑原氏生二男。長成信嗣。次英三別成家。初余之遇先生于長崎也。在安政丁己之歲。一見知其爲名士。爾後海內多故。音問不通。唯聞幕府有平山謙二郎。明治中興。余官於朝。先生亦在東京。於是日夕過從。益悉其爲人。而與成信君最親善。頃者君持狀來諗曰先考小祥忌將至。知先考莫如公者。願不朽之。嗚呼先生既竭力於國家。又翼賛名敎。可謂克成初志者矣。因不辭而表之。

明治二十四年五月

省齋遺稿卷上

男　平山成信子明編錄

安政元年甲寅春正月。奉旨赴相之浦賀。時花旗國船提督被理入港。

誰道他山石。把來玉可磨。笑而甘鼎鑊。誓欲定山河。烈矣出師表。凛乎正氣歌。回頭相識少。俗吏一何多。

三月。花旗船去港。四月。奉命赴蝦夷。路經野奥之間。少時所曾過。今昔之感殊切。

憶昔單身負笈輕。橋霜店月趁晨程。今日誰知爲小吏。春風到處荷恩行。

柳塘梅塢短長程。處處春流拍岸生。二月上頭京洛路。村村煙雨亂鶯聲。

二月二夜。勢州龜山客舍。感時事而有此作

紛紛五洲亂若麻。獨逸佛郎葡萄牙。中有桀鶩似秦楚。西𠸄咭唎北鄂羅。各有正朔有治方。舊國稱帝新稱王。幾隻巨艦幾門礮。梯山航海互誇張。和則盟約通貿易。戰則連兵迭相僵。夷狄非復昔時比。滿淸不察招創傷。吾國東方一乾坤。絕無外患金甌完。二百餘年皷腹樂。實是祖宗雨露恩。近者綠眼來求好。萬里重譯欵海門。男兒致志在斯秋。熟計只應國恩酬。議者說和或論戰。戰失于剛和失柔。

和者偷安貪寵祿惟避勢餂靦靡羞。日復一日徒蹩躠。覆巢豈有完卵留。王衍秦檜皆國賊。先執此輩刎其頭。膠柱主戰亦迂腐。不審彼已慚孫武。馬服君子易言兵。先人遺矩渾齟齬。峽山公子徒好戰。宿老苦諫輒抗拒。暴虎馮河獨自用。故墟凄涼長榛莽。盡把輿圖仔細看。吾於五洲位中部。正當八蠻鍼路程。捕鯨載貨舶萬數。淼渺洋中絕水薪。颶潮卷船船掀舞。歲葬魚腹幾千人。仰吾港口如慈父。捧書懇籲求通市。長免鯨波覆沒苦。吾若待渠如仇讐。拘囚其人摧其艣。渠亦天地所生民。不啻買怨鬼神怒。萬邦來寇無寧日。衆寡不敵理先睹。士疲奔命民瘁路。折戟枯骨空委土。曲在吾儂直在渠。終遭群狠咬一虎。或謂鎌府斬元使。眞爲千秋大快事。至今嘖嘖說偉功。孰識古今形態異。羯奴乘運呑華夏。瀚海馳命辭傲肆。强逼方物爲藩臣。峻斥固不待神智。日和日戰兩糊塗。其誤國事歸一途。俗吏書生濶時務。安知廊廟有遠圖。草莽遺才皆禮致。蹇蹇鄂鄂贊宏謨。天下何世無具眼。唯須協力同馳驅。寄語山林俊傑士。何不奮躍登雲衢。如今世界一變期。粗似戰國七雄時。虎踞狼視各據土。鷹揚鷙搏交相窺。天文推步極精微。砲艦器械競新奇。敎化獨虧先聖道。回回瑪默基利斯。老死未聞仁義懿。終古不見囊中錐。歷山南翁稱豪傑。竟無唐虞龍鳳姿。閣龍壘瓦强志力。詎望百世帝王師。瞢瞢滔滔獺祭魚。惟智惟力相雄雌。畢竟天降賢聖君。一洗寰宇定鴻基。幸是吾邦峙東海。

天神皇統垂萬載。君臣大義日月明。夐異車書追世改。人口億萬性忠烈。五金九穀用不竭。天祐如斯非偶然。何況列聖愼貽厥。風雲待時圖長征。爲披洪荒掃臊腥。我武維揚文教開。綏撫萬邦乳孩嬰。懋德坤輿霖雨洽。戢暴五洲雷霆轟。克繼上帝化育功。糾合八紘爲主盟。初聞軒豁開胸臆。漸向四方伸羽翼。滿淸覆轍有殷鑒。廓然廣交瀛外國。貿遷有無收國利。充實府庫培兵力。遠航諸洲察盈虛。旁拓窮髮宏疆域。採

彼所長充我用。經綸何敢出蠡測。譬如寒梅冒雪霜。春風
忽破馥郁香。又似神龍混魚鼈。一旦吟雲昇九蒼。天命人
心所與歸。蠻珍海錯輸帝鄉。鴟梟悉化從鸞鳳。宇內稽顙
觀國光。古來忠臣偉績多。勤王勳業勝此麼。君不聞丈夫
不虛生世間。一片丹心誓山河。

偶得

無始已來妄作身。妄身脫了見眞神。無量煩惱雲煙散。方
是乾坤濶步人。

戊午春。同復齋林君。奉旨在洛。既而抵浪華。又歸洛。
旬日間。聚散不一。

(3) 下田

SIMODA FROM THE AMERICAN GRAVE YARD

JAPANESE FUNERAL AT SIMODA

PUBLIC BATH AT SIMODA.

COM. PERRY PAYING HIS FAREWELL VISIT TO THE IMPERIAL COMMISSIONERS AT SIMODA.

下田の弁天神社

KURA - KAWA - KAHAI.
PREFECT OF SIMODA.

PRINCE OF IDZU.

吉田松陰銅像　疋田雪洲作「複製」（霊山歴史館蔵）

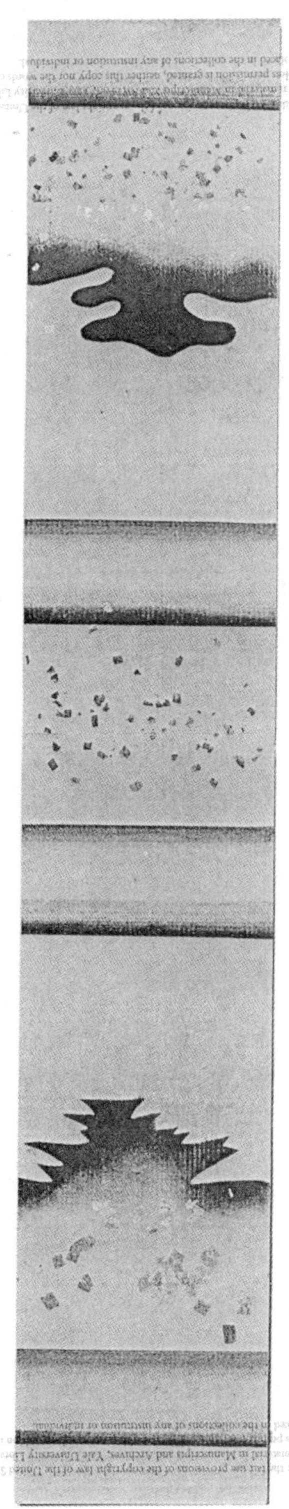

官下田奉行組与力應接掛

日本國江戶府書生、瓜中萬二、市木公太呈書
貴大臣各將官執事、生等賦稟薄弱、軀幹矮小、固自恥列
士籍、未能精刀槍刺擊之技、未能講兵馬鬪爭之法、汎
汎然悠玩愒歲月、及讀支那書、稍聞知歐羅巴、米理駕
風教、乃欲周遊五大洲、然而吾國海禁甚嚴、外國人入
內地與內地人到外國、皆在不貸之典、是以周遊之念勃
々然往來於心胸間、而呻吟蹜跙、蓋亦有年矣、幸
貴國大軍艦連檣來泊吾港口、為日已久、生等熟觀稔察、
深悉
貴大臣各將官仁厚愛物之意、平生之念、又復觸發、今則斷
然决策、將深密請託、假坐貴船中、潛出海外、以周遊五
大洲、不復暇顧國禁也、願執事辱察鄙衷、令得成此事、
生等所能為、百般使役、惟命是聽、夫跛躄者之見行走者、
行走者之見騎乘者、其意之歆羨如何耶、況生等終
身奔走、不能出東西三十度、南北二十五度之外、以是
視夫駕長風、凌巨濤、電走千萬里、隣交五大洲者、豈
特跛躄之與行走、行走之與騎乘之可譬哉、
執事幸垂明察、許諾所請、何恵尚之、惟吾國海禁未除、
以事若或傳播、則生等不徒見追捕召回、刎斬立到無
疑也、事或至此、則傷　貴大臣各將官仁厚愛物之意亦
大矣、執事願許所請、又當為生等委曲包隱、至於開帆
時、以令得免刎斬之慘、若至他年自歸、則國人亦不必追
窮往事也、生等言雖疎漏、意實誠確、執事願察其情、
憐其意、勿為疑、勿為拒、萬二、公太仝拜呈、

我等両人世界致見物度候間、其御船ニ内密ニ
乗込せ呉られよ。尤異国へ渡る事ハ日本之大禁
ニ付、此事を日本之役人達へ御話被成候而ハ甚
當惑仕

右之趣御大将方御承引ニ候ハヽ明晩夜深て
柿崎村之濱邊、傳馬舟壹艘御寄候而御迎ニ
被下候様奉待候

甲寅三月廿二日

市木公太
瓜中萬二

For the incident connected with this paper, see Spaulding's Japan, p. 283, where a translation is inserted.

英雄失意比跡盜賊面縛就捕幽囚累日村長里正倨傲相待其厄亦甚矣雖然俯仰無愧可以見英雄之為英雄也以周遊六十國為未足欲適歷五大洲是吾儕曩日之事也今一旦失計陷於半閉之室食息坐臥不得少出範圍泣則近痴笑則近黠嗚呼默〻而已矣

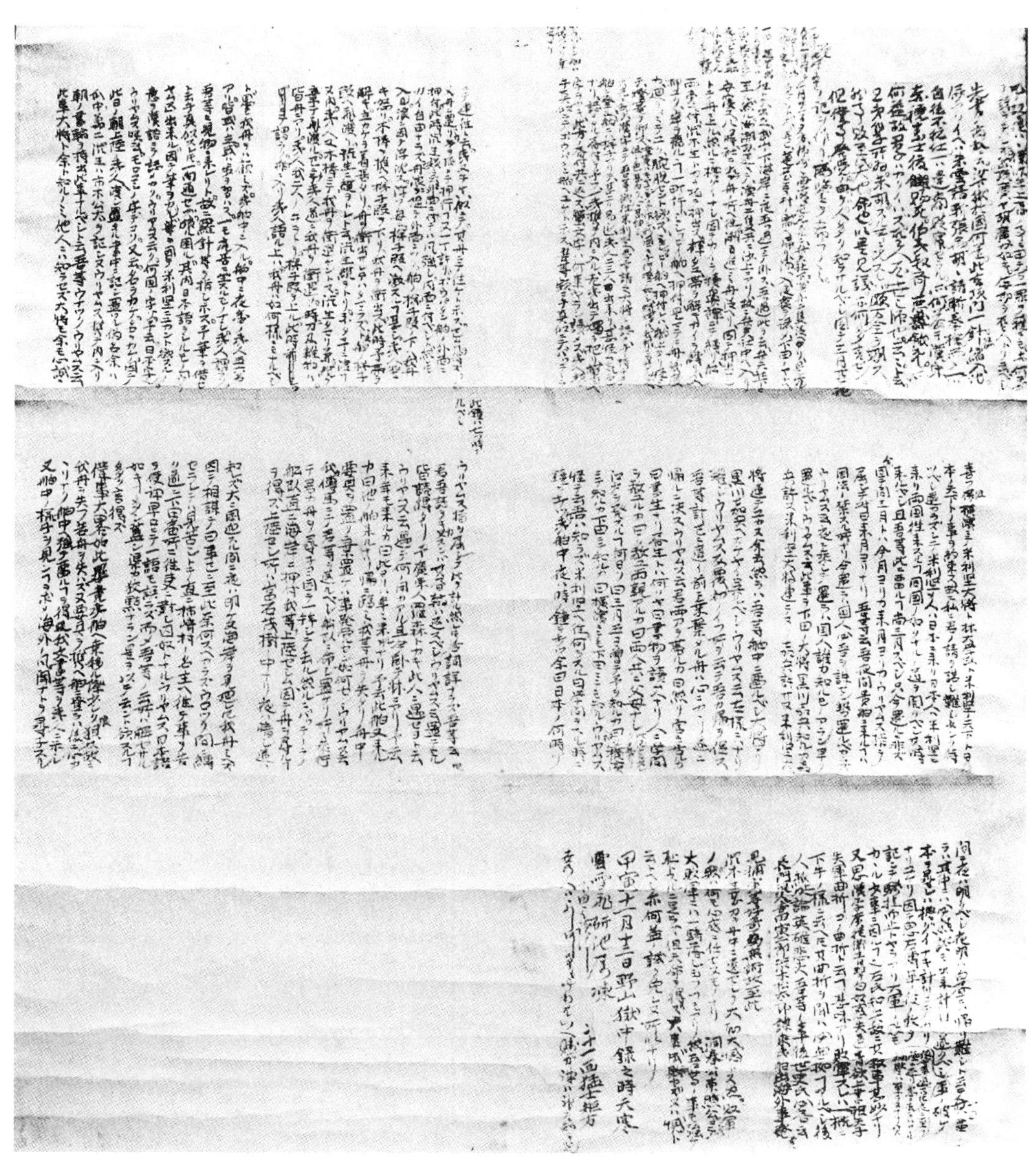

象山佐久間先生著
海舟勝義邦先生校
省諐錄
辛未晚冬
聚遠樓藏梓

省諐錄
象山平大星 啟又名子明氏
嘉永甲寅夏四月。大星以事下獄。在繫七月。
省愆之餘。弗無所述。然獄中禁筆研。不能存
藁。故久而多忘。既出而錄其所曉記。藏諸巾
笥。以貽子孫。如其弊以示衆。則吾豈敢。
所行之道。可以自安。所得之事。可以自樂。罪之有
無。在我而已。由外至者。豈足憂戚。若以忠信受
譴為辱。則不義而富且貴。亦在其所榮耶。
有人於此。憂君父之疾病。而求之藥。幸而得之。且

知其必有效也。則不問其品之貴賤。名之美惡。
必請之於君父矣。君父惡其名而不許。則多方
謀之。竊有進之乎。抑亦坐而俟其斃乎。是歟。臣
子至誠惻怛之情。固不可坐視其病患。則雖知
後逢其怒。亦豈得不竊進之哉。
人所不及知。而我獨知之。人所不及能。而我獨能
之。是亦荷天之寵也。荷天之寵如此。而惟為一
身計。不為天下計。則其負天也。豈不亦大乎。
自古懷忠被罪者。何限。吾無怨焉。但獨可及為之
時。而不為。將使病弊至於不可復救。是則可悲

已。
縱予今日死。天下後世。當有公論。予又何悔何恨。
身雖在囹圄。心無愧怍。自覺方寸虛明。不異平日。
人心之靈。與天地上下同流。夷狄患難。累他不
得。亦可驗也。惟北闈年滿八十。飲食坐臥。非予
不安。自予遠繫。音問不通。動靜不知。其憂慮苦
悶。當如何哉。一念及之。尤難為情。然亦以理排
遣。不至累心。
吾不履此境。無此省覺。經一跌。長一知。果非虛語。
振拔特立。可也。激昂忿戾。不可也。

心戒走作

心曰隶。曰操。亦是時時提撕。以理勝之之謂。

吾雖久從事格物。内而家庭。外而鄉黨親朋。異時傳調處置。頗以為當者。徐而省之。往往有大過不及不滿人意。皆是工夫未熟。人情世故未得通徹故也。可不策勵哉。

格物之於天地造化。却易。於人情世故。却難。吾人須不可狃其所易而倦其所難

行身規矩。則不可不嚴。此治己之方也。治己。即所以治人。待人規矩。則不可過嚴。此安人之道也。安人。即所以自安。

凡讀書須熟誦。不然。寔甚受用。予來此中。書卷不得攜。與端居書室。左右厨子。所欲檢查。輒隨手抽繹。全然不同。日日默念。而因以為藥石。為針砭者。不過平素所精讀暗記者。少時專務博涉。多讀羣書。幸皆若存若亡。今欲記起而卒不能。雖多亦奚以為。他日幸得放還。當以諭後生。且以自警也。

予自來此。勉勵克治。鍛鍊身心。未嘗虛度時日。古人云。僮間居真不空過日月。彼錮我者。皆成我

也。旨哉。

予雖門葉衰薄。亦生長飽暖之中。未經窮鍊寒苦之境。常恐一旦國家有急。起居飲食多所不勝。然去夏彌利堅船突到江都。戒嚴。予為藩邸經理軍務。不得睡者七晝夜。精神倍奮。今歲得罪下獄。飲麁食。嚼鹽與重囚為伍。數旬。恬然安之。精神活潑。身亦健康。此二事少自試驗。得益不細。亦可謂天之賜矣。

外邪襲人。多在睡眠之時。故中夜就寢。不得熟眠。為令速寤。常當係意在醒。若支體有所不安。或以手摩之。或隨意轉側。務令血氣無所停滯。若咽喉不滑。或運舌嚥津。或深息閉氣。少焉放之。如是行之。外邪亦侵不得。

内定心志。外運血氣。晝節飲食。夜少睡眠。脩養祕訣。果無多子。

聞關西地震。勢賀之間。更甚。城垣衛署驛亭民屋傾塌無算。樹木倒植。井水乾涸。人民壓死。殆不知其數。丁未信州地大震。予在鄉里。親閱其變。慘毒之劇。殆不忍言。信中變後。地下每作雷聲。時亦搖撼。經久不止。後七年有小田原之變。又

关西地震在六月十四日而做中传之在二十四五日闲季校致还后次第此录至十一月四日东海道地又大震蘂城郭坏蘗舍民伤无数因窃书寄于江都所亲告以此条大意谓都下恐亦不免作之耳。嘉有所戒备明年十月二日夜江都果有大震火又从之其余烈甚之前之数莫超过数倍矣而予旧所亲又多传深全虽是天意亦不无小资于予言 乙卯冬记

一年。今後有關西之變。嘗記清人雜書所載云其地常動。至數年後。有大震萬家樂土。忽變叢然。則地震固有連數年者矣。古來漢儒。以地震爲蠻夷侵陵之兆。占候之說。洋學所不取。雖然天人合應之理。不可謂必無之。丁未以來地震之變。以時事驗之。漢儒之言。似不可誣。今夷虜之志。未知其所極。則震之相連。而尚有劇甚者。亦不能無慮焉。

君子有五樂。而富貴不與焉。一門知禮義。骨肉無釁隙。一樂也。取予不苟。廉潔自養。內不愧於妻孥。外不怍於衆民。二樂也。講明聖學。心識大道。隨時安義。處險如夷。三樂也。生乎西人啟理窟之後。而知古聖賢所未嘗識之理。四樂也。東洋道德。西洋藝術。精粗不遺。表裏兼該。因以澤民物。報國恩。五樂也。

抗孔聖浮雲之志。養鄒叟浩然之氣。寵辱不驚。俛仰不怍。究天地之際。觀古今之變。玩萬物之理。贊人身之紀。雖在困極。樂亦有在焉。饑而食。渴而飲。坐而思。倦而睡。逌然自得。又不知身在囹圄之中矣。

敏一字。是爲學之法。而爲治之要。亦莫若焉。天下可學可爲之務。如此其廣。如彼其大。故學與治。皆不可以不敏。彼終身于學。而空跡無用。終身于官。而因仍無功者。坐其勤力不敏。十常八九。孔子之聖。猶且發憤忘食。敏以求之。何況吾輩。日晷一移。千載無再來之今。形神既離。萬古無再生之我。學藝事業。豈可悠悠。

射有禮射武射之別。然其初也。專爲防禦而設。防禦之事。蓋男子立身第一義也。故其生。桑弧蓬矢。以射天地四方。然後敢用穀。亦示第一義也。

自銃礮興。弓矢長兵。皆失其爲利。男子生乎今之世。不知銃礮。其可乎。於其初生。亦宜以礮換弧矢。發於上下四方。以志於其所有事也。

予久留意於海防。其所發明。自謂前人有未及者。然卒由此取禍。亦非常之原。常人興焉耳。君相如有省悟時。則吾志之行必矣。

凡學問必以積累。非一朝一夕之所能通曉。海防利害。亦是一大學問。自非講究有素者。未易遽得其要領。人雖提耳告之。而不解。蓋亦由此。不令外夷開易侮之心。是防禦之至要也。邊海防

堵。皆不得其法。所陳銃器。皆不中其式。所接官吏。皆凡夫庸人。胸無甲兵。如此而欲無開夷人悔心。寧可得乎。

有敵國外患。而詑本根未固。形勢未成。進無果決之勇。退持遷延之計者。其所欲縻敵。適足以啟敵而自縻。其所欲緩寇。適足以資寇而自緩。其所欲從容補綴。而全其捍禦之備者。亦將徒為文具。而國家之勢。愈至於不可支矣。而古來當局者。曾不深省。誤家國天下。如出一塗。可勝歎哉。

今之當將帥之位者。非公侯貴人。即膏粱氏族。平日以飲酒歌舞為娛。不知兵謀師律為何事。一旦有國家之急。誰能為軍士之所服。而遏敵人之衝突。是今之深患也。故予嘗欲倣西洋武備之大略。於天下兵籍外。結故家世族忠勇剛毅。一可當十者。以為義會。一以保國護民為志。其初入會。校試磐攷。果不憚艱苦。方始聽入焉。推有韜畧謀猷統馭之才者。為之長。遇警急之日。則鳩集成師。以待官之指揮。庶乎攘寇植勲。或居於在兵籍者之上也。

欲戰必勝。不守必固。不可。欲守必固。不陣必定。不可。魏侯問陣必定之道。吳子曰。君能使賢者居上。不肖者處下。則陣已定矣。今天下諸國。賢者未必居上。不肖者未必處下。然則陣未定也。陣未定而其守必固。戰必勝者。未之有也。有志之主。尚其知所警省哉。

教練不精。賞罰不明。又無能用之者。縱有億萬之衆。其於戰守。所謂伏鷄乳犬。如其貍與虎何哉。

同力度德。同德量義。雖稱文王之美。亦不過云大國畏其力。小國懷其德。無其力而能保其國者。

自古至今。吾未之見也。誰謂王者不尚力耶。不知彼。不知已。每戰必敗。固也。然知彼知已。在今時。未可言戰。悉善彼之所善。而不喪已之所能。然後始可以言戰。

詳證術。為學之基本也。泰西發明此術。兵畧亦大進。竟然與往時別。所謂下學而上達也。孫子兵法。度量數稱勝。亦其術也。然漢與我。有孫子以來。莫不誦習而講說。而其兵法依然如舊。不得與泰西比肩。是無他。坐於無下學之功也。今真欲脩飭武備。非先興此學科不可。

士大夫必有過人之膽量。方能奪戎狄之氣。而伸本國之威。如郭汾陽之單騎見虜。是矣。必有過人之學問才辯。而能屈戎狄之辭。而存本國之體。如富文忠之郤獻納二字是矣。今　天朝搢紳。數與夷使接者。果有汾陽之膽量乎。果有文忠之學問才辯乎。吾竊危之。

人不見其可畏。則必慢易之。一啟其慢易之心。又何以能治之也。故君子必臨之以莊。正其衣冠。尊其瞻視。出辭氣斯遠鄙倍。皆所以為莊之方也。今士大夫往往有舉措輕佻。言辭鄙猥。以自

喜者其意益謂不如是。難以通人情而服人。嗟乎通人情而服人者。自有其道在焉。今不以其道而露此醜態。吾恐其欲服人者。適足以導其慢易也。

人譽己。於己何加。若因譽而自怠。則反損。人毀己。於己何損。若因毀而自強。則反益。

有人之過。有事之過。事之過。未可以觀人。人之過可以觀人。

今之所謂儒者。果何為者耶。本朝　神聖造國之道。堯舜三代帝王之治。兼明而默識之乎。禮樂

刑政。典章制度。以至兵法師律械器之利。講論而皆得其要乎。土境之形勢。海陸道路之險夷。外蕃之情狀。防戍之利害。城堡堵堞控援之略。推算重力幾何詳證之術。並究而悉之乎。吾未之知也。然則今之所謂儒者。果何為者耶。

讀書講學。徒為空言。不及當世之務。與清談廢事。一間耳。

有之無所補。無之無所損。乃無用之學也。有用之學。譬如夏時之葛。冬時之裘。既無為之者。則生民之用闕矣。

帝王之政。藏財於民。有餘而取。不足而與。故不聚斂百姓。而上獨富足。亦不能逸百姓。而國獨貧寠。故曰百姓足。君孰與不足。百姓不足。君孰與足。此天下古今不易之道也。

本邦金貨米粟。號為富饒。然疆域不大。故以邦內所生之財。享邦內所為之用。無甚有餘。乃若海防之事。則起乎外者也。置防堵數百所。造大艦數百艘。鑄巨礮數千門。其費亦浩矣。而皆非永存之物。每一二十年。必待脩繕改造。況外之有應接給資之用。內之有餉糧賜賞之費。凡如此

相房間。其情固為難測。因有纂輯皇國同文鑑若干卷。以通歐羅諸國語之志。而荷蘭久為互市之國。邦人亦多知讀其國書。故欲先刊荷蘭部。先是官有命。凡刊行書籍。必經官看詳。迺嘉永己酉冬。來江都。呈稿本以請。遷延彌年。卒不得允。其在江都日。始獲魏氏之書而讀之。亦欲內地設學。專譯夷書夷史。瞭悉敵情。以補於駕馭。是又其見之與予相符者。第不識彼國今日能用其言否耳。

海防之要。在礮與艦。而礮最居首。魏氏海國圖識中。輯銳礮之說。類皆粗漏無稽。如兒童戲嬉之為。凡事不自為之。而能得其要領者無之。以魏之才識。而是之不察。當今之世。身無礮學。貽此謬妄。反誤後生。吾為魏深惜之。

去夏墨虜。以兵艦四隻。護送其國書。抵浦賀澳。其舉動詞氣。殊極悖慢。辱國體不細。聞者莫不切齒。時某人鎮浦賀。屏氣負屈。遂無能為。虜退後。自抽小刀。寸斷其所遺虜主畫像以洩怒。昔宋曹瑋謫官陝西。聞趙元昊為人。乃使善畫者圖其貌。觀之知其英物必為邊患。欲預講邊備。蒐

之類。將安取其給哉。夫労濟困窮之家。多得賓客。屢設宴饗。則其資財空乏。卒至於不可復繼也必矣。今之時事。何以異乎是。然則其所以經理之者何術。有志於經世者。所宜先審計。

予礮卦之著。不但有益於武學生徒。兼有裨於國家武備。往日官阻其鐫版。吾不知其何意。

先公登相臺。嗣管防海事。時英夷寇清國。聲勢相逮。予感慨時事。上書陳策。實天保壬寅十一月也。後觀清魏源聖武記。亦感慨時事之所著。而其書之序。又作於是歲之七月。則先予上書厪四月矣。而其所論。往往有不約而同者。嗚乎。予與魏。各生異域。不相識姓名。感時著言。同在是歲。而其所見。亦有闇合者。一何奇也。真可謂海外同志矣。但魏云。自上世以來。中國有海防。而無海戰。遂以堅壁清野。杜絕岸奸。為防海家法。予則欲盛講礮艦之術。而為邀擊之計。驅逐防截。以制賊死命於外海。是為異耳。

馭夷俗者。莫如先知夷情。知夷情者。莫如先通夷語。故通夷語者。不惟為知彼之楷梯。亦是馭彼之先務也。予竊深念。頃年諸蕃記事。屢寄舶於

聞人才。後果如其言。然則觀其肖影。亦可以見其能否。而資吾豫備矣。其人知慮不及此。毀而滅之。可惜巳。嗚乎。均夷人也。均畫像也。或無而求之。或有而毀之。其知之深淺。謀之長短。一何遠哉。

今春墨虜之來。　官設便坐於横濱。以為應接之所。命松城小倉二藩。發兵以護衛之。且令聽約束於接待官吏。初吾　公之受命也。以為真備虜之不避也。乃發野戰礮二門。牛角大礮三門。銃卒百名。刀槍士五十名。以國老望月貫恕督之。予參其軍議。謂接待官吏知兵。令吾與小倉一横一直以陣。銃手可以逞威。若其不知兵。使相對而陣。則銃不可用。惟短兵利之。與虜相接咫尺。變起倉卒。彼雖精銃技。我以利兵乘之。一薙可斫斷數頭。乃別備長卷二十把以從吾兵至金川。官吏使人謂曰。大礮必寘前驛。莫引入横濱地。望月對曰。吾藩奉命護衛應接之場。大礮所以備變。寘之隔地。變發非時。難以應卒。敢辭。官吏曰。今茲應接。萬萬可保其無變。不幸將有變。即時發官丁。搬運礮器。決不〻。貴藩有缺

之。今以大礮入横濱。夷人或憚其守衛之嚴。請移於他地。官之累也。望月不得巳從之。退曰。官命使聽約束者。幾是乎。及相護衛之地。官吏曰。東起于海濱。西行二百步。折而北行又如之。是其所也。予聞之驚駭。詳其地。南距應接便坐。不下二百步。有民屋樹林在其間。初在江戶。竊意官吏雖不諳兵。自有國體。且得二藩兵。當密圍繞便坐。以嚴警禦。不圖其區處之陋至斯也。因建議曰。大礮則官吏停之。今所有者。小銃而巳。小銃逞力。非百步內不可。且銃卒不踰百名。執短兵者不過五十名。距夷虜集會之所。遠陣於二百步之外。又散守三四百步之間田。不惟無益於警禦。適足以導虜之侮慢。去歲浦賀應接。護衛無法。夷虜嗤之。邦人恥之。而不少省悟。今又為此兒戲。官吏不肖。固不足道。本藩武功盛名。為此輩壞隳。豈可忍邪。乃與望月謀。使人謂之曰。如公等所區處。是非以我兵備於夷虜。為夷虜禁呵邦民耳。禁呵邦民者。固不可煩士大夫。亦無用於兵器。每逕路出健兒一二名。執青竹杖。誰何之。足矣。但江戶所受之命。則不可

二月廿日夜。聞下田議畧定。翌朝早起。詣望月曰。下田本邦要地。其形勢可比全世界之喜望峰。夷虜僦之屯駐以為巢穴。其害不可言。且 大城在江戶。而人口衆多。米穀布帛皆資海運。不幸有警。海路格塞。江戶首受其禍。伊豆之為州天城之險。隔絕其中。而下田在其南端。一旦變起。陸路出兵。厰隊為嶮所沮。不可以行。海路則我無堅艦。他日縱得造作。虜有海陸之形勝。而我反喪之。主客易位。攻守殊勢。非計也。夫善制事者。常令其利在我。其害在彼。今不得已。而假

以廢應接之日。吾藩當別出士卒。整陣於山間。以備於非時之變耳。此不敗公等之事。又不墜吾職。豈不亦兩得乎。官吏復曰。言皆當理。然官發兩藩人士之事。吾輩既告之夷人。若不出其人。設陣於隱僻之地。夷人必疑吾有異志。應接不諧。是亦 官之累也。必曲從吾言。如其布陣收散離合。唯意所命。吾輩不敢掣肘。予與望月。雖憤惋不樂。亦無可奈何。當日作一哨。置之田畝間。以塞其責。嗚呼。耗損國用。勤勞士卒。盡思慮計畫。而同為兒戲。可付浩歎也已。

敵人地宜為他日計。擇海陸得進兵之處。竊覺橫濱之地勢。甚稱之。且使虜船常在此。去江戶甚邇。則人人嘗膽坐薪之念。自不能已。警衛守禦之方。亦自不得不嚴。又親觀彼之所長。可以速進我之智巧。是其所以為多利。如退下田。則人心必弛。守衛必懈矣。而虜船迅速。難以繫禦。在橫濱。與在下田。其為江戶腹心之患。則間不能以髮。故吾謂不如以橫濱假之之為愈也。是天下之大計也。君總士卒在茲。不可以默。上書乞 公有獻策。可也。望月曰。然然。吾上書不如

子之上言。乃命予還江戶。告之於 公。有沮者。不果。 公許予自為之。於是竊有所建白。又使門人長岡小林虎上書其主侯。開陳大計。又使之見阿部閣老所親幸。為論其利害。欲得因時規諫。有所挽回。並皆不行。小林生以此獲主侯之譴。遂辭歸國。

曩予偕一二友生。為鎌倉之遊。遂泛海。過荒岬。抵城島。泊三崎。歷松輪。宿宮田。次浦賀。上猿嶼。觀於金澤。出本牧而還都。其往來所由。觀設防堵備海寇。無慮十餘所。而錯置皆不得法。無一可

當防截之選者。至此不覺仰天浩歎。撫胸流涕者。久之。夫江都。天下之咽喉也。富津洲觜。雖稱曰天險。海口猶濶。非有戰艦水軍。固難以遏敵人侵攘窺伺。今是之不務。設為癡堵呆堞。高揭之於海表。此示我無謀於海外也。頃年東西諸蕃寄舶遊偵。豈不開輕我之心哉。吏員庸流。固不足譏。其金鞍華韉。綾衣肉食。自謂高出等類者。不知天下之大計。糜國財用。以為此無益之務。抑何歟。有如虜舶馳突。將何以折衝禦侮。因欲上疏論海防利病。冀以裨時政之萬一。具草請之　先公。先公不許。遂止。是嘉永庚戌之首夏也。後四年。果墨夷之事起。登時　先公忌予上書者。益懼觸忤抵罪也。其蓋覆之仁。亦大矣。今日使　先公在世。知予拘囚。則其為憂勞。又當何如。

川路司農自大坂市尹轉任。與聞防海事。予舊有學交。因出擬上書舊稿示之。極言近都防堵修築無法不適實用。司農亦未甚信之。及墨夷事興。無一不如予嘗所論。於是始深納予言。一日謂予曰。予欲有所言。吾能達之於閣老。予曰。僕

所欲言者。為君傾倒幾盡。君能言之。君能行之。天下之福也。僕但求天下之福耳。上書釣名。非其本心也。及論選人材。購船於海外之策。司農有沮色。予曰。是當今先務之急。而君猶牽掣故常。不能發言。他尚何望。僕當上書以道之。乃條疏急務十事。因司農上之阿部閣老。不報。至吉田生獄起。亦不少蒙明察。故常之不易變。時勢之不可明。如此。不知天下之大計。將何日而能立也。

江戶海口。不可無礮臺。予亦嘗數數言之。夫海口之防戰。利在礮臺。其形勢所缺。不可不寘。此以補焉。然其得力之處。全在別備礮艦。相機策應。故能得其要。海中唯置一二區而足。不必多築之。荷蘭諳厄児之策。可據也。如今所為。陸續相連。是陸軍為壘以自屛之法。非海口以待洋寇之術也。蓋陸戰攻中寓守。守中寓攻。方其守也。以壘自屛。方其攻也。出壘以衝。其守與攻。並係壘中之人。故其人衆固不能不多。其壘雖多。其壘亦不相障礙。如海口之戰則不然。礮臺之兵。不操礮艦。礮艦之兵。不在礮臺。故礮臺不貴多。

而礮艘不厭多也。蓋礮臺多則兵分。兵分則用士衆。而左者不能拯右。右者不能救左。不幸賊船出于中間。左右之臺相為障礙。不能用礮。惡在其為利也。且礮艘匱乏。進剿無術。如賊連船於相旁間。以絶我海運。何以却之。當是時。縱令内港有百礮臺。亦屬無用。雖欲無不戰而屈。不可得也。若乃多備礮艘。訓練以時。開戰策應。無所不可。足以讋服洋賊。而制其死命。又何苦而海中以此許多之礮臺為哉。多事之際。其經費亦甚可惜矣。某地縣令某氏。小有才。斬素無學問。見西洋陸戰壘圖。而不知其解。杜撰牽合。以成守海口策。當道亦不深究之。以為是而施行。予深識其非。屢言之川路司農。司農稍信然予言。然而遂弗能救。是亦可慨也。

千羊之皮。不如一狐之腋。而千金之裘。又非一狐之皮。今欲為千金之裘。徼之屠羊之家。而可乎。苟得其心。五州之人。皆可得而使也。學而利之。導而舍之。敵間之來間我者。亦為我用矣。何況我民。

予年二十以後。乃知匹夫有繫一國。三十以後。乃

知有繫天下。四十以後。乃知有繫五世界。

以上十七條

附録上

省諐賦

墨人既得志。以下田箱館二澳。為貿易之所。歲四月。予得罪下獄。始予潛心防海。十數年。思出位言踰分。當止而不止。宜乎其卒至于此。雖然憂國之心。遭艱益深。省諐之餘。思念前古當今將來之事。乃為賦曰。

余蹈世之險阸兮。欻跋盭以離尤。意忼慨而激昂兮。心維結而增愁。何衆人之嘻嘻兮。獨出類而嗟若。世恬然而康娛兮。亦疾首而蹙頞。非病狂而喪

心兮悁煩毒之相憑。微至仁與大知兮。孰云察吾之中情。始余學而閱志兮。知同力之以度德。弗經技而曲撓兮。何謀猷之能淑。値蠻狄之切憂兮。將隱潛以效忠。得吾黨之狂士兮。欣蘭臭之無壅。臨岐路而申命兮。謂回旋必有酬。壯者固果于事為兮。犯時制之不休。忽拘繫而幽阻兮。對鄙訊之紛挐。竭忠悃而遻罰兮。亶天命之謂何。雖辮連而在縶兮。瑩余心其如冰。所循私而違道兮。指天日以為正。依 往聖以節中兮。招百神而目聽。署山川使在列兮。戒周孔以為證。昔 聖皇之樂靈兮。睍

西隣而不盡。暨吳女之綺巧兮。豈維鴆夫典籍。後后承而祗敬兮。庶丕變而熙怡。非王道之無偏兮。胡瞻文明之而今。彼洋儒之深潛兮。啟造物之鐍閟。何黨人之暋昧兮。紛交疾而妬忌。鄙堂阼之明聰兮。不服長而求師。禍機迫而靡寤兮。猶護疾而諱醫。輴世守之至重兮。滯損益之反時。儇吾氓之間敵兮。頤導賊而給資。思國其莫我忠兮。卒忘身之匪任。慷憤歎而壹志兮。嘖煩言而不猒。多操術而無私兮。羗衆工之所雠也。憂國蹇而計身咎兮。又羣咍之所繇也。惟天靈之發曚兮。俟百聖而

不惑。苟 宗社之有裨兮。雖顛隕其焉恻。重曰。西伯幽囚。宣尼拘止。管相負良。擯海隅止。窮達之運。聖愚同止。定心廣志。何所恫止。民生秉彝。欽醇德止。千齡萬世。罔窮極止。往者不可援。願勿追止。徠者可繼。吾將有期止。

讀孟子

醫之治病也。其過于實者。泄之。瀉之。其虛者而補之。要在濟夭死以保其康寧耳矣。聖賢救世之言。亦猶是也。當孟子之時。天下以攻伐為務。民苦於塗炭。故曰我善為陣。我善為戰。大罪也。又曰。善戰

者服上刑。又曰。我能為君約與國。戰必克。今之所謂良臣。古之所謂民賊也。皆救世之言也。今也海外諸蕃。其智巧技能。與往時殊。若耆老之與童孺不同科也。其兵威之所加。駸駸乎隔海之國。而莫之能遏也。而吾邦儒者。誤讀孟子。不審天下之形勢。不察萬國之情狀。兵力萎薾。而不知奮也。械器濫惡。而不知精也。外蕃改銃礮。變兵法。而我不肯講矣。造火輪。革城制。而我不肯效矣。曰。何以礮艦技巧為哉。亦有仁義而已矣。是猶治病虛者。而不知所以補之。幾何其不殺人也。去歲以來。彌利堅

之事與。彼加我屢以無禮。而我不能動手。至于忍國大耻。假地以紓禍。夫誰使之然耶。吾恐世之儒者。終亦不能逃其罪也。

又

孟子曰。得道者多助。失道者寡助。寡助之至。親戚畔之。多助之至。天下順之。以天下之所順。攻親戚之所畔。故有不戰。戰必勝矣。是固也。雖然。我果得道而多助與。彼果失道而寡助與。我果為天下之所順與。彼果為親戚之所畔與。是未可知也。則其戰必勝。豈可期乎。信能行王政。則鄰國之民。仰之若父母矣。率其子弟。攻其父母。自生民以來。未有能濟者也。是固也。雖然。鄰國之民。仰我果若父母與。視其君果若仇讎與。是未可知也。則其無能濟。豈可保乎。施仁政於民。省刑罰。薄稅斂。深耕易耨。壯者以暇日脩其孝悌忠信。入以事其父兄。出以事其長上。可使制梃以撻秦楚之堅甲利兵矣。是固也。雖然。我之民果樂於效死與。彼之民果樂歸於我與。是未可知也。則其制梃以傳勝。豈可許乎。故凡有敵國外患者。不知彼。不知已。不知時勢。惡可乎。乃孟子。則不但以其道。且知其時勢而言之

二十三

也。然當時諸侯。猶以為迂濶。而孟子實未嘗迂濶也。今我新得一大敵國。禍且不測。而讀孟子者。拘執文辭。不察時勢。訑訑却以夷懍夷之計。欲制梃以撻彼之大艦巨礮。是則迂濶之甚者也。甲寅之春。華聖東又發八大兵艦。來近江都。下錨内港。甚無狀。門人長門吉田某。奇士也。奮然欲私索虜之情實以立事功。不遂。官捕之。余亦逮錄下獄。自訟之餘。時誦孟子。不能無感焉。因遂著諸言。

跋孟子舜發畎畝章

鐵之將為劍也。入鑪承鞴。坐碪受鎚。塗灰汙泥。淬于寒水。歛于趣砥。其為鐵亦苦矣。玉之未成器也。錐破其璞。鑿治其瑕。雕之琢之。磨之礱之。其為玉亦艱矣。然使鐵與玉。樂安佚。憚煩燠。不甘受其艱苦。則安得成就其器。而為君子之佩哉。惟人亦然。久挾其術。志則不行。素有所能。言則不聽。運籌進策。莫然其謀。竭誠致悃。莫察其忠。有羣小之慍。有逐斥之讒。有纍囚之辱。窮困拂鬱。激動勞苦。而後增成其材。予自得罪下獄。日誦孟子此章。以自力焉。曰天其有意於用我與。不然。此物奚宜至哉。斯道遼遠。繇邈未能必信。雖然。天意固未可知也。則

二十四

吾之處困戹。豈可不奮發而激勵乎、甲寅閏七月二十八日。

夢有得魯公爭坐帖者、與予共之。適甚、因為跋其尾。覺而記之。

此帖有無限姿態、無限精神。譬如太牢滋味。愈嚼而愈無窮。假令出他人之蹟、愛玩摹臨。足為樂事、況於魯公精忠貫天地。大節與日月爭光者乎。使吾人居圍牆之中。而恣纍囚之艱者、非此帖也歟。

兵要

漢土兵家之書。莫高於孫子、而其為書空言無事實者邈乎矣、未可以治兵也。何以言之。曰、善戰者。先為不可勝、以待敵之可勝、其不可勝。何以致之。善守者藏於九地之下。善攻者。動於九天之上。其藏於地下、動於天上。何以得之、善戰者。先立於不敗之地、而不失敵之敗。其立於不敗之地。何以能之。如此之類、吾未覩其有事實也。而世徒賦其文。不求其實、萬口一致。稱為兵法而不疑。吾甚怪之。趙括讀父書傳、縱談兵事。以天下莫能當。而卒喪趙軍、其亦有以也耶。至閱漢書藝文志。吳孫子兵法有圖九卷。乃知其事實。蓋有在焉。而今亾矣。可勝。惜哉。然兵之性、革也。明理察事。因時而革。亦猶天道之於曆也。故曆而不革。不足為曆。兵而不革。不足為兵。至歐邏巴諸國。發揮火礮以為元戎。務於攻伐吞幷。兵制大革。設令孫子圖傳于世。亦惟存古法耳。何補於今之事實哉。故當今之時。求得兵之事實。莫若學洋兵。洋兵之法、其科有五。一曰將畧。二曰陣法。三曰器學。四曰守國。五曰軍用。將畧者、其言類如孫吳司馬所道。陣法者。有步騎礮之別。有步騎礮之合。而戰術存焉。器學者、以操教為主。而械器之制。與其得失之辨、莫不備焉。守國者。築城壘。鑿溝池。善保其民之術也。軍用者、糧食硝彈兵甲戰具之屬。是也。凡此五者、莫不有事實。而操教尤為當務之急。令勇者不能獨進。怯者不能獨退。非操教不能也。其形如決積水、其勢如轉圓石。非操教不能也。擊其首而尾至。擊其尾而首至。擊其中而首尾俱至。非操教不能也。故曰有制之兵、無能之將、不可以敗。無制之兵。有能之將。不可以勝。故良將之於操教也。盡心焉耳矣。蓋不以操教。而易言之以能濟其事者。自古及今。未之有也。趙括之敗。可以鑒矣。

孫子說二則

孫子火攻。以火佐攻。今則以火攻守。是古今之變也。古者以油薪之火佐攻。故行火有因。有時日。內外之應。晝夜之風。皆在所詳。今用大小神器之火。以為攻守。故不由因。不擇時日。不論內外。不問風之有無。皆可用之。而震擊之威。焚燒之慘。非古者油薪之可比也。我攻守用火。敵攻守用火。火火之變不可勝窮。非天下之至明。其孰能參於此。惟理勢可坐譚也。選練不可空論也。此尤主將之所宜慮修。讀孫子者其亦知之哉。

間之於軍。猶瞽之相聾之史乎。瞽而無相。則前有水火而不知。聾而無史。則後有車馬而不省。軍而無間。則敵之所以謀吾啗吾者。吾皆茫然。甚則敵國之形勢。敵主之仁暴。敵將之能否。敵衆之強弱。敵兵之利鈍。並不得其實。所謂廟算者。無所由立。尚何和戰守禦之可言哉。故經考索情。雖曰兵之先著。非初有間諜而得其實。則亦無以施其計也。孫子之書首列始計。而以用間終焉。蓋貞下起元之意也。故軍國之務。莫先於間。事莫重於間。情莫親於間。故曰。微乎微乎。無所不用間也。而世有大

敵在前。而不知用間。爲有勝間之任。而視之如艸芥者。可痛哭也已。

右賦雜文共八首

詩

獄中寫懷二首

久憂邊事歎天遠。忽墜此中悲海深。欲為 皇朝存至計。敢因吾利勞知音。鷄鳴不已晦冥夜。鶴韻應通蓊鬱陰。寄語吾門同志士。莫將榮辱負初心。

不思城下作盟恥。却見忠貞抱忌疑。伯映議疆長崎澳。聖東假地下田湄。異時輕敵已非策。今日伐謀知是誰。幽憤瀰胸無所泄。獄中瀝血寫茲詩。

君恩

君恩如天地。國恩如江海。外患今非一。奮身思有

濟。勉勵十餘年。何問明與晦。在卑欲為池。在高欲為壘。奈何肉食人。頽然若傀儡。苟安愒歲月。般樂敖且怠。當初恃不來。不知恃有待。復不伐其謀。卒然為所詒。假地缺金甌。屈膝甘無禮。反却知彼計束縛直自累。咨余何為者。致忠忽遭逮。幽囚在犴獄。甘心待其罪。松柏有本性。歲寒節不改。忠義許君國。百折何須悔。用間在得人。全勝在知彼。是非不可磨。公論期千載。

敝笱五章 有叟

敝笱在海。魚則唯唯。狄人戲謔。笑言有啞。

比也。笱以竹為器以取魚者也。唯唯出入不制也。啞笑貌。笱當在河。而今在海。況其敝壞者。安得能取魚哉。宜乎其魚之唯唯然。而出入無忌憚也。以比禦侮失策。而致狄人之陵蔑也。

曾欲御冬。亟歸旨蓄。莫碩我勞。反比予于毒。

比也。御當。歸貽。旨美。蓄聚也。曾蓄聚美菜。以為餽貽不一再者。蓋欲使以禦冬月之空乏也。以比安不忘危。治不忘亂。方泰寧之時而深思遠慮。以數數然及邊防戎備之事也。

其霧其霧。曀曀有霾。求言念國。不瑕有害。

比也。其者冀其將然之辭。陰而風曰曀。雨土曰霾。瑕何也。冀其開霽。而卒不開霽。且陰陰冷風雨土蒙霧。以比衰替之世。欲有奮發改革。而狃習因循流弊愈深。近患又生也。

幽室陰陰。不日不月。言思君子。如饑如渴。

嗟爾君子。靡知臧否。懷私之故。有似充耳。

並賦也。靡不也。充耳塞耳也。謂耳聾之人。

泄泄八章

我艦未牢。我辭未矗。將者泄泄。蠻方孔棘。

艦之未牢。猶可治之。辭之未矗。猶可為之。將者泄泄。云如之何。

積薪如陵。火發于下。載笑載言。晏然以處。

匪風飄揚。匪瀾澎湃。念彼　神京。竊歎有慨。

憂思如燬。其誰知之。悲憤如噎。其誰思之。

人不我諒。請勿復敢思。人不我信。請勿復敢悲。

雖欲無思與　君為體。雖欲無悲與國為系。

夏夜之短。耿耿如年。摽擗不寐。泣涕漣漣。

敝卦

予嘗演敝卦。敝卦即睽卦也。爾來竊省予所遭遇。無一非睽者。亦云奇矣。圖事揆策。

而莫用其謀。睽也。竭忠盡力。而反招罪戾
睽也。言辭確寔。而不免疑猜。睽也。貲財橫
散。而家道困迫。睽也。雖然物窮則變。變則
通。居以正道。固無終睽之理。且天地睽而
其事同也。男女睽而其志通也。萬物睽而
其事類也。處睽之世。合睽之用。亦在自強
之耳。

少小窮易理。中年研斅火。融會著斅卦。推演訓蒙
者。斅卦本是睽。乖戾諧情寡。通來我所為。拂亂躑
而跛。憂國竭忠精。反自求飛禍。一與卦象應。或天

其誠我。志因勞苦堅。行以勇決果。前脩皆如茲。猛
省砭頑惰。

故園

夠繫十旬心不平。秋風忽動故園情。濃陰但見狐
烏影。攏隙空望日月明。繞壑林泉何改色。傍門松
菊不忘榮。水清石秀曾遊地。野鶴溪猿有舊盟。

秋思

幽室日如年。廻風揚塵埃。時節值秋晏。愁來不可
排。名都何鬱鬱。飛閣臨通街。日夕絃歌起。音響隨
風來。曲調苦且怨。沉吟激餘哀。理曲知爲誰。無迺

蕩子妻。身貞反見棄。歡愛何時諧。盛年不再至。華
容日益衰。意合忘情異。感同難自持。掩耳請勿聽。
重聽不勝悲。

秋風

秋風浙浙霜眇眇。木葉辭條蘭蕙槁。日景不至廣
室冥。虛櫳危檐飛塵杳。潛無鱗兮舉無翰。兀兀中
處將安還。

黠虜

黠虜先聲已得志。旌帆來去更縱橫。久歎天下無
豪傑。誰道胸中有甲兵。終古禁人偵彼實。連年許

敵探吾情。謀猷顛倒今如此。不識何時見掃平。

漫述

兩風月如晦。猘犬吠成羣。是亦尋常事。利害何足
云。
謗者任汝謗。嗤者任汝嗤。天公本知我。不覓他人
知。

右古今詩共十二首

The Commodore, upon being made aware of this treatment of his officers, felt greatly indignant, as it was in violation of the stipulations of the treaty, and he determined to bring the authorities of Simoda, whom he held responsible, to account. He accordingly dispatched his flag lieutenant and his two interpreters on shore, to call upon the prefect and lay before him certain complaints, which were specified in a memorandum in which the Commodore expressed his dissatisfaction at the manner in which his officers were treated on going ashore, and protested against their being followed by soldiers, the dispersion of the people, and the closing of the shops. These, he declared, were at variance with the stipulations of the treaty; and threatened, if the annoyances should continue, that he would sail to Yedo with his whole squadron and demand an explanation. The Commodore also took occasion to insist upon a suitable place being set apart on shore for a resort for himself and officers; and as he proposed a visit to the island of Oho-sima, requested that proper provisions should be made for the journey, a junk be provided, and certain Japanese officials selected to accompany the American expedition.

The prefect, upon hearing this protest of the Commodore, replied, that the Dutch at Nagasak were always followed by twelve or fourteen Japanese soldiers, and seemed to think that such a precedent should be a rule of conduct for the Americans. He was, however, told, that the treatment of the Dutch was not to be taken for a moment as a criterion by which the Japanese authorities were to judge of what was proper in their relations with the Americans, who had a "treaty of amity and intercourse" with Japan; and coming, as they did, to Simoda as friends, they would insist upon being treated as such, and suffer no infringement of privileges which had been guarantied by a solemn compact. The prefect, moreover, was told that the Americans intended no harm to the people, but, on the contrary, desired the most friendly relations with them, and the freest intercourse, without being watched and restrained by soldiers, acting under the orders of their superiors. Such a surveillance as had hitherto been practised was what Americans were not accustomed to, and particularly as it would seem to indicate that they were intent upon the commission of some outrage.

This resolute language produced its desired effect upon the prefect, who excused his conduct upon the plea that he had left Yoku-hama before the signing of the treaty, and had, in consequence, not been aware that it contained the clause "free intercourse." He would be obliged, he continued, to refer to his superiors at Yedo for instructions on this point, and ascertain how they construed that article; but, in the meanwhile, he would give orders that the houses should not be closed, and try the experiment of allowing the officers to visit the shore without being followed by soldiers.

The prefect then readily acceded to the Commodore's demands in regard to a place of resort and the visit to Oho-sima, saying that any of the temples were at his disposition, where the best accommodation Simoda afforded would be prepared for him, and that a junk, two boats, and certain Japanese attendants would be immediately provided for those persons of the squadron the Commodore wished to send to Oho-sima. After an expression from the prefect of courtesy, and the hope that trifles would not be permitted to interrupt the friendly feeling subsisting between the Americans and the Japanese, the interview closed.

The various officers of the squadron now visited the shore daily, and for a time there was apparently less disposition to interfere with their movements, or watch their proceedings. On one of these occasions a party had passed out into the country beyond the suburbs, when they found two Japanese following them; but, as they were supposed to be a couple of spies on the

提督は旗艦付副官と2人の通訳を陸上に派遣して、監督官を訪問させ、苦情を明記した覚書を提出させた。提督はそのなかで、部下の士官が上陸した際の処遇のされ方について不満の意を表明し、兵士につきまとわれること、住民を追い散らし、店を閉めることに抗議した。これは条約の規定にもとるものであると断言し、いやがらせが続くのであれば、全艦隊を率いて江戸に向かい、釈明を求めるつもりだと脅した。また、提督はこの機会をとらえ、自分と部下の士官が休息する適当な場所を陸上に確保するよう強く主張し、さらに、大島を訪れる予定なので、この旅行に要するしかるべき食料および船1隻を提供すること、アメリカ遠征隊に同行する日本役人若干名を選ぶことを要求した。

監督官は、提督の抗議を聞くと、長崎のオランダ人には常に12人から14人の日本兵がつき従っていると答え、このような慣例はアメリカ人にも適用すべき規則だと考えているようだった。そこで、われわれは次のように言った。すなわち、オランダ人に対する処遇を、日本当局はすでに「和親条約」を結んだアメリカ人との関係においても適切な基準であると判断しているが、われわれはそのような基準を絶対に受け入れない。知ってのとおり、われわれは下田に友人として訪れているのであるから、友人として待遇されることを主張し、厳粛な協約によって保証されている特権に対する侵害を甘受するつもりはない。アメリカ人には住民に危害を加える意図はなく、むしろ住民ときわめて親しい関係を結び、上司の命によって行動する兵士から監視や束縛を受けることなく、まったく自由に交際することを望んでいるのだ。これまで行なわれてきたような監視は、アメリカ人の習慣にはないものであり、ことに、なんらかの違反行為を意図しているかのように監視されることは、かつてないことである、と。

この断固とした言葉は、望み通りの効果をあげ、監督官は、自分が横浜を発ったのは条約調印の前であり、したがって条約中に「自由な交際」という条項が含まれていることを知らなかったと言って、自分の行為を弁解した。さらに監督官は、この件について指令を受けるため江戸にいる上司に問い合わせ、上司たちがこの条項をどのように解釈しているのか確かめなければならないと思うが、とりあえず家屋を閉めないよう命令し、こころみに兵士の随伴なしに士官たちの陸上訪問を許可してみようと言った。

そして監督官は、休息所と大島訪問に関する提督の要求に快く応じ、どの寺院を使ってもよいし、そこでは下田でなしうる最善の便宜を提供しよう、また提督が大島に派遣しようとしている乗組員のために、ただちに船1艘、小舟2艘および若干の日本人従者を用意すると言った。監督官からの慇懃な挨拶と、つまらないことで日本人とアメリカ人の友情が傷ついてはいけないとの希望の表明があったのち、この会見は終了した。

こうして、艦隊のさまざまな士官たちが毎日上陸し、しばらくの間は行動を束縛されることも、一連の動きを監視されることもなくなったように見えた。ある日、このような上陸のさなか、一行が郊外を抜けて田舎を歩いていたところ、2人の日本人があとをつけてくるのに気づいた。はじめは2人組の密偵が監視しているのだろうと思い、ほとんど注意を払わなかった。ところが、この2人はひそかに近寄ってくるようだし、こちらと話す機会をうかがっているように見えるので、アメリカ士官たちは彼らがやってくるのを待った。近寄ってきた2人を見て、この日本人が地位と身分のある人物であることが分かった。いずれも高い身分を示す2本の刀を

watch, little notice was at first taken of them. Observing, however, that they seemed to be approaching as if stealthily, and as though desirous of seeking an opportunity of speaking, the American officers awaited their coming up. On being accosted, the Japanese were observed to be men of some position and rank, as each wore the two swords characteristic of distinction, and were dressed in the wide but short trowsers of rich silk brocade. Their manner showed the usual courtly refinement of the better classes, but they exhibited the embarrassment of men who evidently were not perfectly at their ease, and were about doing something of dubious propriety. They cast their eyes stealthily about as if to assure themselves that none of their countrymen were at hand to observe their proceedings, and then approaching one of the officers and pretending to admire his watch-chain, slipped within the breast of his coat a folded paper.* They now significantly, with the finger upon the lips, entreated secresy, and rapidly made off.

During the succeeding night, about two o'clock, a. m., (April 25th,) the officer of the mid-watch, on board the steamer Mississippi, was aroused by a voice from a boat alongside, and upon proceeding to the gangway, found a couple of Japanese, who had mounted the ladder at the ship's side, and upon being accosted, made signs expressive of a desire to be admitted on board.

They seemed very eager to be allowed to remain, and showed a very evident determination

---

* This paper proved to be a letter in Japanese, of which the following is a literal translation by Mr. Williams, the interpreter of the squadron:

" Two scholars from Yedo, in Japan, present this letter for the inspection of 'the high officers and those who manage affairs.' Our attainments are few and trifling, as we ourselves are small and unimportant, so that we are abashed in coming before you; we are neither skilled in the use of arms, nor are we able to discourse upon the rules of strategy and military discipline; in trifling pursuits and idle pastimes our years and months have slipped away. We have, however, read in books, and learned a little by hearsay, what are the customs and education in Europe and America, and we have been for many years desirous of going over the 'five great continents,' but the laws of our country in all maritime points are very strict; for foreigners to come into the country, and for natives to go abroad, are both immutably forbidden. Our wish to visit other regions has consequently only 'gone to and fro in our own breasts in continual agitation,' like one's breathing being impeded or his walking cramped. Happily, the arrival of so many of your ships in these waters, and stay for so many days, which has given us opportunity to make a pleasing acquaintance and careful examination, so that we are fully assured of the kindness and liberality of your excellencies, and your regard for others, has also revived the thoughts of many years, and they are urgent for an exit.

" This, then, is the time to carry the plan into execution, and we now secretly send you this private request, that you will take us on board your ships as they go out to sea; we can thus visit around in the five great continents, even if we do in this, slight the prohibitions of our own country. Lest those who have the management of affairs may feel some chagrin at this, in order to effect our desire, we are willing to serve in any way we can on board of the ships, and obey the orders given us. For doubtless it is, that when a lame man sees others walking he wishes to walk too; but how shall the pedestrian gratify his desires when he sees another one riding? We have all our lives been going hither to you, unable to get more than thirty degrees east and west, or twenty-five degrees north and south; but now when we see how you sail on the tempests and cleave the huge billows, going lightning speed thousands and myriads of miles, skirting along the five great continents, can it not be likened to the lame finding a plan for walking, and the pedestrian seeing a mode by which he can ride? If you who manage affairs will give our request your consideration, we will retain the sense of the favor; but the prohibitions of our country are still existent, and if this matter should become known we should uselessly see ourselves pursued and brought back for immediate execution without fail, and such a result would greatly grieve the deep humanity and kindness you all bear towards others. If you are willing to accede to this request, keep 'wrapped in silence our error in making it' until you are about to leave, in order to avoid all risk of such serious danger to life; for when, by-and-bye, we come back, our countrymen will never think it worth while to investigate bygone doings. Although our words have only loosely let our thoughts leak out, yet truly they are sincere; and if your excellencies are pleased to regard them kindly, do not doubt them nor oppose our wishes. We together pay our respects in handing this in. April 11."

A small note was enclosed, of which the following is a translation: "The enclosed letter contains the earnest request we have had for many days, and which we tried in many ways to get off to you at Yoku-hama, in a fishing boat, by night; but the cruisers were too thick, and none others were allowed to come alongside, so that we were in great uncertainty how to act. Hearing that the ships were coming to Simoda we have come to take our chance, intending to get a small boat and go off to the ships, but have not succeeded. Trusting your worships will agree, we will, to-morrow night, after all is quiet, be at Kakizaki in a small boat, near the shore, where there are no houses. There we greatly hope you to meet us and take us away, and thus bring our hopes to fruition. April 25."

420

帯び、幅広で短い立派な錦襴の袴をはいていた。彼らは上流階級に共通する礼儀正しく洗練された物腰をしていたが、明らかに落ち着きがなく、なにかやましいことをしているような、当惑の様子が見てとれた。自分たちの行動を見ている日本人が近くにいないかどうか確かめるように、ひそかに周囲に目配りしてから、士官のひとりに近づいて、時計の鎖をほめるような振りをしながら、畳んだ紙を士官の上着の胸に滑り込ませた。* 2人は意味ありげに唇に指を押し当て、秘密にしてくれと懇願してから、足早に立ち去った［この2人こそ、吉田松陰と金子重之助である］。

---

*この紙は日本語で書いた手紙であることが判明した。艦隊の通訳ウィリアムズ氏がこの手紙を次のように逐語訳している。［原文は漢文。参考のため要所に原文を書き下した訳注を入れた。］

「日本国江戸府の2人の書生は、この書を『高位の士官および有司の方々』［原文は「貴大臣、各将官の執事」］の閲覧に供します。われらは微賤の身でありますから、その才芸は乏しく、取るに足らぬものであり、貴下らの前にまかりでるのを恥じております［もとより自ら士籍に列するを恥ず］。われらは武器の使用に習熟せず、兵法や軍隊を論じることもできず、些々たる用務と怠惰な逸楽のうちにいたずらに歳月を過ごしてきました。しかしながら、われらは書物を読み、風聞によりヨーロッパとアメリカにおける習慣と教育をいささか知りましたので［風教を聞知し］、長年の間『五大陸』［五大州］を周遊したいと願っておりました。しかし、わが国の法律はあらゆる海事上の問題についてはなはだ厳しく、外国人の入国と日本人の渡航とは、いずれも同様に禁じられております。そのため、他国を訪れたいとのわれわれの願いは、呼吸を妨げられ、歩行を束縛された者のごとく、ただ『たえざる衝動のうちに胸中を揺れ動く』［勃々然として心胸の間に往来し］ばかりでありました。幸いにも、多数の貴国の艦船がこの海上に到着し、久しく滞在しているので、われらは親しく接して［熟観］入念に調査する機会を与えられ、貴下らの親切と寛容、他者に対する貴下らの心遣い［仁厚愛物の意］を十分に確かめ、多年の思いをふたたび触発されました。それは活路を求めてやみません。

そこで、いまこそ計画を実行に移すときであり［今すなわち断然策を決し］、艦隊が出航する際には、われらを貴船中に同乗させてくださるよう、ひそかにこの私的な願いを貴下らに書き送るものであります。たとえそうすることが国禁を軽んじることになろうとも、かくしてわれらは五大陸を周遊できるのです［海外に潜出して、もって五大州を周遊せんとす、また国禁をも顧みざるなり］。有司の方々が、われらの願いを実現するにつき、なんらかの憂慮を覚えることのないよう［願わくは執事、辱くも鄙衷を察して、此の事成るを得しめられよ］、われらは船中においてなしうる限り喜んで使役に務め、命令に服従いたします。歩けない人間が他人の歩くのを見て、自分も歩きたいと願うのは疑いのないことです。しかし歩行者が他人の騎馬を見るとき、どうしてその願望を充たせばよいのでしょうか。われらは終生奔走しても、東西30度、南北25度の外に出ることはできませんでした。しかるに、いま貴下らが嵐に帆を掲げ、巨涛をしのいで、千万里を電光のごとく疾走し、五大州を周航するのを見るとき、それは歩けない者が歩行の方法を見いだし、歩行者が騎馬の方法を見ることにもたとえられるのではないでしょうか。もし有司の方々が、われらの願いを考慮してくださるならば、その御恩は生涯忘れません。ただし、わが国の禁令はいまなお存在し、このことが世の知るところとなれば、われらはいたずらに追捕され、連れ戻されてただちに処刑されることは間違いありません。このような結果は、貴下らがこの願いを聞き入れてくださるならば、貴下らが退去するときまで『われらが犯している過ちを沈黙のうちに包み隠し』て［まさに生等のために委曲包隠して］、このような深刻な生命の危険［刎斬の惨］を免れさせてくださるようお願いいたします。いつかわれらが帰国するころには、わが国の人々も、過去の行為を追及するに値するものとは考えなくなっているでしょう。われらの言葉は粗野で意中を吐露するに足りませんが、われらの心は真に誠実であります。［以下、原文通りに］執事、願わくは其の情を察し、其の意を憐れみ、疑うことを為すなかれ、拒むことを為すなかれ。万二［瓜内万二。吉田松陰の偽名］、公太［市木公太。金子重之助の偽名］同じく排呈す。4月11日」

一通の短い添え書が同封してあった。それを翻訳すると次の通りである。［ここでは原文の書き下しを掲載する］

「本書内に開列、懇請するところは、生等これを思うこと累日、多方に策を求む。横浜に在りては、かつて商漁の船隻をやとい、暗夜に乗じて貴船に近づかんと欲す。しかれども地方の巡邏ははなはだ密。官船を除くほかは一切近づき前むを許さず。これがためにゆきなやむ。貴船まさに此の地に来るべしと聞き、期に先んじて来り待ち、一小舟を掠めて、もって貴舟に近づかんと欲すれども、いまだ能わず。よって願わくは貴船の各大員合議して、請うところを許允せられなば、すなわち明夜人しずまる後、脚船一隻を発し、柿崎村海浜の人家なき処に至りて、生等を邀えられよ。生等もとより、まさに約に先んじて該地に至り相待つべし。切に約信たがうことなく、生等の望むところに副われんことを祈る。4月25日」

not to return to the shore, by the desire they expressed of casting off their boat, utterly regardless of its fate. The captain of the Mississippi directed them to the flag-ship, to which, on retiring to their boat, they pulled off at once. Having reached her with some difficulty, in consequence of the heavy swell in the harbor, they had hardly got upon the ladder and mounted to the gangway, when their boat got adrift, either by accident, or from being let go intentionally. On their reaching the deck, the officer informed the Commodore of their presence, who sent his interpreter to confer with them and learn the purpose of their untimely visit. They frankly confessed that their object was to be taken to the United States, where they might gratify their desire of travelling, and seeing the world. They were now recognised as the two men who had met the officers on shore and given one of them the letter. They seemed much fatigued by their boating excursion, and their clothes showed signs of being travel worn, although they proved to be Japanese gentlemen of good position. They both were entitled to wear the two swords, and one still retained a single one, but they had left the other three in the boat which had gone adrift with them. They were educated men, and wrote the mandarin Chinese with fluency and apparent elegance, and their manners were courteous and highly refined. The Commodore, on learning the purpose of their visit, sent word that he regretted that he was unable to receive them, as he would like very much to take some Japanese to America with him. He, however, was compelled to refuse them until they received permission from their government, for seeking which they would have ample opportunity, as the squadron would remain in the harbor of Simoda for some time longer. They were greatly disturbed by this answer of the Commodore, and declaring that if they returned to the land they would lose their heads, earnestly implored to be allowed to remain. The prayer was firmly but kindly refused. A long discussion ensued, in the course of which they urged every possible argument in their favor, and continued to appeal to the humanity of the Americans. A boat was now lowered, and after some mild resistance on their part to being sent off, they descended the gangway piteously deploring their fate, and were landed at a spot near where it was supposed their boat might have drifted.

On the afternoon of the next day, Yenoske, the chief interpreter, who had come to Simoda from Yedo for the express purpose of requesting the postponement of the expedition to Oho-sima, which was conditionally granted by the Commodore, came on board the Powhatan, and requested to see the flag-lieutenant, to whom he stated, that "last night a couple of demented Japanese had gone off to one of the American vessels," and wished to know if it had been the flag-ship; and if so, whether the men had been guilty of any impropriety. The flag-lieutenant replied, that it was difficult to retain any very precise recollection of those who visited the ships, as so many were constantly coming from the shore in the watering boats and on business, but he assured the interpreter that no misdemeanor could have been committed, or he would have been aware of the fact. The interpreter was then asked, whether the Japanese he referred to had reached the shore in safety, to which the very satisfactory answer that "they had" was received.

The Commodore, upon hearing of the visit of the interpreter and the apparent anxiety of the Japanese authorities in regard to the conduct of the two strange visitors to the ships, sent an officer on shore in order to quiet the excitement which had been created, and to interpose as far as possible in behalf of the poor fellows, who it was certain would be pursued with the utmost rigor of Japanese law. The authorities were thanked for the solicitude they had expressed lest the Americans should have been inconvenienced by any of their people, and assured that

421

翌日の夜、午後2時ごろ（4月25日）、蒸気艦ミシシッピ号の艦上で夜間当直をしていた士官は、舷側についた小舟から聞こえてくる人声に呼び起こされた。舷門にいって見ると、2人の日本人がすでに舷側の梯子を登ったところだった。話しかけると、乗艦させてほしいと身振りで示した。

彼らはなんとしても艦上にとどまることを許可してほしいと願っているらしく、乗ってきた小舟を惜し気もなく放棄する意志を表わして、海岸には戻らないとの決意をはっきりと示した。ミシシッピ号の艦長が旗艦に行くよう指示すると、彼らは小舟に引き返して、すぐさま旗艦に漕いでいった。港内の波が高かったため、いくぶん苦労しながら旗艦に達し、梯子にすがって舷門に登るやいなや、故意か偶然か、小舟は舷側を離れて漂い去った。甲板に着くと、士官が提督に2人の日本人が現われたことを報告した。提督は通訳を送り、2人と話し合い、不意の訪問の目的を聞き出させた。彼らは率直に、自分たちの目的は合衆国に連れていってもらうことであり、そこで世界を旅して、見聞したいという願望を果たしたいのだと打ち明けた。こうして、士官たちと陸上で出会い、そのひとりに手紙を渡したのは、この2人の人物だったことが分かった。舟を漕いできたため、2人ともひどく疲れているようだった。彼らが立派な地位にある日本の紳士であることは明らかだったが、その衣服はくたびれていた。2人とも2本の刀を帯びる資格があり、ひとりはまだ1本をさしていたが、残りの3本はすべて小舟の中に置いてきたので、舟とともに流されてしまっていた。彼らは教養ある人物であり、標準中国語を流暢かつ端麗に書き、物腰も丁重で非常に洗練されていた。提督は彼らの来艦の目的を知ると、自分としても何人かの日本人をアメリカに連れていきたいのはやまやまだが、残念ながら2人を迎え入れることはできない、と答えさせた。そして、2人が日本政府から許可を受けるまでは、受け入れを拒絶せざるをえないが、艦隊は下田港にしばらく滞在する予定だから、許可を求める機会は十分にあるだろうと言って聞かせた。提督の回答に2人は大変動揺して、陸に戻れば首を斬られることになると断言し、とどまることを許してもらいたいと熱心に懇願した。この願いはきっぱりと、しかし思いやりを込めて拒絶された。長い話し合いが続いた。彼らは自分たちを支持してくれるようあらん限りの議論をつくし、アメリカ人の人道心に訴え続けた。結局、1艘のボートが降ろされ、送り帰されることになった。2人は穏やかながら多少抵抗したあと、運命を嘆きながら悄然と舷門を下り、小舟が流れ着いたと思われる場所の近くに上陸させられた。

翌日の午後、大島遠征の延期を要請するため（提督は条件つきでこれを認めた）急遽江戸から下田にやってきた首席通訳［森山］栄之助がポーハタン号に来艦して、旗艦付副官に面会を求め、「昨夜、発狂した2人の日本人がアメリカ艦船の1隻に近づいていった」と話し、旗艦にやってきたかどうか、もしそうなら、その男たちがなにか不都合なことをしなかったかどうか教えてほしいと言った。副官は、まことに大勢の人々が給水や業務でたえず海岸からやってくるので、来艦した2人を正確に覚えているわけではないが、と答えてから、なんの悪行も犯されなかったし、そんな素振りも見えなかったと断言した。そして通訳に、いま話に出た日本人は、無事に海岸にたどり着いたかとたずね、「着いた」との答えに大いに安堵した。

提督は通訳の来艦を聞き、日本当局が2人の見知らぬ訪問者の行動に懸念を抱いているらしいと知り、ひと

they need not trouble themselves for a moment with the thought that so slight a matter had been considered otherwise than a mere trivial occurrence unworthy of any investigation. The Japanese were further informed that they need give themselves no anxiety for the future, as none of their countrymen should be received on board the American ships without the consent of the authorities, as the Commodore and his officers were not disposed to take advantage of their confidence or act in any way that would be inconsistent with the spirit of the treaty. If the Commodore had felt himself at liberty to indulge his feelings, he would have gladly given a refuge on board his ship to the poor Japanese, who apparently sought to escape from the country from the desire of gratifying a liberal curiosity, which had been stimulated by the presence of the Americans in Japan. There were other considerations which, however, had higher claims than an equivocal humanity. To connive at the flight of one of the people was to disobey the laws of the Empire, and it was the only true policy to conform, in all possible regards, to the institutions of a country by which so many important concessions had already been reluctantly granted. The Empire of Japan forbids the departure of any of its subjects for a foreign country under the penalty of death, and the two men who had fled on board the ships were criminals in the eye of their own laws, however innocent they might have appeared to the Americans. Moreover, although there was no reason to doubt the account the two Japanese gave of themselves, it was possible they were influenced by other and less worthy motives than those they professed. It might have been a stratagem to test American honor, and some believed it so to be. The Commodore, by his careful efforts to impress upon the authorities how trifling he esteemed the offence, hoped to mitigate the punishment to which it was amenable. The event was full of interest, as indicative of the intense desire for information on the part of two educated Japanese, who were ready to brave the rigid laws of the country, and to risk even death for the sake of adding to their knowledge. The Japanese are undoubtedly an inquiring people, and would gladly welcome an opportunity for the expansion of their moral and intellectual faculties. The conduct of the unfortunate two was, it is believed, characteristic of their countrymen, and nothing can better represent the intense curiosity of the people, while its exercise is only prevented by the most rigid laws and ceaseless watchfulness lest they should be disobeyed. In this disposition of the people of Japan, what a field of speculation, and, it may be added, what a prospect full of hope opens for the future of that interesting country!

Some days subsequently, as a party of officers were strolling in the suburbs, they came upon the prison of the town, where they recognized the two unfortunate Japanese immured in one of the usual places of confinement, a kind of cage, barred in front and very restricted in capacity. The poor fellows had been immediately pursued upon its being discovered that they had visited the ships, and after a few days they were pounced upon and lodged in prison. They seemed to bear their misfortune with great equanimity, and were greatly pleased apparently with the visit of the American officers, in whose eyes they evidently were desirous of appearing to advantage. On one of the visitors approaching the cage, the Japanese wrote on a piece of board that was handed to them the following, which, as a remarkable specimen of philosophical resignation under circumstances which would have tried the stoicism of Cato, deserves a record:

"When a hero fails in his purpose, his acts are then regarded as those of a villain and robber. In public have we been seized and pinioned and caged for many days. The village elders and head men treat us disdainfully, their oppressions being grievous indeed. Therefore, looking up while yet we have nothing wherewith to reproach ourselves, it must now be seen whether a hero

りの士官を陸に派遣して、引き起こされた騒ぎを鎮め、厳重きわまる日本の法律で追及されるに違いない哀れな2人のために、できる限り仲裁の労をとろうとした。提督の使者は、いかなる日本人にもアメリカ人に迷惑をかけさせないという当局の配慮に感謝の意を表わしつつ、調査するに足らないほんのささいな出来事を大げさに考えて心配する必要はまったくないと確言した。さらに提督とその士官は、信頼につけこんだり、条約の精神に反するような行為をするつもりはなく、当局の同意がない限り日本人はひとりもアメリカ船に迎え入れることはないので、今後も心配は無用であると伝えた。もし提督が、自分の感情のおもむくままに自由に事を進めてよいと思うのであれば、アメリカ人が日本に現われたために刺激され、自由な好奇心を満たしたいとの一心から、日本を脱出しようとしたらしい哀れな日本人を、喜んで艦内にかくまってやっただろう。しかし、曖昧な人道心より高度な考慮を必要とする問題があった。ひとりの人民の逃亡を黙認することは、日本帝国の法律に背くことであり、すでに多くの重要な譲歩を意に背いて行なった国の規範に、できる限り顧慮を払って従うことが、唯一の正しい政策だった。日本帝国では死罪をもって自国民が外国に赴くことを禁じている。艦隊内に逃れてきた2人の男は、アメリカ人には無実だと思われても、日本の法律に照らせば罪人なのだ。そのうえ、2人の日本人が自ら述べた説明を疑う理由はないにしても、彼らが主張する動機とは別の、もっと不純な動機がはたらいていた可能性もある。それはアメリカ人の節義を試す策略であったのかもしれず、そう思った者もいたのである。提督は、自分がこの事件をまったくささいなことと見なしていると役人に印象づけるよう注意深く努力して、この犯行に課される刑罰が軽減されるよう望んだ。この事件は、知識を増すためなら国の厳格な法律を無視することも、死の危険を冒すことも辞さなかった2人の教養ある日本人の激しい知識欲を示すものとして、実に興味深かった。日本人は間違いなく探求心のある国民であり、道徳的、知的能力を広げる機会を歓迎するだろう。あの不運な2人の行動は、同国人の特質であると思うし、国民の激しい好奇心をこれほどよく表わしているものはない。その実行がはばまれているのは、きわめて厳重な法律と、法に背かせまいとするたえまない監視のせいにすぎない。この日本人の性向を見れば、この興味深い国の前途はなんと可能性を秘めていることか、そして付言すれば、なんと有望であることか！

その数日後、士官の一行が郊外を散歩しているとき、たまたま町の牢獄にさしかかり、あの不幸な2人の日本人が、通常の拘禁所、すなわち前に閂(かんぬき)をかけられた、ひどく狭苦しい一種の檻の中に、監禁されているのが見えた。哀れな2人は、艦隊を訪れたことが発覚するとただちに追跡され、数日後には捕らえられて投獄されたのである。彼らは自分の不運を偉大な平静さで耐え忍んでいるようで、アメリカ士官の訪問を非常に喜んで、その目を引こうとしているのが明らかに見てとれた。訪れた士官の1人が檻に近寄ると、日本人は板切れに次のようなことを書いて渡した。この文章はカトー［ローマの政治家］にも比すべき冷徹さを試される状況での、哲学的な諦念の注目すべき見本として、ここに記載する価値がある。

「英雄ひとたびその企図を失すれば、彼の行為は悪漢や盗賊の所業と見なされる。われらは衆人の面前で捕らえられ、縛められ、多日にわたり投獄されている。村の長老や首長のわれらを遇するに、侮蔑的その抑圧は

will prove himself to be one indeed. Regarding the liberty of going through the sixty States as not enough for our desires, we wished to make the circuit of the five great continents. This was our hearts' wish for a long time. Suddenly our plans are defeated, and we find ourselves in a half sized house, where eating, resting, sitting, and sleeping are difficult; how can we find our exit from this place? Weeping, we seem as fools; laughing, as rogues. Alas! for us; silent we can only be.

"ISAGI KOODA,
"KWANSUCHI MANJI."

The Commodore, on being informed of the imprisonment of the two Japanese, sent his flag lieutenant on shore to ascertain unofficially whether they were the same who had visited the ships. The cage was found as described, but empty, and the guards of the prison declared that the men had been sent that morning to Yedo, in obedience to an order from the capital. They had been confined, it was stated, for going off to the American ships, and as the prefect had no authority to act in the matter, he had at once reported the case to the imperial government, which had sent for the prisoners, and then held them under its jurisdiction. The fate of the poor fellows was never ascertained, but it is hoped that the authorities were more merciful than to have awarded the severest penalty, which was the loss of their heads, for what appears to us only liberal and a highly commendable curiosity, however great the crime according to the eccentric and sanguinary code of Japanese law. It is a comfort to be able to add, that the Commodore received an assurance from the authorities, upon questioning them, that he need not apprehend a serious termination.

The large Buddhist temple, the Rio-shen-zhi, or great peace monastery, was the place appropriated by the authorities, in accordance with the demands of the Commodore, for his use, and another was provided for that of his officers. Most of the Japanese temples have apartments separate from the ecclesiastical part of the establishment, which are used for lodging and entertaining strangers and distinguished visitors. They are also employed occasionally for various public gatherings, on festival and market days; and bazaars, for buying and selling, are not unfrequently opened; thus converting the temple into a place for the free exercise of all the roguery of trade, if not literally into a "den of thieves." As the supply of furniture was scant in the lodging department of the Rio-shen-zhi, chairs and other appliances of comfort were brought from the ships, and the quarters were made tolerably luxurious. In order to familiarize the Japanese people with their presence, the Commodore and his officers frequently resorted to their apartments on shore, and found a walk in the pleasure grounds which surrounded them, and on the wooded hills at the back, a pleasant diversion from the routine of ship's duty.

There was, notwithstanding the promise of the prefect, very little improvement in the conduct of the authorities, and the Americans still found their liberty much restricted, and their privacy interrupted by the jealous watchfulness and intrusive officiousness of the soldiers and spies. The Commodore himself, on one occasion, when proceeding through the town in company with several of his officers, found that he was constantly preceded by two Japanese functionaries, who ordered all the people they met to retire within their houses and close the doors. The shopmen were evidently forbidden to sell their wares to the strangers, for the most trifling articles which they might desire to purchase could not be obtained on any terms. The Commodore found it necessary again to protest against this illiberal treatment, and sent his flag-lieutenant to the prefect to lay before him certain complaints and to insist upon their causes being immediately removed. The prefect was accordingly called upon, and informed that it appeared that he was

実に過酷である。しかし、顧みて身にやましいところはなく、いまこそ英雄の英雄たるゆえんが試されるときである。日本六十州を自由に踏破しても、わが大望満たされず、われらは五大州の周遊を希求した。これこそ、われら多年の心願であった。突如、わが企図はくじかれ、狭い檻に閉じ込められ、飲食も、休息も、安座も、睡眠もままならぬ。われらはこの窮境をいかにして脱しえようか。泣けば愚人と見られ、笑えば悪漢と見なされる。ああ、われらには沈黙あるのみだ。

市木公太

瓜中万二」

提督は、2人の日本人が投獄されているという報告を受けると、旗艦付副官を陸上に派遣して、2人が艦を訪れた者と同じ人物であるかどうかを非公式に確認させた。牢獄は前述のとおりだったが、囚人はいなかった。牢番の申し立てによると、その朝2人は首府からの命令によって江戸に送られたとのことだった。2人はアメリカ船に出向いたために拘禁されたが、監督官にはこの事件を処理する権限がないので、ただちにこの事件を帝国政府に報告し、政府から囚人を引き取りにきたので、2人は政府の司法管轄下に置かれることになったという。哀れな2人の運命がどうなったのか、確かめることはまったくできなかったが、当局者が寛大であり、斬首という最も重い刑に処すことのないように望む。なぜなら、並はずれて残忍な日本の法典によれば大罪であっても、われわれには自由で大いに賞賛すべき好奇心の発露としか見えないからである。ちなみに、提督からの問いに答えて、当局が深刻な結末を懸念する必要はないと保証したことは、せめてもの慰めであった。

大きな仏教寺院である了仙寺、すなわち大いなる平安の僧院は、当局が要求に応じて提督の使用に供した場所であり、部下の士官には別の寺があてられた。たいていの日本の寺院には、宗教上の施設とは別個の部屋があり、外来者および身分の高い来訪者の宿泊や接待に使われる。それはまた、祝祭や市の日などさまざまな公共の集まりにも利用されている。交易のための市はしばしば開かれるので、寺院は文字通り「泥棒の巣窟」ではないにしろ、商売上のあらゆるいかさまが自由に行なわれる場所にもなる。了仙寺の宿所には家具が不足していたので、艦から椅子その他の生活を快適にする家具を運び入れ、かなり豪勢に仕立て上げた。アメリカ人の存在を日本人になじませるため、提督と士官たちはしばしば陸上の宿所に出入りして、まわりの庭園や背後の樹木の茂った丘陵を散歩して、きまりきった艦上勤務の気晴らしを楽しんだ。

監督官との約束にもかかわらず、当局の態度はほとんど改善されなかった。アメリカ人は依然として自由をかなり拘束され、プライバシーは兵士や密偵の疑り深い監視と、差し出がましいおせっかいによって侵害された。提督自身、ある日士官数人を伴って町を歩いているとき、たえず2人の日本役人が先行していることに気づいた。役人は出会う住民をかたっぱしから家に追い戻して戸を閉めさせた。商人が外国人に品物を売ることを禁じられているのは明らかで、どんなささいな品物を買おうとしても、まったく手に入れることができなかった。提督はふたたびこの狭量な処遇に抗議しなければならないと思い、旗艦付副官を監督官のもとに派遣し、いくつか苦情を申し立て、即刻このような扱いをやめるよう要求させた。副官は監督官に対し、次のように通

約附

使節日本國合衆國提督被理同日本大君之全權林大學頭、井戶對馬守、伊澤美作守、都筑駿河守、鵜殿民部少輔、竹內清太郎、松崎滿太郎、與國政府以立條約附錄、

一下田鎮台支配、其境亦仍舊設爲関所巡守、但亞美理駕人既條約議定于日本數里、七里之境則任從往來、出入境界之事、或有人悖犯日本法度、則能緝捕而送回船、

一下田港或有商船、鯨魚船、須築石繞三個、一築于下田、一築于柿崎、一築于港內中央小島之東南濱邊、以便上落、合衆國人民必要日本官吏而禮待之、

一上陸之亞美理駕人、若無相請、則不得闖入武館、人家、若寺廟、舖店則隨便可入、

一徘徊而欲休息者、亦未設便旅店、可于下田之了仙寺、柿崎之玉泉寺二處以定休息、

一柿崎玉泉寺境内以一地與亜美理駕人埋葬、既立墳墓、必無毀壞之、

一横濱所議之條約、于箱館得取石炭、但因箱館地遠、運渡石炭甚難、今提督許諾、回奏致知日本國政無於箱館取石炭、

一向後兩國政府或有公文往来示告、須用和蘭語傳譯、若無蘭語亦能以漢文取用、

一下田之港已設締役一人、港内案内者三人、置定引水

一凡有人于市店所撰之品、買主乃寫名于品上價記、然後店人送至御用所、以價銀交與日本官吏、而取品物、

一鳥獸遊獵、是日本之禁、所以亜美理駕人亦要遵從此制度、

一此度箱館之境以日本里数五里為亜人行之限、而法度亦

傚附録之第一條、

一横濱之條約、俟後亜國批准、日本君主不論委任誰人、可以收換、

一此後附録之條、或有以為不合横濱之條約、則必依于横濱之條約為准而不變、

右條約附録英語、日本語取認名判、蘭語飜譯、其書面合衆國與日本全權官守互換為據、

嘉永七年五月廿二日　下田立

SKETCH OF SIMODA,
mentioned in the Treaty.

亜墨利加合衆国と
日本国と議定之書面
於豆州下田におゐて取替
之儀を井上信濃守江委任
せしむるもの也
右
大君之命を以て

安政四年五月　阿部伊勢守
牧野備前守
松平和泉守
松平伊賀守
久世大和守
内藤紀伊守

Now therefore, I, Franklin Pierce, President of the United States of America, having seen and considered the said Treaty, do, in pursuance of the aforesaid advice and consent of the Senate, by these presents accept, ratify and confirm the said Treaty and every clause and article thereof.

In faith whereof, I have caused the seal of the United States of America to be hereunto affixed.

Given under my hand at the City of Washington, this seventh day of August in the year of Our Lord one thousand eight hundred and fifty-four, and of the Independence of the United States the seventy-ninth.

By the President: Franklin Pierce

W. L. Marcy, Secretary of State

（4）箱馆

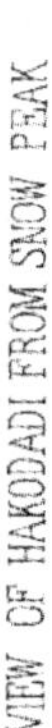

VIEW OF HAKODADI FROM SNOW PEAK

HAKODADI FROM TELEGRAPH HILL

ENTRANCE TO A TEMPLE AT HAKOTADI.

CHIEF TEMPLE HAKODADI

STREET IN HAKODADI.

日本の駕籠

Eng. by E. Brown Jr   T. Sinclair's lith Phil^a

BUNGO OR PREFECT HAKODADI

Sub-prefect of Hakodadi with Attendants.

Dag. by E. Brown   Ackerman Lith 379 Broadway N.Y.

DEPUTY OF THE PRINCE OF MATSMAY

CONFERENCE ROOM HAKODADI.

松前勘解由

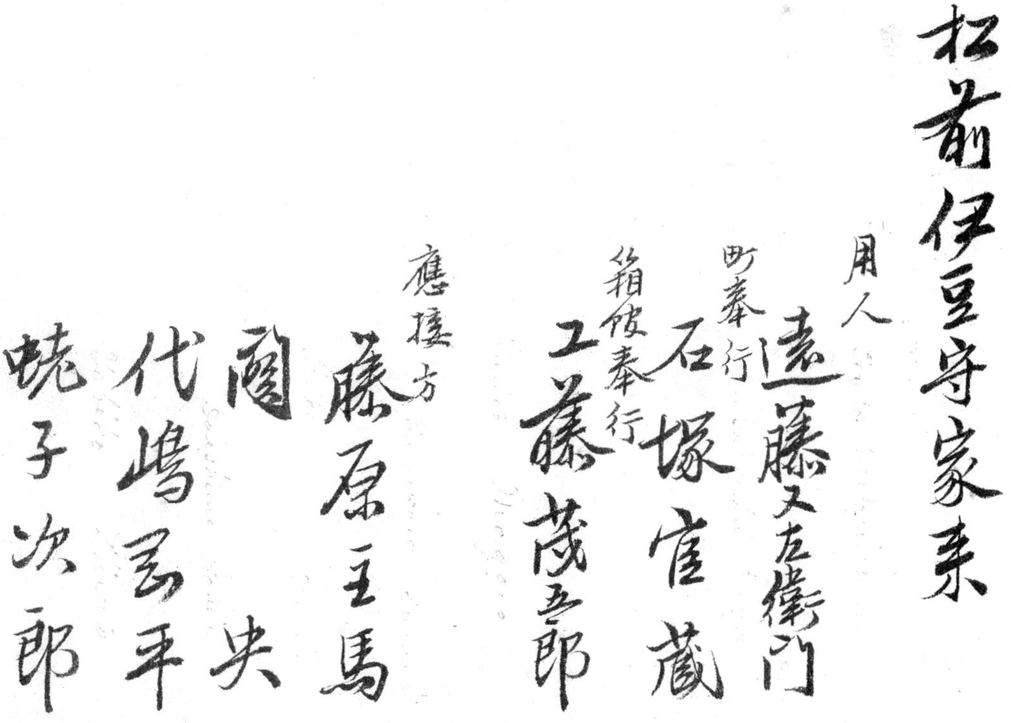

今般御帰帆ニ
候ニ付亜墨利加船
損傷無之哉見合候得共
候ハゝ急度
其節ハ遣し有之候ニ付
右方候右ニ相成候
以来難忘候
千秋万年平穏
三月十日

松前伊豆守家来

用人　遠藤又左衛門

町奉行　石塚官蔵

箱館奉行　工藤茂五郎

應接方　藤原主馬

関　央

代嶋剛平

蛯子次郎

日本國政府司農曹安間純之進鑒察参
謀平山謙二郎等與
亜美理駕合衆國欽差全權大臣及諸將
官會話余等奉
官命將赴哈剌土島途聞
貴國船到箱館港覩其奥内一事固係
前日橫濱之議惟遠境未詳其事或有
差誤乃請長官併日而至如橫濱議
與聽焉然長官取路海上已赴哈剌
島余等不可後當限三日而與公等
話併候崇安

...ed at
...i, June 1st 1854,
...a Zhiunnoshin &
...ma Kenzhiro.

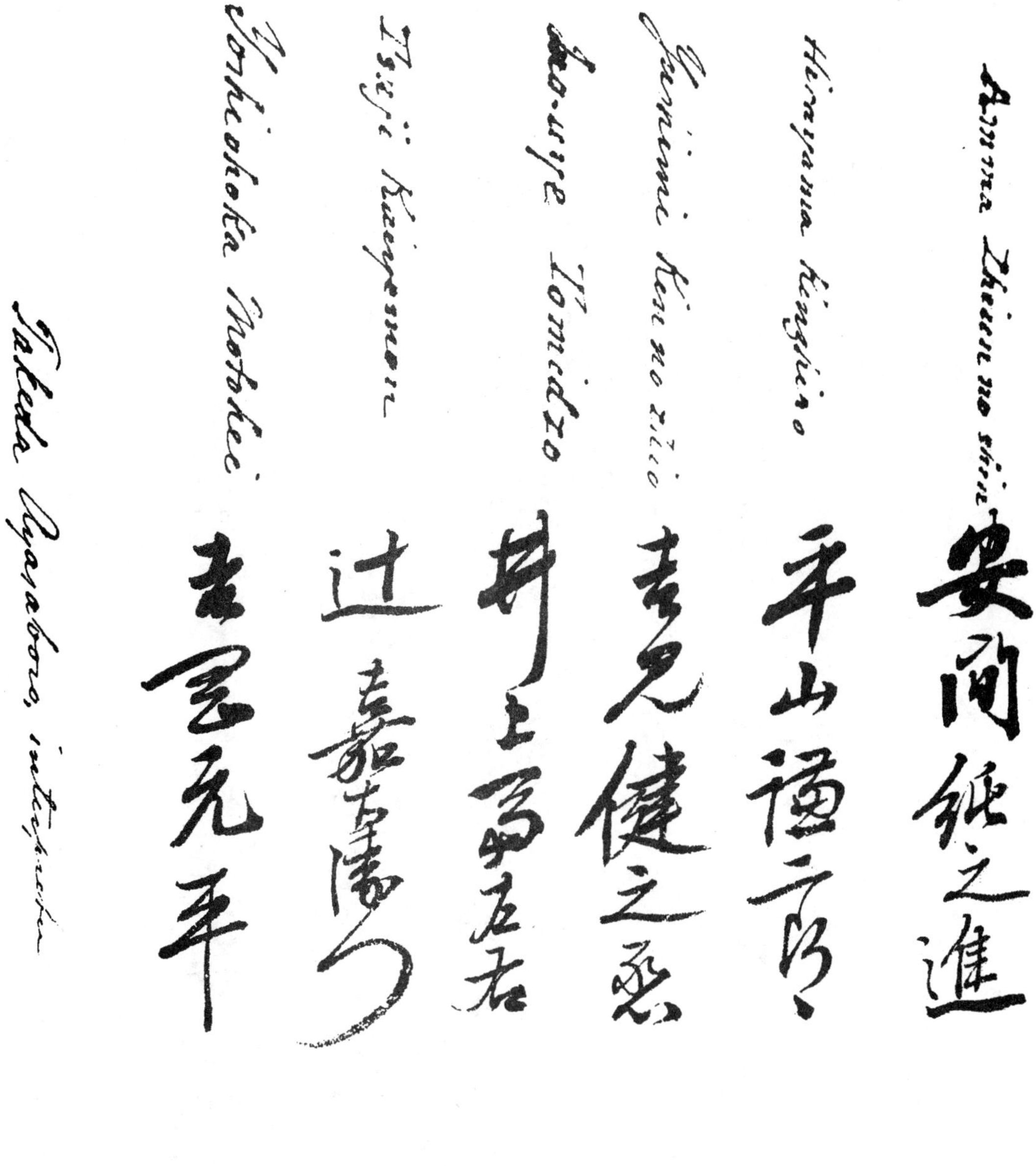

Anma Zheiun no shin 安間純之進

Hirayama Kingiiro 平山謙二郎

Yoshimi Ken no zio 吉見健之丞

Ino-uye Tomidzo 井上富左右

Tsuji Kiuyemon 辻嘉右衛門

Yoshioka Motokei 吉岡元平

Takeda Ayaboro, interpreter

今提督説你貴官至此必然有權力能為條約之事、故欲速與你相議且聞貴官今欲在此商議乎、抑或要往下田而商議乎、

惟令所與之筆牘皆有未通。請

回答

我松前公、不得江户朝廷之命、則不能來此地而

相會、本大臣 雖到松前、亦不得私相見、徒費時日

而已、至買賣之事、於此地方[illegible]可能、

今言不可得見松前〻公、則不能相議條約各款、今大臣是來見也、不能議各款之事因此處官不同其品級本大臣不欲如此回音、或因有別款之事商議、不在箱館、則要在松前酌議也、因為前時在橫濱、曾與林大學商議以定條約、今江戶無官至此、我難久待、故必要往松前〻公以定各款也、亦或我公所管辖地方，皆奉政府之命而守之耳，行步一件，極是重事，不得政府之命，則不能定之，無已則聞之於政府，而後回答之。

江户政府下令曰、亜国船要到箱舘見其地方、此係到神奈川亜国船、故遣你到箱舘、以待遇之、必毋失禮、

昨夜有一官從江户政府来、說、政府遣官二員不日到箱
館、其官責於平山名村二子、將與提督議定約事也、提督 何
用費貨往江户乎、我大夫切想提督費思慮、故俟天明而
報之、

如横濱條約我大夫可能議定

大夫答如横濱條約俟来年三月而後可能定此欵也

條約有云若箱舘港行步之規應俟日後量度較定今時（日後、即由江戸至此之日也、量度較定、今之定也、）提督要定之似與條約異如何貴國非欺騙我者、然國土各異其風習、以貴國之風習、比之我日本、則判一大鴻溝、箱舘行步之規、吾以為大事、自不得政府之命、則不能違此欵也、横濱二官到箱舘、不止貴國待之而已、此二官必奉政府之命而到箱舘、吾亦企足之日望之、此二官不到、則事々不明晰、吾難之、甚前日提督贈伊豆守及各名貴邦西産佳好諸物皆共運輸之扵前伊豆守展視之思有報故不腆諸物致之貴船各名亦皆致不腆諸物聊表芳志耳　請勿辭

自弘化三年至嘉永三年外國船遭飄爛到我境内者凡五回皆送之於長崎寄託和蘭人而傳致其國無丁人在日本者弘化三年五月亜美理駕人七員駕小舟漂到江登呂府嘉永元年五月亜美理駕人十三員駕小舟三隻漂到江良町村嘉永二年二年亜美理駕船到哈良土上船人三員於岸而去嘉永三年四月英吉利船遭飄爛漂到麻毘溜者三十二人其在何処漂爛也不可知

展視横濱條約有云、若箱舘港行步之規、應俟後日量度較定、然昨各船人市街舗店、隨意横行、或有入屋而慱者、或有踰垣墻而亂進者、我地方之人無得禁止、又條約中有云各船人所取薪水食料及缺之諸物、皆應從該地官吏等幹辦、凡一支一収、皆不得私下相與也、然昨各船人市街舗店所有什物、任意取之、不待報知價直而以洋金洋銀私投而去者有焉、此兩件與横濱條約相矛盾、貴國既在横濱、與日本大臣商量議定、各船人自應謹守條約、而在此地方如此、何故敢問

今日各船人上街、所為甚於昨日、

呈

翰林院編修通理官衛廉士

要地方百姓開店貴國既有前言則與作故恐驚慌百姓可知我不敢拒任縱貴國人買物是我政府未下以故不能允准唯市店所有之名物貴國人隨意取之若夫問銀價本官負後適議之

問於前道途水陸所由我何有所隱于貴國因記如左

海陸共二十五里

發給食物事則借館事件彼此未有定議則不能議之借館事件則不知上館者幾負歇息者幾日或唯有午飯而無夜宿乎否則未可議也是係昨本官負所問必待貴答而後舉議之可乎

公等每事動照下田規矩下田切近政府每事必得政府之許可而後行之如箱館距政府道途悠遠每事聞政府而行之則非數月間之所能辦也今我大夫權行其事而暫任從公等之意然事々必有不適公等之意者公等亦坦懷察之

如箱館壤土僻遠小民頑囂前聽貴船之來老幼相携逃於遠地地方官令無散無逃去既過半今貴国欲廣大其土地衆多其人民必不有掠略亂進之為但小民頑囂不可再提面誨其勢至如此昨見貴官員上街人情益恟々不安生業自今而後貴官員見地方者則無攔阻其他毋緩漫上街

箱館之為地如彈丸黑子而其前岸土壤曠漠不毛庶民之食料皆取給於他邦毋以下田浦賀一樣例看其所產物品識別簡略諒察之恐不能適於請之意也其所致各船上之物必不要價直

昨你道以朋友之情相待蓋朋友之誼彼此相利而無窒碍之事今我公奉廟堂之命守此地安此民至重大之事件則不得私斷若不待廟堂之令而順從貴國所議之條約則必適貴國之意無廟堂自有典型在我公必受嚴譴衆庶無所措手足貴國知此等事而再三強之恐非朋友相待之情願慊其意恕其不恭

夫舉大事謀國益者、宜觀德服衆心也　提督將神妙之機略
航滄溟到我　日本者、其事在廣互市之道、以建不測之功、傳芳於
萬世也、豈驚慌異方之民、奪其生産者乎、今也、　貴國人士遊
街者、或上寺廟博奕、或入肆店、從恣其藏貨、或超垣墻、闌入於
官舍、粗暴殆如狂者之為、是以地方小民等棄業閉戶、號訴日
不絶、哀歎滿路、或以為西國無度律、無禮義、戶戶相傳、人人相罵、皆
曰、後來　貴國人到此港者、皆如此、吾輩終餓死于道路、吾官員等謂
貴國新與我和親、已有橫濱條約相示、其宜有禮待也、其宜有懇切
也、故貴國人士遊街者、必為之先導、必為之後從　貴國人士縱令有放恣
不敢強制之、唯恐土民對貴國人有不恭蓋　貴國與本邦相去千萬里、
雖習俗異、恒情同、雖動作不同、禮意豈違乎、唯以異狀易驚、異言
難喻、我官員等日為之洶洶淵亂、唯非　提督嚴制之不能止也、若
提督謂無禮是我風、粗暴是我俗、我安禁之、則已矣、然粗暴不
能成其志、無禮不能久其功、自古然、　提督豈不知之哉、乃知
提督不罪我所言、而深恕小民之憂苦、以永保其不朽之功、

大臣要往覧火山此事群官會議而回答之
貴國官員持鳥鎗打鳥此地方極偏小民人見之驚慌益甚
願勿有此事
漆器瓷器之各品大臣待上此地方而供觀覧不取價乎
取

大抵以忠厚禮義相交。則太平和平和好之真者也。或以暴粗貪墨。則爭狠所由伏者。而人民亦不相親愛。此天理之自然。不容於疑者也。如衛康士。高明之士。須了當這箇道理。不消曉曉。

展視橫濱條約有云、若箱館港行步之規、應俟後日量度較定、
然昨各船人市街鋪店隨意橫行、或有入屋而慱者、或有踰垣墻
而亂進者、我地方之人無得禁止、又條約中有云、各船人所取薪水食
料及缺乏之諸物、皆應從該地官吏等幹辦、凡一支一収、皆不得私下相與
也、然昨各船人市街鋪店所有什物、任意取之、不待報知價直、而以洋金洋
銀私投而去者有焉、此兩件與橫濱條約相矛盾、貴國既在橫濱與日本大臣
商量議定、各船人自應謹守條約、而在此地方如此、何故敢問
今日各船人上街、所為甚於昨日、

呈

翰林院編修通理官衛廉士

貴國非欺騙我者、然國土各異其風習、以貴國之風習、比之我日本、則判一大鴻溝、箱舘行步之規、吾以為大事、自不得政府之命、則不能定此數也、橫濱二官到箱舘、不止貴國待之而已、此二官必奉政府之命、而到箱舘者、亦企足日望之、此二官不到、則事々不明晰、吾、難之、甚

聞説提督自從至箱舘、與這裏吏人往來、甚歡悦云〻、
余等亦不堪喜、但于行街見舖戶閉門、而婦人女子不
在家、此一事嘗在横濱、而如今榮之助譯説者、我邦
風習未嘗遇外國之人、官吏雖諭安撫誨之、亦不敢信、多
之疑矣、如嘗在横濱、提督步行遊、余等相信之日、亦在里
正家、偶見一婦人耳、如余等亦未得看見、乃至如下田、則
頗見兒女遊行、庶民安業、漸董陶貴國人也耳、如這境則
距江戶數百里、人民積習之固、未可遽化也、豈敢仇視貴國
人等者乎、且説看官吏且不慣觀焉、如觀余等亦奔走畏縮、
前後跟隨、乃我邦之風習、未可遽化者也、然如夫男兒、
則有忠剛尚義之節、婦人則有閑雅貞烈之操、蓋輙
看人亦稍似有淳風耳、公等幸勿怪、

DESCRIPTION OF THE TOWN OF HAKODADI, IN JAPAN,

One of the Two Ports opened by Treaty to American Trade,

BY S. W. WILLIAMS.

The town of Hakodadi, or Hakodate, lies on the southern coast of the island of Yesso, in latitude 41° 49′ 22″ N., and longitude 140° 47′ 45″ E., on the western shores of a small peninsula, which forms one side of the secure harbour before the town, and in full view of the Straits of Sangar. It belongs to the imperial fief of Matsmai, and is situated near the eastern boundary of the country of the Ainos, or aborigines of Yesso ; beyond which, a different mode of government commences. There are few or none of these people now left within the limits of this principality, and none are to be seen in the town. Hakodadi is a place of considerable native commerce, a large part of the supplies for the Ainos and the Japanese residents and people living among them, being stored here, as well as great quantities of produce brought in to exchange for these importations from the south. It lies about thirty miles eastward from Matsmai, the chief town in the principality, and is the second in importance on the island ; the two are connected by a well-made road, running along near the sea-coast, and both of them carry on a large trade with several small towns on the south side of the Straits of Sangar (or more properly Tsugaru), and other ports farther south in Nippon.

The word *Hakodadi* means "*Box Shop,*" applied to the town because it is little else than a warehouse or shop for the goods and boxes imported into it from Nippon and elsewhere ; the spelling *Chakodade* used in "*Golownin's Recollections*" is incorrect. The town contains about 8000 inhabitants, living in 1000 or 1100 houses, which are mostly stretched along for three miles, in one main thoroughfare near the sea-side ; the remainder form two or three parallel streets further up the hill. The shape of the peninsula on which it lies bears a slight resemblance to that on which Macao is situated, but the whole extent of the town being seen at once, added to the greater height of the hills behind it, renders the view much more imposing when coming in from the sea. The highest peak just behind the town, is about 1000 feet, the other three are upwards of 600, all of them bare upon the summits, and have their slopes covered with a low growth of shrubs and underbrush, and a few patches of pine trees. The groves of pines, maples, and fruit-trees behind the town, add much to its picturesque appearance, and with the large buildings in it, give the impression of its being a place of wealth and taste.

The peninsula is joined to the mainland by a low isthmus, on which a few patches of vegetables and some garden plants are seen, but most of the soil in this direction is too sandy for tillage. The rocks seem to be mostly volcanic, a coarse hard trachyte of a reddish or whitish tint, which is quarried in several spots for stone for sea-walls and pavements, for jetties, dykes, foundations, and other building purposes. Blocks of whitish porphyry or basalt are brought into town from a short distance, and used in constructing the walls of fire-proof storehouses. Hewn blocks and slabs of granite, for pillars, tomb-stones, temple candelabra, and other ornamental purposes, are brought from Nippon.

The buildings are of one story, with an attic or loft of different heights, occasionally making a commodious upper-chamber, but usually forming only a dark cock-loft, where goods are stored or servants lodged. The height of the roof is seldom over twenty-five feet from the ground ; the gently sloping sides are covered with pine shingles, not much larger than one's hand, which are kept in their places by bamboo nails and long slips of board, and over these are laid rows of cobble-stones, sometimes so thickly spread as to cover the entire surface. One object in using these stones, it was said, was to hasten the melting of the snow from the roofs. This heavy covering is supported by a framework of joists and tie-beams. The singular appearance which this tiling gives the houses, is increased by the tub of water placed on the gable-peak, which, rising above the porch, fronts the street in Dutch style ; the tub has a broom or two stuck in it, with which to wet the house in case of fire. A foreigner landing and seeing these for the first time, however, thinks that he has at last reached the end of the world, and has fairly got to the land where the witches take their nightly rides on broomsticks, perched up here for their convenience. In the street, the many rows of buckets and tubs filled with water near the houses, with a small fire-engine and hose seen here and there, shewed the dread of fires, and the precautions taken against them. Fire-alarms, made of a thick piece of plank hung under a little roof on posts at the corners, to be struck by watchmen, exhibited the mode of arousing the inhabitants when a fire broke out ; while the charred timbers and heaps of ashes still lying about where a hundred houses had stood only a few months ago, proved the need there was of all these precautions.

A few of the better houses and the temples are neatly roofed with brown wedge-shaped tiles, laid in gutters like the Chinese ; while the poor are content to shelter themselves in thatched hovels. The thatch in many cases is covered with a crop of vegetables and grass, growing from seeds planted by crows and other birds, and presenting sad evidence of the poverty or unthriftiness of the inmates. The abundance of crows flying about the town, reminds one of Bombay and other places in Southern India. Other birds were seen in great variety, both land and sea fowl, but not in large numbers, except gulls and sparrows.

The dwellings are generally built of pine boards, nailed against the framework on the two sides; in front and rear, boards or upright doors slide in grooves in which they are barred at night for security, and taken out by day to allow light to shine through the papered frames behind them. The roof projects beyond the house in front and rear four or five feet, making a porch that affords shelter from the sun or rain to persons passing along the street, or to goods placed there, and a convenient place in rear for carrying on many household duties, or depositing various utensils. None of the Japanese houses are painted, and in the humid climate of Hakodadi, these pine boards soon look rusty and contract mould, and the whole town consequently has an old, decayed look, which does not fairly indicate its age. The earth is beaten smooth inside to protect the house from dampness, and the floor is laid on a frame about two feet above it; leaving a path through to the rear, and one along the front entrance, both of which serve also as convenient places for depositing rough articles or tools. In shops, the whole front is sometimes taken out to display the goods; but in dwellings, there is usually a barred lattice in front to protect the inmates from observation, the papered shutters being removed in pleasant weather. Every house has a charm placed upon the lintel or door-post, consisting of the picture of a god, a printed prayer, or a written paper, designed to protect the dwelling.

The raised floor, which occupies nearly the whole area of the house, is covered with stuffed mats, and can be partitioned off into two, three, or more rooms by sliding panels, and folding screens, according to the wants of the inmates. In the centre is a brick fire-place, about three feet square, tiled around the edge and filled with ashes; the charcoal and wood are commonly brought in thoroughly ignited, and then burned on a brazier or handiron in the centre of this fire-place. There is not much smoke when it is burned in this manner, but in the cottages the annoyance from the smoke is almost intolerable. In a few houses a hole in the roof or side allows the escape of some of the smoke, and then, cooking is carried on in the same place. It may easily be imagined what gloomy abodes these are in rainy wintry weather, having no glass windows to admit light, or chimneys to carry off the smoke, and the wind whistling through every crevice and panel, upon the shivering inmates. The poor spend much of their time in winter cuddling around the fireplace, while the rich are unable to make themselves comfortably warm with it, and lade themselves with clothes to protect their bodies from the cold. In the largest establishments, there are small open courts between the rooms, sheltered from the wind, by which a dim light can be admitted through the windows; but the best houses in this town are cheerless abodes compared with even the glazed, warm, comfortable cottage of an English peasant; and one is surprised to see, among a people who have carried many arts to a high degree of excellence, so little progress made in the art of living comfortably.

Connected with the greater part of the dwelling-houses is a yard, either in front or rear; in many of them a kitchen or stable is seen; it is also used for storing wood, for rearing vegetables, or cultivating a few flowers; sometimes a kitchen garden with fruit and shade trees, indicated the greater taste as well as wealth of the occupant. In the houses of the officers, there was an arbor or fancy rock-work garden at the entrance, which shewed invitingly to the passer, and did credit to the tenant. The shops along the main street are often connected with the family residence in the rear, but quite as frequently with a mechanic's room. The goods in shops are packed in boxes or drawers as much as possible, only the coarsest pottery, grains, sandals, and other common articles, being exposed. The ceiling is about seven feet high, and the beams are hung with a large part of these articles.

Besides the shops, are numerous warehouses, built higher and with more care, and made as nearly fireproof as possible. Their walls are two feet thick, faced with stone, and made of mud or rubble-stone, securely tiled on top, and entered only by two or three large doors. Some of them have a loft; the window-shutters are of plank sheeted with iron. Some of them are entirely covered with fine plaster instead of stone on the outside; and their substantial appearance stands in strong contrast to the unpainted, flimsy, pine-board dwellings near them.

The shops in Hakodadi are stored with goods, mostly of a cheap sort, such as a poor people require. Coarse thick cottons, common earthen and chinaware, lacquered bowls, cups, and stands, durable silks, cutlery, and ready-made clothes, constitute the greatest portion of the stocks. Furs, leather, felted cloths, glassware, or copper articles, are rarely seen, nor are books and stationery very common. The provision stores contained rice, wheat, barley, pulse, dried and fresh fish, seaweed, salt, sugar, saki, soy, charcoal, sweet potatoes, and flour, with other less necessary articles, and to all appearance in ample quantities. There is no public market, as neither beef, pork, nor mutton, are eaten, and not many fowls, geese or ducks;

vegetables are occasionally hawked about. The artisans are chiefly blacksmiths, carpenters, barbers, shipwrights, lacqueredware-makers, potters, and stonecutters.

The signs of the shops are written on the paper windows or doors in various well known devices and cyphers; some were in Chinese characters, and others in Japanese, or a combination of the two. The streets are about thirty feet wide; and wooden fences, thrown across them at intervals, with gateways, divide off the several neighbourhoods. No wheeled carriages are seen in them, and they are kept commendably clean, sprinkled and swept frequently. The yards are surrounded with board fences, built close and high to conceal the interior; hedges and stone-walls are occasionally substituted. The streets present a remarkable contrast to those in Chinese towns, indicating less energy and traffic: no vociferous coolies or stalwart chair-bearers here thrust the idler aside, no clamorous dealers claim the preference of the passer-by for their wares and viands, no busy peddlers cry their goods, or industrious craftsmen work their trade, along the side of the way; but a quiet reigns through all the streets, broken now and then by a stout horseboy hallooing to his unruly beasts, an official attendant crying out to the people to prostrate themselves to the great man coming, or the clang of a busy forgeman in a neighbouring shop. Yet the general impression is made upon the visitor, that Hakodadi is a town of considerable wealth and trade; and the droves of pack-horses passing through the streets with their produce, the hundred junks at anchor off the town, their boats and fishing smacks passing from ship to shore and about the harbour, the tidy streets, and gentlemen with two swords riding through them on horseback, all tend to increase and strengthen this impression.

The peninsula on which the town is situated affords only a few score acres of arable land, lying on the eastward slope of the highest hill, near the fishing-village of Shirasawabi on the seaside. It is cultivated with vegetables for the town. The flat land on the isthmus is mostly left untilled, though it might be rendered productive with a little labour; farther north, the crops are greater, but the sandy flat plain extending far beyond the town northerly, hardly repays the farmer for his culture. Even those patches near the town which were under cultivation, had not yet been ploughed by the first of June.

There are several copses of pines and maples near the town, and the vegetation is vigorous on the hills. A variety of northern plants—oak, birch, willow, sassafras, viburnums, honeysuckles, wake-robins, angelica, and others—clothe their sides, and afford fuel to the poor. On the summits of the hills, stone images of Budha are erected, about four feet high, elevated on a small pedestal; offerings of copper cash, rags, flowers, and written paper, are seen strewed before them —evidences of both the poverty and devotion of worshippers, who felt interest enough to climb to these heights, to prevent, by such simple oblations, storms or disasters, which they supposed these weather-beaten, moss-covered stone idols had control over. The Japanese regard such spots as favourite locations for their gods, and many of them are enshrined in niches or small temples, erected on the summits or sides, to which devotees continually resort.

There are four large Budhist temples in Hakodadi, one of which, called the *Zhiogen zhi*, or the Country's Protector, is a good specimen of Japanese architecture. It was built about twenty years' since, and is elaborately carved and gilded in the principal room, and throughout is kept in good repair. The tiled roof rises fully sixty feet from the ground, and is supported by an intricate framework of girders, posts, and tie-beams, resting on varnished pillars; this roof is one of the most conspicuous objects seen when coming into the harbour. The carving on the altar, niches, and cornices, represents dragons, phœnixes, and other mythological subjects, and is done in a superior style of workmanship; some of it is in wood and some in brass. The main room, elevated five feet above the ground, and covered with stuffed mats, contains three shrines, all with small images; the cornice is so built that each shrine can be easily partitioned off with folding-screens placed under it, whenever an occasion required. The scrupulous neatness of the whole establishment attracted the praise of every visitor. It may be here observed, that temples, in Japan as well as in China, are often used for places of concourse or entertainment, on which occasions the shrines and altars are covered or removed, and the spacious room so changed in appearance, that no one would imagine it belonged to a temple. At Simoda, one of these buildings was set apart for a bazaar, and the priests derive a portion of their revenue from other uses than a religious. In the yard before this temple stood several stone candelabra, a goddess with a child in her arms, and a shed containing six small stone images, besides other out-houses and shrines, and several large trees. These six images each wore a skull-cup, like a Chinese winter cap, and looked most comically in them, mewed in their narrow stall. This goddess and the images in the temples had each a copper nimbus around their heads, in the same style as those in Romish churches.

Next to this temple, southerly, is the *Zhetsu-gio-zhi*, or True Acting temple, an older and somewhat dilapidated building. The yard contains several small sheds (one of which covers a subscription-box) and stone candelabra; and there is a neat garden in the rear, where the priests have shewn some taste in the arrangement of a group of rock-work and fish-pools, and planting some pines, flowers and dwarfed trees. The candelabra are stone sculptures about four feet high, provided with an open receptacle at the top for containing a lamp on festival days, and surmounted with a cover; they are usually of granite, and are sometimes tastefully carved, and of a graceful shape.

Near the main street stands the *Korio zhi,* or High Dragon temple, a large and costly edifice, but now falling to decay. It derives its name from a huge dragon carved on the front, where also is a carp fish, neatly cut in wood, six or eight feet long, placed head upwards on the right side of the porch. The front yard of this temple is nearly filled with various statues, gateways, sculptures, candelabra, out-houses, and shrines, some of which are elaborate and even beautiful pieces of work. Several trees also add to the general pleasing effect of the ornaments in this inclosure.

The fourth, called the *Shio-mio zhi,* or Budha's Name temple, presents nothing of particular interest. In addition to these, there are three Sintoo temples, called the *Shim-mei,* the *Hachiman,* and the *Penten,* dedicated to the national deified heroes and gods, but less expense is laid out on them than on the Budhistic. They are less resorted to than those; no burial-grounds are attached to them. The curator and his family usually reside on or near the premises. The roof of the second of these *miá* presents a peculiarity in architecture, the only thing of the kind seen. It is a projection in the centre like a dormer window, covering an entablature underneath, on which are a few carvings; the effect was good, as it relieved the dullness of the expanse of the roof, and was in harmony with the rich carvings on and below the eaves. In front of this temple are several gateways and stone ornaments, extending down the hill-side, but not surrounded by an inclosure, as the area is all occupied on the annual festival, and the public road passes through it. The building is not so large as the Budhist temples, but is kept neatly, and exhibits the peculiarities of Japanese architecture better than almost any other edifice in town.

Near the Budhist temples are extensive grave-yards, the tombs and monuments in which are peculiarly national, and their epitaphs offer an interesting subject for study. Near each grave are posts or boards, on which are written prayers, the names of the deceased, quotations from Budhist canonical books, and lines of poetry, which refer to the deceased, and their present felicity in Budha's heaven, the shortness of life, the folly of setting one's mind on this world, and such like homilies. These poles add much to the instructive interest of these spots, as their inscriptions illustrate the feelings and expectations of the Japanese, in reference to a future state, even more than the epitaphs carved on the tombs. One was observed, in which an iron ring was inserted, running on an axle, which, like the machines in use among the Mongols and Buriats, when turned around once, was considered as being equivalent to saying the prayers on the post.

The environs of Hakodadi present little to attract the visitor. Beyond the town eastward are two forts, dug out of the ground, and intended to guard the entrance to the harbour. Stakes are driven along the cuttings to retain the earth from caving in, and two wooden buildings, apparently connected with magazines underground, stand in the excavated area, which is paved with stones. Embrasures for only two guns are opened in the seaward embankment, and these are each nearly four feet wide. There is a building at the eastern end of the main street on the beach, which seems intended for a fort, but the absence of cannon and other appointments for such a place made it doubtful whether it was a fort or parade-ground. These rude works should not be taken as the best attempts of the Japanese in fortification, for several forts exist near Uraga, constructed on better principles; though there are probably none in the country which could withstand a slight cannonading from foreign ships-of-war, or even an attack from a few armed boats.

Beyond the earth-forts is a small neglected burying-ground, a portion of which has been set apart and fenced off for the interment of Americans who may die in port. It is a pretty spot, commanding an extensive view of the harbour and adjacent coasts and straits; and the interest of the place or the delights of the prospect, will no doubt often attract the footsteps of foreigners resorting to the port. About a mile beyond this spot, on the edge of the beach, is a steep cliff, within which is a cave of considerable size, open to the sea, and approachable only in ship's boats. A few rods further along the beach, which is here strewed with immense quantities of seaweed, is a spring of sulphur water, of a pleasant quality, and running from the clayey ledge in a little rill into a tub set in the ground. The only use made of it by the natives, apparently, is for washing themselves.

The climate of Hakodadi is probably not subject to the same extremes as the coast of Manchuria in the same latitude, though the snow still lingering on the western hills on the first of June, showed that it is colder than the towns of New Bedford or Boston on the Atlantic coast, about as far north and with a similar exposure. At this date, the peach and apple trees were in full bloom, the wake-robin, sassafras, maple, willow, and snow-ball in blossom, and some of the trees around the town not yet fully leaved out.

The animal food of the inhabitants chiefly consists of fish, clams, crabs, shell-fish, and other marine productions. Salmons are caught in the harbour in the month of June, of a delicious flavour, besides herring, perch, plaice, shad, and eels. Poultry, eggs, and ducks, and perhaps a little rabbit or venison, afford a small additional variety ; and dogs, cats, and crows are numerous, but none of them are eaten, so far as could be ascertained. The dog is like the common Chinese variety, and is very common. The horses are small limbed, and some of those belonging to the officers resembled barbs, but most of the pack-horses appeared only half-fed and over-worked. The price of one of the latter is from $25 to $35, while a fine riding horse was rated over $200. No waggons or carts were seen, and all the internal freight is carried on horses, of which nearly a thousand were seen in the streets on one occasion.

Wheat, rice, pulse of various kinds, greens, and barley, with a great assortment of seaweed, principally a species of *laminaria*, form the staples of vegetable diet. No fruits or fresh vegetables were in season when the American squadron was in port. Fully one-half of the food of the people of this town comes from the sea, and the rank odour of drying fish and seaweed, met one on the skirts and seashore of the town. The hamlet of Shirasawabi, on the eastern shore of the peninsula, was insufferable from the stinking fish around it ; and its inhabitants presented a squalid, dirty appearance, which may probably be taken as the average condition of the people of Yesso rather than that of the well-fed and clean townsfolk in Hakodadi. It should also be mentioned, that not a beggar was seen among them.

The people are stout, thick-set, more sturdy than those of Simoda, and if anything not so fawning or immoral. Their average height is about five feet three inches ; heavy beards are very common, but none are worn. They are mostly engaged in trade and shipping, depending on their importations for their supplies of bread-stuffs. Junks come from several places on the south side of the Straits of Sangar, from Sado I, lying south of Matsmai, Yedo, Yechigo, Noto, Nagasaki or Simonoseki towards the western end of Nippon, and even Ohosaka and Owari on the south. The harbour contained more than a hundred junks, though it was the dullest season, as the south wind had not yet begun to bring vessels up from these ports ; and the authorities regretted they could not supply what we wanted. They declined to sell any rice or wheat or flour, on account of the uncertainty of the arrival of fresh stocks. Rice, sugar, spirits, cotton cloth, silk, iron, porcelain, and hewn stone, are brought, for which they send in exchange, dried and salted fish, seaweed, charcoal, wheat, barley, deer's-horns, timber, and other produce of Yesso.

There is not much likelihood of the port soon becoming a place of much trade in American ships, but it can easily furnish supplies of wood, water, fish, especially fresh or dried salmon and perch, sugar, boards, eggs, poultry, and other articles, the variety of which will doubtless increase as there is a demand for them.

As a place for a retreat from the heats of Shanghai and Canton, Hakodadi may by and by attract visitors, who will by that day doubtless be allowed to investigate the resources and topography of the whole island.

LATEST NEWS FROM JAPAN.

The following is the most extended account of the transactions of *His Excellency Commodore Perry* at *Japan* that has been made public.

FROM "THE FRIEND OF CHINA EXTRA," *Hongkong*, 3d *April*, 1854.—"The return to Hongkong yesterday of the U.S.S.S. *Susquehanna*, Captain Buchanan, has placed us in possession of a few more particulars of the United States and Russian expeditions to Japan. The American fleet, it will be remembered, left this harbour on the morning of the 14th of January last. On the 7th of February the Steamers left Loochoo, the sailing vessels having left that place about a week before. On the 12th the *Susquehanna*, bearing the flag of Commodore Perry, anchored in a bay a little to the south of Yeddo, where she found the Frigates *Macedonian* and *Vandalia*—and the Store ship *Lexington* in sight beating in. (The *Southampton* Store ship, was afterwards found to have arrived in the Bay of Yeddo on the same day.) The *Macedonian* had got on a reef, but a tug from one of the Steamers, all three of which arrived together, placed her in deep water the same afternoon. She is not supposed to have received any material injury.

"On the 13th February the Steam Frigates *Susqushanna*, *Mississippi*, and *Powhatan*, with the *Macedonian*, *Vandalia* and *Lexington* in tow, steamed up to within twenty miles of Yeddo, bringing up in a place which, on the previous visit, was designated the "American Anchorage." The whole of the surrounding country, including a high volcanic peak called *Fudsi Jamma*, was found covered with snow; the thermometer was down to 30° and water froze on the decks.

"On the 18th February Commodore Perry shifted his flag to the *Powhatan*, on board of which vessel negotiations commenced;—the *Vandalia* proceeding to *Uraga*, where it was intended by the Japanese an interview between the respective Commissioners should take place. A succession of gales prevented the vessels from proceeding further up the bay until the 24th, on which day the Squadron got under weigh and ran up off a large town called *Kanagawa*, from twelve to fifteen miles from Yeddo by water,—nine only by land. The houses of Yeddo were plainly enough visible from the mast heads, and boats from the Squadron sounded up to within three miles of the wharves. The *Vandalia's* visit to Uraga was rendered unnecessary; it being determined, in her absence, to have the Council house erected at a small fishing village called *Yo-ko-ha-ma*, not far from the town off which the Squadron had anchored.

"On the 1st of March His Excellency *Yeizaimou* Deputy Governor of Uraga and some other high officers were entertained on board the *Susquehanna*. The bearing of these officials is said to have been frank and friendly in the extreme. Toasts were drank and speeches made, interpretation being rendered by means of intermediate Dutch; and by all that could be ascertained from the temper of the guests, there was every reason to believe that the reply of the Emperor of Japan to the letter from the President of the United States would be as favourable as might reasonably be expected. At first it was understood that the report circulated by the Russians of the death of the Emperor was altogether without foundation. From subsequent inquiry, however, the report was found to be true; though no attempt was made to postpone negotiations on mortuary account, as the Russians asserted would be the case; an excuse there is some reason to believe that had effect so far as they (the Russians) were concerned; the Japanese denying most positively that any treaty had been made with them. The Emperor of Japan was 83 years of age when he died—His Majesty's son has been proclaimed successor, though he is not yet crowned.

"The Sloop *Saratoga* arrived in the Bay of Yeddo on the 4th of March, and was ordered to prepare for a trip to the Sandwich Islands, by which route, thence to Panama, His Excellency the Commodore announced his determination to forward the earliest report of the result of his negotiations. Early in March, an Interpreter arrived direct from Yeddo, and on the 5th visited the flag ship. He is said to have been able to converse quite fluently in both Dutch and English, and could read and write our language with facility. He spoke freely of the Emperor, his master, and of His Majesty's willingness to accord commercial advantages to foreign nations. Of coal he said there was plenty, which should be brought from the mines to a depot to be selected by the Americans. This Interpreter had only recently returned from Nanga-saqui where he said, the Russians were point blank refused any promise of a Treaty.

"On the 8th of March, at noon, under an Ambassador's salute from one of the ships, Commodore Perry landed for his promised interview with the Imperial Japanese Commissioners. His Excellency's barge was accompanied by boats from the various vessels of the squadron, to the number of twenty eight, and besides the boats' crews, four hundred seamen and Marines were conveyed to the shore to form His Excellency's escort. The weather was magnificent, and the landing was effected most successfully. Two other salutes, one for the Emperor, another for the Commissioners were fired by the boat squadron after His Excellency was on shore.

"The result of this first interview can only be generalized into the report that the disposition evinced was most favourable to American wishes. Other meetings were determined on, and a Warehouse was erected for the special reception of presents for the Emperor, Empress, and Court, which were landed on the morning of the 13th. From the size of the building prepared to receive these presents the Japanese appeared to have expected a bulkier, if not a more valuable, assortment. A plot of ground was cleared, too, for laying down the miniature Railroad, and a line was arranged for working the electric telegraph; of both of which, as forming part of the intended presents to the Japanese Court, our readers will, no doubt, already have heard."

"March 15th 1854—A Red Letter day in the annals of Japan—saw the Emperor's reply to the President's requests under perusal on board the flag ship; and on the 17th Commodore Perry again landed for his second interview with the four Commissioners appointed to negotiate a Commercial Treaty. The names and rank of these Officers are said to be as follows.—First Commissioner, His Highness the Prince Councillor HAYASHI; Second Commissioner, IDO Prince of *Tsussima;* Third Commissioner, IZAWA Prince of *Mima-sa-ki;* Fourth Commissioner, His Excellency UDONO a Member of the Board of Revenue.—The names of the Japanese Interpreters of the respective legations are Mr. Mats-ma-ke Mich-i-ta-ro and Dr. Samuel Wells Williams."

"March 20th. The store ship *Supply* arrived from Shanghae, conveying to Commodore Perry the report left by the *Vostock* of the successes in Japan of the Russian Admiral;—but the period of a year *fixed by the Russians* for the opening of Japan to the world was said by the Japanese to be entirely a figment of Russian imagination. The Japanese would only admit that the Russians said *they* would be back in a year."

"On the morning of the 24th March Commodore Perry had his third interview with the Japanese Commissioners, a few days before having despatched the *Vandalia* and *Southampton* to examine the harbour of *Sho-di-ma* about seventy miles south of Yeddo, one of the places indicated by the Japanese as fitting for a factory.

"Were we to give in this journal, as certain facts, the whole of what we have heard as having been effected by Commodore Perry in his negotiations, it would speak ill for American diplomacy in having allowed so much to transpire. Without infringing any reasonable requirement, however, we are permitted to say that the following detail is not far from a correct summary of the principal advantages."

"Two Ports are given to trade—*Matsmai** in Yeso, and *Sho-di-ma*† before mentioned;—and in addition to these places with trading residents, another location is promised contiguous to the Coal country. At first the Japanese Commissioners spoke of one year for the Coal station, and five for the trading places, as periods within which they promised the warm endeavour of their government to prepare the people for the new regulations. The laws of the Empire they said were very strict against trading of any kind excepting at Nanga-saqui with the Dutch. To these lengthy periods, however, His Excellency Commodore Perry temperately, though firmly, objected—insisting on the Coal depot at once, and trading ports within a year."

"As regards the terms of treaty the basis of that with China is said to form the leading feature. This we think is to be regretted. Ports in Japan as well as in China, should be as free as the harbour of Hongkong, where duty on our Island's sole production—Granite, is collected by the Government from the stone quarry farmer. Commodore Perry it is said offered to embody a clause in the treaty for participation by all the world in the advantages he desired; but to this proposition the Japanese Commissioners demurred; expressing, however, a willingness to make separate treaties on similar terms with any other nations who migh seek them in a peaceful manner. Directly the Treaty is concluded Capt. Adams in the *Saratoga* will leave with despatches; but as it is said Commodore Perry intends to remain on the Japanese Coast for at least two or three months, we presume His Excellency is prudently determined upon doing what is to be done in a quiet, steady manner, and without any unnecessary haste."

"The miniature Railway, and five miles of Magnetic telegraph, created great astonishment. Arranged with Japanese characters there was much amusement among the natives at the extremes of the line at the rapidity and ease with which a conversation could be carried on, additional wires being ordered to be prepared immediately, so that they might carry the communication right up to the capital. The railway was taken round a circus of some fifty yards in diameter—or nearly a tenth of a mile in length. The locomotive, with its tender and car was made to travel at the rate of forty miles an hour. Of course the action of these machines was only intended as a small exhibition of Western science. The curiosity of the Japanese appears to have been highly excited by the beautiful symmetry of the *Macedonian*, and artizans were engaged in measuring her, as they said, for the purpose of building her counterpart."

"One of the Marines of the *Mississippi* dying while the squadron was lying in the Bay of Yeddo, an occasion was given to apply for ground for a cemetery. Sufficient space for ten interments being allotted, the Marine was buried with all the honours of war. In conclusion we have only to say that the *Susquehanna* reports her own and the crews of the rest of the Squadron, as in excellent health and fine spirits. She was eight days on the run from Yeddo to this port."

---

* *Matsmai*, a large town, with 50,000 inhabitants, situated on a bay at the south-west point of the island of Yeso. Its harbour is constantly filled with merchant vessels, and it has a flourishing trade.—*Malte Brun*.

† *Osaka* a capital city of *Niphon* is also mentioned as one of the ports to be thrown open.

Movements of American Vessels of War.

" On the departure of the Commodore, the command of the U. S. Squadron in the East devolves on Captain Abbott. The store-ship *Supply* sailed on the 2d instant for the United States *viâ* Batavia and the Cape of Good Hope. The steamer *Susquehanna*, with the store-ship *Southampton* in tow, left on the 4th instant for Japan. The *Susquehanna* proceeds to San Francisco, and from thence to Philadelphia *viâ* Cape Horn; as does also the *Southampton*, after the *Mississippi* relieves her of the coal not taken by the *Susquehanna*. The *Lexington* sailed on the 9th for the States, touching at Mauritius and the Cape. The *Mississippi* leaves for Japan to-day, and having coaled there from the *Southampton*, will go home *viâ* Sandwich Islands and San Francisco. The steamer *John Hancock* and schooner *Fenimore Cooper* have been temporarily detached from the Surveying Expedition, for the service of the U. S. Commissioner, and sailed for Shanghae on the 9th; to be followed on the 16th or 17th by the steamer *Powhatan*, leaving the sloop *Macedonian* in Hongkong. The *Vandalia* is at Shanghae; and the sloop *J. P. Kennedy*, and steamer *Queen* (whose charter has been renewed,) are at Canton. The *Vincennes* and *Porpoise* leave to-day (12th) for Corea and the Bonin Islands, on a surveying cruize."—*China Mail, September 14th*, 1854.

Proclamation.

Whereas, in the present disturbed state of the city of Canton, the lives and property of American citizens here are greatly exposed in going to and from this city:—and, Whereas the Authorities of the United States have found it necessary to place vessels of war in the Canton river, for the protection of American citizens residing at Canton, and conducting their commercial business at this city, and thence to the anchorage of the ships of commerce at Whampoa Reach:—and Whereas this action on the part of the authorities of the United States has not been properly understood or appreciated, and while innumerable falsehoods are circulated concerning the purpose and object of the authorities of the United States in disposing of the naval force of that country, frequent occasions occur when disorders are permitted to involve the safety, and security, and commercial rights of American citizens:—Wherefore this Proclamation is issued to notify all concerned that the ships of war of the United States of America, now stationed in the Canton river, are there for the sole object of protecting the lives and property of American citizens, and that any assault upon them, or any interference with their just rights as secured by Treaty, come from whatever quarter, will be summarily chastised. The authorities of the United States in China have everywhere manifested their honorable fidelity to existing treaty obligations, avoiding all interference with the domestic strife that now disturbs the peace and tranquillity of the Chinese Empire, and this neutrality shall be adhered to in the future, unless an imperious necessity shall demand another policy.

ROBERT M. M'LANE,
Commissioner of the United States of America to China.

Canton, 11th September, 1854.

The Treaty with Japan.

The following is a copy of the Treaty negotiated by Commodore Perry with the Emperor of Japan, and recently confirmed by the Senate.

Treaty between the United States of America and the Empire of Japan, done at Kanagawa, the 31st day of March, in the year of our Lord Jesus Christ, 1854; and of Kayei, the seventh year, third month and third day.

The United States of America and the Empire of Japan, desiring to establish firm, lasting and sincere friendship between the two nations, have resolved to fix, in a manner clear and positive, by means of a treaty or a general convention of peace and amity, the rules which shall in future be mutually observed in the intercourse of their respective countries; for which most desirable object the President of the United States has conferred full powers on his Commissioner, Matthew Calbraith Perry, special ambassador of the United States to Japan, and the august Sovereign of Japan has given similar full powers to his Commissioners, Hayashi, Dai-gaku-no-kami; Ido, Prince of Tsus-sima; Izawa, Prince of Mimasaki; and Udono, a member of the Board of Revenue;—and the said commissioners, after having exchanged their said full powers, and duly considered the premises, have agreed to the following articles:

Art. I.—There shall be a perfect, permanent, and universal peace, and a sincere cordial amity between the United States of America on the one part, and the Empire of Japan on the other part, and between their people respectively, without exception of persons or places.

Art. II.—The port of Simoda, in the principality of Idzu, and the port of Hakodadi, in the principality of Matsmai, are granted by the Japanese as ports for the reception of American ships, where they can be supplied with wood, water, provisions, and coal, and other articles their necessities may require, as far as the Japanese have them. The time for opening the first named port, is immediately on signing this treaty; the last named port is to be opened immediately after the same day in the ensuing Japanese year. [*Note.*—A tariff of prices shall be given by the Japanese officers of the things which they can furnish, payment for which shall be made in gold and silver coin.]

Art. III.—Whenever ships of the United States are thrown or wrecked on the coast of Japan, the Japanese vessels will assist them and carry their crews to Simoda or Hakodadi, and hand them over to their countrymen appointed to receive them; and whatever articles the shipwrecked men may have preserved, shall likewise be restored, and the expenses incurred in the rescue and support of Americans and Japanese who may thus be thrown upon the shores of either nation, are not to be refunded.

Art. IV.—Those shipwrecked persons and other citizens of United States shall be free as in other countries, and not subjected to confinement, but shall be amenable to just laws.

Art. V.—Shipwrecked mariners and other citizens of the United States, temporarily living at Simoda and Hakodadi, shall not be subject to such restrictions and confinement as the Dutch and Chinese are at Nagasaki, but shall be free at Simoda to go where they please within the limits of seven Japanese *ri* (or miles), from a small island in the harbor of Simoda, marked on the accompanying chart hereto appended; and will in like manner be free to go where they please at Hakodadi, within limits to be defined after the visit of the United States squadron to that place.

Art. VI.—If there be any other sort of goods wanted, or any business which shall require to be arranged, there shall be careful deliberation between the parties in order to settle such matters.

Art. VII.—It is agreed that ships of the United States resorting to the ports open to them, shall be permitted to exchange gold and silver coin and articles of goods, for other articles of goods under such regulations as shall be temporarily established by the Japanese government for that purpose. It is stipulated, however, that the ships of the United States shall be permitted to carry away whatever articles they are unwilling to exchange.

Art. VIII.—Wood, water, provisions, coal, and goods required, shall only be procured through the agency of Japanese officers appointed for that purpose, and in no other manner.

Art. IX.—It is agreed that if at any future day the government of Japan shall grant to any other nation or nations privileges and advantages which are not herein granted to the United States and the citizens thereof, that these same privileges and advantages shall be granted likewise to the United States and to the citizens thereof, without any consultation or delay.

Art. X.—Ships of the United States shall be permitted to resort to no other ports of Japan but Simoda and Hakodadi, unless in distress or forced by stress of weather.

Art. XI.—There shall be appointed by the government of the United States, consuls or agents to reside in Simoda, at any time after the expiration of eighteen months from the date of the signing of this treaty, provided that either of the two governments deem such arrangement necessary.

Art. XII.—The present convention having been concluded and duly signed, shall be obligatory and faithfully observed by the United States of America and Japan, and by the citizens and subjects of each respective Power; and it is to be ratified and approved by the President of the United States, by and with the advice and consent of the Senate thereof, and by the august Sovereign of Japan; and the ratifications shall be exchanged within eighteen months from the date of the signature thereof, or sooner if practicable. In faith whereof, we, the respective plenipotentiaries of the United States of America and the Empire of Japan, aforesaid, have signed and sealed these presents.

Done at Kanagawa, this thirty-first day of March, in the year of our Lord Jesus Christ, one thousand eight hundred and fifty-four; and of Kayei, the seventh year, third month, and third day.

—*From the New York Courier.*